The authors wish to dedicate this reader to our students—

those we have taught, those we have learned from,
and those whom we will meet.

PREFACE

While the European twentieth century has ended, the legacy of that "Age of Conflict" will continue well into this new, twenty-first century. The twentieth-century legacy includes the rise of Marxist-Leninism and its decline and death. Mussolini and Hitler's fascism briefly captured European and world attention. Nationalism struggled with European unity—a struggle that will continue.

How each of these movements came about, how they evolved, and how they have survived or have not survived into this new century are some of the subjects of the fifty-three essays presented in this third edition of *An Age of Conflict: Readings in Twentieth-Century European History.*

This revised reader is a natural continuation from the first and second editions. It is intended to supplement, not to replace, a course's main study textbook. The overall topics have been retained: reorientation of social thought as the century began, the origins of World War I, the Bolshevik Revolution and the rise of Stalinism, the short-lived triumphs of fascism, the tragedy of the Holocaust, the steps toward European unity. However, this third edition takes into account the continuing controversies over the Holocaust, the ongoing fallout over the collapse of Yugoslavia, and new developments in the struggle for European unity.

Although the Holocaust came to an end more than fifty years ago, its origins and impact still inspire lively debate among scholars. The chapter on the Holocaust has therefore been expanded to include controversial interpretations from two scholars on the subject, Daniel Jonah Goldhagen and David S. Wyman. The chapter on European unity has been complemented by recent selections from Bill Lucarelli, who depicts three future scenarios for the European Community, and Elizabeth Pond, who considers its future in partnership with the North Atlantic Treaty Organization (NATO). Crises ensuing over the collapse of Yugoslavia, and specifically the wars in Bosnia and Kosovo, have been at the forefront of European politics and diplomacy during the greater part of the last decade of the twentieth century. Interpretations of the causes and course of these conflicts are consequently indispensable in a reader such as this one. These interpretations are presented by Laura Silber and Allan Little, Sabrina Petra Ramet, and James J. Sadkovich. In the new final chapter, readings from Paul M. Kennedy and Francis Fukuyama ask students to ponder the future of European unity and the overall impact of nationalism.

Each of the readings, both those retained from previous editions and the new ones, has been selected not only for the information it provides, but also to show how historians writing on the same subject differ, and how once-popular interpretations can give way to different views. For example—and at the risk of oversimplification—one historian describes the Nazis as the product of the German past; another sees them as criminals relied on by capitalists who had forsaken parliamentary means to preserve their assets; a third sees Nazism as not essentially different from communism; and a fourth regards it as a desperate effort by the middle classes to maintain economic and social respectability. Students can consider how each interpretation may fit a particular period or ideological orientation and ask whether it was only coincidental that the "Nazism-as-Germanism" school gained prominence during World War II, the "Nazism-as-not-different-from-communism" school during the cold war, and so on.

The readings also provide some more recent analyses: Roy A. Medvedev's essay on Stalinism, Jill Stephenson's essay on how German women fared under Nazi rule, Walter Laqueur's and David S. Wyman's essays on why the Allies—and particularly the Americans—did nothing to stop the Holocaust, as well as the selections mentioned previously on the Kosovo conflict and the European Community. Hence, the anthology provides a breadth of supplementary readings and a modest introduction to the history of historical writing on twentieth-century Europe. In so doing it informs the student, whether "major" or "nonmajor," about the nature of the discipline. Chapter introductions provide an overview of the topic and a context for each of the readings to follow. Then in short introductions to each reading, students are encouraged to evaluate the author's viewpoint and contrast it with that given by the previous or next author.

Are "readers" such as *An Age of Conflict* still appropriate? We would obviously suggest they are. At a time when book costs continue to soar, students cannot be expected to purchase the number of separate books required even to begin exploring the literature relevant to each particular topic found in studying European history. The Internet, though potentially useful, does not yet provide the complete, legitimate, and reputable range of readings required. Although we do admit that any instructor can compile a list of readings from various sources, place those sources on reserve at the library, and require students to go to the library to read each and every one, is that always practical? Does the library have the source? Is there more than one copy, so students do not have to wait in line? Do all students have the time? Through this selection of readings, we hope that instructors will find the basis for stimulating student interest and thought and that students will find in one convenient source the lessons gleaned from a variety of viewpoints as historians look at the major events of the twentieth century.

We wish again to express our appreciation to colleagues and friends who made numerous helpful suggestions for the first two volumes, particularly Robert Paxton, John O'Sullivan, Samuel Portnoy, and Irwin Wall, as well as many others. We are especially grateful to the students on whom these readings were tested. Indeed it was their enthusiasm that encouraged us and their suggestions for improvement that have strengthened the book. For this third edition, we would also like to thank Donald Schwartz (California State University at Long Beach), Ronald J. Granieri (Furman University), and Richard B. Spence (University of Idaho). Their comments have been valuable. We also wish to acknowledge the editors at Harcourt College Publishers, especially David Tatom (executive editor), steve Norder (developmental editor), Matt Townsend (project editor), Garry Harman (art director), and Diane Gray (production manager) for their assistance on this project.

Leslie Derfler
Patricia Kollander
April 2001

CONTENTS

AN AGE
OF CONFLICT

Readings in
Twentieth-Century
European History

Third Edition

1

THE OPENING OF THE TWENTIETH CENTURY

The Reorientation of Social Thought

Many older texts on twentieth-century European history provided only a political and economic survey of conditions in the decade prior to World War I. They described and generally applauded Europe's favored position that gave her worldwide economic, technological, and artistic supremacy. Before 1914 Europeans were secure, showed confidence, and set the standards by which the rest of the world was measured. The year 1914 was seen as a dividing line, bringing to an end an equilibrium "so stable as almost to give an illusion of permanence."[1] Then with the publication of H. Stuart Hughes' *Consciousness and Society* (1958), Gerhard Masur's *Prophets of Yesterday* (1961), and other works, the awareness emerged of a prewar climate of "cultural revolt," "intellectual disquiet," and movement "toward a new consciousness."[2] These analyses suggested that "Victorian certainties" were no longer appropriate; the "competitive power of the individual" was no longer seen as "a source for progress"; belief in the "superiority of European culture" was shaken. Historians began to wonder whether cultural disharmony played as important a part in bringing on World War I as the discredited alliance system and whether it accounted for the

---

[1] Frank P. Chambers, *The Age of Conflict: The Western World: 1914 to the Present* (New York: Harcourt Brace, 1962), p. 4. In the next sentence, however, the author states that "the illusions concealed the reality."

[2] David Sumler, *A History of Europe in the Twentieth Century* (Homewood, Ill: Dorsey, 1973); Felix Gilbert, *The End of the European Era: 1890 to the Present* (New York: Norton, 1984); and Robert O. Paxton, *Europe in the Twentieth Century*, 3rd ed. (Fort Worth: Harcourt Brace, 1997). Taken from chapter and section headings.

younger generation's enthusiasm for war and willingness to endure the unparalleled horror and destruction that followed.

During the quarter century that preceded the outbreak of the war, advanced sectors of the European climate of opinion indeed underwent tremendous change. Intellectuals no longer offered ultimate answers and doubted they could be found. Certitudes, absolutes, and established codes of conduct no longer seemed relevant. Einstein's insistence on relativity destroyed forever Newton's mechanistic worldview; the belief in an orderly universe governed by predictable laws was shattered. Nietzsche questioned the basis of Judeo-Christian morality. Ibsen exposed the hypocrisy of that bastion of stability and order, the bourgeoisie. In psychology and sociology Freud and Weber contended that rather than controlling their environment, people were products of it. Such innovative thinkers, regardless of their intentions, rejected the positivist tradition that so well complemented much of Europe's march toward industrial progress—a tradition that emphasized rational and objectively verifiable thought. According to the new school, people did things not as a result of rational decision making, but because of unconscious processes they did not even understand.

Existing values were challenged on all sides. In addition to Nietzsche's repudiation of the scriptural bases of morality, Bergson maintained that the impetus of life transcended rationalism. Freud taught that thinking was a circuitous path toward the goal of wish fulfillment. Sorel believed that myths and not reason accounted for great collective movements. Artists, too, joined in intellectual revolt: The paintings of Fauvists, cubists, and futurists violated all traditional standards; in music, the first atonal work was composed in 1908; in literature, Joyce and Proust developed new forms based on the workings of the subconscious, while Mann and Galsworthy wrote of the decay of great bourgeois families as symbolic of larger European decay.

The three readings that follow address this intellectual revolution in different ways. H. Stuart Hughes defines this "reorientation" of thought, distinguishing it from the romanticism that prevailed near the beginning of the nineteenth century. Robert Wohl looks especially at the generation that accepted the teachings of these cultural rebels and tries to assess the impact of this acceptance. Zeev Sternhell is more interested in the political consequences; he sees similarities between these avant-garde beliefs and the fascism that emerged between the two world wars. If he is right, the revolution in thought that preceded World War I—specifically the antirationalism and nationalism it engendered—had profound consequences for subsequent twentieth-century history.

Consciousness and Society

H. STUART HUGHES

H. Stuart Hughes, who taught at Harvard and the University of California, San Diego, was perhaps the most influential American intellectual historian of his generation, a reputation he established with the publication in 1958 of *Consciousness and Society*. His grasp of the relationship between ideas and political and social realities issues from varied experiences in public life: He headed the State Department's Division of Research for Europe, was an independent candidate from Massachusetts for the U.S. Senate, and cochaired the National Committee for a Sane Nuclear Policy. Questions to keep in mind while reading are the following: How does Hughes characterize the revolution in European thought? Why does he object to describing this movement as "neo-romanticism"?

There are certain periods in history in which a number of advanced thinkers, usually working independently one of another, have proposed views on human conduct so different from those commonly accepted at the time—and yet so manifestly interrelated—that together they seem to constitute an intellectual revolution. The decade of the 1890s was one of such periods. In this decade and the one immediately succeeding it, the basic assumptions of eighteenth- and nineteenth-century social thought underwent a critical review from which there emerged the new assumptions characteristic of our own time. "A revolution of such magnitude in the prevailing empirical interpretations of human society is hardly to be found occurring within the short space of a generation, unless one goes back to about the sixteenth century. What is to account for it?"

Nearly all students of the last years of the nineteenth century have sensed in some form or other a profound psychological change. Yet they have differed markedly in the way in which they have expressed their understanding of it. In the older, more aesthetically oriented interpretations (we may think of Henry Adams), the 1890s figured as the *fin de siècle:* it was a period of overripeness, of perverse and mannered decadence—the end of an era. We need not stop to ask ourselves how much of this was simply an artistic and literary pose. For our present purposes, it is irrelevant: the *fin de siècle* is a backdrop, nothing more.

Somewhere between an aesthetic and a more intellectual interpretation, we might be tempted to characterize the new attitude as neo-romanticism or neo-mysticism. This formulation has considerable plausibility. Unquestionably the turn toward the subjective that we find in so much of the imaginative and spec-ulative writing of the quarter-century between 1890 and the First World War recalls the aspirations of the original Romanticists. It is not difficult to think of writers who in the 1890s or early 1900s felt that they were reaching back over a half-century gap to restore to honor those values of the imagination that their immediate predecessors had scorned and neglected. It was writers such as these who established the cult of Dostoyevsky and Nietzsche as the literary heralds of the new era. There is a pathetic paradox in the fact that the year of Nietzsche's madness—1889—coincides with the time at which his work, after two decades of public neglect, first began to find wide acceptance. Again and again in the course of the present study we shall find one or another social thinker elaborat-ing more rigorously and systematically the suggestions with regard to uncon-scious strivings and heroic minorities which Nietzsche had thrown out in fragmentary form.

Yet to call Nietzsche a neo-romantic is surely misleading. Any such charac-terization does less than justice to the critical and Socratic elements in his thought. And when it is applied to the social thinkers of the early twentieth century, it fits only a very few—and these are minor figures like Péguy and Jung. The truly great either were hostile to what they took to be neo-romantic ten-dencies or, like Freud and Weber, sought to curb the romanticism they discov-ered within themselves. Durkheim was perhaps the most categorical of his contemporaries in protesting against what he called a "renascent mysticism," but he was not an isolated case. It was rather the "mystic" Bergson (whom Durkheim may have been aiming at) who was less typical. Indeed, of the major new doctrines of the period, the Bergsonian metaphysics was unique in having frankly mystical aspects—and even this doctrine was couched so far as possible in acceptable philosophic terminology. It was on the "lower" levels of thought, rather—on the level of semipopular agitation—that the neo-romantic tenden-cies were to have their greatest effect. And it was here that their application to politics eventually produced that "betrayal of the intellectuals" which Julien Benda assailed with such telling effect three decades later.

If not "romanticism," will "irrationalism" serve as a general description? It is neat, it is frequently used, and it at least begins to suggest the real concerns of early twentieth-century social thought. Unquestionably the major intellectual innovators of the 1890s were profoundly interested in the problem of irrational motivation in human conduct. They were obsessed, almost intoxicated, with a rediscovery of the nonlogical, the uncivilized, the inexplicable. But to call them "irrationalists" is to fall into a dangerous ambiguity. It suggests a tolerance or even a preference for the realms of the unconscious. The reverse was actually the case. The social thinkers of the 1890s were concerned with the irrational only to exorcise it. By probing into it, they sought ways to tame it, to canalize it for constructive human purposes. Even Sorel, who has often been held up as the supreme irrationalist, had as his life's goal the enunciation of a political formula that would fit the new world of industrial logic and the machine.

Sorel, Pareto, Durkheim, Freud—all thought of themselves as engineers or technicians, men of science or medicine. It is obviously absurd to call them irrationalists in any but the most restricted sense. As a substitute, the formula "anti-intellectualist" has sometimes been employed. This characterization is both flexible and comprehensive. It suggests the revulsion from ideology and the *a priori,* from the abstract thought of the century and a half preceding, which served to unite writers otherwise so far apart as Durkheim and Sorel. It recalls the influence and prestige of William James—an influence at the same time comparable, opposed, and complementary to that of Nietzsche. "Anti-intellectualism," then, is virtually equivalent to Jamesian pragmatism. It offers a satisfactory common denominator for grouping a large proportion of the intellectual innovations of the 1890s.

Yet it is at the same time too broad and too narrow. It fails to take account of the unrepentant abstraction and intellectualism in the thought of Benedetto Croce—or, to take quite a different example, the later elaboration by Max Weber of social theory in terms of "ideal types." It suggests, moreover, that the turn from the principles of the Enlightenment was more complete and decisive than was actually the case. The main attack against the intellectual heritage of the past was in fact on a narrower front. It was directed primarily against what the writers of the 1890s chose to call "positivism." By this they did not mean simply the rather quaint doctrines associated with the name of Auguste Comte, who had originally coined the term. Nor did they mean the social philosophy of Herbert Spencer, which was the guise in which positivist thinking was most apparent in their own time. They used the word in a looser sense to characterize the whole tendency to discuss human behavior in terms of analogies drawn from natural science. In reacting against it, the innovators of the 1890s felt that they were rejecting the most pervasive intellectual tenet of their time. They believed that they were casting off a spiritual yoke that the preceding quarter-century had laid upon them.

As a preliminary characterization, to speak of the innovations of the 1890s as a revolt against positivism comes closest to what the writers in question actually thought that they were about. Yet even this last formula has its pitfalls. We must be on guard against the tendency of someone like Croce to use positivism as a philosophic catch-all, to embrace under this epithet every doctrine for which he had a dislike. We must not forget the number of influential thinkers of the period—men like Durkheim and Mosca—who remained essentially in the positivist tradition. And, finally, we must take proper account of the others, like Freud, who continued to use mechanistic language drawn from the natural sciences long after their discoveries had burst the framework of their inherited vocabulary.

❈ ❈ ❈

So much for the cultural setting. Against this background we may outline in preliminary and schematic form the major ideas that were initially stated in the 1890s, preparatory to their fuller elaboration in the first decade of the twentieth century.

1. Most basic, perhaps, and the key to all the others was the new interest in the problem of consciousness and the role of the unconscious. It was the problem implicit in the title of Bergson's first book, the *Essay on the Immediate Data of Consciousness*. In it he had tried to distinguish between a "superficial psychic life" to which the scientific logic of space and number could properly be applied, and a life in the "depths of consciousness" in which "the deep-seated self" followed a logic of its own: He had come to the conclusion that the world of dreams might offer a clue to this secret and unexplored realm. "In order to recover this fundamental self," he had added, "a vigorous effort of analysis is necessary." A decade later, and proceeding from a philosophic and professional preparation almost totally in contrast to that of Bergson, Freud began to carry out the program that the former had outlined. Freud's first major work, *The Interpretation of Dreams*, built on his own "vigorous effort" of self-analysis a theory of unconscious motivation to which the life of dreams offered the key.

2. Closely related to the problem of consciousness was the question of the meaning of time and duration in psychology, philosophy, literature, and history. It was the problem to which Bergson was to return again and again in an effort to define the nature of subjective existence as opposed to the schematic order that the natural sciences had imposed on the external world. It represented one aspect of the task that Croce had set himself in trying to establish the qualitative and methodological differences

between the realm of history and the realm of science. In somewhat different form it was the problem with which the natural scientists were themselves contending in postulating a universe that no longer strictly conformed to the laws of Newtonian physics. Finally it was the dilemma that obsessed the novelists of the first two decades of the new century— Alain-Fournier, Proust, Thomas Mann—the tormenting question of how to recapture the immediacy of past experience in language that in ordinary usage could reproduce no more than the fragmentized reality of an existence that the logical memory had already stored away in neat compartments.

3. Beyond and embracing the questions of consciousness and time, there loomed the further problem of the nature of knowledge in what Wilhelm Dilthey had called the "sciences of the mind." In the early 1880s Dilthey had attempted to establish rules that would separate the areas in which the human mind strove for some kind of internal comprehension from the realm of external and purely conventional symbols devised by natural science. A decade later Croce had resumed the task, with his first important essay, *"La storia ridotta sotto il concetto generale dell'arte."* Croce soon abandoned the simple solution of including history among the arts. But his conviction of the radical subjectivity of historical knowledge remained. By 1900 it was apparent to the more imaginative of Croce's contemporaries that the nineteenth-century program of building an edifice of historical and sociological knowledge by patient accumulation and painstaking verification no longer sufficed. By such means it would prove forever impossible to penetrate beneath the surface of human experience. One had, rather, a choice between the exercise of the sympathetic intuition postulated in Croce's neo-idealistic theory of history, and the creation of useful fictions, as Max Weber was later to elaborate them, as models for critical understanding.

4. If the knowledge of human affairs, then, rested on such tentative foundations, the whole basis of political discussion had been radically altered. No longer could one remain content with the easy assurances of the rationalistic ideologies inherited from the century and a half preceding—liberal, democratic, or socialist as the case might be. The task was rather to penetrate behind the fictions of political action, behind what Sorel called the "myths," Pareto the "derivations," and Mosca the "political formulas" of the time. Behind these convenient façades, one could postulate the existence of the actual wielders of power, the creative minorities, the political élites. The discussion of politics, then, had been pushed back from the front of the stage to the wings—from the rhetoric of public discussion to the manipulation of half-conscious sentiments.

Such, indeed, is the most general characterization we may give to the new intellectual concerns of the 1890s. They had displaced the axis of social thought from the apparent and objectively verifiable to the only partially conscious area of unexplained motivation. In this sense the new doctrines were manifestly subjective. Psychological process had replaced external reality as the most pressing topic for investigation. It was no longer what actually existed that seemed most important: it was what men thought existed. And what they felt on the unconscious level had become rather more interesting than what they had consciously rationalized. Or—to formulate the change in still more radical terms—since it had apparently been proved impossible to arrive at any sure knowledge of human behavior—if one must rely on flashes of subjective intuition or on the creation of convenient fictions—then the mind had indeed been freed from the bonds of positivist method: it was at liberty to speculate, to imagine, to create. At one stroke, the realm of human understanding had been drastically reduced and immensely broadened. The possibilities of social thought stretched out to infinity. It was perhaps this that Freud had in mind when in 1896 he spoke of "metapsychology"—the definition of the origin and nature of humanity—as his "ideal and problem child," his most challenging task for the future.

█ █ █

In the retrospect of [World War I], the year 1905 most clearly offered the watershed. It marked the first time for a quarter-century that all Europe seemed astir. The revolution in Russia had come as the first major social disturbance since the Paris Commune of 1871—and for a moment the Socialist parties of France and Germany, Austria and Italy, had faced the embarrassing prospect that they might be obliged to give reality to the Marxist professions that had gradually been transformed into little more than a litany for the faithful. The revolutionary danger soon passed. But the effects of the other decisive event of the year—the First Moroccan Crisis—were not to be eradicated so quickly. From 1905 on, one diplomatic crisis followed on another in regular succession. The shock of Tangiers—as Péguy put it—"within the space of . . . two hours" introduced a new epoch in his own life, as it did in the history of his country and of the world. For the next decade the youth of Europe lived and breathed in an atmosphere of impending war.

It was this prospect of war service which most sharply marked off the new generation from those who had reached intellectual maturity in the 1890s. By 1905, men like Freud and Weber, Durkheim and Bergson, Mosca and Croce, were already getting too old for front-line duty. Of them, Weber alone put on a uniform during the war, and even he was not permitted to engage in actual combat. The war, when it came, was not *their* war: it was their sons' war. For

them the decisive experience had been the intellectual renewal of the 1890s—
or perhaps, in the case of the French, the defense of Captain Dreyfus. For the
generation of their sons the great event was obviously the war itself. Here we
find a dramatic instance of the contrasting experiences that serve to demarcate
one age group from another in intellectual history.

Living as it did in a state of nearly constant war alert, the new generation
was more impatient than that of its fathers. It respected its elders: in this it differed from the conventional image of a younger generation. But it was looking
for something more arresting and dogmatic than its seniors had provided. It admired the discoveries they had made—but it understood these discoveries in
cruder fashion. Where the writers of the 1890s had restricted themselves to a
questioning of the potentialities of reason, the young men of 1905 became
frank irrationalists or even anti-rationalists. This crucial distinction, which so
often remains blurred in the history of ideas in our century, was largely a matter
of contrasting age groups. The younger men were no longer satisfied with the
urbane detachment of their elders. Everywhere they were in search of an ideal
and a faith.

Thus in Germany they began to apply the teachings of Nietzsche in the
sense of direct action, and thought of themselves as that "first generation of
fighters and dragon-slayers" whom he had called on to establish the "Reich of
Youth." One of Nietzsche's self-styled disciples—Stefan George—became their
poet: from George they learned to regard themselves as a new spiritual aristocracy, with a lofty if ill-defined mission. The newly formed youth groups gave
them an organizational outlet and an intoxicating sense of physical and spiritual liberation. Ten months before the outbreak of the war, in October 1913,
representatives of the Free German Youth assembled on the Hohen Meissner
hill in central Germany and drew up a melodramatic pledge to "take united action . . . under any and all circumstances . . . for the sake of . . . inner freedom."
It was young people of this sort that Weber encountered four years later, when,
at a gathering at Burg Lauenstein in Thuringia, he declined to serve as the
prophet for whom they longed.

In Italy the years between the turn of the century and the First World War
brought into prominence new writers, new reviews, and new political organizations. The reaction from positivism that in Croce's case had expressed itself in
rational and measured form, with the younger generation became a kind of
spiritual explosion. Nationalism in politics, dynamism and "Futurism" in literature, above all the example—both artistic and personal—of the flamboyant
word-magician Gabriele D'Annunzio, marked the changed temper of Italian
youth. It was not until the review *La Voce* was founded in Florence in 1908 that
some of the new writers were able to collaborate with their elders in reconciling
a moderate type of nationalism with the older liberal tradition.

❊ ❊ ❊

It was in France, however, that the cleavage between generations was most self-consciously delineated, and it is from here that we shall chiefly draw the literary evidences of a changed temper. In France after the turn of the century, as in Germany a decade earlier, the young people began to declare themselves Nietzscheans. André Gide's *The Immoralist,* published in 1902, is an early example. Subsequently, still younger writers like Alain-Fournier were to recognize the influence, either explicit or unconscious, of Nietzsche on their own thought. But in France the Nietzscheans were only a minority. It was Bergson, rather, who ranked as the tutelary deity of the new generation. After 1905 the educated youth of France became militantly "Bergsonian."

The young people seized hold of Bergson with avidity and interpreted him according to their own tastes. They read into his teaching the notion of direct-action politics—usually of the Right—which was distinctly in contrast with his own convictions, and of dogmatic religion, on which his personal position still remained obscure. As so often has happened in the history of ideas, the originator of the doctrine lost control of his own creation: his disciples escaped from his tutelary guidance. For the half-decade before the First World War, "Bergsonism" was living a life of its own, almost independent of its founder.

It was a curious phenomenon, this new generation in which the sons were more conservative than the fathers. The latter had done battle for the innocence of Dreyfus and fought the power of the "reactionaries" and the clergy. Their children were as likely as not to embrace the neo-royalism of Charles Maurras and the *Action Française,* or the milder version of conservative nationalism preached by the novelist Maurice Barrès. At the Ecole Normale Supérieure the influence of Lucien Herr, the librarian, and of Jean Jaurès, the great Socialist alumnus, began to wane: Léon Blum—who three decades later was to be prime minister of France, but who at this period still ranked only as a brilliant lawyer and a rather precious *littérateur*—was one of the last of their great converts. And, to the more critical of the younger minds, Blum seemed rather superficial: he still took Jaurès's rolling periods seriously.

❊ ❊ ❊

In 1900, in intellectual circles, it had been bad form to be a practicing Catholic. By 1910, while the majority still consisted of unbelievers—philosophical positivists for the most part—a growing minority of the sensitive and discriminating spirits were returning to the faith in which they had been baptized. A few great conversions had served as examples—the poet Paul Claudel from the elders, the philosopher Jacques Maritain in the younger generation. It was the latter who was to appeal in vain with the anti-clerical wife of Péguy to ease her husband's torments of conscience by letting her children be baptized.

⧖ ⧖ ⧖

   With this contrast, we touch the central ambiguity in the generation of 1905. In France—and the same was true in Germany—during the years just before the outbreak of the war there reigned among the youth a spirit that combined respect for authority with the cult of spontaneous creation. Depending on where they have chosen to lay their emphasis, historians of the epoch have judged it very differently. On the one hand, they have found in it a threatening proto-fascist atmosphere, on the other hand a renaissance of culture and of living brutally cut off at its start. This was the generation of French and Germans of whom the best were to perish in battle—or so, at least, their contemporaries saw it. And the tragic irony of the matter was that they greeted the outbreak of the slaughter with enthusiasm. The more bellicose felt at last within their grasp the life of action for which they had longed. The more reflective welcomed it as a deliverance from unfruitful anticipation: "Better that war should come," they repeated, "than to go on with this perpetual waiting."

The Generation of 1914

ROBERT WOHL

Robert Wohl, who teaches at the University of California, Los Angeles, has published a comprehensive study of the origins of French communism. The work from which the following is taken is interesting both for its conceptual approach and for the information it provides. According to Wohl, what constitutes an "historical generation"? Compare Wohl to Hughes in regard to the nature of avant-garde thought at the turn of the century. To what extent does the psychological rebellion of the younger against the older generation explain the former's willingness to accept theories it knew its parents rejected? Finally, why did the "generation of 1914" welcome, rather than draw back from, the prospect of war?

Generational theorists worked hard to devise a reliable and scientifically respectable method of determining the chronological limits of generations. Their goal was a periodic table that would set forth the history of modern Europe in a succession of quantifiably delimited generations. These efforts were in vain because they rested on a misconception of the generational phenomenon. A historical generation is not defined by its chronological limits or its borders. It is not a zone of dates; nor is it an army of contemporaries making its way across a territory of time. It is more like a magnetic field at the center of which lies an experience or a series of experiences. It is a system of references and identifications that gives priority to some kinds of experiences and devalues others— hence it is relatively independent of age. The chronological center of this experiential field need not be stable; it may shift with time. What is essential to the formation of a generational consciousness is some common frame of reference that provides a sense of rupture with the past and that will later distinguish the members of the generation from those who follow them in time. This frame of reference is always derived from great historical events like wars, revolutions, plagues, famines, and economic crises, because it is great historical events like these that supply the markers and signposts with which people impose order on their past and link their individual fates with those of the communities in which they live.

What allowed European intellectuals born between 1880 and 1900 to view themselves as a distinct generation was that their youth coincided with the opening of the twentieth century and their lives were then bifurcated by the Great War. Those who survived into the decade of the 1920s perceived their lives as being neatly divided into a *before,* a *during,* and an *after,* categories most of them equated with the stages of life known as youth, young manhood, and maturity. What bound the generation of 1914 together was not just their experiences during the war, as many of them later came to believe, but the fact that they grew up and formulated their first ideas in the world from which the war issued, a world framed by two dates, 1900 and 1914. This world was the "vital horizon" within which they began conscious historical life.

The primary fact of this world—and the first thing that young people noticed about it—was that it was being rapidly transformed by technology. Europeans were being freed increasingly from the traditional constraints imposed on mankind by nature. Life was becoming safer, cleaner, more comfortable, and longer for most sectors of the population. Death had not been vanquished (though many death-bearing diseases had), but its arrival was now more predictable, and the physician, along with the engineer, had been elevated to the priesthood of the new civilization.

At the same time that life was becoming more secure, its pace quickened and the sense of distance among people shrank. Even rest became recreation. Instead of picnicking *sur l'herbe* or strolling on resort boardwalks, Europeans began to pedal, swim, ski, and scramble up the sides of mountains. The great events of the era, from a technological point of view, were the invention and diffusion of the automobile, the motorcycle, and the airplane. Speed still implied romance and adventure and had yet to be connected with traffic fatalities, tedium, and pollution. It is difficult to determine the precise effects that these changes of velocity had on the sensibility of intellectuals growing up in early twentieth-century Europe. Certainly, though, the acceleration of movement enhanced the feeling of novelty and encouraged the conviction that the twentieth century would be fundamentally different from its predecessor, if only because it would be faster.

The second characteristic of the prewar world, prominently featured on the front page of every daily newspaper, was that it was undergoing a revolutionary change in political and social structures. Old empires were under attack in Central and Eastern Europe. Oppressed peoples were clamoring for statehood. Workers were insisting on higher wages and shorter hours. Peasants were demanding land or more favorable sharecropping arrangements. Everywhere in Europe there was a movement to open political participation to larger groups of people. The old systems of deference were under attack, and the old elites were being pressed to make concessions. Authority, whether exercised by landlords, factory owners, clergymen, or fathers within their own families, was being angrily disputed. As Ortega was later to complain, people were no longer content to occupy the place that destiny had assigned them. And since the number of people in Europe was increasing at a rapid rate, there was much talk about "the masses" and what they were likely to do. The great political and social movement of the day was Socialism. It seemed certain that Socialism would play as important a role in the twentieth century as liberalism had played in the nineteenth. In 1900, though, it was far from clear what that role would be. The still unsatisfied ambitions of the subordinate classes and their organization into groups that challenged the forces of public order on the streets of Europe's capitals meant that the threat of revolution hovered menacingly on the horizon of the middle- and upper-class mind. But the commitment of the most prominent Socialist leaders to democracy and peace and their often professed abhorrence of violence kept alive the hope that the transition to a new society could be made painlessly and with benefit to all.

A third characteristic of this world—one that is especially difficult to grasp today—is that while it stood under the cloud of threatening war, its inhabitants viewed the possibility of this war from the perspective of a century in which warfare in Europe had been kept within such narrowly circumscribed limits that it had never interfered with improvements in the quality of life. War among the major European powers seemed both inevitable (because of Germany's determination to dominate the continent and challenge England's control of the world's seas and markets) and impossible (because of the complex economic interrelationships that bound the great powers to each other and made the prosperity of one dependent on the prosperity of all). This was the paradox that defined European international relations between 1900 and 1914. There was no lack of signs that conflict was coming. Major European crises erupted with regularity almost every year after 1895. The Boer War, Faschoda, the Russo-Japanese War, Agadir, the Balkan wars—these were the events with which the generation of 1914 grew up. But somehow the final breakdown of the system was averted, and war became in people's minds a dangerous sport, like big game hunting, that some particularly adventurous Europeans practiced outside or on the periphery of Europe. These conditions of increasing ease of life, along with increasing sources of domestic and international conflict, explain how among Europeans of the ruling classes optimism about the future could be "allied insanely" with the expectation of Armageddon.

This was the world that young people growing up between 1900 and 1914 encountered; this was the vital horizon within which they had to act. To understand what they thought about that world, we must look at the prevailing state of culture. Toward the end of the nineteenth century, European high culture began to split into two related but mutually antagonistic camps. On the one hand, there was the official bourgeois culture; on the other hand, there was the culture of the trailblazing vanguard. Middle-class intellectuals born during the last two decades of the nineteenth century reacted fiercely and self-consciously against the first and gave their allegiance to the second. It was from the leaders of the avant-garde that young intellectuals learned how to interpret their world; and it was from them that they took their criticism of contemporary society and their visions of the future. These cultural innovators were in the process of redefining and restructuring European culture. Men like Bergson, Poincaré, Sorel, Freud, Weber, James, Blondel, Mosca, Pareto, and Croce had brought about a radical change in the way European intellectuals thought and the way they viewed the products of thought. The very possibility of achieving sure knowledge had been called into question. Philosophers of science and society showed that the laws linking subject and object were fictions, thus not really laws at all, unless legislated into fleeting reality by human will. Time was redefined in subjective terms to free experience from the determinism of sequence. The standard of truth was abandoned in favor of the idea of efficacity. The bridges between the individual consciousness and the outside world were blown up. Even the unity of the self was thrown into doubt. Descartes's *Discourse on Method* became a favored example of faulty thinking, the product of an age now disappeared.

The new culture was, in one of its most important aspects, a "culture of Anti-Necessity." Varieties of neoidealism competed for the allegiance of the European intellectual elite, and the prophets of these systems of belief dedicated the major part of their energies to demonstrating that no self-respecting intellectual could assume a materialistic outlook on the world. Reality, they said, was a perspective and a construction rather than a verifiable fact or a thing. Man was not the executor of natural and historical laws, but a creator of his life with no limits on him but those imposed by lack of imagination and weakness of will. Scientific analysis was considered to be a mental instrument of severely limited validity; intuition into the multiplicity of human realities took its place; and action rather than contemplation was recommended as a source of knowledge. With organized religion in retreat and reason exposed as the greatest of illusions, it became essential to find new bases for life and new systems of morality by which to judge men's actions. No longer was it possible to count on the beneficence of history or to rely on receiving steady dividends handed out by progress. The mind became an instrument with which intellectuals dominated and took possession of the world; civilization, a precarious achievement of the spirit that must constantly be renewed through the process of destruction and re-creation.

These attitudes represented a break with the main tradition of European rationalism. Yet the very intellectuals who prided themselves on being liberated from the illusions of progress and the mystique of science remained strangely indentured to determinisms of various kinds, determinisms, furthermore, that were themselves inspired by scientific theories. For some, it was the determinism of biology; for others, the determinism of geography; for still others, the determinism of history or race. Whatever the determinism chosen, however, it led toward the acknowledgment of a painful contradiction: that man was free to create his own life, as the novelist creates a fiction; and yet was a slave to the material conditions of his existence. Most European intellectuals of the late nineteenth century sought escape from this dilemma by asserting that man could master the determinisms that bound him only by raising them to consciousness, accepting them, and living life with vitality and passion.

Some intellectuals were quick to perceive the political implications of these attitudes and to push them to their most extreme consequences. Democracy and Socialism, they noted not unhappily, were based on faulty premises. All societies were dominated by aristocracies and all civilizations were doomed to collapse. Why, then, get concerned about the misery of the masses? Suffering was the price that peoples paid for culture. Progress, insofar as it existed, took place in individual minds. Better, then, the cultivation of one truly successful human being than the futile, life-destroying pursuit of an impossible egalitarian utopia. Since life was struggle, truth was a matter of perspective, and annihilation awaited us at the end, we ought to endeavor, as Unamuno put it, "to stamp others with our seal, to perpetuate ourselves in them and in their children by dominating them, to leave on all things the imperishable impress of our signature." War was the seedbed of culture, the foundation of morality, and the form of social intercourse that brought men closest together. Peace came at a cultural price too high to pay. This was the message that many people derived from Nietzsche's teachings; and if, for some reason, they were put off by the mists of Teutonic terminology that surrounded Nietzsche's aphorisms or the intimations of derangement with which the message was relayed, they could get the same complex of ideas from a dozen other sources, for the notions of an aristocracy of intellect and a tragic sense of life were everywhere in the air.

Naturally, the new culture was not taught in schools. It remained the possession of a small elite: that literary and artistic vanguard living in the great capitals of Europe that Hugo von Hofsmannthal called the "conscience" of the young generation. But it was discovered and disseminated among young intellectuals during the years immediately preceding the war. The spiritual guides and mentors acknowledged by the members of the generation of 1914—Barrès, Péguy, Sorel, and Romain Rolland in France; Nietzsche, Langbehn, and Moeller van den Bruck in Germany; Shaw, Wells, and Hardy in England; Unamuno, Azorín, and Baroja in Spain; D'Annunzio, Croce, Gentile, and Pareto in Italy; Ibsen and Strindberg in Scandinavia—were all proponents of the new culture. Their syntheses of neoidealism and biological determinism, their elitism, their pessimism about the future of Western culture, and their critiques of democracy and socialism were the ideas that seemed most up-to-date between 1900 and 1914. The existence of this new culture, and the excitement it produced, contributed to the consciousness of a generational rupture among people born between 1880 and 1900; yet, paradoxically, the generational idea concealed the extent to which the new culture was a creation of the intellectuals of the preceding generation. "I could not have defined what all this was about that had laid so strong a spell on me," Carl Zuckmayer (1896) later wrote, "but it was *our* time, *our* world, *our* sense of life that came rushing upon me, falling upon me, and suddenly I awakened to a consciousness of a new generation, a consciousness that even the most intelligent, most aware and unbiased parents could not share." What Zuckmayer and other young intellectuals like him did not realize was that the intellectuals in the generation of their parents had created that new art and those new ideas which his generation experienced as a "revelation" and an "illumination."

Thus it was from intellectuals among the age-group of their fathers that men born between 1880 and 1900 learned to think of themselves as a generation. Massis inherited the idea from Barrès; Ortega took it from Unamuno and Azorín; Prezzolini and Papini found it in Croce and D'Annunzio. Moreover, it was these same intellectuals who taught their disciples what to think about the society in which they lived. Prewar European intellectual youth grew up in revolt against the comfort, coziness, and predictability of modern life. They feared that they had been born into a declining world, and they longed after risk, danger, and brutal contact with the elemental realities of life, as they imagined that life was lived outside of European cities. The first images of the generation of 1914, devised during the decade or so before the outbreak of the war, were nothing but a reversal of the qualities that young intellectuals disliked or feared in the generation of their parents. The previous generation had been thinkers; they would be doers. The previous generation had floundered in moral relativism; they would seek assurance in calm faith. The previous generation had been weak and indecisive; they would be strong and vital. This supposed change in character was rendered superficially plausible by the spread of team sports, the quickening of the pace of life, greater possibilities for travel, and the weakening of the authority of fathers over their sons as society became more complex and opportunities for employment and careers became more varied.

The sentiment of generational unity grows out of and is nourished by an even deeper feeling. What draws young people together and ignites the sparks that join them is a sense of common grievance. This does not happen regularly, as some generational theorists assumed. But when it does, groups of coevals will form to set the world aright. The complaint voiced most often by young intellectuals during the period before 1914 was that they had the misfortune to be born into a dying world that lacked energy, vitality, and moral fiber. It was characteristic of this age-group of European intellectuals that they perceived the problem of decadence in connection with a crisis of the nation. The nation was perceived as being weak, morally flabby, a shaky structure that might at any time collapse into its constituent parts. The desire for a reform of the nation and a renewal of its spiritual resources was ordinarily allied with a profound ignorance of the realities of national life. Young intellectuals generally knew little about the people or their problems. But their longing for regeneration was nonetheless strong, and it was a feeling capable of inspiring action. Hence the prevalence of national revivals and the popularity of nationalist movements during the decade preceding the Great War. The nation, they believed, must somehow be whipped into action; its classes and contending factions must be reconciled; its citizens must learn to subordinate their corporatist and selfish interests to the spiritual interests of the national community conceived as a whole. This was what Ortega meant in 1914 when he said that Spanish society must be nationalized; but his program for backward Spain was an ideal shared by Massis and Prezzolini and others like them all over Europe.

Partisans of national revival perceived two ways by which their goal of national regeneration could be accomplished. One was to implement the Socialist program, which called for the democratization of political institutions, the extension of political participation, the elimination of social inequities, and the defense of international peace. Between 1900 and 1914 most young intellectuals felt some attraction toward this program; many called themselves Socialists and even joined their country's Socialist party. Among these converts to Socialism were Brooke, Ortega, and Gramsci. But most middle-class intellectuals of this generation withheld their adherence from Socialist parties, or withdrew soon after joining, because of their feelings that Socialism was a plebeian movement in which intellectuals had no place and their fear that Socialism's victory would destroy elitist values and undermine the cohesion of the nation. Socialism, Henri Franck confided to a friend in 1908, could be the salvation of life, sensibility, and art. It could create new values and bring about the renewal of civilization. But if the Socialists remained bound to a "sterile Marxism" and a "base materialism," if their movement resulted only in "appetite, envy, and hate," and if they were not willing to give their lives to defend "that ensemble of feelings of veneration that is called France," then everything would be finished. "There is something more important yet than the success of the working class; it's the preservation of France."

The other way the nation could be rejuvenated and civilization saved from decadence was through a sudden trauma or blow of fate. The only deliverance from the languor of bourgeois complacency that most young Europeans could imagine was the outbreak of a general war. Hence some leaped to the treacherous assumption that it was on the field of battle and in the stress of national emergency that a sense of national consciousness would develop and that a new, more ethical, less commercial man would emerge to replace the bourgeois and the proletarian, both products of the hateful and selfish society into which young intellectuals cursed themselves for having been born. This idea may seem strange and even demented; but it will appear less so when we remember that all European wars since 1815 had been short, progressive in their effects, and, in memory at least, heroic. One did not have to be a reactionary like Walter Flex to believe that war offered a means of breaking the impasse of prewar politics, of creating a sense of national unity where none existed, and of nourishing "those virtues of sacrifice, fortitude, and boldness that constitute the essence of the combatant and that make of the fighting man, with all his excesses and brutality, a type infinitely superior to that shrewd sybarite who finds in the cult of peace the best expression of his sensual concept of life."

Attitudes like these explain the feverish enthusiasm with which large sectors of European intellectual youth greeted the outbreak of war in 1914. European youth did not actively want war; but many young European intellectuals desperately wanted change and were willing to risk their lives (and those of others) to achieve it. More than one prewar intellectual had gazed into the future and sensed that something new and wonderful was coming. "It is brooding heavily in the air as a storm does, and soon, oh, very soon, it will thunder upon the world. Flashes of lightning have appeared on the horizon, the echoes of thunder have been heard in the air, but the great reckless storm, the storm that will make us abandon mediocrity and will set us free from pettiness, has not yet come—yet soon it will break over us." When war did break over Europe, it was interpreted by intellectuals as an hour of redemption, a rite of purification, and a chance, perhaps the last, to escape from a sinking and declining civilization. This is why Rupert Brooke could sing "Now, God be thanked Who has matched us with His hour"; why the German poet Bruno Frank could shout "Rejoice, friends! that we are alive"; why the Italian writer Giani Stuparich was so happy that he wept with joy; why Drieu la Rochelle remembered the outbreak of the war as a marvelous surprise and the unexpected fulfillment of his youth; and why Ortega immediately interpreted the news of war on August 5, 1914, as the end of one world and the birth of another. "History," he wrote, "is trembling to its very roots, its flanks are torn apart convulsively, because a new reality is about to be born."

Neither Right nor Left

Fascist Ideology in France

ZEEV STERNHELL

Zeev Sternhell is an Israeli who studied at the University of Paris and has published works on French nationalism and French fascism. He now heads the political science department at Hebrew University in Jerusalem. This excerpt comes from his book on fascism in France. Compare his insistence on the "cult of instinct" and the "subordination" of the role of the individual to Hughes' and Wohl's analyses of social thought at the turn of the century. What in Sternhell's view is the relationship between rationalism and political liberalism, or, put another way, how does the belief that man is irrational help undermine the foundations of democracy?

The thirty years that preceded the First World War and the decade that followed it formed a truly revolutionary period in the history of Europe. In the space of less than half a century the condition of society, the form of life, the rate of technological progress, and in many respects people's way of looking at themselves underwent a greater change than at any other time in modern history. The growth of industry and technology transformed manners and morals, radically altered the pace of life, brought into being great metropolitan cities, and had a profound effect on life in the provinces.

In the second and third decades of our century, there was a strong and widespread awareness of living in a world that was changing with unprecedented

From Zeev Sternhell, *Neither Right nor Left: Fascist Ideology in France,* University of California Press. Copyright © 1986 The Regents of the University of California. Reprinted by permission of the University of California Press and the author.

rapidity. As Henri De Man wrote, "In reality, there are not many qualitative changes in the history of mankind that can be compared, as regards their revolutionary significance for society and culture, with the change from mechanical movement to electrical movement, from the technique of the lever to the technique of waves, from the cogwheel to the electric wire and wireless transmission, from material to energetic work processes, from mechanistic thought to functional thought." De Man felt that the world of that period was a world in gestation, "which differed as much from the world of our grandparents as that differed from the world of their ancestors six thousand years ago." And he concluded, in a manner very characteristic of his generation, "We are living in the midst of the greatest social revolution that history has ever known. There is an old world that is passing away and a new world that is being born."

However, if it was only in the interwar period that this consciousness of the new situation became practically universal, a presentiment of the upheavals that were to overtake an entire civilization already existed at the end of the nineteenth century. Indeed, in the sphere of ideas, that period was already deeply affected by a resurgence of irrational values, by a cult of instinct and sentiment, and by an affirmation of the supremacy of the forces of life and the affections. The rationalist and "mechanistic" explanation of the world that had been dominant in European thought from the sixteenth century onward now gave way to an "organic" explanation, and the new importance given to historical values and various idealistic factors amounted to a condemnation of rationalism and individualism. The role of the individual was made subordinate to that of society and of history. To state the matter differently, for the generation of 1890— Le Bon, Barrès, Sorel, Georges Vacher de Lapouge, and others—the individual had no value in himself, and therefore society could not be regarded simply as the sum of the individuals who composed it. This new generation of intellectuals was violently opposed to the rationalistic individualism of the liberal order, to the dissolution of social bonds that existed in bourgeois society, and to the "utilitarianism and materialism" that prevailed there. It was precisely in this desire to overturn the prevailing order of values that the most clear-sighted fascist intellectuals of the interwar period perceived the origins of fascism. Gentile defined fascism as a revolt against positivism.

That revolt, which was also an attack on the way of life produced by liberalism, an opposition to the "atomized" society, led to a glorification of the institution that was felt to represent the element of unity—the nation. This glorification of the nation, the emergence of a nationalism involving a whole system of defenses and safeguards intended to assure the integrity of the national body, was a natural outcome of the new conception of the world. The new school of thought, rejecting the system of values bequeathed by the eighteenth century and the French Revolution and assailing the foundations of liberalism and democracy, had a very different image of things: "The selection-ist morality gives one's duty toward the species the position of supremacy that Christianity gives one's duty toward God," wrote Vacher de Lapouge.

Here we must insist on something of great importance for an understand-ing of subsequent developments. The antirationalist reaction that questioned the underlying principles of both Marxism and democracy was not the mere product of a literary neoromanticism that affected only the world of arts and letters. These principles were challenged in the name of science, and this was the real significance of the intellectual revolution of the first quarter of the twen-tieth century. When one sees them in this context, one can understand the na-ture and scope of the new directions taken in many fields in this period: the new humanistic and social sciences, Darwinian biology, Bergsonian philosophy, Ernest Renan and Hippolyte Taine's interpretation of history, Le Bon's social psychology, and the so-called Italian school of political sociology—Pareto, Gaetano Mosca, and Michels—all opposed the basic premises of liberalism and democracy. The new social sciences, which inherited many aspects of social Darwinism (this was especially true of anthropology and social psychology), created a new theory of political conduct. They thus contributed to an intellec-tual climate that helped to undermine the foundations of democracy and to enable fascism to come to power.

The positivist character of their scientific method cannot alter the fact that the objective criticisms of given realities of Mosca, Pareto, and Michels amount, in actuality, to sweeping attacks on democracy. The rational explanation of the irrational provided by the theory of elites constitutes a bridge between social re-search and fascist practice. This explanation by the Italian school of political so-ciology contributed to the development of revolutionary syndicalism and nationalism, and in many respects represented the meeting point of these two schools of thought. A conception of man as being essentially motivated by the forces of the unconscious, a pessimistic idea that human nature is unchange-able, led to a static view of history: Human conduct cannot change, since psy-chological motivations always remain the same. According to this view, in all periods of history, whatever the current ideology, under whatever regime, human behavior is unchanging, and therefore the character of a regime is fi-nally of little importance in itself. Moreover, these three authors, like Max Weber at a later date, were agreed that the social sciences could not provide a basis for value judgments either of political structures or of ideologies. This sci-entific objectivism, based on a vision of man as an essentially irrational being, thus played an important role in undermining the foundations of democracy, and the theory of elites associated with Mosca, Pareto, and Michels remained until the forties one of the most formidable offensive weapons against both Marxism and democracy. Their writings influenced every form of rebellion against democracy, liberalism, and Marxism; nationalists, syndicalists, and nonconformists of every kind referred to them, but in fact, from the end of the nineteenth century, all the social sciences contributed to the erosion of the spirit of optimism, of faith in the individual and in progress, without which it is difficult to conceive of the survival of democracy.

Here we must mention another important factor. From Mosca and Pareto at the turn of the century and Michels on the eve of the First World War up to De Man and Déat, the social sciences—sociology, anthropology, political science, psychology, and Bergsonian philosophy—were working toward what seems, at least in retrospect, to have been an attempt to create an alternative system to Marxism—a system that could give a total explanation of things comparable to the one given by Marx's. But this long-drawn-out competition with Marx involved not only people like Pareto, Michels, and Mosca but also Weber and even, by implication, Émile Durkheim and Freud. De Man's revision of Marxism was based on psychology, and it was by no means fortuitous that his major work was called, in the best tradition of Gustave Le Bon, *Zur Psychologie des Sozialismus.*

Throughout the interwar period, the influence of these modern disciplines was enormous. They were the only ones with enough authority to be able to speak, along with Marxism, in the name of science, and they were the only ones to provide revisionism with its conceptual foundations.

Thus, at the beginning of the century, these new social sciences, particularly psychology and anthropology, which in turn influenced sociology, political science, and historical research, provided both the anti-liberal and the anti-Marxist reactions with their conceptual framework. They also helped to fuse the ideas of the generation of 1850 (Darwin, Arthur de Gobineau, Wagner) and those of the generation of 1890 into a complete and coherent system. The old romantic outlook, the old historicist tendencies, the old theory of the unconscious origins of the nation, the idea of living forces that make up the soul of the people thus received scientific legitimation. One sees the reappearance, modernized and adapted to the requirements of mass society, of the old principles of the subordination of the individual to the collectivity and the integrity of the national body. These new theories completely rejected the traditional mechanistic conception of man that made human behavior dependent on rational choices. The idea became prevalent that feelings and the unconscious played a far greater role in politics than did reason, and this, by a logical process, engendered a contempt for democracy, its institutions, and its machinery.

The biological and psychological determinism of Le Bon, Vacher de Lapouge, Barrès, Drumont, and even Taine, and of innumerable publications in every field of intellectual endeavor led finally to racism.

According to Le Bon, a people's life, its institutions, its destiny are "simply the reflection of its soul," or, that is to say, the "moral and intellectual characteristics" that "represent a synthesis of its whole past, the heritage of all its ancestors, the motivation of its conduct." "Human conduct," he said, "is inexorably pre-determined" because "each people is endowed with a mental constitution that is as fixed as its anatomical characteristics," and these "fundamental, unchanging characteristics" derive from a "special structure of the brain." Here Le Bon introduced the idea of race that, he said, "is becoming increasingly prevalent and tends to dominate all our historical, political and social conceptions." He often returned to this theme, claiming that race "dominates the special characteristics of the soul of crowds," and represents the influence of past generations on the living.

The critical attitude to individualism, democracy and its institutions, parliamentarianism, and universal suffrage owed a great deal to this new view of man as an essentially irrational being, confined by historical and biological limitations and motivated by sentiments, associations, and images, never by ideas.

The belief in the dominance of the unconscious over reason, the stress on deep, mysterious forces led, as a natural and necessary consequence, to an extreme anti-intellectualism. To rationalism, to the critical spirit and its manifestations, the rebels of the end of the nineteenth century opposed intuitive feelings, emotions, enthusiasms, an unthinking spontaneity welling from the depths of the popular subconscious. Thus, for the generation of 1890, as for the generation that emerged from the trenches, the motive force of political conduct was the unconscious will of the people. This anti-intellectualism was paralleled, moreover, by a demogogic populism that decried intelligence and the use of words and glorified action, energy, and force. Barrès, for instance, no longer asked which doctrine was true, but which force would enable one to act and be victorious. This was the basis of the new nationalism that came into being at the end of the last century and hardly altered until the time of Munich.

The new nationalists sang the praises of every source of power, and all its forms: vitality, discipline, social and national cohesion. Convinced that nothing can be accomplished unless one joins the majority, the crowd, Barrès, the committed intellectual par excellence, was able to "savor deeply the instinctive pleasure of being part of a flock." He deliberately sacrificed the values of the individual to collective values: "What gives an individual or a nation its values is that its energies are tensed to a greater or lesser degree," he maintained. Thus, the new nationalism of the turn of the century was a mass ideology par excellence, designed to embrace and to mobilize the new urban strata.

Based on a physiological determinism, a moral relativism, and an extreme irrationalism, nationalism, in the definitive form it assumed at the beginning of this century, well expressed this new intellectual direction. The new ethics that Barrès developed in the last years of the nineteenth century and that he opposed to the Jacobin mystique at the time of the Dreyfus affair was perhaps the most striking expression of the transformation of French nationalism. To be sure, it was Péguy's achievement to have stamped an important fringe of that nationalism with the mark of his universalistic genius, but his voice was scarcely audible among the chorus of such journalists, writers, and agitators as Rochefort, Drumont, Gustave Tridon, Barrès, and Maurras and such scientists as Jules Soury, Le Bon, and Vacher de Lapouge, for it was this form of determinism that provided the conceptual framework for the nationalism of the end of the century, and its underlying racial argument was precisely the main legacy of the generation of 1890 to the generation of 1930.

These two generations had another point of resemblance: Like the neonationalists of the 1890s, the fascists of the interwar period rejected the political and social consequences of the industrial revolution and of liberal and bourgeois values. Moreover, just as the turn-of-the-century nationalists could not imagine their revolt without the support of the masses, so the fascist ideology was a mass ideology par excellence. One could multiply these parallels. Was not fascism also an anti-intellectual reaction, a reaction of the feelings against the rationality of democracy? Was it not a kind of reflex of the instincts? Did it not also have a cult of physical force, of violence, of brutality? All this explains the importance attached to the setting, the attention paid to decor, great ceremonies, parades—a new liturgy that substituted songs, torches, and processions for deliberation and discussion. In this respect, fascism seems a direct continuation of the neoromanticism of 1880–90, but the scale of that revolt was determined by the mass society that the generation of 1890 was only beginning to glimpse.

However, the intellectual malaise, the political tensions, the social conflicts that characterize the end of the nineteenth century and the beginning of the twentieth were already manifestations of the enormous difficulties experienced by liberalism in adapting itself to the age of the masses. It was toward the end of the century that one began to feel the full impact of the intellectual revolution effected by Darwinism, of the industrialization and urbanization of the European continent, and, finally, of the long-drawn-out process of the growth of a popular nationalism.

Contemporaries had no doubt that they were entering a new period. "The age we are entering will be truly the ERA OF THE MASSES," wrote Le Bon. "It is no longer in the councils of princes but in the heart of the masses that the destiny of nations is being prepared." The entry of the new urban masses into the political arena posed problems for the liberal regime that had not previously existed. Liberalism is an ideology based on rationalism and individualism; it is the product of a society that was supposed to have stopped undergoing structural changes, and in which political participation was necessarily very limited. At the end of the century, an increasing number of people questioned the usefulness of an ideology in which the new social strata, the millions of workers and wage earners of all categories crowded together in the great industrial centers, could find no place. The crisis of liberalism had its roots in the enormous contradictions that existed between the idea of individualism and the way of life of the urban masses, between the traditional concept of the natural rights of man and the new laws of existence that the generation of 1890 discovered in social Darwinism. The great changes that took place after the First World War are really comprehensible only if one examines them against the background of this first prewar period.

2

THE ORIGINS OF WORLD WAR I

In spite of repeated international crises and, in some quarters, dissatisfaction with material and cultural conditions, most Europeans wished to preserve peace. Peace organizations thrived; *Lay Down Your Arms,* a pacifist novel by Austrian writer Bertha von Suttner, became a best-seller. Two peace conferences took place at The Hague in 1899 and 1907 with the aims of bringing about arms reductions and finding ways to settle international affairs. Yet little was accomplished, mutual distrust remained unchecked, and aside from agreements over Germany's railway plans in the Middle East and British and German interests in Portugal's African colonies, few genuine understandings were reached.

If few people actively wanted war, many came to expect it and prepared accordingly. "I only meet people who assure me that an early war with Germany is certain, in fact, inevitable," a Belgian envoy reported from Paris in 1913. "People regret it, but they accept it."[1] Their resignation becomes more understandable if we realize that only a handful anticipated conflict on the scale that was to come. War in the nineteenth century had been acknowledged as a legitimate means of pursuing defined objectives and all conflicts had been short in duration and limited in scope. The losers were perhaps embarrassed and made to pay in the form of reparations, or territory, or both, but none of these wars escalated beyond their original geographic limits.

When war broke out in the aftermath of the assassination of Archduke Franz Ferdinand, heir to the Austro-Hungarian throne, by a Bosnian nationalist, what initially had started as a local struggle rapidly escalated into widespread European conflict as each nation was convinced it was fighting in defense of vital and legitimate rights. The Entente powers feared the extension of German

[1]Andreas Dorpalen, *Europe in the Twentieth Century* (New York: Macmillan, 1968), p. 10.

hegemony; the Central powers believed they were struggling for survival. Indeed, the news that war had come was greeted with some relief; after years of recurring crises the hour of decision had finally arrived, and inasmuch as almost everyone expected a short war, the risks did not seem great. In the summer of 1914 few could imagine the devastation in lives and property that Europeans were bringing upon themselves by accepting a military solution.

Precisely because of the unparalleled dimensions of the cataclysm that ensued, and because the victors held the losers morally guilty of having unleashed it, no subject in history has evoked more discussion and debate than the origins of and the responsibility for the outbreak of World War I. The Treaty of Versailles blamed Germany and her ally Austria-Hungary. To counter these accusations, the Germans—soon followed by the British, the French, and the Austrians—published volumes of documents demonstrating the guilt was not theirs alone, thus making the half-century between the end of the Franco-Prussian War and the start of World War I the most richly documented period in diplomatic history.

In the 1920s, as the wave of retribution receded and many within Britain, France, and the United States rejected what they considered the excesses of a "Carthaginian" peace, some historians sought to revise the treaty's judgment, contending that every country shared at least some blame. One of the most noted "revisionist" historians was Sidney B. Fay, whose conclusions are cited in this chapter. Also revisionist, but in a wholly different way, was the Communist party of the Soviet Union, whose official history emphasized the imperialism engendered by the capitalist systems of wartime belligerents—systems that ensured war was essential to achieve redivision of imperial gains. Also significant in this history is the opinion that capitalist Europe wanted to suppress proletarian revolution by persuading workers to accept nationalist goals.

Responsibility for World War II was attributed to Germany's Nazi government, headed by Adolf Hitler. Consequently, during and after World War II the question of responsibility for World War I was linked to the origins of World War II. Whether through insinuation or demonstration, many historians concluded that German refusal to accept the 1919 settlement made the interwar period a "long armistice" with the foreign policy of Hitler's Germany marking a continuation of the foreign policy of the Kaiser's Germany. Anglo-Saxon and French historians found few difficulties in accepting this interpretation, but conservative German historians, who acknowledged German guilt for the 1939 war, could not accept unilateral German guilt for the 1914 war.[2] Hence when in 1961 German historian Fritz Fischer published his *Griff nach der Weltmacht* (translated in shortened form as *Germany's Aims in the First World War* but more literally meaning "Grab for World Power"), these traditionalists were outraged,

---

[2] James Joll, *The Origins of the First World War* (New York: Longman, 1984), pp. 4–5.

because Fischer's book showed not only the extent of German annexationist aims in World War I but also suggested that the German government deliberately went to war in 1914 in order to attain them. To compound matters, Fischer's next book, *Krieg der Illusionen* (translated as *War of Illusions: Germany's Policies from 1911 to 1914*), published in 1975, developed the theme that domestic political and social problems are inextricably linked to and often responsible for a country's foreign policy—a thesis that generated considerable reexamination of the European domestic scene before 1914. This belief in the primacy of *innenpolitik* (domestic policy) in contrast to *aussenpolitik* (foreign policy) was reinforced by the fact that in the 1960s many Americans were examining the origins of the cold war and the Vietnam War in terms of economic matters, and they did the same for pre-World War I Europe. Arno J. Mayer's essay on the domestic causes of World War I reflects this thinking. Mayer cites the numerous problems faced by the soon-to-be belligerents at home—problems generated not only by the left but by militant conservatives, who in radicalizing moderate elements threatened effective government—as at least partly responsible for their governments' decision to risk war in order to divert attention from internal turbulence.

What then can be concluded from this discussion of the origins of World War I? That there will never be agreement on the question of responsibility? That the underlying causes of the war—such as nationalism, imperialism, the alliance system, the arms race, and coordination of military plans in the event of war—were more significant than the immediate cause, the assassination of the archduke? Such historians as the highly respected Pierre Renouvin have shown that the alliance system effectively preserved peace in a number of prewar crises: for example, the imbroglio that issued from the Austrian annexation of Bosnia-Herzegovina in 1908 and the second Moroccan crisis in 1911. Most divisive imperialist rivalries, Renouvin argued, like British opposition to Germany's proposed Berlin–Baghdad railroad, had been resolved by the summer of 1914.[3] Doesn't an arms buildup create a deterrent, and is it not the military's function to make preparations for war? Whether put in political, social, or economic terms, the causes examined by these historians gloss over the antirationalism discussed in the previous chapter. How should we evaluate the importance of ideas in this context? Which are of greater significance in the determination of foreign policy, internal or external matters? How crucial is the role of individual diplomats and statesmen? Finally, how inevitable was World War I?

---

[3] Pierre Renouvin, *De 1871 à 1914. L'apogée de l'Europe*, vol. 6, part 2 of *Histoire des relations internationales*, ed. Pierre Renouvin (8 vols.) (Paris: Hachette, 1953–1958), pp. 380–84.

The Origins of the World War

SIDNEY B. FAY

※

Sidney B. Fay was educated in Germany and wrote on the history of eighteenth-century Prussia. Even though he has been charged with showing a pro-German bias, his two-volume history *Origins of the World War* admirably reflects the revisionist view. What follows is his conclusion, in which he assesses the responsibility of all the participants. His account will be more intelligible if the personalities referred to are identified: Pashitch headed the Serbian government; Berchtold was the Austro-Hungarian minister for foreign affairs; Bethmann was the German chancellor; Sazonov, the Russian foreign minister; Grey, the British foreign secretary; and Poincaré, the president of France. In contrast to the immediate cause of the war, what importance does Fay attach to underlying causes? Why was Fay's revisionism more acceptable in the 1920s than in subsequent decades?

None of the Powers wanted a European War. Their governing rulers and ministers, with very few exceptions, all foresaw that it must be a frightful struggle, in which the political results were not absolutely certain, but in which the loss of life, suffering, and economic consequences were bound to be terrible. This is true, in a greater or less degree, of Pashitch, Berchtold, Bethmann, Sazonov, Poincaré, San Giuliano and Sir Edward Grey. Yet none of them, not even Sir Edward Grey, could have foreseen that the political results were to be so stupendous, and the other consequences so terrible, as was actually the case.

Nevertheless, a European War broke out. Why? Because in each country political and military leaders did certain things which led to mobilizations and

Reprinted with the permission of Scribner, a Division of Simon & Schuster, Inc., from *Origins of the World War*, Volume II, by Sidney B. Fay. Copyright ©1930 by The Macmillan Company; copyright renewed 1958 by Sidney Bradshaw Fay.

declarations of war, or failed to do certain things which might have prevented them. In this sense, all the European countries, in a greater or less degree, were responsible. One must abandon the dictum of the Versailles Treaty that Germany and her allies were solely responsible. It was a dictum exacted by victors from vanquished, under the influence of the blindness, ignorance, hatred, and the propagandist misconceptions to which war had given rise. It was based on evidence which was incomplete and not always sound. It is generally recognized by the best historical scholars in all countries to be no longer tenable or defensible. They are agreed that the responsibility for the War is a divided responsibility. But they still disagree very much as to the relative part of this responsibility that falls on each country and on each individual political or military leader.

Some writers like to fix positively in some precise mathematical fashion the exact responsibility for the War. This was done in one way by the framers of Article 231 of the Treaty of Versailles. It has been done in other ways by those who would fix the responsibility in some relative fashion, as, for instance, Austria first, then Russia, France and Germany and England. But the present writer deprecates such efforts to assess by a precise formula a very complicated question, which is after all more a matter of delicate shading than of definite white and black. Oversimplification, as Napoleon once said in framing his Code, is the enemy of precision. Moreover, even supposing that a general consensus of opinion might be reached as to the relative responsibility of any individual country or man for immediate causes connected with the July crisis of 1914, it is by no means necessarily true that the same relative responsibility would hold for the underlying causes, which for years had been tending toward the creation of a dangerous situation.

One may, however, sum up very briefly the most salient facts in regard to each country.

Serbia felt a natural and justifiable impulse to do what so many other countries had done in the nineteenth century—to bring under one national Government all the discontented Serb people. She had liberated those under Turkish rule; the next step was to liberate those under Hapsburg rule. She looked to Russia for assistance, and had been encouraged to expect that she would receive it. After the assassination, Mr. Pashitch took no steps to discover and bring to justice Serbians in Belgrade who had been implicated in the plot. One of them, Ciganovitch, was even assisted to disappear. Mr. Pashitch waited to see what evidence the Austrian authorities could find. When Austria demanded cooperation of Serbian officials in discovering, though not in trying, implicated Serbians, the Serbian Government made a very conciliatory but negative reply. They expected that the reply would not be regarded as satisfactory, and, even before it was given, ordered the mobilization of the Serbian army. Serbia did not want war, but believed it would be forced upon her. That Mr. Pashitch was aware of the plot three weeks before it was executed, failed to take effective steps to prevent the assassins from crossing over from Serbia to Bosnia, and then failed to give Austria any warning or information which might have averted the fatal crime, were facts unknown to Austria in July, 1914; they cannot therefore be regarded as in any way justifying Austria's conduct; but they are part of Serbia's responsibility, and a very serious part.

Austria was more responsible for the immediate origin of the War than any other Power. Yet from her own point of view she was acting in self-defense— not against an immediate military attack, but against the corroding Greater Serbia and Jugoslav agitation which her leaders believed threatened her very existence. No State can be expected to sit with folded arms and await dismemberment at the hands of its neighbors. Russia was believed to be intriguing with Serbia and Rumania against the Dual Monarchy. The assassination of the heir to the throne, as a result of a plot prepared in Belgrade, demanded severe retribution; otherwise Austria would be regarded as incapable of action, "worm-eaten" as the Serbian Press expressed it, would sink in prestige, and hasten her own downfall. To avert this Berchtold determined to crush Serbia with war. He deliberately framed the ultimatum with the expectation and hope that it would be rejected. He hurriedly declared war against Serbia in order to forestall all efforts at mediation. He refused even to answer his own ally's urgent requests to come to an understanding with Russia, on the basis of a military occupation of Belgrade as a pledge that Serbia would carry out the promises in her reply to the ultimatum. Berchtold gambled on a "local" war with Serbia only, believing that he could rattle the German sword; but rather than abandon his war with Serbia, he was ready to drag the rest of Europe into war.

It is very questionable whether Berchtold's obstinate determination to diminish Serbia and destroy her as a Balkan factor was, after all, the right method, even if he had succeeded in keeping the war "localized" and in temporarily strengthening the Dual Monarchy. Supposing that Russia in 1914, because of military unpreparedness or lack of support, had been ready to tolerate the execution of Berchtold's designs, it is quite certain that she would have aimed within the next two or three years at wiping out this second humiliation, which was so much more damaging to her prestige than that of 1908–09. In two or three years, when her great program of military reform was finally completed, Russia would certainly have found a pretext to reverse the balance in the Balkans in her own favor again. A further consequence of Berchtold's policy, even if successful, would have been the still closer consolidation of the Triple Entente, with the possible addition of Italy. And, finally, a partially dismembered Serbia would have become a still greater source of unrest and danger to the peace of Europe than heretofore. Serbian nationalism, like Polish nationalism, would have been intensified by partition. Austrian power and prestige would not have been so greatly increased as to be able to meet these new dangers. Berchtold's plan was a mere temporary improvement, but could not be a final solution of the Austro-Serbian antagonism. Franz Ferdinand and many others recognized this, and so long as he lived, no step in this fatal direction had been taken. It was the tragic fate of Austria that the only man who might have had the power and ability to develop Austria along sound lines became the innocent victim of the crime which was the occasion of the World War and so of her ultimate disruption.

Germany did not plot a European War, did not want one, and made genuine, though too belated efforts, to avert one. She was the victim of her alliance with Austria and of her own folly. Austria was her only dependable ally, Italy and Rumania having become nothing but allies in name. She could not throw her over, as otherwise she would stand isolated between Russia, where Panslavism and armaments were growing stronger every year, and France, where Alsace-Lorraine, Delcassé's fall, and Agadir were not forgotten. Therefore, Bethmann felt bound to accede to Berchtold's request for support and gave him a free hand to deal with Serbia; he also hoped and expected to "localize" the Austro-Serbian conflict. Germany then gave grounds to the Entente for suspecting the sincerity of her peaceful intentions by her denial of any foreknowledge of the ultimatum, by her support and justification of it when it was published, and by her refusal of Sir Edward Grey's conference proposal. However, Germany by no means had Austria so completely under her thumb as the Entente Powers and many writers have assumed. It is true that Berchtold would hardly have embarked on his gambler's policy unless he had been assured that Germany would fulfil the obligations of the alliance, and to this extent Germany must share the great responsibility of Austria. But when Bethmann realized that Russia was likely to intervene, that England might not remain neutral, and that there was danger of a world war of which Germany and Austria would appear to be the instigators, he tried to call a halt on Austria, but it was too late. He pressed mediation proposals on Vienna, but Berchtold was insensible to the pressure, and the Entente Powers did not believe in the sincerity of his pressure, especially as they produced no results.

Germany's geographical position between France and Russia, and her inferiority in number of troops, had made necessary the plan of crushing the French army quickly at first and then turning against Russia. This was only possible, in the opinion of her strategists, by marching through Belgium, as it was generally anticipated by military men that she would do in case of a European War. On July 29, after Austria had declared war on Serbia, and after the Tsar had assented to general mobilization in Russia (though this was not known in Berlin and was later postponed for a day owing to the Kaiser's telegram to the Tsar), Bethmann took the precaution of sending to the German Minister in Brussels a sealed envelope. The Minister was not to open it except on further instructions. It contained the later demand for the passage of the German army through Belgium. This does not mean, however, that Germany had decided for war. In fact,

Bethmann was one of the last of the statesmen to abandon hope of peace and to consent to the mobilization of his country's army. General mobilization of the continental armies took place in the following order: Serbia, Russia, Austria, France and Germany. General mobilization by a Great Power was commonly interpreted by military men in every country, though perhaps not by Sir Edward Grey, the Tsar, and some civilian officials, as meaning that the country was on the point of making war—that the military machine had begun to move and would not be stopped. Hence, when Germany learned of the Russian general mobilization, she sent ultimatums to St. Petersburg and Paris, warning that German mobilization would follow unless Russia suspended hers within twelve hours, and asking what would be the attitude of France. The answers being unsatisfactory, Germany then mobilized and declared war. It was the hasty Russian general mobilization, assented to on July 29 and ordered on July 30, while Germany was still trying to bring Austria to accept mediation proposals, which finally rendered the European War inevitable.

Russia was partly responsible for the Austro-Serbian conflict because of the frequent encouragement which she had given at Belgrade—that Serbian national unity would be ultimately achieved with Russian assistance at Austrian expense. This had led the Belgrade Cabinet to hope for Russian support in case of a war with Austria, and the hope did not prove vain in July, 1914. Before this, to be sure, in the Bosnian Crisis and during the Balkan Wars, Russia had put restraint upon Serbia, because Russia, exhausted by the effects of the Russo-Japanese War, was not yet ready for a European struggle with the Teutonic Powers. But in 1914 her armaments, though not yet completed, had made such progress that the militarists were confident of success, if they had French and British support. In the spring of 1914, the Minister of War, Sukhomlinov, had published an article in a Russian newspaper, though without signing his name, to the effect, "Russia is ready, France must be ready also." Austria was convinced that Russia would ultimately aid Serbia, unless the Serbian danger was dealt with energetically after the Archduke's murder; she knew that Russia was growing stronger every year; but she doubted whether the Tsar's armaments had yet reached the point at which Russia would dare to intervene; she would therefore run less risk of Russian intervention and a European War if she used the Archduke's assassination as an excuse for weakening Serbia, than if she should postpone action until the future.

Russia's responsibility lay also in the secret preparatory military measures which she was making at the same time that she was carrying on diplomatic negotiations. These alarmed Germany and Austria. But it was primarily Russia's general mobilization, made when Germany was trying to bring Austria to a settlement, which precipitated the final catastrophe, causing Germany to mobilize and declare war.

The part of France is less clear than that of the other Great Powers, because she has not yet made a full publication of her documents. To be sure, M. Poincaré, in the fourth volume of his memoirs, has made a skilful and elaborate plea, to prove *"La France innocente."* But he is not convincing. It is quite clear that on his visit to Russia he assured the Tsar's Government that France would support her as an ally in preventing Austria from humiliating or crushing Serbia. Paléologue renewed these assurances in a way to encourage Russia to take a strong hand. He did not attempt to restrain Russia from military measures which he knew would call forth German counter-measures and cause war. Nor did he keep his Government promptly and fully informed of the military steps which were being taken at St. Petersburg. President Poincaré, upon his return to France, made efforts for peace, but his great preoccupation was to minimize French and Russian preparatory measures and emphasize those of Germany, in order to secure the certainty of British support in a struggle which he now regarded as inevitable.

Sir Edward Grey made many sincere proposals for preserving peace; they all failed owing partly, but not exclusively, to Germany's attitude. Sir Edward could probably have prevented war if he had done either of two things. If, early in the crisis, he had acceded to the urging of France and Russia and given a strong warning to Germany that, in a European War, England would take the side of the Franco-Russian Alliance, this would probably have led Bethmann to exert an earlier and more effective pressure on Austria; and it would perhaps thereby have prevented the Austrian declaration of war on Serbia, and brought to a successful issue the "direct conversations" between Vienna and St. Petersburg. Or, if Sir Edward Grey had listened to German urging, and warned France and Russia early in the crisis that if they became involved in war, England would remain neutral, probably Russia would have hesitated with her mobilizations, and France would probably have exerted a restraining influence at St. Petersburg. But Sir Edward Grey could not say that England would take the side of France and Russia, because he had a Cabinet nearly evenly divided, and he was not sure, early in the crisis, that public opinion in England would back him up in war against Germany. He could resign, and he says in his memoirs that he would have resigned, but that would have been no comfort or aid to France, who had come confidently to count upon British support. He was determined to say and do nothing which might encourage her with a hope which he could not fulfil. Therefore, in spite of the pleadings of the French, he refused to give them definite assurances until the probable German determination to go through Belgium made it clear that the Cabinet, and Parliament, and British public opinion would follow his lead in war on Germany. On the other hand, he was unwilling to heed the German pleadings that he exercise restraint at Paris and St. Petersburg, because he did not wish to endanger the Anglo-Russian Entente and the solidarity of the Triple Entente, because he felt a moral obligation to France, growing out of the Anglo-French military and naval conversations of the past years, and because he suspected that Germany was backing Austria up in an unjustifiable course and that Prussian militarists had taken the direction of affairs at Berlin out of the hands of Herr von Bethmann-Hollweg and the civilian authorities.

Italy exerted relatively little influence on the crisis in either direction.

Belgium had done nothing in any way to justify the demand which Germany made upon her. With commendable prudence, at the very first news of the ominous Austrian ultimatum, she had foreseen the danger to which she might be exposed. She had accordingly instructed her representatives abroad as to the statements which they were to make in case Belgium should decide very suddenly to mobilize to protect her neutrality. On July 29, she placed her army upon "a strengthened war footing," but did not order complete mobilization until two days later, when Austria, Russia, and Germany had already done so, and war appeared inevitable. Even after being confronted with the terrible German ultimatum, at 7 P.M. on August 2, she did not at once invite the assistance of English and French troops to aid her in the defense of her soil and her neutrality against a certain German assault; it was not until German troops had actually violated her territory, on August 4, that she appealed for the assistance of the Powers which had guaranteed her neutrality. Belgium was the innocent victim of German strategic necessity. Though the German violation of Belgium was of enormous influence in forming public opinion as to the responsibility for the War after hostilities began, it was not a cause of the War, except in so far as it made it easier for Sir Edward Grey to bring England into it.

In the forty years following the Franco-Prussian War, as we have seen, there developed a system of alliances which divided Europe into two hostile groups. This hostility was accentuated by the increase of armaments, economic rivalry, nationalist ambitions and antagonisms, and newspaper incitement. But it is very doubtful whether all these dangerous tendencies would have actually led to war, had it not been for the assassination of Franz Ferdinand. That was the factor which consolidated the elements of hostility and started the rapid and complicated succession of events which culminated in a world war, and for that factor Serbian nationalism was primarily responsible.

But the verdict of the Versailles Treaty that Germany and her allies were responsible for the War, in view of the evidence now available, is historically unsound. It should therefore be revised. However, because of the popular feeling widespread in some of the Entente countries, it is doubtful whether a formal and legal revision is as yet practicable. There must first come a further revision by historical scholars, and through them of public opinion.

War's Origins

Marxist-Leninist View

SOVIET UNION

The *History of the Communist Party of the Soviet Union*, revealing the official Marxist-Leninist version of events, placed emphasis on the contradictions contained within capitalism, on the need of advanced (monopoly) capitalism to resort to imperialism, on class conflict in general, and on the role of the Soviet proletariat guided by its party in particular. To what extent is evidence cited in support of the conclusions reached?

The imperialist world war broke out on August 1 (July 19, old style), 1914: It was the cumulative result of sharp imperialist contradictions.

The distinctive feature of imperialism, the highest and last stage of capitalism, is the domination of monopolies—syndicates, trusts and similar organisations of a handful of millionaires controlling vast amounts of capital. Not content with the home market, the capitalists made their way into the colonies and economically underdeveloped countries in search of profit. By the beginning of the century the whole world had already been divided among a small group of leading capitalist powers.

But under capitalism, an even course of development is impossible. Individual enterprises, industries and, indeed, countries overtake and outstrip others, which have to give way to their more successful competitors; or the latter themselves yield place. Imperialism, with its domination of giant monopolies, accentuates this unevenness, both in the economic and political

From the *History of the Communist Party of the Soviet Union*, Moscow, 1963, pp. 181–183. Originally reprinted by permission of the Soviet Copyright Agency.

fields. The development of capitalism becomes spasmodic, and this uneven development constantly upsets the international equilibrium, changing the relative economic and military strength of the powers. And the greater their strength, the more insistent becomes their demand for more markets and for new colonies, because in a society based on private ownership of the means of production, division of spoils is always in accordance with strength or capital. With the world already divided up among the biggest capitalist states, its redivision could only take place at the expense of one or another of these states, that is, through war.

Lenin pointed out that the emergence of powerful capitalist monopoly associations and their struggle for an economic redivision of the world which was already divided territorially was bound to lead to imperialist wars.

The imperialists had, in fact, long been preparing for a war to redivide the world. The most bellicose in this respect were the German militarists, who considered that they had been cheated out of their share of colonies. By the close of the last century, Germany had overtaken Britain in industrial development and was ousting her from her traditional markets. Germany's aim was a radical redivision of the world in her favour. This contradiction between British and German imperialism was in fact the root cause of the war. However, a big part was also played by the imperialist contradictions between Germany and France, Russia and Germany, etc. Long before the war, in 1879–82, Germany had formed an alliance with Austria-Hungary and Italy against Russia and France. The latter retaliated by forming an alliance of their own, and the British imperialists, fearing Germany's advance to world domination, concluded an agreement (Entente) with France to combat Germany by joint effort. In 1907 Russia concluded a treaty with Britain, as a result of which Russia joined the Entente. The two mutually opposed imperialist blocs in Europe thus took final shape.

Economically dependent, mainly on French and British capital, Russia was drawn into the war on the side of the Entente. But the tsarist government had its own reasons for taking part in the imperialist war. The Russian capitalists strongly resented German competition in the domestic market. The dominant classes of Russia wanted new markets in which there would be no competition. The Russian imperialists were out to gain possession of Constantinople and the straits leading from the Black Sea to the Mediterranean; they wanted to seize Turkish Armenia and thereby bring the whole of Armenia under Russian rule. This clashed with German imperialist plans in the Middle East: Germany was penetrating into Turkey and Iran and had secured a concession for a railway from Berlin to Baghdad. Russo-German contradictions in the Middle East became especially keen in the twentieth century.

Another major cause of the war was the imperialists' desire to suppress the revolutionary movement, which in the past ten years had grown to powerful dimensions. The Russian revolution of 1905–07 had greatly stimulated the working-class struggle in Europe and America and set off a national liberation movement in the East. The governments of the leading powers—and the tsarist government first and foremost—feared a further spread of the revolution, and believed that war would sidetrack the masses from revolutionary struggle. The imperialists hoped that by instigating the workers of different countries against each other they could split the international proletarian movement, poison it with the venom of chauvinism, physically annihilate a big section of the advanced workers and in this way crush, or at any rate weaken, the revolutionary pressure of the masses.

Germany's Aims in the First World War

FRITZ FISCHER

Fritz Fischer is a professor of history at the University of Hamburg. He has lectured widely in the United States and was a member of the Institute for Advanced Studies at Princeton. The excerpts that follow come from his book, *Germany's Aims in the First World War.* Described as possibly the most important historical work, certainly one of the most controversial, to come out of Germany since World War II, it contains a wealth of documentation from previously unused archives. How may Fischer's arguments be compared to those of Fay? Whose do you find more persuasive? Why?

The fundamental changes in economic conditions, the wide-spread prosperity, the rapid growth of the population, the swift expansion in all branches of economic life, combined to create a general conviction, which was reinforced by nation-wide propaganda, that Germany's frontiers had become too narrow for her, but that the ring of powers round her would never consent to their extension. The diplomatic campaign to 'split the Entente' by peaceful means cannot be understood without a glance at these structural changes.

Germany's claim to world power was based on her consciousness of being a 'young,' growing and rising nation. Her population had risen from about 41 millions in 1871 to about 68 millions in 1915, while that of France, with a larger area, had remained almost stationary, reaching only 40 millions in 1915. Moreover, more than one-third of the population of Germany was under fifteen years of age, and this gave the national consciousness a dynamic element which further reinforced the demand for *Lebensraum,* markets and industrial expansion. Although emigration had been high (1.3 million persons emigrated between 1881 and 1890), the population figures for 1910 were nevertheless far more favourable than, for example, those of France: an excess of births over deaths of 800,000 (8.9 per 1,000 against 3.4 per 1,000 in France), while the expectation of life was increasing and infant mortality on the decline. With increasing industrialisation, internal migration was beginning to replace migration overseas and immigrants were beginning to come in from Austria, Italy, Russian Poland and other European countries. Germany was developing more and more into a highly industrialised exporting country, and the problem of finding markets and raw materials to support her population was growing increasingly urgent.

⊠ ⊠ ⊠

Economic expansion was the basis of Germany's political world diplomacy, which vacillated in its methods between rapprochement and conciliation at one moment, aggressive insistence on Germany's claims the next, but never wavered in its ultimate objective, the expansion of Germany's power.

⊠ ⊠ ⊠

In spite of all the surface calm, the feeling, or conviction, that a great European conflict could not be long postponed had become general in Europe. Germany found herself, as Moltke put it, 'in a condition of hopeless isolation which was growing ever more hopeless.' Her confidence in the invincibility of her military strength had been deeply shaken by the increases in the French and Russian armies (of which the latter would in 1917 reach its maximum peacetime strength of 2,200,000 men), and the idea of a 'preventive war' was acquiring an increasing appeal, especially in military circles. 'We are ready, and the sooner it comes, the better for us,' said Moltke on June 1, 1914. At about the same time, Moltke asked Jagow to precipitate a preventive war as soon as possible. Jagow refused, but admitted later that he had never wholly excluded the idea of a preventive war and that Moltke's words had influenced him during the crisis of July–August, 1914. Another element of danger was the fact that Conservative circles had come, especially since the Reichstag elections of 1912, to regard war as a 'tempering of the nation' and calculated to strengthen the Prusso-German state. Bethmann Hollweg, who in December, 1913, had already rejected the suggestion passed on to him by the crown prince, and emanating from the pan-Germans, that a *coup d'état* should be carried out against the Social Democrats, spoke out again just six months later against these speculations on the internal political consequences of a war. He told Lerchenfield, the Bavarian minister, at the beginning of June, 1914, that:

> There were still circles in the Reich which looked to war to bring about an improvement, in the conservative sense, of internal conditions in Germany. He thought that the effects would be the exact opposite; a world war, with its incalculable consequences, would greatly increase the power of Social Democracy, because it had preached peace, and would bring down many a throne.

A month later the Chancellor agreed on foreign-political and military grounds to take the risk of a great war, while recognising—unlike the Conservatives—that the war could not be carried on without the co-operation of Social Democracy.

❀ ❀ ❀

There is no question but that the conflict of military and political interests, of resentment and ideas, which found expression in the July crisis, left no government of any of the European powers quite free of some measure of responsibility—greater or smaller—for the outbreak of the war in one respect or another. It is, however, not the purpose of this work to enter into the familiar controversy, on which whole libraries have been written, over the question of war guilt, to discuss exhaustively the responsibility of the individual statesmen and soldiers of all the European powers concerned, or to pass final judgment on them. We are concerned solely with the German leaders' objectives and with the policy actually followed by them in the July crisis, and that only in so far as their policy throws light on the postulates and origins of Germany's war aims.

It must be repeated: given the tenseness of the world situation in 1914—a condition for which Germany's world policy, which had already led to three dangerous crises (those of 1905, 1908 and 1911), was in no small measure responsible—any limited or local war in Europe directly involving one great power must inevitably carry with it the imminent danger of a general war. As Germany willed and coveted the Austro-Serbian war and, in her confidence in her military superiority, deliberately faced the risk of a conflict with Russia and France, her leaders must bear a substantial share of the historical responsibility for the outbreak of general war in 1914. This responsibility is not diminished by the fact that at the last moment Germany tried to arrest the march of destiny, for her efforts to influence Vienna were due exclusively to the threat of British intervention and, even so, they were half-hearted, belated and immediately revoked.

It is true that German politicians and publicists, and with them the entire German propaganda machine during the war and German historiography after the war—particularly after Versailles—have invariably maintained that the war was forced on Germany, or at least (adopting Lloyd George's dictum, made for political reasons, that 'we all stumbled into the war') that Germany's share of the responsibility was no greater than that of the other participants. But confidential exchanges between Germany and Austria, and between the responsible figures in Germany itself, untinged by any propagandist intent, throw a revealing spotlight on the real responsibility.

A few weeks after the outbreak of war, during the crises on the Marne and in Galicia, the Austrians asked urgently for German help against the superior Russian armies facing them. It was refused. Count Tisza then advised Berchtold to tell the Germans: 'That we took our decision to go to war on the strength of the express statements both of the German Emperor and of the German Imperial Chancellor that they regarded the moment as suitable and would be glad if we showed ourselves in earnest.'

※ ※ ※

The official documents afford ample proofs that during the July crisis the Emperor, the German military leaders and the Foreign Ministry were pressing Austria-Hungary to strike against Serbia without delay, or alternatively agreed to the dispatch of an ultimatum to Serbia couched in such sharp terms as to make war between the two countries more than probable, and that in doing so they deliberately took the risk of a continental war against Russia and France. But the decisive point is that, as we now know—although for a long time it was not admitted—these groups were not alone. On July 5 and 6 the Imperial Chancellor, Bethmann Hollweg, the man in whom the constitution vested the sole responsibility, decided to take the risk and even over-trumped the Emperor when he threatened to weaken. That this was no 'tragic doom,' no 'ineluctable destiny,' but a deliberate decision of policy emerges beyond doubt from the diary of his private secretary, Kurt Riezler, who recorded in it his conversations with the Chancellor in the critical days (and, indeed, over many years). These diaries have not yet been published, but the extracts from them which have seen the light furnish irrefutable proof that during the July crisis Bethmann Hollweg was ready for war. More than this, Riezler's entry for the evening of July 8, after Bethmann Hollweg's return to Hohenfinow (where Rathenau was also stopping) shows what advance calculations the leaders of Germany were making in respect of the situation produced by the Sarajevo murder. According to his secretary, the Chancellor said: 'If war doesn't come, if the Tsar doesn't want it or France panics and advises peace, we have still achieved this much, that we have manoeuvred the Entente into disintegration over this move.'

In other words, Bethmann Hollweg reckoned with a major general war as the result of Austria's swift punitive action against Serbia. If, however, Russia and France were again to draw back (as in 1909 and 1911)—which he at first regarded as the less probable eventuality—then at least Germany would have achieved a signal diplomatic victory: she would have split Russia from France and isolated both without war. But war was what he expected, and how he expected its course to run we learn from his predecessor in the Chancellorship, Bülow, who had a long discussion with him at the beginning of August. Bethmann Hollweg told Bülow that he was reckoning with 'a war lasting three, or at the most, four months . . . a violent, but short storm.' Then, he went on, revealing his innermost wishes, it would 'in spite of the war, indeed, through it,' be possible to establish a friendly relationship with England, and through England with France. He hoped to bring about 'a grouping of Germany, England and France against the Russia colossus which threatens the civilisation of Europe.'

Bethmann Hollweg himself often hinted darkly during the war how closely Germany had been involved in the beginning of the war. He was less concerned with the 'staging' of it than to register the spirit of the German leaders who had made it possible for the war to be begun even after the premises for it had collapsed. The following bitter words are taken from his address to the Central Committee of the Reichstag at the beginning of October, 1916, during the sharp debate on the initiation of unlimited submarine warfare; they outline Germany's real 'guilt,' her constant over-estimation of her own powers, and her misjudgment of realities:

> Since the outbreak of the war we have not always avoided the danger of underestimating the strength of our enemies. The extraordinary development of the last twenty years seduced wide circles into over-estimating our own forces, mighty as they are, in comparing them with those of the rest of the world . . . in our rejoicing over our own progress (we have) not paid sufficient regard to conditions in other countries.

The July crisis must not be regarded in isolation. It appears in its true light only when seen as a link between Germany's 'world policy,' as followed since the mid-1890s, and her war aims policy after August, 1914.

Domestic Causes of the First World War

ARNO J. MAYER

Arno J. Mayer taught at Princeton University. His books, which have shown how foreign and domestic policies are necessarily intertwined, reveal an interest in the peacemaking process and in the diplomacy practiced after World War I. He has also published on what he calls the persistence of monarchical conservatism well into the modern period; his most recent book reexamines the Holocaust. This excerpt from an essay on the domestic tensions that may have affected diplomatic decision making in 1914 comes from an anthology compiled in honor of the distinguished historian of Germany, Hajo Holborn. How close to a Marxist view is it to state that errors are inherent in capitalism and that the internal contradictions of capitalist society in 1914 increased the likelihood of war? Does this make the argument any less legitimate? Compared to the Communist party history, does Mayer offer evidence in support of his conclusions?

When analyzing the origins of the Great War, diplomatic historians continue to focus on two sets of underlying and precipitant causes: those rooted in the dysfunctions of the international system and those rooted in the mistakes, miscalculations, and vagaries of the principal foreign-policy actors. These historians assume that in a multiple-state system the balancing of power is a natural and essential method of control, notwithstanding its inherent uncertainties. In other words, they do not question or criticize the balancing-of-power system or process as such. Instead, they tilt their lances at four developments that complicated, if not obstructed, its smooth operation: 1. the alliance system, which became increasingly polarized and rigidified, thereby threatening to transform any limited, local conflict into an unlimited, general war; 2. the attendant armaments race, which exacerbated mutual hostility, fear, and distrust; 3. the new military metaphysics, which inclined civilian foreign-policy actors to become increasingly responsive to the military leaders and their ironclad timetables; and 4. public opinion, expressed and mobilized through the daily press, notably the yellow and jingoist dailies, which were impatient with accommodation.

In addition to diagnosing these four dysfunctions in the balancing-of-power system or process, diplomatic historians also probe into the personal attitudes, motives, and objectives of the principal foreign-policy actors—heads of state, chief executives, foreign ministers, permanent foreign office officials, ambassadors, and military and naval officers. Not surprisingly, each major historian tends to have his favorite villain. Rather than indict entire nations, scholars tend to return verdicts against individual actors of a given nation or alliance. Three categories of charges are most commonly preferred: 1. that they made grave mistakes in diplomatic tactics; 2. that they miscalculated the responses of potential enemies; and 3. that they pursued objectives that were incompatible with the maintenance of the European equilibrium. But whatever the charge, in the last analysis their actions and judgments are said to have been warped by personal ambition, caprice, pique, or lack of backbone in the face of ruthless warmongers.

Admittedly, this framework of orthodox diplomatic history, tempered by amateur psychology, has been used to good advantage. It has served to uncover a great deal about the origins of the First World War in particular, and about the causes of international conflict in general.

Just the same, this time-honored approach has some rather grave limitations. In particular, it slides over: 1. the proclivity of key foreign-policy actors to risk war in general, and preventive war in particular; 2. the degree to which they realized that any localized conflict was likely to develop into a major all-European or even world war; and 3. the extent to which they entertained recourse to external war for internal political purposes.

This third limitation stems very largely from the diplomatic historian's disposition to detach foreign policy hermetically from domestic politics; and to disconnect foreign-policy and diplomatic actors rigorously from the political and social context from which they originate and in which they operate.

Admittedly, this twofold dissociation, for analytic purposes, may not fatally handicap the study of the international politics of the relatively calm and elitist mid-eighteenth century. There seems little doubt, however, that this dual disjunction hinders the examination and understanding of foreign policy and diplomacy in such revolutionary eras as 1789 to 1815 and in such brief revolutionary spasms as 1848–50.

This interconnection of domestic politics and foreign policy is exceptionally intense under prerevolutionary and revolutionary conditions. Characteristically, in the prewar years domestic tensions rose sharply at the same time that the international system became increasingly strained. Moreover, this symbiotic growth of domestic and international tensions occurred in that part of the world in which, for the first time in recorded history, government policies, including foreign policies, were shaped in the crucible of organized party, pressure, and interest politics.

In other words, on the eve of war the major European politics were far from quiescent; and both the making and the conduct of foreign policy had ceased to be the private preserve of an encapsulated élite free of political pressures and neutral in the explosive domestic controversies of their respective societies. Accordingly, the 50 percent increase in military spending in the five prewar years may not have been exclusively a function of mounting international distrust, insecurity, and hostility. In some measure it may also have been a by-product of the resolve by conservatives and ultraconservatives to foster their political position by rallying the citizenry around the flag; and to reduce the politically unsettling cyclical fluctuations of the capitalist economies by raising armaments expenditures. In this same connection it should be stressed that the chief villains of July–August 1914—those foreign-policy actors whom diplomatic historians identify as having practiced reckless brinkmanship—were intimately tied in with those social, economic, and political strata that were battling either to maintain the domestic status quo or to steer an outright reactionary course.

To attenuate if not overcome the limitations of diplomatic history's conventional approach to the causes of war its analytic framework should be recast to accommodate three aspects of the historical and immediate crisis that conditioned and precipitated hostilities in July–August 1914: 1. the dysfunctions in the international system; 2. the domestic dysfunctions in the would-be belligerent nations; and 3. the inextricable interplay between these two sets of dysfunctions.

Whereas the dysfunctions in the international system and the diplomatic rivalries among the major powers have been studied exhaustively and are well-known, the same cannot be said about the prewar domestic dysfunctions, notably about their all-European scope.

During the decade, including the weeks immediately preceding July–August 1914, the European nations experienced more than routine political and social disturbances. Even Britain, that paradigm of ordered change and constitutionalism, was approaching the threshold of civil war. Judging by the Curragh incident, Carson and the Ulster volunteers had the sympathy if not outright cooperation of influential civil and military leaders in their defiance of Parliament; and the Triple Alliance of railwaymen, miners, and transport workers, among whom militant syndicalists were ascendant, threatened a paralyzing

general strike in case their minimum demands were not met by the fall of 1914.
Whereas Ulster became the rallying issue and symbol for an influential con-
glomeration of conservatives and reactionaries, the strike project of the Triple
Alliance roused extensive support throughout the restless Labour movement.
The resulting polarization, along with the shift from debate in Westminster to
direct action in the streets, eroded the vital center so essential for the politics of
compromise and accommodation. Indeed, historians have wondered whether if
external war had not come in 1914 England might not have become caught up
in civil strife, with fatal damage to her time-honored parliamentary system.

In France, meanwhile, the struggle between the right and the left raged
with unabated intensity around the twin issues of the three-year draft and the
progressive income tax. As in England, the center of the political spectrum,
which in France was multiparty in nature, was being eroded in favor of the two
opposing extremes. In particular, the left's strident antimilitarism, which the
right construed as a pressing social threat, frightened not only moderate republicans but also radicals into a common political front with the right. In turn,
the *enragés* of the left made it increasingly difficult for the socialists to cooperate
with the center-left, which stood accused of truckling to antirepublicanism.
And, indeed, the right and center joined forces in support of the three-year
draft, capitalizing on the appeals of nationalism to impugn the patriotism of
the socialists, who advocated a two-year draft. This reordering of political part-
nerships was reflected in acute cabinet instability and in the antirepublican and
protofascist right becoming the backstop for a conservative-leaning regime
putting order and defense ahead of reform.

In Italy prewar political and labor disturbances culminated in the explosive
Red Week of early June 1914. Especially once this strike wave subsided, and as
usually happens in the wake of misfired rebellions, the Italian middle-class nationalists assumed a position of intransigent hostility to the left—including the
moderate left—which in 1915 took the form of taking Italy into the war against
the will of the vast majority of the Italian nation.

As for Germany's semi-parliamentary system, which was the privileged preserve of conservative nationalists, it was heavily besieged by those parties—the
Social Democrats, the *Zentrum,* the Progressives, and the moderate wing of the
National Liberals—that denounced Prussia's three-class franchise and clamored
for the cabinet's subordination to the Reichstag. Paradoxically, the mounting
militancy in certain key trade unions scared off potential converts to political
reform. In any case, according to Arthur Rosenberg, the political and social tensions in prewar Germany were "typical of a pre-revolutionary period," and if
Germany had not gone to war in 1914 "the conflict between the Imperial Government and the majority of the German nation would have continued to in-
tensify to a point at which a revolutionary situation would have been created."

The power élites in both halves of the Dual Monarchy faced increasingly explosive nationalistic unrest which, in itself, was an expression of spiraling political, economic, and social dysfunctions. Both Otto Bauer and Victor Bibl have argued convincingly that fear of southern Slav insurgency and of intensifying Austro-Czech tensions drove Vienna's political class into trying to overcome its permanent internal crisis by recourse to external war.

Simultaneously the Russian government, firmly controlled by unbending conservatives, confronted rising labor unrest in the major industrial centers alongside heightened restlessness among the peripheral national minorities. It was a sign of the times that during the first seven months of 1914 industrial unrest reached unparalleled scope and intensity, much of it politically and socially rather than economically motivated.

Great care must be taken to distinguish between, on the one hand, the actual scope and intensity of these internal tensions and disturbances, and, on the other hand, their perception, evaluation, and exploitation by the political contestants of the time. It is characteristic of prerevolutionary situations that hardened conservatives and counterrevolutionaries deliberately exaggerate all disorders, including the imminence of their transmutation into full-scale insurrection, in order to press and justify energetic precautionary measures. In turn, advanced reformers and revolutionaries similarly distort and distrust the intentions and actions of their domestic antagonists, charging them with pre-emptive counterrevolutionary designs. But this mutual misrepresentation itself contributed to the polarization between the intransigent forces of order and the revolutionary forces of change, at the expense of the moderate, compromise-seeking center.

In Britain, France, and Italy parliamentary liberalism—the locus of this vital center—was heavily besieged, if not on the verge of collapse. The moderately reformist administrations of all three countries found it increasingly difficult to secure governing majorities. They were buffeted constantly by the parliamentary as well as extraparliamentary pressures of the militant counterrevolutionary right and the militant revolutionary left. In Germany, Austria-Hungary, and Russia, where the ruling power élite considered even the advocates of integral parliamentarism dangerous revolutionaries, the vital center was almost completely emasculated.

It would seem that in these as in other prerevolutionary eras, the specter of revolution precipitated an active counterrevolutionary response among vulnerable status groups—the landed aristocracy, the petty nobility, the petite-bourgeoisie, the artisans, and the bypassed entrepreneurs. In fact, there may well be a certain parallelism between the attitudes and actions of such crisis strata in domestic politics and the attitudes and actions of foreign-policy actors who consider their nation's international power and prestige to be declining. In both instances the threatened parties are particularly prone to force a pre-emptive showdown—armed repression or insurrection at home or preventive war abroad—with the resolve of thereby arresting or reversing the course of history, which they claim to be turning against them.

Admittedly, much has been written about the antiwar agitation that was such a prominent aspect of the prewar thunder on the left. Considerably less is known about the superpatriotic agitation that was so central to the corresponding thunder on the right. To be sure, conventional diplomatic historians have noted the upsurge of nationalism before the war, and its further inflammation during and immediately following the July crisis. Few, however, have bothered to examine systematically the social, economic, and political background of the political organizers and social carriers of this nationalist revival. Surely it is not without significance that nearly all the superpatriots who clamored for preparedness and foreign-policy pugnacity held reactionary, ultraconservative, or protofascist views on domestic affairs. Before the war there were few if any liberal conservatives or reformers in the Navy League, the Tariff Reform League, and the pro-Entente wing of the Unionist and Liberal parties in England; in the *Action française*, the *Ligue des patriotes*, and the *Fédération des gauches* in France; in the Nationalist Party and the *fasci* in Italy; in the Pan-German League and the Conservative Party in Germany; in the war party centering around the Archduke in Austria-Hungary; and in the Assembly of the Russian People and the Black Hundreds in Russia.

Evidently foreign-policy issues became highly politicized, since notwithstanding governmental appeals, the primacy of foreign policy is inoperative under prerevolutionary conditions. Whereas the campaign against the arms race was an integral part of the struggle against the forces of order, the campaign for preparedness was a central feature of the struggle against the forces of change. All along the superpatriots of the two opposing camps did each other's bidding in that they exploited and fomented the mutual suspicion, fear, hostility, and insecurity that quickened the European arms race. The Pan-German League and the *Action française* unwittingly helped each other at the expense of heightening international tensions. Domestically, meanwhile, they were instrumental in frightening liberal conservatives and reformists into supporting national preparedness, thereby eroding the vital center. In the parliamentary nations of Western Europe as well as in the autocratic empires of Central and Eastern Europe the prewar governments were particularly responsive to superpatriotic blandishments whenever moderate and advanced reformists threatened a united front, as was the case when Caillaux and Jaurès explored the basis for cooperation. In brief, the center increasingly relied on the right as a backstop, with the powerful encouragement of the upper echelons of the army, the foreign offices, the diplomatic corps, the ministry of the interior, and—in most cases—the church. Almost without exception these time-honored institutions were strongholds of the threatened and intransigent crisis strata rather than of the self-confident and supple business and banking grande-bourgeoisie.

To a not inconsiderable degree, then, throughout Europe the rising international tensions were accompanied by rising internal tensions—by mounting social, political, and economic struggles that radicalized the extremes, eroded the center, and inclined the governments to push preparedness and diplomatic obduracy as part of their efforts to maintain a precarious domestic status quo.

3

THE BOLSHEVIK REVOLUTION

The overthrow of the tsarist government in March 1917 came as no surprise. For months the regime had hovered on the point of collapse. Corruption and incompetence at home, defeat and demoralization at the front, had caused widespread discontent. "Revolution was in the air," wrote Buchanan, the British ambassador in Petrograd, "and the only moot point was whether it would come from above or below." The revolution was popular and spontaneous, issuing from food riots and street demonstrations, and it was triumphant, in view of the soldiers' refusal to fire on the crowd. Under the aegis of a provisional government, all political forces were free to compete for power. What came as a surprise, a scant eight months later, was the victory of the Bolshevik wing of the Russian Social Democratic Workers party, the smallest and least impressive of the contenders, whose leaders returned to Russia from abroad or from internal exile after the collapse of the empire. The unexpected victory, which brought the Bolsheviks (or, after they changed their name, the Communists) to the power that they were able to maintain for the next three-quarters of a century, has been the subject of countless inquiries and serves as the focus of the three readings that follow.

Less closely examined (perhaps because losers in history do not receive quite the same attention as winners) is the question of why revolutionary socialism, with a short-lived exception or two, failed elsewhere in Europe. In Germany, with the prolongation of war misery, Social Democrats and Independent Social Democrats were demanding liberal constitutional reforms and peace without annexations, while a small group on the far left known as the Spartacists openly agitated for revolution. When German sailors refused to set out against the British fleet on a mission they regarded as suicidal and intended only to save the honor of a vanquished navy, and when an independent socialist republic was proclaimed in Bavaria, successful revolution seemed imminent.

Although events did not go so far in France, Britain, or Italy, it was nevertheless true that formidable labor unrest would soon lead to general strikes in France, have the red flag flying over such industrial centers as Glasgow, and bring about the seizure of factories by workers in northern Italy. Yet revolution, certainly from the left, failed outside of Russia. In his analysis of Bolshevik success, Theodore H. Von Laue compares conditions in Russia with those in Western and Central Europe and explains why it was only in the former that revolution succeeded.

In the debate over the issue of "inevitability," Von Laue believes that liberal democracy could not have survived in Russia, regardless of whether the provisional government remained faithful to her wartime allies. Other historians have emphasized it was the government's insistence on continuing to fight a losing war that lacked popular support. George F. Kennan asks why the Allies, who had hailed the overthrow of the tsar and at once recognized the provisional government, convinced that a popular regime could muster support for a flagging war effort, insisted that the government continue to fight. He concludes that the reasons were not only military ones. In any event, the decision by the government—and its chief minister, Alexander Kerensky—to remain in a wholly unpopular war accounts for the popularity of the Bolsheviks, who could point to the army as already having voted for peace "with its feet" through wholesale desertions. Jerry F. Hough, in a revision of a well-established book by Merle Fainsod, downplays the belief that superior party organization and German financial support allowed Lenin and the Bolsheviks to prevail.

One might have expected considerable scholarly attention to be given to Lenin and the part he played in the November uprising. Was he the "hero" in this history who by dint of forceful character and strategic brilliance transformed the uncertainties of a chaotic situation into Bolshevik success?[1] Was this success a consequence of his party's superior organization, for which, admittedly, he was responsible? Or was the Bolshevik victory the result of his masterful ability to exploit popular unrest by siding with a public opinion he had no intention of following in the future? Given the imperatives of the day, would the results have been the same without Lenin?

The historians cited are providing answers to somewhat different aspects of the larger question of why the Bolsheviks were victorious. Kennan examines the failure of the Western allies to respond to the dilemma faced by the provisional government; Von Laue considers why democracy could not have survived in Russia regardless of what the government did; and Hough and Fainsod

---

[1] Sidney B. Hook, *The Hero in History* (New York: Transaction, 1955), pp. 184–228. By "hero," Hook is not making a value judgment; he is referring to "the individual to whom we can justifiably attribute preponderant influence in determining an issue or event" and he devotes a chapter to Lenin to refute the deterministic view of history in orthodox Marxism.

ask why the Bolsheviks, though never able to secure a majority, enjoyed substantial popular support.

While reading their analyses, particularly before rushing to judgment on Kerensky and the provisional government, it may be useful to keep the following question in mind: Could this government, under its first chief Prince Lvov, a kindly Tolstoyan type who believed in "non-resistance to evil" and in "bloodless revolution," and then under Kerensky, formerly a bourgeois lawyer who had joined the Socialist Revolutionary party after the tsar's downfall, have undertaken significant reform? It tended in the best liberal tradition to defer decisions to a future constituent assembly, and the reforms agreed to—political amnesty, removal of religious and racial distinctions, and assorted civil liberties—were relatively harmless and readily supported. More controversial issues, especially those of land reform and unilateral withdrawal from the war, were neglected. Under the socialist and former pacifist Kerensky, attempts at sweeping political change were too few and too late; the Achilles' heel of his moderate socialist regime was his stubborn dedication to the war effort, a policy already rejected by the vast majority of Russian people.

Can we simply conclude that at the heart of the matter is the fact that Lenin was the ultimate revolutionary, that is, prepared to behave as the ultimate opportunist: to take popular stands, to make promises he had no intention of keeping, and to enter into alliances he had no intention of maintaining, regardless of how illegal or immoral his actions? This would explain his willingness to violate the promises made to the Allies by previous governments (no matter how irrelevant the promises), to take land from its lawful owners for popular redistribution before lengthy discussions about compensation could be held, and to acquiesce in what amounted to the disintegration of the country by supporting demands for independence by the various ethnic minorities (no matter how legitimate the demands). Lenin defined morality as "that which serves the destruction of the old exploiting society."[2] Law-abiding liberal that he was, Kerensky could not do these things. He was not a revolutionary.

---

[2] V. I. Lenin, "The Tasks of the Youth Leagues," *Collected Works*, vol. 31 (April–December 1920), (Moscow: Progress Publishers, 1966), p. 293.

Why Lenin? Why Stalin?

THEODORE H. VON LAUE

Theodore H. Von Laue was born in Germany and received graduate degrees from Princeton University. He taught at the University of California, Riverside, and at Clark University. A
recipient of Guggenheim and Fulbright fellowships, he has published a number of books including studies on the German historian Von Ranke and the Russian statesman Sergei Witte. In
the book from which this excerpt is taken, Von Laue contends
that the Russian Revolution is made intelligible only by understanding the internal and external pressures under which the
Russian state and society operated. Why does Von Laue believe
that the failure of democracy in Russia was "inevitable"? How
does he account for the success of radical revolution in Russia
and its failure—or absence—in Western Europe?

Liberal democracy in Russia—using the term broadly—had proved unequal to
the task. Since March it had given the country every opportunity to speak its
will, and the result had been division, violence, and a breakdown of government. Spontaneity, leaving the population to its own devices, had produced anarchy. The invisible resources of unity and social discipline, which in the western
democracies restrained liberty from degenerating into license and made possible
not only effective government in peace but also unprecedented voluntary sacrifices in war, were found wanting in Russia. A few years later they were equally
found wanting in Italy, Spain, Poland, or Germany (to mention but a few parallel cases). None of these countries had had a chance in the past of knitting the
tight habit of subconscious unity before they copied western democracy. Russia

Excerpt from *Why Lenin? Why Stalin? Why Gorbachev?* By Theodore H. Von Laue. Copyright ©
1993 by Theodore H. Von Laue. Reprinted by permission of Addison-Wesley Educational Publishers, Inc.

was merely the first case in a long series of similar breakdowns, the one that occurred under the most exceptional circumstances.

Viewing the events of the summer of 1917 in this perspective, we must conclude that the failure of democracy in Russia was inevitable, if not in 1917 then surely in the years following (assuming that a Russian state still survived). Only decades, if not centuries, of relative immunity to the pressures of power politics and an active internal melting pot might have helped the discordant elements to grow together. Now there was no time. In the extreme moments of the twentieth century, a country either possessed that cohesion or had to create it artificially, if it did not want to fall apart.

After the July days, the sole question of Russian domestic politics was whether the heir to autocracy would be a dictator of the right or of the left. The wave of reaction favored the former. It brought to the fore General Kornilov, a distinguished officer whom merit had raised from the peasantry to his high rank and who was by no means a reactionary. He was convinced that only a military dictatorship could save Russia from Germany and from disintegration, an opinion which by now many members of "privilege Russia" (including some socialists) shared. With such backing he began, toward the end of August, to move supposedly reliable army units toward Petrograd, ostensibly in order to strengthen Kerensky but secretly prepared to go further if opportunity opened. Yet as his men approached the capital, they were met by agitators sent by the Soviet, under whose persuasion even the most loyal soldiers lost heart. Against the Petrograd Soviet, Kornilov's troops melted away as had the armies at the front, and his *coup* collapsed. No dictatorship of the right could stem the tide of revolutionary spontaneity as embodied in the soviets. On the contrary, Kornilov revived its impetus, somewhat checked after July, and prepared the way for the dictatorship of the left.

The dictatorship of the proletariat had, of course, been the goal of the Bolsheviks ever since Lenin returned to Russia. At every opportunity, he pressed home the argument that the war was an imperialist war and that it could be stopped, with all its savage hardships, only if the "capitalist" governments in Russia and elsewhere were overthrown. In his eyes, all those Russians who sought to continue the war—and this included Kerensky, the Mensheviks, and most Social Revolutionaries—were "capitalist" warmongers. He gambled on the inability of the Provisional Government to carry out its staggering tasks and on the growing revulsion against the war.

Of all political parties, thus only the Bolsheviks cast their lot with the revolutionary torrent. Their slogan was "All power to the Soviets" until July, when the Soviet leadership turned against the masses. Then they allied themselves with the more radical elements represented in the Petrograd district soviets and the factory committees. In the fall, when they gained control of the city soviets in many parts of Russia, they proclaimed as their goal the dictatorship of the proletariat. They alone dared to profess what the unruly masses wanted and were already trying to achieve by themselves: immediate peace for the soldiers, land to the peasants by Black Partition, self-determination for the minority groups, bread for the hungry, and social justice on their own terms for all those who felt oppressed and exploited. They alone were willing to descend to the language of the *Lumpenproletariat* and, when necessary, to incite its passions to fever pitch. "The Bolsheviks," Trotsky wrote in retrospect, "not afraid of those backward strata now for the first time lifting themselves from the dregs, took people as history had created them." Mercilessly they exploited the ignorance of the masses.

Yet while they placed themselves midstream in the revolutionary tide, they would not be carried away by it. As a revolutionary elite, they had a will of their own. They thought of themselves as the engineers of revolution, harnessing the revolutionary steam power created by the historic conditions of the moment to its true purpose which only revolutionary Marxists could perceive. Whatever the Bolsheviks would do, for their own benefit and that of Russia, they would do through the masses, never against them. But they would also remain inwardly apart, as manipulators, not agents, of the popular will. In this manner, they solved the first of the underlying necessities of modern Russian development, identifying the people with their government and in turn identifying themselves with the people.

❊ ❊ ❊

Let us ignore at this point the fact that the Bolsheviks were not firmly established for several years, but rather draw a few conclusions about their ascent to power. In the first place one can hardly deny that theirs was a democratic revolution. It established a government that could hope to speak—at least at this fleeting moment—for a majority of Russians. It was a government of "Soviet Russia," as this term has been used here, close to the political instincts of the bulk of the people.

Secondly, the overthrow of the Provisional Government—and of "privilege Russia" in general—was not entirely of the Bolsheviks' own making. It was the result of the elemental torrent of liberation that had broken loose after March. The existing bonds of government and society were all snapping by themselves, in the countryside, the army, the factories, the national minorities, everywhere. No authority was strong enough to stem that tide. All that could possibly be attempted—and that with great difficulty—was to direct it from within until it had run its course.

Thirdly, the elemental revolt aiming at the smashing of the old state machinery was a phenomenon possible only in Russia (or underdeveloped countries like China). Only there did the run of the population still live in relative self-sufficiency, with hardly a stake in the government. "Soviet Russia" had little to lose from the overthrow of the government, neither protection of property or status, nor social security, nor extensive public education, nor any other boon of government. In urban-industrial Europe, on the other hand, the majority of the population had long since acquired such a stake. State, society, and the economy were interwoven a thousandfold; all citizens were patently interdependent for their very livelihood. Thus nearly everyone had a vested interest in order and security, regardless of his political views. Threaten him, in time of crisis and internal disunity, with the overthrow of the government and he would rush headlong into the arms of a Mussolini or Hitler. And if he longed for a change of regime, he would still insist that the transition be accomplished "legally," without disturbing the continuity of the public services. There would never be a chance, in other words, of a Bolshevik revolution in the West.

The Bolshevik seizure of power—to take at this point a long look both backward and forward—marked for Russia the end of an era of revolution from below. The tide of liberation, which assumed hurricane proportions in the fall of 1917 and continued to rage for several years more, had been rising since the start of the century. Autocracy had sacrificed the "Witte system" to it but had itself been forced to give ground in 1905. While seemingly recovering most of its losses, it never succeeded in reestablishing its authority. The trend continued to run against it, even under the pressure of the war. The defeats deepened and strengthened the upsurge until it finally broke all bounds after the sudden fall of the monarchy.

The new freedom liberated the long-suppressed spontaneity of the peoples of Russia. It did not lead, unfortunately, to the self-discipline needed for an effective democratic policy or an industrial economy. Liberation meant throwing off the hated restraints of the old order and being able, for once, to act according to one's deepest feelings.

The war, on which the Bolshevik victory is so often blamed, had rather little to do with that extremist turn of events. It may have contributed to the savagery of the revolt, but it destroyed neither liberal democracy nor Russian "capitalism." Freedom, the heady freedom of the new regime, did that. Given its own ideals, liberal democracy in Russia could never have been more than a brief transition phase. It would always have led to "Soviet democracy," the freedom of the "black people," which signified, under existing conditions, spontaneity carried to the point of anarchy.

By the same logic, however, freedom was bound to destroy itself. If Russia was to survive as a Great Power, with the same universal appeal as the others— these were the harsh terms of the competition—it needed the discipline of cooperation under both government and an industrial economy.

Here lay the central quandary of modern Russia. It was a backward country at the mercy of powerful neighbors. The essence of its backwardness rested in the fact that its people, left to their own devices, could manage neither effective government nor a productive modern economy. Was the Russian Empire then to be dissolved? For the Bolsheviks, at any rate, and many non-Bolsheviks as well, the answer was a passionate No! They craved power for their own survival, for the future of world socialism, and for the integrity of their territorial base in Imperial Russia which they dearly loved. Thus from November, 1917, onward the suppression of spontaneity began anew, slowly at first under Lenin, furiously at last under Stalin. The new harness of Communist rule proved to be far tighter than the tsarist one. The dangers to the country were greater, the ambitions of its rulers bolder, and the progress of the "advanced" countries undiminished; they would not mark time while Soviet Russia tried to catch up.

The essence of industrialism, which stands at the base of modern power, is interdependence and voluntary cooperation throughout the length and breadth of society. Lenin's sociology, although clumsy and extreme, took its cue from the "capitalist" order. Every advanced industrialized society constitutes a vast workshop. Its members voluntarily coordinate their activities under a common law and government—never perfectly, to be sure, yet sufficiently so as to produce a remarkable flow of goods and services. They do this with no more drastic compulsions than submitting to majority rule and earning a living, and sometimes with much nonpecuniary zeal. Submitting to the discipline of their jobs and their political order, they ordinarily do not even feel constricted in their freedom; they are spurred on by the opportunities (the current talk of alienation notwithstanding).

Woe now to a country that requires the results of modern industrialism without possessing among its inhabitants the necessary motivation and self-discipline. It has no choice but to replace the spontaneous self-discipline of the West by a process of deliberate substitution replacing lacking motivation by compulsion. The scope of Communist totalitarianism, as it developed over the years, indicates to what extent, in the judgment of its leaders, the Soviet population still lacks the spontaneous motivation needed for competitive power in world affairs. What it lacks has to be replaced by an artificial, external discipline.

The Bolsheviks would never admit, of course, that they were sacrificing freedom for the sake of power. Their determination to become a superior universal model required that they make an additional effort to represent their Russia as the embodiment of a freedom greater than that found in the "capitalist" West. They had to overtake their model in *all* attributes of superiority, even at the price of stretching the vocabulary of freedom and spontaneity beyond all recognition.

Russia and the West under Lenin and Stalin

GEORGE F. KENNAN

George F. Kennan accompanied Ambassador Bullitt to Moscow to reopen the American Embassy in 1933. He also was second secretary, minister-counselor, and from 1952 to 1953 ambassador to the Soviet Union. After twenty-five years in the foreign service, he turned to the writing of diplomatic history. His books have won Pulitzer and Bancroft Prizes for history as well as a National Book Award. Contrast Kennan with Von Laue on the importance of World War I in explaining the Bolsheviks' success.

But Russia was the first great country to crack under the strain of the World War. This meant social and political instability. And the Bolsheviki, being a Russian party, starved for power and success, could not resist the temptation to take advantage of this instability and to make the bid for power. They knew that Russia was scarcely ripe for socialism, in Marxist terms; but they rationalized their action by persuading themselves that a successful seizure of power by Communists in Russia would ignite the smoldering tinder of social revolution in Germany as well.

The Bolsheviki were, of course, by no means the only faction struggling for exclusive power in Russia in 1917. The sudden disintegration of the Tsarist régime had roused to frantic and desperate activity every other political faction active on the Russian scene. In view of the narrow intolerance which has always characterized Russian political thought and activity, the penalty for failure in Russian political life, at crucial moments, can very well be destruction at the hands of others. Once the disintegration of Tsarist power set in, conditions of self-preservation alone would thus have forced every one of these Russian factions to exert its utmost effort, even had ambition for predominance not had this same effect. The result was that Russia was plunged, from the beginning of 1917, into a tremendous domestic-political crisis: probably the greatest that country had ever experienced—certainly the greatest since the so-called "time of trouble" at the end of the sixteenth century. The struggle of the tiny, fanatical Bolshevik faction against all the others was at first only one portion of this huge upheaval.

The things involved in this crisis were of greatest conceivable importance to every individual Russian. The social structure, the system of land ownership, the privileges and property interests of entire classes, were now at stake. There was not a single Russian for whose fate the outcome of this crisis would not have momentous, intimate personal significance.

This being so, it was, of course, the internal crisis which preoccupied the individual Russian from the beginning of 1917 on. The World War had nowhere near the same significance in his eyes. It is difficult, in fact, to see what stake the common people of Russia ever did have in the outcome of the war. A Russian victory would presumably have meant the establishment of Russia on the Dardanelles. For this, the Russian peasant could not have cared less. A German victory would obviously have affected the prestige of the Tsar's government. It might have led to limited territorial changes, and to some German commercial penetration. That any of this would have affected adversely the situation of the Russian peasant is not at all clear; in any case, he was not convinced that it would. Not only this, but he was by now, as a rule, heartily tired of the struggle: of the losses, the hardships, the deprivation. And if this detachment from the issues of the war was true of the ordinary people, how much more true it was of the Bolsheviki, for whom this was the great moment of political existence. They had never had anything but contempt, anyway, for the issues over which people claimed to be fighting in this imperialist war in the West.

How different all this was in the Western countries! Here, war fervor had by 1917 attained a terrific intensity. The Western democracies had by this time convinced themselves, as embattled democracies have a tendency to do, that the entire future of civilization depended on the outcome of the military struggle.

There is, let me assure you, nothing in nature more egocentrical than the embattled democracy. It soon becomes the victim of its own war propaganda. It then tends to attach to its own cause an absolute value which distorts its own vision on everything else. *Its* enemy becomes the embodiment of all evil. Its own side, on the other hand, is the center of all virtue. The contest comes to be viewed as having a final, apocalyptic quality. If *we* lose, all is lost; life will no longer be worth living; there will be nothing to be salvaged. If we win, then everything will be possible; all problems will become soluble; the one great source of evil—*our* enemy—will have been crushed; the forces of good will then sweep forward unimpeded; all worthy aspirations will be satisfied.

It will readily be seen that people who have got themselves into this frame of mind have little understanding for the issues of any contest other than the one in which they are involved. The idea of people wasting time and substance on any *other* issue seems to them preposterous. This explains why Allied statesmen were simply unable to comprehend how people in Russia could be interested in an internal Russian political crisis when there was a war on in the West. Did the Russians not realize, it was asked in Paris and London, that everything depended on the defeat of the Germans, that if Germany was successful, no one could ever conceivably be happy again, whereas if Germany lost, everyone would somehow or other receive what he wanted?

You saw this well illustrated in the first reaction of President Woodrow Wilson to the news of the seizure of power in Russia by the Communists, in November 1917. "It is amazing to me"—he said—

> that any group of persons should be so ill-informed as to suppose, as some groups in Russia apparently suppose, that any reforms planned in the interests of the people can live in the presence of a Germany powerful enough to undermine or overthrow them by intrigue or force.

There was, of course, an important substantive difference between the issue that interested the early Bolsheviki and that which interested the warring powers in the West. The first was ideological, with universal social and political implications. The Bolsheviki believed that questions of social organization—in particular the question of ownership of the means of production—had an importance transcending all international rivalries. Such rivalries were, in their eyes, simply the product of social relationships. This is why they attached so little importance to the military outcome of the struggle in the West.

▨ ▨ ▨

The myopia of the Western capitals in the face of Russia's growing agony was well illustrated by the Allied diplomatic conference which took place in Petrograd in January 1917, just one month before the first Revolution. The purpose of this gathering was to stimulate the Russians to new efforts on the eastern front and to co-ordinate these efforts with Western war strategy. Lord Milner and Sir Henry Wilson attended for Great Britain. The French Minister of Colonies, Gaston Doumergue, was there for the French. The Americans were of course not represented, being not yet in the war.

The conference afforded an excellent opportunity for the Allied statesmen to acquaint themselves with the seriousness of the situation in Russia and to take measures betimes to mitigate its effects. Had they looked carefully at the

Russian scene at that moment, they could have discerned in it the dilemma that was to be basic to their problem of policy toward Russia throughout the following two years. This dilemma consisted in the fact that not only had Russia become involved in a great internal political crisis, but she had lost in the process her real ability to make war. The internal crisis was of such gravity that there was no chance for a healthy and constructive solution to it unless the war effort could be terminated at once and the attention and resources of the country concentrated on domestic issues. The army was tired. The country was tired. People had no further stomach for war. To try to drive them to it was to provide grist to the mill of the agitator and the fanatic: the last people one would have wished to encourage at such a dangerous moment. The sad fact is that from 1916 on, the demands of the political situation in Russia were in conflict with the demands of the Allied war effort.

At the time of the inter-Allied conference in January 1917, the Russian bureaucracy, themselves partially blind to these realities, had no desire that the Allied governments should pry too deeply into Russia's weaknesses and embarrassments. They were reluctant, in particular, to admit to the real exhaustion of their war effort, being fearful of losing Allied military aid and future support at the peace conference. Instead, therefore, of confessing their real plight, they made efforts to conceal it. They defended themselves against Allied curiosity and Allied demands in the traditional manner: by a combination of extravagant promises of military performance, on the one hand, and a formidable barrage of banquets and other social ordeals on the other. This was a combination guaranteed, by the experience of centuries, to get even the most sanguine Western visitor out of town—exhausted, bilious, empty-handed, but grateful for his escape—within a matter of weeks, if not days. It is a technique, incidentally, which the Soviet government has not hesitated to borrow from its predecessors.

⊠ ⊠ ⊠

I shall not attempt to describe to you the dramatic circumstances of the February Revolution. I should like only to tell you of two incidents which to my mind reveal the deficiencies of the Allied reaction to what was going on and illustrate the extent to which, as I said earlier, the Russians and the Westerners were preoccupied with different things. Both concern the French ambassador, Paléologue. While he was, as I say, an intelligent man, with much understanding for what was happening, he was first and foremost the representative of his government; he had to follow in his utterances the line his government had laid down for him; and like all Frenchmen he felt very strongly about the war in Europe.

At one point, walking through the streets amid the kaleidoscopic events of the February Revolution, Paléologue found himself surrounded by a group of celebrating students, half-curious, half-suspicious. They evidently first thought

him to be some distinguished member of the old regime, and took a hostile attitude. On learning that he was the French ambassador, they called upon him
to accompany them to the Tauride Palace, the home both of the Duma and of
the Petrograd Soviet, and to do homage there to the red flag of the Revolution
which now waved over the building. His answer was eloquently revealing: "I
can render no better homage to Russian liberty," he said, "than by asking you to
join me in shouting 'Vive la Guerre.'" In other words, "Forget about your Revolution; think of the war."

The second incident took place a few days later. The head of the Russian
Duma, Mikhail Rodzyanko, appealed to Paléologue for advice as to the course
the Russian moderates should now adopt. Rodzyanko and his friends were men
deeply attached to the Allied cause. They really needed advice and help. But
Paléologue had to evade the issue. No one in Paris, he realized, would have
much understanding for the problems of these men. The words with which he
put them off were again revealing. "As ambassador of France," he said, "the war
is my principal preoccupation."

In these simple words the principal reason for the bankruptcy of Allied
policy in the face of the Russian Revolution—namely, the inability to believe
that anything other than the war in Europe could be of real importance—became visible at the start.

✠ ✠ ✠

Aside from its ideological implications, the Bolshevik seizure of power
was, of course, a complete disaster from the standpoint of the Allied war effort. The Bolsheviki were committed to taking Russia out of the war—committed to this not just by their own promises but by the very methods they
had used to come into power. They had worked hard and successfully at the
demoralization of the armed forces. They had done this in order that the Provisional Government should not have under its control at the crucial moment
any sizable body of armed men which could be used as a defense against the
violent usurpation of power by the Communists. To this end the Bolsheviki
had played for all it was worth the purely demagogic card of land reform,
promising the peasant soldier the division of the larger farms and estates and
encouraging him to leave the trenches and go back to the village to get his
share. This agitation had begun to take effect well before the Bolshevik seizure
of power. For days and weeks, the army had been streaming away from the
trenches and making its way home as best it could. It was this that caused
Lenin to say triumphantly that the army had voted against the war with its
feet. By mid-November, when the Communist seizure of power in the main
centers was complete, it would have been physically impossible and politically
suicidal for the Bolshevik leaders to do anything else but sue for peace. It was
therefore natural that the first act of foreign policy of the new regime, taken

on the very day of the Revolution, should have been the issuance of the Decree on Peace, calling on all the belligerent peoples and their governments to open negotiations for an immediate cessation of hostilities on the basis of no annexations and no indemnities. With this act, the departure of Russia from the war was really sealed.

Please note how intimately the causes of Kerensky's failure were connected with his effort to continue Russia's participation in World War I. Had he been able to demobilize the Petrograd garrison, and to get its members out of town, he presumably would never have been faced with the July insurrection; nor would the Bolsheviki have been able to organize the final seizure of power in November. But the fact that there was a war on prevented this. Had he not undertaken the summer offensive, he might have permitted the army to demobilize peacefully without raising the fateful problems of military discipline and authority by which he and his regime were bound to be crushed. Had he not endeavored to hold the armed forces together for a military purpose, he might have been able to compete with the Bolsheviki in encouraging the soldiers to return to their villages and in carrying out a prompt and politically effective land reform. The Bolsheviki had, after all, largely stolen the agrarian program of the Socialist-Revolutionary Party, to which Kerensky himself nominally belonged. The only reason they were able to exploit this issue successfully was that they, uninhibited by any loyalty to the war effort, were willing to put this agrarian program into effect at once, whereas Kerensky and his associates felt obliged to ask for delay in deference to the needs of the war effort. In every respect Kerensky's political position would have been eased, and his prospects for resistance to Bolshevik pressure would have been improved, had he been able to take the country out of the war at once.

The question may legitimately be asked: If all this was so, why did Kerensky attempt to continue the war at all? Why did he not flout the wishes of the Allies and address himself exclusively to his internal political problem? I am not sure that I can answer this question. Trotsky alleges that the Provisional Government clung to the tie with the Allies as a means of protecting themselves against the full sweep of the Revolution. This sounds to me forced and unconvincing. Kerensky and other members of the Provisional Government felt themselves bound to the Allies by many bonds. They had no sympathy for the Germans. Feelings of national pride made them reluctant to abandon outright the coalition with which they had been associated. They were urged to continue the war not just by conservative circles in the West but also by the Western Socialists and the representatives of Western labor. Finally, they were well aware that the country over which they presided was at the end of its economic and financial rope; and I am sure that they hesitated to face the future without the assurance that they would have some claim on Western economic assistance after the war.

Like everything else that had to do with the Russian Revolution and Soviet power, Kerensky's final defeat exercised a highly divisive effect on Western opinion. The French and British governments, still swayed predominantly by their interest in the war, tended to sympathize with Kornilov and to blame Kerensky for frustrating what they felt to be the only serious attempt to restore the discipline and fighting capacity of Russia's armed forces. American circles in Russia, on the other hand, had less natural sympathy for the upper classes, and appreciated dimly the fact that the old Humpty Dumpty of Tsarist Russia could never be put together again. They thought Kornilov's venture doomed to failure in any case. They considered it the height of folly for the Allies to support it: this, they considered, only estranged the workers and peasants without whose support a war effort was unthinkable.

If history has any comment to make on these arguments, from the perspective of forty years, it is that all the parties to these disputes were wrong. The premise from which they all departed—namely, that Russia could and should be kept in the war—was an impossible premise. The sad fact is that by the spring of 1917 nothing the Allies might have done could have made Russia once more a serious factor in the war. The entire Russian economic and political system had by this time been overstrained by the military effort. The prerequisites for a continuation of this effort—spiritual, psychological, and political as well as economic—were simply no longer there. From this standpoint the policies of Paléologue, of Milyukov, and of Kerensky were as futile as those of Buchanan, President Wilson, or Elihu Root. Whichever had been adopted, the results would have been substantially the same, so far as the Russian war effort was concerned. The only point at which Allied statesmanship might, with different policies, have produced a different result was in the political field. It was inevitable that Russia should leave the war in 1917. It was not inevitable that this should have occurred under the chairmanship of the Bolsheviki. This, surely, was at least in part the effect of the blunders of Western statesmanship.

When we inquire, then, into the causality of the Russian Revolution—when we ask ourselves why it was that the Russian political structure broke down in 1917 and why the ensuing situation degenerated within a few months into the rigidities and extremisms of Bolshevism—we see that in each case it was the World War, and specifically the Allied cause in the World War, which was the determining factor. Whatever it may be said to have been that the Western Allies were fighting for, it was this to which the real needs of Russia in these crucial years were sacrificed. The Russian Revolution and the alienation of the Russian people from the Western community for decades to come were only a part of the staggering price paid by the Western people for their insistence on completing a military victory over Germany in 1917 and 1918.

Can it conceivably have been that the end in view was worth this price? I should like to let the discussion of Allied policies toward the Provisional

Government rest with this question. The impression I gain after three or four years of immersion in these problems is that in attaching such enormous value to total military victory in 1917 and 1918, the Western peoples were the victims of a great misunderstanding—a misunderstanding about the uses and effects of the war itself. And I suspect that this misunderstanding also lies at the heart of those subsequent developments which have carried the Western community in the space of forty years from a seemingly secure place at the center of world happenings to the precarious and isolated position it occupies today, facing a world environment so largely beyond its moral and political influence.

How the Soviet Union Is Governed

JERRY F. HOUGH
AND MERLE FAINSOD

Merle Fainsod was a Harvard professor of political science whose groundbreaking analysis of the organization of power in Russia, *How Russia Is Ruled,* was published in 1953. In order to take into account recent events and statistics, and to make use of the great amount of scholarly work published since the 1960s, the book was extensively revised and enlarged by Jerry F. Hough, who is a professor of political and policy sciences at Duke University and a senior fellow at the Brookings Institution. It is from this revision that the following excerpt comes. Why, in the opinion of the authors, did the Bolsheviks succeed in winning power in, and after, November 1917?

On no other major event in recent Russian history is there so much general agreement among leading western specialists as there is on the revolution of 1917. Although there are some differences in emphasis and some variation in interpretation on narrower points, the same general picture emerges from the magnificent and long-standard *The Russian Revolution* written by William Henry Chamberlin in the 1930s, from *How Russia Is Ruled* in the early 1950s, and from the more recent work of such scholars as Robert Daniels, John Keep, and Alex Rabinowitch. The educated population in the United States also holds a common view of the Bolshevik revolution, one that is shared by many scholars (including a number in Russian and Soviet studies). Such unexpected consensus would be the source of great rejoicing were it not for one unfortunate fact—namely, that in almost all important respects the consensus of the educated public is radically different from that of those who study the revolution.

In the image of the educated public and many scholars, two revolutions occurred in Russia in 1917—a democratic revolution in March (or February, according to the Russian calendar of the time) and a Communist coup d'état that overthrew the democratic regime in November (or October, by the old calendar). The Bolsheviks succeeded, it is believed, not because of popular support (their 25 percent vote in the Constituent Assembly election of November 1917 is often cited), but because of their "organizational weapon." The Bolshevik success is attributed to the "fact" that the party of *What Is To Be Done?* had the unity of views, the military discipline, the narrow elite membership, and the great conspiratorial leader needed for seizing the levers of power in a time of chaos and indecisive governmental leadership.

Scholars studying the revolution more seriously, however, have tended to see only one revolution in Russia in 1917—a continuing surge of unrest that overthrew the tsar in March and that, with short periods of abatement, grew in intensity as the year wore on. It was a time of conflict, breakdown of authority, polarization of opinion of a type observed more recently in Chile. These scholars would say that the party was, indeed, fairly well organized in comparative terms, but they find the Bolsheviks of 1917 to be a much-divided mass party quite unlike that depicted in *What Is To Be Done?* In their explanations of the Bolshevik success, they emphasize much more the nature of the Bolshevik program. While acknowledging the failure of the party to win majority support, these scholars would argue that the Bolsheviks did have a program that won the support of half of the inhabitants of Russian cities and the soldiers stationed near the major urban centers and that satisfied the basic desires of the peasantry. In this view, the Bolsheviks won because they were the only party whose radicalism really matched the spirit of the urban majority and the army. Indeed, if the Bolshevik victory is dated by the successful completion of the Civil War in 1921 rather than by the seizure of power in November 1917 (in many ways, the most reasonable viewpoint), then one should no doubt give more attention to the millions of peasants who joined the Red army of the Communists instead of their opponents, the Whites.

The contrast between the specialists' view of the revolution and that of the nonspecialist has created a serious problem for western understanding of the Soviet experience. If the social forces that produced the Bolshevik revolution are neglected, as they often are in generalizations about the Soviet system, the new regime inevitably assumes the appearance of a totally alien agent that has grafted itself, like a tumor, onto a helpless organism. The ability of the regime to survive such shocks as collectivization, the Great Purge, and World War II becomes quite incomprehensible, except perhaps in terms of some almost mystical and superhuman totalitarian control. Moreover, of course, if Communist movements in general are seen in light of the nonspecialist's image of the Bolshevik revolution, we may be led into a fundamental misunderstanding of the dynamics of Communist movements in the Third World, sometimes with unfortunate consequences in the foreign policy realm.

※ ※ ※

Reasons for the Bolshevik Success in 1917

In the brief period of eight months, a tiny band of underground revolutionaries, numbering fewer than 25,000 men on the eve of the March revolution, had gained sufficient support to catapult themselves into a governing authority over nearly 150,000,000 people. The success of the Bolsheviks can be explained on many levels. In one sense, of course, the crucial factor was the revolutionary mood of the time and the way in which the Bolsheviks' opponents responded—or failed to respond—to it. If the Provisional Government had been able to withdraw from the war and carry through a land settlement satisfactory to the peasantry, it is highly doubtful that the Bolsheviks could have been so successful.

Yet, to state this alternative, so plausibly reinforced by hindsight, is to miss the tragic imperatives of 1917. Each of the parties which maneuvered for ascendancy in the months between March and November was the prisoner of its own illusions, its own interests, and its own visions of the future. To a Kadet leader like Miliukov it was inconceivable that Russia could betray her allies and her own national interests by suing for a separate peace; consequently, it was all too easy to believe that his own sense of patriotic exaltation and dedication were shared by soldiers, workers, and peasants who had lost their taste for war. To SRs of the right like Kerensky, who in a measure shared Miliukov's illusions, the successful prosecution of the war was paramount, with the agenda of economic reforms to be postponed until properly constituted legal bodies could be assembled to deal with them. To SRs of the center and left, who were much closer to the aspirations and expectations of the villages, land reform brooked no delay. Frustrated by the procrastinations of the Provisional Government, the Left SRs were thrown into the arms of the Bolsheviks. For Mensheviks of all shades, still loyal to the orthodox Marxist two-stage panorama of capitalist development, the socialist revolution had to be postponed until the bourgeois-democratic revolution was completed. They were left with a program of the establishment of a bourgeois order they described in the harshest of terms and a policy of conducting legal opposition to it—hardly a program for which the wretched and disinherited could develop more than qualified enthusiasm.

Until the arrival of Lenin from exile, the Bolsheviks too were prisoners of ancient formulas. They oriented their policies on a perspective not very different from that of Menshevism. Lenin reversed this course and set the party on the road to the conquest of power. With an unswerving faith in his goal and a readiness to take any measures whatever to realize it, Lenin, frequently over bitter opposition, managed to transform the party into an instrument that carried out his will.

Despite all its divisions and disorganization, despite all the lack of real direction given to the organization of the revolution in the provinces, despite the fact that "there was little [that was] systematic about Bolshevik Party organization during this period," the party still had a sense of discipline that was relatively greater than that of its rivals. On October 30, when a debate on the insurrection broke out at a meeting of Petrograd borough leaders, Sverdlov could say, "The decision of the Central Committee on the uprisings has been made. . . . We have not gathered to set aside a decision of the Central Committee, but to consider how we ought to carry it out." It was an appeal that was peculiarly effective to men who had accepted the principle of "democratic centralism" in joining the party. The Central Committee certainly felt that it had the right to debate Lenin's proposals and to disagree with them (as it clearly did, according to the principles of democratic centralism), and the continued presence of a man like Kamenev in the Central Committee despite his opposition to Lenin since April indicates a willingness to maintain a diversity of views within that body. Even the two "strike-breakers" returned to party discipline with the "compromise" of November 2 and Kamenev at least was present at the planning sessions through the night of November 6–7.

Nevertheless, as Fainsod emphasized, the success of the Bolsheviks is to be explained not nearly so much by their discipline as by Lenin's "remarkable talent as a revolutionary strategist . . . [his] unerring sense for the deeply felt dissatisfactions of the masses and a genius for finding the slogans to catalyze grievances into revolutionary energy."

> Except for his insistence on striking at the right moment, Lenin had relatively little to do with the actual mechanics of the insurrection. His great contribution was to set the stage for insurrection by identifying Bolshevism with the major forces of mass discontent in Russian society. Lenin did not create the war-weariness which permeated the army and the nation: the material was at hand; his task was to exploit it. With one word—peace—Lenin and the Bolsheviks fused it into a revolutionary amalgam. The land-hunger of the peasants was an ancient grievance of which all parties were aware. The SRs built their ascendancy in the villages on the promise to satisfy it, but, while they temporized, Lenin stole their program from under their noses. . . . With one word—land—Lenin insured the neutrality of the villages. . . . With two slogans—bread and workers' control—Lenin captured the allegiance of substantial sections of the industrial workers from the Mensheviks.

The nature of the Bolshevik support—and the limitations on it—were clearly revealed in the elections to the Constituent Assembly, which were held (on the whole) on November 25 to 27—three weeks after the uprising in Petrograd. All parties participated in the election, and the vote was generally free—a fact attested to by the 25 percent vote that the Bolsheviks received.

While the Bolsheviks were not a majoritarian movement, they did have important pockets of strength. They claimed that they were the party of the proletariat, and it was a claim that they could generally substantiate. The Mensheviks received only 3 percent of the vote in Moscow and Petrograd, and only 1.5 percent of the total vote outside of the Transcaucasus (where they were strong) and a district in which voters were compelled to vote for the Menshevik candidate. In Petrograd and Moscow, the Bolsheviks received 45 percent and 48 percent of the vote respectively, but the Kadets—the party of the middle class and the bourgeoisie—were their major competition here, receiving 26 percent and 35 percent of the vote respectively in the two metropolises.

The Bolsheviks also had strong support among a number of the army units. The Baltic fleet remained a Bolshevik center (63 percent of the vote), as did the army units at the western front (67 percent of the vote) and at the northern front (56 percent of it). In a pattern that was repeated in the peasant vote, the Bolshevik vote declined sharply in units more distant from the metropolitan centers where they had had much less opportunity to present their case. The Bolsheviks received only 30 percent of the vote at the southwest front and only 15 percent of the vote at the Rumanian front, which was the most remote of all. Similarly, the sailors of the Black Sea fleet presented only 20 percent of their votes to Lenin's party.

The picture in the countryside is more mixed. The SRs "won" the election in that they received 38 percent of the total vote, and the bulk of this support came from the peasants. In remote rural areas such as Siberia and the Central Black-Earth region (for example, Kursk and Voronezh), their vote exceeded 75 percent of the total, but in the central and western provinces, where peasant families had more contact with the cities and the army units, the Bolsheviks garnered a substantial number of peasant votes. The latter won 43 percent of the vote in the eleven central and northwest Russian guberniias, and actually carried the rural guberniia of Smolensk with 55 percent of the vote and rural Belorussia with 59 percent. It is hard to avoid the conclusion that the Bolshevik program had strong support among the Russian peasantry whenever the latter were exposed to it in a substantial way.

Social revolution is seldom a matter of winning majority support. In all revolutions there are large numbers who are uninterested, and in the Russian provinces in particular "what emerges," to quote Fainsod, "is a picture of utmost confusion in which passivity and apathy played a much larger role than is commonly assumed." Revolutions are made by active minorities who tap groundswells of discontent, and this the Bolsheviks were able to do; they are successful when the military force supporting the old regime melts away or defects, and this too the Bolsheviks were able to achieve. Russia of 1917 had much in common with the disorder and polarization of the last months of the Allende regime in Chile, but in Chile the soldiers carried out the orders of the "Chilean Kornilov." In Russia they did not, and the war and the war-weariness were surely crucial in this respect.

As William Chamberlin emphasized many years ago, the essence of Lenin's great insight in September and October was an understanding of the meaning of the failure of the Kornilov affair:

> There is no period in Lenin's life when his stature as a leader and his capacity to grasp accurately the basic facts of a new and changing political situation appear so vividly as in the few weeks which elapsed between the Kornilov affair and the Bolshevik stroke for power. He recognized immediately that Kornilov's defeat was Bolshevism's opportunity. . . . Living in hiding . . . it was only natural that his judgment should be faulty in connection with some of the details of the projected uprising. . . . He seems to have been precipitate with his suggestion that the uprising should have begun at the time of the Democratic Conference, and in his single-track insistence on the organization of insurrection at the earliest possible moment he was somewhat too contemptuous of the expediency of linking up the uprising with the meeting of the Second Congress of Soviets, with its assured Bolshevik majority. But these were minor miscalculations of detail, which could be and were corrected in the development of the action. Lenin's indisputable claim to greatness as a revolutionary leader lies in the fact that he realized immediately after the collapse of Kornilov that the time for action had come, that he drove home this view . . . and that he never relaxed his pressure on the Party Central Committee . . . until the opposition was crushed and the Party organization had swung into line behind his proposals.

To repeat a crucial point, however, the real test of the Bolsheviks came not in November, but in the coming three years. They had to demonstrate an ability to rule that no one expected this group of fractious extremists to have; they had to build an army from a war-weary population after having promised peace; they had to win a Civil War while extracting grain by force from peasants in the countryside, while attempting to reinstitute authority relations in the army and the factory, and while ending the wildly free politics of 1917 and emasculating the soviets in whose name they came to power. It was in 1917–1921 that the Bolshevik revolution was really won.

4

STALIN AND STALINISM

One of the most intriguing aspects of President Mikhail Gorbachev's *perestroika,* or restructuring program, was his call for a large-scale return to private farming. Though he had stopped short of rejecting the Soviet experience of agricultural collectivization as a total failure, Gorbachev boldly detailed the human horror and economic folly of Stalin's rapid collectivization strategy after 1928.

The collectivization of farms was first attempted during the war communism that followed the Bolsheviks' seizure of power. Together with the five-year plans it marked an essential component of Stalin's "Socialism in One Country." State involvement in the economy, however, antedates the Russian Revolution. Peter the Great proposed a five-year plan, and state initiative under the last tsars instigated the industrialization for which the Communists later took credit.

Certainly in the 1920s there was need for drastic economic modernization after years of foreign and civil war. Losses were horrendous: population, which had been 171 million in 1914, was 132 million in 1921, and the loss of Finland, Poland, and the Baltic states also meant a loss of industrial plants, railroads, and farms. Manufacturing in 1920 was thirteen percent of what it had been in 1913. The middle classes had been decimated, and seventy-eight percent of the population worked in (private) agriculture.[1] In the absence of any foreign investment, Stalin believed collectivization was the only way to raise funds for industrial development and to create the substantial military establishment he regarded as vital to confront an anticipated capitalist onslaught.

It also seemed to Stalin the only way to increase the productive capacity of the land. Because primitive methods—plowing with wooden plows, sowing by hand, reaping with sickles, threshing with flails—were still used and the output per acre was among the lowest in Europe, the gathering of scattered holdings

---

[1] Figures cited in Paul Kennedy, *The Rise and Fall of the Great Powers* (New York: Random House, 1987), pp. 321–322.

into large collective farms *(kolkhozy),* well managed and provided with access to government-owned, up-to-date tractors and other machinery, seemed an attractive alternative.

Equally desirable among Stalin's far-reaching aims was the great transformation of the petty-bourgeois peasant, a change that would bring the very individualistic, stubborn, and intractable peasant into conformity with the Party's image of the new Soviet man.

What dismayed observers was the frantic haste, the vast increase in state power, the mass terror waged against the *kulaks* (the allegedly well-to-do farmers), the prohibition of all opposition in or out of the Party, and the colossal human costs stemming from forced collectivization and industrialization. The consumers' share of the gross national product was driven down to levels unmatched in modern history, resulting in deprivation of the basic necessities of life. If productivity goals were not achieved, the Party blamed "saboteurs" or "imperialist agents" (including many "Old Bolsheviks"), who were framed, hauled into Soviet courts, and later "liquidated" or consigned to the forced labor camps of the "gulag." The widespread destruction of life (Stalin himself estimated that ten million peasants had died in the famine of 1932–1933 alone, which came in the wake of refusals to turn land or draft animals over to the state), agriculture's failure to feed the population adequately, and the loss of individual freedoms for at least the next two generations were not too high a price to pay for Stalin, who, in spite of inflated production figures, could point to many real gains. By the late 1930s, the Soviets' industrial output exceeded that of such nations as France, Japan, Italy, and probably Great Britain, and their military force enabled the USSR to face World War II as a great industrial and military power.

Assessments, appreciations, and criticisms of this so-called second revolution—Stalin's revolution—are found in the readings that follow. In exile Trotsky published a scathing condemnation of Stalin for having betrayed the ideals of Bolshevism. Isaac Deutscher is much less harsh, and while deploring such excesses as the persecution of the old "intelligentsia," finds much to admire in Stalin's achievements. Roy Medvedev contrasts Stalin unfavorably with Lenin, and Bernice Rosenthal traces the changing fortunes of women during the period of Stalinist rule. While reading these interpretations, bear in mind the great historical question of whether Stalin's revolutionary changes marked a continuation or a perversion of the work begun by Lenin and whether, in view of the human costs incurred, these changes can, as Deutscher argues, be justified.

The Revolution Betrayed

LEON TROTSKY

Leon Trotsky, once Lenin's second-in-command and heir apparent, the military genius of the Revolution, a significant contrib-
utor to Communist theory, defeated by Stalin in the ideological
struggles of the 1920s, vilified and hounded into exile, and ultimately murdered by Stalin's agent, was indeed a titanic but
tragic figure in Russian and twentieth-century history. What is
the basis of Trotsky's condemnation of Stalin? How does he distinguish between Stalin and Lenin? On what does he blame the
degeneration of the Bolshevik party? Inasmuch as Trotsky had
initially called for collectivization himself, how, specifically, does
he criticize Stalinist collectivization?

The Degeneration of the Bolshevik Party

The Bolshevik party prepared and insured the October victory. It also created
the Soviet state, supplying it with a sturdy skeleton. The degeneration of the
party became both cause and consequence of the bureaucratization of the state.
It is necessary to show at least briefly how this happened.

The inner regime of the Bolshevik party was characterized by the method
of *democratic centralism.* The combination of these two concepts, democracy
and centralism, is not in the least contradictory. The party took watchful care
not only that its boundaries should always be strictly defined, but also that all
those who entered these boundaries should enjoy the actual right to define the
direction of the party policy. Freedom of criticism and intellectual struggle was
an irrevocable content of the party democracy. The present doctrine that Bolshevism does not tolerate factions is a myth of the epoch of decline. In reality

the history of Bolshevism is a history of the struggle of factions. And, indeed, how could a genuinely revolutionary organization, setting itself the task of overthrowing the world and uniting under its banner the most audacious iconoclasts, fighters and insurgents, live and develop without intellectual conflicts, without groupings and temporary factional formations? The farsightedness of the Bolshevik leadership often made it possible to soften conflicts and shorten the duration of factional struggle, but no more than that. The Central Committee relied upon this seething democratic support. From this it derived the audacity to make decisions and give orders. The obvious correctness of the leadership at all critical stages gave it that high authority which is the priceless moral capital of centralism.

The regime of the Bolshevik party, especially before it came to power, stood thus in complete contradiction to the regime of the present sections of the Communist International, with their "leaders" appointed from above, making complete changes of policy at a word of command, with their uncontrolled apparatus, haughty in its attitude to the rank and file, servile in its attitude to the Kremlin. But in the first years after the conquest of power also, even when the administrative rust was already visible on the party, every Bolshevik, not excluding Stalin, would have denounced as a malicious slanderer anyone who should have shown him on a screen the image of the party ten or fifteen years later.

The very center of Lenin's attention and that of his colleagues was occupied by a continual concern to protect the Bolshevik ranks from the vices of those in power. However, the extraordinary closeness and at times actual merging of the party with the state apparatus had already in those first years done indubitable harm to the freedom and elasticity of the party regime. Democracy had been narrowed in proportion as difficulties increased. In the beginning, the party had wished and hoped to preserve freedom of political struggle within the framework of the Soviets. The civil war introduced stern amendments into this calculation. The opposition parties were forbidden one after the other. This measure, obviously in conflict with the spirit of Soviet democracy, the leaders of Bolshevism regarded not as a principle, but as an episodic act of self-defense.

The swift growth of the ruling party, with the novelty and immensity of its tasks, inevitably gave rise to inner disagreements. The underground oppositional currents in the country exerted a pressure through various channels upon the sole legal political organization, increasing the acuteness of the factional struggle. At the moment of completion of the civil war, this struggle took such sharp forms as to threaten to unsettle the state power. In March 1921, in the days of the Kronstadt revolt, which attracted into its ranks no small number of Bolsheviks, the tenth congress of the party thought it necessary to resort to a prohibition of factions—that is, to transfer the political regime prevailing in the state to the inner life of the ruling party. This forbidding of factions was again regarded as an exceptional measure to be abandoned at the first serious improvement in the situation. At the same time, the Central Committee was extremely cautious in applying the new law, concerning itself most of all lest it lead to a strangling of the inner life of the party.

However, what was in its original design merely a necessary concession to a difficult situation, proved perfectly suited to the taste of the bureaucracy, which had then begun to approach the inner life of the party exclusively from the viewpoint of convenience in administration. Already in 1922, during a brief improvement in his health, Lenin, horrified at the threatening growth of bureaucratism, was preparing a struggle against the faction of Stalin, which had made itself the axis of the party machine as a first step toward capturing the machinery of state. A second stroke and then death prevented him from measuring forces with this internal reaction.

The entire effort of Stalin, with whom at that time Zinoviev and Kamenev were working hand in hand, was thenceforth directed to freeing the party machine from the control of the rank-and-file members of the party. In this struggle for "stability" of the Central Committee, Stalin proved the most consistent and reliable among his colleagues. He had no need to tear himself away from international problems; he had never been concerned with them. The petty bourgeois outlook of the new ruling stratum was his own outlook. He profoundly believed that the task of creating socialism was national and administrative in its nature. He looked upon the Communist International as a necessary evil which should be used so far as possible for the purposes of foreign policy. His own party kept a value in his eyes merely as a submissive support for the machine.

❊ ❊ ❊

Of party democracy there remained only recollections in the memory of the older generation. And together with it had disappeared the democracy of the soviets, the trade unions, the co-operatives, the cultural and athletic organizations. Above each and every one of them there reigns an unlimited hierarchy of party secretaries. The regime had become "totalitarian" in character several years before this word arrived from Germany. "By means of demoralizing methods, which convert thinking communists into machines, destroying will, character and human dignity," wrote Rakovsky in 1928, "the ruling circles have succeeded in converting themselves into an unremovable and inviolate oligarchy, which replaces the class and the party." Since those indignant lines were written, the degeneration of the regime has gone immeasurably farther. The G.P.U. has become the decisive factor in the inner life of the party. If Molotov in March 1936 was able to boast to a French journalist that the ruling party no longer contains any factional struggle, it is only because disagreements are now settled by the automatic intervention of the political police. The old Bolshevik party is dead, and no force will resurrect it.

⊠ ⊠ ⊠

Bonapartism as a Regime of Crisis

The question we previously raised in the name of the reader: "How could the ruling clique, with its innumerable mistakes, concentrate unlimited power in its hands?"—or, in other words: "How explain the contradiction between the intellectual poverty of the Thermidorians and their material might?"—now permits a more concrete and categorical answer. The Soviet society is not harmonious. What is a sin for one class or stratum is a virtue for another. From the point of view of socialist forms of society, the policy of the bureaucracy is striking in its contradictions and inconsistencies. But the same policy appears very consistent from the standpoint of strengthening the power of the new commanding stratum.

The state support of the kulak (1923–28) contained a mortal danger for the socialist future. But then, with the help of the petty bourgeoisie the bureaucracy succeeded in binding the proletarian vanguard hand and foot, and suppressing the Bolshevik Opposition. This "mistake" from the point of view of socialism was a pure gain from the point of view of the bureaucracy. When the kulak began directly to threaten the bureaucracy itself, it turned its weapons against the kulak. The panic of aggression against the kulak, spreading also to the middle peasant, was no less costly to the economy than a foreign invasion. But the bureaucracy had defended its positions. Having barely succeeded in exterminating its former ally, it began with all its power to develop a new aristocracy. Thus undermining socialism? Of course—but at the same time strengthening the commanding caste. The Soviet bureaucracy is like all ruling classes in that it is ready to shut its eyes to the crudest mistakes of its leaders in the sphere of general politics, provided in return they show an unconditional fidelity in the defense of its privileges. The more alarmed becomes the mood of the new lords of the situation, the higher the value they set upon ruthlessness against the least threat to their so justly earned rights. It is from this point of view that the caste of parvenus selects its leaders. Therein lies the secret of Stalin's success.

⊠ ⊠ ⊠

The progressive role of the Soviet bureaucracy coincides with the period devoted to introducing into the Soviet Union the most important elements of capitalist technique. The rough work of borrowing, imitating, transplanting and grafting was accomplished on the bases laid down by the revolution. There was, thus far, no question of any new word in the sphere of technique, science or art. It is possible to build gigantic factories according to a ready-made Western pattern by bureaucratic command—although, to be sure, at triple the normal cost. But the farther you go, the more the economy runs into the problem of quality, which slips out of the hands of a bureaucracy like a shadow. The Soviet products are as though branded with the gray label of indifference. Under a nationalized economy, *quality* demands a democracy of producers and consumers, freedom of criticism and initiative—conditions incompatible with a totalitarian regime of fear, lies and flattery.

Behind the question of quality stands a more complicated and grandiose problem which may be comprised in the concept of *independent, technical* and *cultural creation.* The ancient philosopher said that strife is the father of all things. No new values can be created where a free conflict of ideas is impossible. To be sure, a revolutionary dictatorship means by its very essence strict limitations of freedom. But for that very reason epochs of revolution have never been directly favorable to cultural creation: they have only cleared the arena for it. The dictatorship of the proletariat opens a wider scope to human genius the more it ceases to be a dictatorship. The socialist culture will flourish only in proportion to the dying away of the state. In that simple and unshakable historic law is contained the death sentence of the present political regime in the Soviet Union. Soviet democracy is not the demand of an abstract policy, still less an abstract moral. It has become a life-and-death need of the country.

If the new state had no other interests than the interests of society, the dying away of the function of compulsion would gradually acquire a painless character. But the state is not pure spirit. Specific functions have created specific organs. The bureaucracy taken as a whole is concerned not so much with its function as with the tribute which this function brings in. The commanding caste tries to strengthen and perpetuate the organs of compulsion. To make sure of its power and income, it spares nothing and nobody. The more the course of development goes against it, the more ruthless it becomes toward the advanced elements of the population. Like the Catholic Church it has put forward the dogma of infallibility in the period of its decline, but it has raised it to a height of which the Roman pope never dreamed.

The increasingly insistent deification of Stalin is, with all its elements of caricature, a necessary element of the regime. The bureaucracy has need of an inviolable superarbiter, a first consul if not an emperor, and it raises upon its shoulders him who best responds to its claim for lordship. That "strength of character" of the leader which so enraptures the literary dilettantes of the West, is in reality the sum total of the collective pressure of a caste which will stop at nothing in defense of its position. Each one of them at his post is thinking: *l'état*—c'est moi. In Stalin each one easily finds himself. But Stalin also finds in each one a small part of his own spirit. Stalin is the personification of the bureaucracy. That is the substance of his political personality.

Caesarism, or its bourgeois form, Bonapartism, enters the scene in those moments of history when the sharp struggle of two camps raises the state power, so to speak, above the nation, and guarantees it, in appearance, a complete independence of classes—in reality, only the freedom necessary for a defense of the privileged. The Stalin regime, rising above a politically atomized society, resting upon a police and officers' corps, and allowing of no control whatever, is obviously a variation of Bonapartism—a Bonapartism of a new type not before seen in history.

Caesarism arose upon the basis of a slave society shaken by inward strife. Bonapartism is one of the political weapons of the capitalist regime in its critical period. Stalinism is a variety of the same system, but upon the basis of a workers' state torn by the antagonism between an organized and armed soviet aristocracy and the unarmed toiling masses.

As history testifies, Bonapartism gets along admirably with a universal, and even a secret, ballot. The democratic ritual of Bonapartism is the *plebiscite*. From time to time, the question is presented to the citizens: *for* or *against* the leader? And the voter feels the barrel of a revolver between his shoulders. Since the time of Napoleon III, who now seems a provincial dilettante, this technique has received an extraordinary development. The new Soviet constitution which establishes *Bonapartism on a plebiscite basis* is the veritable crown of the system.

In the last analysis, Soviet Bonapartism owes its birth to the belatedness of the world revolution. But in the capitalist countries the same cause gave rise to fascism. We thus arrive at the conclusion, unexpected at first glance, but in reality inevitable, that the crushing of Soviet democracy by an all-powerful bureaucracy and the extermination of bourgeois democracy by fascism were produced by one and the same cause: the dilatoriness of the world proletariat in solving the problems set for it by history. Stalinism and fascism, in spite of a deep difference in social foundations, are symmetrical phenomena. In many of their features they show a deadly similarity. A victorious revolutionary movement in Europe would immediately shake not only fascism, but Soviet Bonapartism. In turning its back to the international revolution, the Stalinist bureaucracy was, from its own point of view, right. It was merely obeying the voice of self-preservation.

Stalin and the Second Revolution

ISAAC DEUTSCHER

Isaac Deutscher's biography of Stalin, first published in 1949, remains one of the most important accounts of the leader's rise to power and of his various accomplishments. Although the author of an essential three-volume biography of Trotsky and a one-time Trotskyist himself, Deutscher attempts to provide a balanced view of Stalin. He acknowledges the abuses practiced, but argues that the dictator's policies were no different from those of earlier rulers and that the steps taken to bring Russia into the twentieth century—steps that constituted a "second Russian revolution"—were comparable to policies taken earlier in English history. Do you agree with this analogy and with the conclusions drawn from it? How does Deutscher evaluate Stalin's policy of forced labor?

Perhaps the most important aspect of his social policy was his fight against the equalitarian trends. He insisted on the need for a highly differentiated scale of material rewards for labour, designed to encourage skill and efficiency. He claimed that Marxists were no levellers in the popular sense; and he found support for his thesis in Marx's well-known saying that even in a classless society workers would at first be paid according to their labour and not to their needs. Nevertheless, a strong strand of equalitarianism had run through Bolshevism. Under Lenin, for instance, the maximum income which members of the ruling party, even those of the highest rank, were allowed to earn equalled the wages of a skilled labourer. That the needs of industrialization clashed with 'ascetic' standards of living and that the acquisition of industrial skill was impeded by the lack of material incentives to technicians, administrators, and workers can hardly be disputed. But it is equally true that, throughout the thirties, the differentiation of wages and salaries was pushed to extremes, incompatible with the spirit, if not the letter, of Marxism. A wide gulf came to separate the vast mass of unskilled and underpaid workmen from the privileged 'labour aristocracy' and bureaucracy, a gulf which may be said to have impeded the cultural and industrial progress of the nation as a whole, as much as the earlier rigidly equalitarian outlook had done.

It was mainly in connexion with Stalin's social policy that his opponents, especially the exiled Trotsky, denounced him as the leader of a new privileged caste. He indeed fostered the inequality of incomes with great determination. On this point his mind had been set long before the 'great change.' As early as 1925 he enigmatically warned the fourteenth congress: 'We must not play with the phrase about equality. This is playing with fire.' In later years he spoke against the 'levellers' with a rancour and venom which suggested that in doing so he defended the most sensitive and vulnerable facet of his policy. It was so sensitive because the highly paid and privileged managerial groups came to be the props of Stalin's régime. They had a vested interest in it. Stalin himself felt that his personal rule was the more secure the more solidly it rested on a rigid hierarchy of interest and influence. The point was also so vulnerable because no undertaking is as difficult and risky as the setting up of a new hierarchy on ground that has just been broken up by the mighty ploughs of social revolution. The revolution stirs the people's dormant longings for equality. The most critical moment in its development is that at which the leaders feel that they cannot satisfy that longing and proceed to quell it. They get on with the job which some of their opponents call the betrayal of the revolution. But their conscience is so uneasy and their nerves are so strained by the ambiguity of their role that the worst outbursts of their temper are directed against the victims of that 'betrayal.' Hence the extraordinary vehemence with which a Cromwell, a Robespierre, or a Stalin, each hit out against the levellers of his time.

❊ ❊ ❊

It was only in the late thirties that the fruits of the second revolution began to mature. Towards the end of the decade, Russia's industrial power was catching up with Germany's. Her efficiency and capacity for organization were still incomparably lower. So was the standard of living of her people. But the aggregate output of her mines, basic plants, and factories approached the level which the most efficient and disciplined of all continental nations, assisted by foreign capital, had reached only after three-quarters of a century of intensive industrialization. The other continental nations, to whom only a few years before Russians still looked up, were now left far behind. The industrial revolution spread from central and western Russia to the remote wilderness of Soviet Asia. The collectivization of farming, too, began to yield positive results. Towards the end of the decade the grain crops were thirty or forty million tons higher than those that had been obtained under individual farming. Industry was at last able to supply tractors, harvester combines, and other implements in such numbers that Soviet farming achieved the highest degree of mechanization. The outside world was more or less unaware of the great change and the shift in the international balance of power which it implied. Spectacular failures of the first five-year plan induced foreign observers to take a highly sceptical view of the results of the second and the third. The macabre series of 'purge' trials suggested economic and political weakness. The elements of weakness were undoubtedly there; and they were even greater than may appear when the scene is viewed in retrospect from the vantage point of the late forties. But the elements of strength were also incomparably greater than they were thought to be in the late thirties.

The achievement was remarkable, even if measured only by the yard-stick of Russian national aspirations. On a different scale, it laid the foundations for Russia's new power just as Cromwell's Navigation Act had once laid the foundation for British naval supremacy. Those who still view the political fortunes of countries in terms of national ambitions and prestige cannot but accord to Stalin the foremost place among all those rulers who, through the ages, were engaged in building up Russia's power. Actuated by such motives even many of the Russian White émigrés began to hail Stalin as a national hero. But the significance of the second revolution lay not only and not even mainly in what it meant to Russia. To the world it was important as the first truly gigantic experiment in planned economy, the first instance in which a government undertook to plan and regulate the whole economic life of its country and to direct its nationalized industrial resources towards a uniquely rapid multiplication of the nation's wealth. True enough Stalin was not the originator of the idea. He borrowed so much from Marxist thinkers and economists, including his rivals, that often he might well be charged with outright plagiarism. He was, nevertheless, the first to make of the abstract idea the practical business of government. It is also true that an important beginning in practical planning had been made by the German Government and General Staff in the First World War; and that Lenin had often referred to that precedent as to a pointer to future experiments. What was new in Stalin's planning was the fact that it was initiated not merely as a wartime expedient, but as the normal pattern of economic life in peace. Hitherto governments had engaged in planning as long as they had needed implements of war. Under Stalin's five-year plans, too, guns, tanks, and planes were produced in great profusion; but the chief merit of these plans was not that they enabled Russia to arm herself, but that they enabled her to modernize and transform society.

We have seen the follies and the cruelties that attended Stalin's 'great change.' They inevitably recall those of England's industrial revolution, as Karl

Marx has described them in *Das Kapital*. The analogies are as numerous as they are striking. In the closing chapter of the first volume of his work, Marx depicts the 'primitive accumulation' of capital (or the 'previous accumulation,' as Adam Smith called it), the first violent processes by which one social class accumulated in its hands the means of production, while other classes were being deprived of their land and means of livelihood and reduced to the status of wage-earners. The process which, in the thirties, took place in Russia might be called the 'primitive accumulation' of socialism in one country. Marx described the 'enclosures' and 'clearings' by which the landlords and manufacturers of England expropriated the yeomanry, the 'class of independent peasants.' A parallel to those enclosures is found in a Soviet law, on which Stalin reported to the sixteenth congress, a law which allowed the collective farms to 'enclose' or 'round off' their land so that it should comprise a continuous area. In this way the individual farmers were either compelled to join the collective farms or were virtually expropriated. Marx recalls 'the bloody discipline' by which the free peasants of England were made into wage-labourers, 'the disgraceful action of the state which employed the police to accelerate the accumulation of capital by increasing the degree of exploitation of labour.' His words might apply to many of the practices introduced by Stalin. Marx sums up his picture of the English industrial revolution by saying that 'capital comes [into the world] dripping from head to foot, from every pore, with blood and dirt.' Thus also comes into the world—socialism in one country.

In spite of its 'blood and dirt,' the English industrial revolution—Marx did not dispute this—marked a tremendous progress in the history of mankind. It opened a new and not unhopeful epoch of civilization. Stalin's industrial revolution can claim the same merit. It is argued against it that it has perpetrated cruelties excusable in earlier centuries but unforgivable in this. This is a valid argument, but only within limits. Russia had been belated in her historical development. In England serfdom had disappeared by the end of the fourteenth century. Stalin's parents were still serfs. By the standards of British history, the fourteenth and the twentieth centuries have, in a sense, met in contemporary Russia. They have met in Stalin. The historian cannot be seriously surprised if he finds in him some traits usually associated with tyrants of earlier centuries. Even in the most irrational and convulsive phase of his industrial revolution, however, Stalin could make the claim that his system was free from at least one major and cruel folly which afflicted the advanced nations of the west: 'The capitalists [these were his words spoken during the Great Depression] consider it quite normal in a time of slump to destroy the "surplus" of commodities and burn "excess" agricultural produce in order to keep up high prices and ensure high profits, while here, in the U.S.S.R., those guilty of such crimes would be sent to a lunatic asylum.'

On Stalin and Stalinism

ROY A. MEDVEDEV

Roy A. Medvedev's exposé of Stalin's dictatorship, *Let History Judge*, the first major study of the Stalin era from within the Soviet Union, was first published in 1969. Medvedev was thereupon expelled from the Communist party. Twenty years later the Party's Control Commission determined that the action was "unfounded," restored his membership, and allowed publication of abbreviated versions of an even more critical revision of the study. In 1989, in the first free election held in the Soviet Union since 1918, Medvedev was sent to both the new Congress of Peoples' Deputies and the Supreme Soviet, the nation's parliament. *On Stalin and Stalinism,* excerpted here, is an assessment of Stalin's character and actions based on sources available only to a Soviet author. Medvedev contends that Stalinism marked a departure from the more benevolent Communism envisaged by Lenin, and hence makes a sharp distinction between the two. How does he contrast Lenin and Stalin? Both Medvedev and Deutscher take note of the "second revolution" as taking place in peacetime. How, nevertheless, do their interpretations of it differ? To what extent is Medvedev in agreement with Trotsky?

Stalin himself constantly maintained that he was first and foremost a loyal disciple of Lenin, merely continuing the work of his teacher, and that his activities in every respect represented the implementation of Leninist designs. The same was repeated by people in Stalin's immediate entourage, who additionally made the point that Stalin was the *best* disciple, the one *most steadfast* in his continuation

Reprinted from *On Stalin and Stalinism* by Roy A. Medvedev, translated by Ellen de Kadt by permission of Oxford University Press Ltd. Copyright © Oxford University Press, 1979.

of Lenin's work. However, many none too objective Sovietologists also find it quite tempting to identify Stalinism with Marxism and Leninism and to portray socialism only in its perverted Stalinist form. This is very much the view proclaimed far and wide by Solzhenitsyn, according to whom there never was any such thing as 'Stalinism,' since Stalin always followed in Lenin's footsteps and was only a 'blind, mechanical executor' of Lenin's will. An approach of this kind is convenient not only for those who would like to discredit every variety of socialism as a matter of principle, but also for those who favour the rehabilitation of Stalin and Stalinism. Nevertheless, it is wrong.

Sometimes the urge to identify Stalinism and socialism, Stalinism and communism, can take on truly perverted forms. Certain writers have expressed what amounts to satisfaction that Stalin existed and thereby helped to discredit Marxism and communism.

※ ※ ※

It should be stated at the outset that the infamous Stalinist system was not the creation of one man alone. Its development was affected by many circumstances and preconditions that were part of Russian life even before the Revolution and also by the experiences of the October Revolution, civil war, and the first six years of Soviet rule. Therefore without making any sweeping generalizations, clearly one cannot avoid identifying some elements of continuity in specific aspects of Leninism and Stalinism, continuity that requires sober, scholarly investigation rather than demagogic assertion. On the whole, Leninism and Bolshevism, both in theory and practice, represented a fundamental departure from the 'classical' social-democratic movements of the nineteenth century, and this allowed Lenin to speak of the creation of a 'party of a new type.' Many of the distinctive characteristics of Leninism resulted from the peculiarities of the Russian environment in which the socialist movement began and developed. Leninism was also influenced by the general international situation: the transition of capitalism to the imperialist stage, the development of monopoly capitalism, the First World War, etc. Quite a number of Lenin's statements and actions were wrong, or appropriate only for specific situations within limited periods of time. Subsequently Lenin admitted some of these errors; others were simply forgotten. But there were certain mistaken notions that he maintained until the end of his life. For example, what Lenin said about communist morality at the Third *Komsomol* Congress can hardly be accepted as a basis for socialist morality: '. . . morality is that which serves the destruction of the old exploiting society. . . . Communist morality is that which serves the struggle [of the proletariat], which unites the workers . . . against every kind of petty ownership . . .'

Furthermore, even in September 1917 Lenin assumed that mass terror and civil war could be averted in the event of a Soviet government coming to power, led by the Bolsheviks. This hope proved to be illusory. Yet the Red terror and the civil war that began in the summer of 1918 were only in part natural measures of self-defence against counter-revolutionary violence and the Intervention; the terror was also intimately connected with serious errors on the part of the first Soviet government in the implementation of important economic and political measures. Government actions provoked opposition and resistance among an overwhelming majority of the petty bourgeois masses of Russia, bringing Soviet power to the brink of catastrophe and compelling those in charge to resort to mass terror.

It is clear that the excesses of this terror were without any justification. Yet we must bear in mind that it is inevitably misleading to judge a revolutionary epoch or wartime situation by the laws and customs normally applicable to peacetime.

If soldiers panic and abandon the trenches under the impact of an enemy onslaught, their commanding officer, brandishing his pistol and shouting 'Go back!,' may shoot three or four soldiers as an example to the others. No one would regard this as a crime if it served to restrain the regiment and make it return to its former position or secure a new line of defence, since otherwise the entire regiment could be killed with nearby regiments and divisions affected as well. In fact, a military tribunal would have the right to try and put before a firing squad a regimental commander who lacked the necessary resolution at the critical moment. However, what was the crime of the unfortunate soldiers who were shot? Were they really more guilty than the others, or did they just happen to be closer to the commander than the real culprits who had been the first to panic? It is perfectly possible that those who were the first to leave the trenches might display exceptional courage in some counterattack only hours later; on the following day they would receive a decoration from the divisional commander or from the same commander of the regiment who had so recently shot down their fleeing comrades. But if the commander of a regiment were to open fire at three or four soldiers in peacetime or on manoeuvres, he would find himself up before a military tribunal.

Considerations of this kind are in many respects applicable to the harrowing years of civil war (1918–20) and to the actions of the Cheka, headed by Dzerzhinsky, and the Council of People's Commissars and the Central Executive Committee, headed by Lenin and Sverdlov. Unfortunately there were a number of situations where Red terror was the only way of avoiding the total destruction of the Soviet state and the triumph of the White terror that would certainly follow. Solzhenitsyn, Shafarevich, and Naum Korzhavin (from his current perspective) understand this well enough—it is simply that they find Kornilov or Denikin preferable to Lenin and Sverdlov, White terror preferable to Red.

But can there really be any comparison between decisions taken at the height of civil war and decisions arrived at in peacetime? Can the Red terror of 1918–20 really be equated with the terror inflicted on the country by Stalin in

1929–32 or in 1936–8? In the first case it was a question of saving the Soviet state from certain downfall; later it was the consolidation of Stalin's one-man dictatorship.

The one-party system was not established without the participation of Lenin, and the same may be said of limitations on freedom of speech and of the press which were introduced immediately after the Revolution and extended during the years of 'war communism.'

※ ※ ※

One could extend the list of Stalinist measures that in some sense were a continuation of anti-democratic trends in Lenin's time, although there is still the question of different historical circumstances and the fact that we have reason to suppose that Lenin would never have gone as far as Stalin in this direction.

It can easily be shown, for example, how skilfully Stalin managed to manipulate for his own purposes two distinctive characteristics of the Bolshevik Party: centralism and discipline. And yet centralism (which was by no means always 'democratic'), strict discipline, and effective organization were essential aspects of the Leninist party before the Revolution and in the period of Revolution and civil war. Centralism and Party discipline were the crucial weapons that provided victory not only in October but also in the extremely precarious conditions of 1918–19 and during the economic and political crisis of 1920–1. Although the harmful consequences of excessive centralism are quite apparent today, this does not mean that it would have been preferable to have avoided centralism from the very beginning. Lenin believed that centralism was indispensable for the success of the socialist revolution, but he never maintained that the organizational principles of the Party were appropriate for a socialist society. Forms of organization change according to circumstances, and no one understood this better than Lenin. In wartime, ordinary citizens are called up for military service and placed under military discipline. But the war comes to an end, and people returning to normal civil existence are once again subject to other laws and regulations. Stalin not only never modified the centralized system of Party organization, but he extended it to the highest degree of absolutism. This may have suited his personal ambitions and the interests of the apparatus, but it certainly did not correspond to the needs of socialist construction or encourage the creation of a truly just society. Stalin behaved like a Roman general who, instead of disbanding his legions when the war was over, as Roman custom demanded, returned to Italy, took his legions to Rome, and seized power in the Republic.

In most respects, however, there is no continuity between Leninism and Stalinism; they are essentially different political phenomena sharing a common 'Marxist' terminology. Stalin's policies were in no way a reflection of Leninist objectives: the abolition of NEP, the hasty implementation of forced collectivization, mass terror against well-to-do peasants in the countryside and 'bourgeois specialists' in the cities, industrialization largely by harsh administrative rather than economic measures, the prohibition of all opposition both within the Party and outside, the revival of the tactics of 'war communism' in utterly different circumstances—in all this Stalin acted in defiance of clear Leninist directives, particularly those that appeared in his last writings of 1921–2.

※ ※ ※

I hardly need mention in this context the mass terror against the basic cadres of Party and state in the second half of the thirties. Starting with the annihilation of the leaders and members of all opposition groupings, this terror caused the deaths of more than one million Party members who had borne the brunt of civil war, the transitional period, and the first Five-Year Plan. I hardly need mention Stalin's policy of subordinating the entire Party to the control of the secret police, its power and authority extended beyond measure. Nor is there any need to mention Stalin's revival of Great Russian chauvinism, the deportation of many peoples of the USSR from their native lands, or his anti-Semitic policies which led to the physical destruction of the most brilliant representatives of Jewish culture and his plans for the deportation of all Jews to remote regions of the USSR. It goes without saying that all these and many other criminal political actions have nothing in common either with Marxism or Leninism.

It is certainly not my intention here to portray Lenin as some kind of saint who never committed political mistakes, who never resorted to cruel expedients in the course of political struggle. Many letters and instructions from the civil war period show that Lenin sanctioned the use of terror on a scale that was entirely unjustified. In one of his telegrams of 1918 he ordered the authorities of Nizhny Novgorod to 'evacuate and shoot the hundreds of prostitutes who are getting the soldiers and commanders drunk.' Even when the civil war had come to an end, Lenin proposed that terror be made legitimate in the Criminal Code of the RSFSR; he also advocated a much broader definition of political crime and counter-revolution.

In the spring of 1918 Lenin wrote: 'So long as revolution in Germany is delayed, our task is to learn from German state capitalism to do everything in our power to imitate it without shying away from dictatorial methods in order to accelerate this process. We must even surpass Peter, who hastened the adoption of Westernism by barbaric Rus without stopping at barbarous means in the struggle against barbarism.' It is doubtful whether anyone in the communist movement today would accept the formula that barbarous means are permissible in the struggle against barbarism. And one can hardly imagine that this approach was suitable for the conditions of 1918. It is difficult to accept Lenin's statements on the relativity of all moral concepts.

⬛ ⬛ ⬛

Undoubtedly Lenin was a man fanatically dedicated to the idea of power, but it was the power of the proletariat, the power of the Communist Party, the power of the workers, and it was never a question of personal power. Lenin was always ready to subordinate his personal interests and ambitions to the interests of the Party, to the interests of the workers, to the interests of the Revolution. Stalin, on the other hand, was fanatically dedicated to the quest for personal power and was quite prepared to sacrifice any other interests in the process, including the interests of the Party, the proletariat, and the peasantry. Therefore the abuse of power under Stalin was not only on a different scale but was also fundamentally different in character from the abuse of power in Lenin's time. Here, too, there is no continuity.

In essence, Lenin and Stalin have almost nothing in common as human beings or as political personalities. Stalin was brutal, unscrupulous, a boundless cynic and contemptuous of others, no matter whether they were political opponents or members of the Party; consumed by the lust for power, he was a man of morbid vanity with an inferiority complex and a taste for spiteful vengeance. Stalin was not just a political criminal but also a criminal in the ordinary sense of the word; he recognized no rules in political struggle and, above all, in the struggle for personal power. Unfortunately it was just this lack of scruple that gave him an enormous advantage over his opponents and helped him to emerge victorious.

But Lenin was an entirely different person. It would be easy to quote from numerous testimonials by Lenin's comrades, friends, and all those who by right consider themselves to be Marxists and communists.

⬛ ⬛ ⬛

Leninism was not merely the application of Marxism to Russian conditions. Many aspects of Marxism were enriched and developed by Lenin, in accordance with prevailing conditions in the first quarter of the twentieth century. At the same time, however, Lenin's conception of Marxism was in certain respects a more narrow, one-sided doctrine than that of its founders. In addition, one must keep in mind the fact that classical Marxism was certainly not free of error. But all this bears little relation to Stalinism. I have received a letter from an Old Bolshevik containing the following passage:

> Conservative tendencies and forces have appeared in the socialist movement of the twentieth century that have acted as a brake on the further development of the socialist revolutionary process, in many cases exerting an anti-revolutionary influence. The most striking manifestation of these forces is Stalinism. Stalinism

is not just a bureaucratic perversion of Marxism-Leninism in general or the theory and practice of socialist construction in particular. It is a total system of social, political, and economic organization. It is pseudo-socialism.

And this is entirely my own view.

☒ ☒ ☒

Of course many features of authoritarian rule developed by Stalin first appeared under Lenin and in some cases he played a direct role in introducing them. The one-party system, restrictions on democracy at large and, later, the restrictions on democratic practices and discussion within the Party are all obvious examples. But these are by no means inherent features of Leninism. At first Lenin visualized Soviet power as a pluralist system, allowing all parties with links to the workers (including Right and Left SRs, Mensheviks, Trudoviki, and Anarchists) to compete freely within the Soviets. Even the ban on parties which stood outside the Soviet system was considered to be temporary. Lenin was convinced that the Bolsheviks would prevail over all other parties in an open competition and that this would certainly be the case after the main popular demands had been realized. Before and immediately after October he believed that the Bolsheviks would be able to govern with minimal use of force even in the first phase of the transitional period.

This is not the place to examine the reasons for the civil war or the Bolshevik mistakes that preceded it. Suffice it to say that, as can be seen from his last works, Lenin regarded as *temporary* phenomena much of what became part of our political life as a result of the civil war. For example, he never expected the ban on Party factions or freedom of speech to last. It was Stalin who extended and transformed what Lenin considered to be special measures into permanent and characteristic elements of the system. Stalin was responsible for the barbarous mass terror, the idolization of the 'leader,' the creation of an absolute personal dictatorship, the omnipotent police apparatus controlling even the Party—all those typical features of the regime that today are associated with the concept 'Stalinism.' To be sure, many achievements of the October Revolution were not totally destroyed by Stalinism; pseudosocialism has not managed to root out all elements of socialism from our social, economic, and political life.

Love on the Tractor

Women in the Stalin Period

BERNICE ROSENTHAL

After the Russian Revolution of 1917, feminists aspired to a wholly restructured society that would see the liberation of women. In her essay, "Women in the Russian Revolution and After," an American historian, Bernice Rosenthal, writes that despite greater representation of women in the professions, these hopes never really materialized. How does she explain the gradual return to traditional roles for women during the collectivization and industrialization of the 1930s, a period when Stalin, embarking on a course of Russian nationalism and chauvinism, made divorce more difficult and abortion (save for medical reasons) a crime? In the mid-1930s women were officially guaranteed equality within the new system. How did reality differ?

Stalin's accession to power brought the institution of a totally planned economy. Bolsheviks had long viewed massive industrialization as the means to equality. The first Five-Year Plan (1929–1934) aimed to build the infrastructure of a modern Communist society. Featuring heavy industry and collectivization of agriculture, it skimped on consumer goods. Subsequent plans followed the same pattern of deliberately holding down consumption in order to maximize resources for investment.

Until mechanization could occur, hands still had to be used, thus creating a demand for labor. In order to enlist women, the party drew up lists of occupations

Excerpted from selection by Bernice Rosenthal, from *Becoming Visible: Women in European History*, First Edition, by Renate Bridenthal and Claudia Koonz. Copyright © 1977 by Houghton Mifflin Company. Adapted with permission.

deemed especially suitable for them (assembly-line work in factories) and strength-ened protective legislation. Each year the percentage of women in the labor force increased: from 24 percent in 1928 to 26.7 percent in 1930, 31.7 percent in 1934, 35.4 percent in 1937. Though many women were peasants displaced by collec-tivization, they made good workers, registering fewer absences, latenesses, and in-dustrial accidents than men did and showing more amenability to factory discipline.

Stalin's first Five-Year Plan had the aura of a military campaign. The slogan "Catch up to and surpass America!" implied that through struggle and sacrifice, Russians could realize their dream of universal prosperity. Despite a sharp drop in the standard of living, they were enthusiastic and believed the privation to be only temporary. In this atmosphere protective legislation was often ignored. Women filled the most arduous jobs: pulling, hauling, digging ditches, main-taining roads. Illiterate and unskilled, they did not qualify for the most attrac-tive positions. Many were simply drafted and sent to work in the wilderness without proper tools, shelters, and food. In four years, young workers, most of them girls, built over 1,500 industrial plants. Popular literature glorified mus-cular heroines who could do anything a man could do: the idea of "woman's work" became obsolete.

In 1931 efforts were made to upgrade the skills of the entire labor force, including women. Wage differentials for skilled workers replaced identical wages for all workers. The factory training schools established female quotas; by 1934 women comprised 50 percent of their students. In 1935, on a technical profi-ciency test compulsory for all workers, women outperformed men in the younger age groups. Women were promoted to supervisory positions and, after 1934, became Stakhanovites (workers who markedly exceed their production norms and are held up as models). On the new collective farms, where model statutes decreed that women be paid in their own name, women became tractor drivers, section managers, brigade leaders, and even chairpersons.

An intensified drive to eradicate illiteracy increased opportunities for both sexes. By 1934 a network of primary schools covered the countryside, and the number of secondary schools increased rapidly. Female quotas in technical train-ing institutes and universities made higher education more accessible to women. Each university department reserved 25 percent of its places for women, partic-ularly benefiting women applicants in science, mathematics, engineering, and agricultural technology. Though accurate statistics on the number of women before the quotas are unavailable, it is clear that previously few women applied for these fields and even fewer had been admitted.

The party itself made sustained efforts to recruit women and to place them in prominent positions on local soviets, people's courts, and factory commit-tees. Though exact figures are unavailable, women did begin to work their way up. We know that the percentage of women in the party rose from 8.2 percent in 1925 to 15.9 percent in 1932 and that by 1933 girls comprised half the members of the *Komsomol* (Young Communist League).

The impact of all these changes varied. For younger women, work provided the means to independence, and increased opportunities for training created the possibility of upward mobility. Many chose not to marry. Jobs and child-care centers in which unmarried women had priority permitted any woman to have children. As a result, some men accused women of flaunting their independence. Older women, on the other hand, expressed bitterness and confusion. They disliked assembly-line work, but for them it was too late to learn new skills. Child-care facilities were included in the first Five-Year Plan, but did not expand rapidly enough to keep pace with demand. Even by 1936 only a small percentage of preschool children could be accommodated, and most married women still did not work. Moreover, the original plan to have twenty-four-hour child-care facilities could not be implemented, so working women could not attend night school or take correspondence courses. As shortages developed, plant managers tended to shift funds from child-care facilities to direct investment in production. By 1935 the hours had been reduced to cover the mother's working time only. Combining work and motherhood became increasingly difficult, and the birthrate plummeted.

Primitive housing conditions may also account for women's increasing reluctance to bear children. The plan did not provide sufficient new housing for the millions of workers flooding into the cities. Often entire families crowded into one room. Few houses had running water or electricity. Hot water and central heating were almost unknown. Carrying water in buckets, chopping wood, hauling fuel for the stove, consumed the woman's time and energy. Factory cafeterias served lunch only. As late as 1935 only 180 laundries existed in all of Russia. Doing the weekly washing involved a full day's work, so working women did it on their day off or at night. Laborsaving devices, like most consumer goods, were not manufactured, and most men refused to help at home with "woman's work." In the newer industrial areas, worse conditions prevailed. At Magnitogorsk, a steel city in the Ural Mountains, tents and dugouts provided the only shelter against the bitter winter winds. Visitors reported waitresses at the workers' cafeteria picking lice out of each other's hair, an example of the abysmal sanitary conditions. At the Dnepestroi Dam site, single women slept on plank beds, in crowded barracks, surrounded by wailing infants.

The family continued to disintegrate. No correspondence existed between formally registering a marriage and its stability, and marriage entailed little status or material advantage for either sex. Being a housewife was condemned, and inflationary pressures created a need for the wife's salary. The economic advantages of shared living expenses, plus sex, were attainable without formal marriage. And marriage did not necessarily denote companionship; industrial plants operated around the clock with no common day off, so a couple working different shifts rarely saw each other. At home, overcrowding frayed the nerves. By 1934, unsupervised children constituted a serious juvenile delinquency problem.

The sexual counterrevolution of the mid-1930s promoted a return to a conventional family structure, a pronatalist policy, and the promotion of a puritanical sexual morality. It resulted from several factors: the hardship suffered by abandoned wives and their children, official dismay at sexual permissiveness, and the precipitous decline in the birthrate after 1934. Sexual individualism and personal hedonism conflicted with the collectivist attitudes desired by the regime.

The 1930 official rehabilitation of the family as a socialist institution turned out to be a harbinger of the new policy. Party theoreticians now emphasized the necessity of a stable family structure but continued to oppose bourgeois patriarchal authority based on women's economic dependence. In 1934, Stalin with great publicity visited his aged mother in the Caucasus and that same year a new law held parents legally liable for the vandalism of their children and gave the entire family collective responsibility for the treason, defection, or state crime of any of its members. Homosexuality became a criminal offense punishable by hard labor. Circular letters had restricted abortion since 1931. At the clinic in Kuznetsk, in eastern Siberia, abortion could be performed only to save the mother's life. The 1936 decrees restricting divorce and abolishing legal abortion culminated the return to traditional morality. "The foul and poisonous idea of the liquidation of the family," Stalin announced in 1936, "is a false rumor . . . spread by enemies of the people." High fees introduced for divorce rose steeply for a second and third instance, and records of divorce were included in the labor books of both parties. The decree abolishing legal abortion stated that since the conditions necessitating the original decree of 1920 had been overcome, "mass abortions for egoistic reasons cannot be tolerated." *Izvestia* and *Pravda* editors scolded women who wrote letters of protest. They denied that childbirth was a personal matter and implied that women who failed to bear many children lacked faith in the socialist future. In a sense, this policy was a logical conclusion of earlier attitudes. Even Kollontai[1] regarded childbearing as a social duty. She believed that a pregnant woman "does not belong to herself . . . she is working for the collective . . . from her own flesh and blood she is producing a new unit of labor." To meet some of the specific protests, Stalin promised increased maternity leave, more and better child-care centers, and improved housing, but not contraceptives. Since Russian women had been using abortion *instead* of birth control, the new law resulted in a steep

---

[1]Alexandra M. Kollontai was born in 1872, the daughter of a tsarist general. She became an early revolutionary and joined the Bolsheviks in 1915. Her moral and cultural radicalism—she advocated "free love"—repelled Lenin. She was also a leader of the so-called Workers' Opposition, which in 1921 urged that all decisions about economic matters be made by the trade unions, an indication of labor's dissatisfaction with the economic dictatorship of the Communist Party bureaucracy—Eds.

rise in the birthrate: 18 percent for Russia as a whole, 100 percent in Moscow. However, in 1938, military preparedness led to the reduction of maternity leave to the pre-1936 level. Women still worked but the new emphasis on motherhood hampered their upward mobility. Anticipating women to be frequently pregnant, managers hesitated to train them. Unallayed domestic responsibilities deflected women's time and energy away from activities leading to promotion. Also, in 1936, Stalin terminated the 50 percent female quotas in the factory training schools and technical institutes. Since women were now equal, he said, special measures were no longer necessary. By 1938 the number of women in technical institutes had dropped to a startling 27 percent; after 1938 these figures ceased to be published. The doors opened to women during the first Five-Year Plan were shut, except to a minority. Only universities made no serious attempt to limit women and their number continued to rise. In 1941 women composed 57 percent of the student body (already reflecting mobilization for the war); they studied teaching, medicine, law, mathematics, agronomy, economics, engineering, and all the sciences. But the majority of women still worked in the lowest-skilled, most easily replaceable job categories, including arduous physical labor.

Literature reflected the new emphasis. Earlier heroines had been almost sexless, the plot being girl meets tractor. Married couples when depicted in bed discussed the Five-Year Plan, their children, if any existed, nowhere in evidence. But the post-1936 female, a kind of superwoman, not only made a "serene home" for her husband but had many children and still equaled her husband's performance on the job. Novels and speeches lauded the joys of motherhood and pitied the childless, while posters of happy, large families appeared all over the Soviet Union. The popular child-care manual, Anton Makarenko's *A Book for Parents,* lauded the large family as the place where collective attitudes are first learned and castigated men who abandoned their wives and children. His pedagogy, stressing discipline and subordination to the group, replaced the more individualistic pedagogy of Lunacharsky, who had been dismissed as commissar of enlightenment in 1931. Makarenko's philosophy emphasized the responsibility of all age groups to society.

Article 122 of the Soviet Constitution of 1936 reads:

Women in the USSR have equal rights with men in all branches of economic, cultural, social, and political life.

The implementation of these rights of women is assured by granting women the same rights as men to work, to pay, to social insurance and education and by government protection of mothers and children, by paid maternity leave, and by a wide network of maternity homes, children's *crèches,* nursery schools and kindergartens.

Like the entire constitution, this article bore little relation to Soviet reality; at best it can be considered a statement of a still remote ideal. In 1936 the "great terror" began. Women, too unimportant to be purged, numbered only 10 percent of the victims. But this 10 percent included women working their way up the hierarchy and almost all the older generation of women activists, thus removing all but a few women from the higher levels of Soviet society. Moreover, women whose husbands were arrested suffered heavy secondary pressures, such as being fired from their jobs or evicted from their lodgings unless they got divorced.

Mobilization, with its new demands for workers, brought about a renewed effort to recruit women into the work force. Once again they were urged to improve their skills, and after 1941 figures on the number of women in key segments of the economy again became available. For example, in one year, 1941–1942, the percentage of women steam engine operators rose from 6 percent to 33 percent and similar dramatic increases occurred among tractor drivers, locomotive engineers, steam compressor operators, electricians, and welders—all highly paid occupations. By 1945 women composed 56 percent of the labor force, a majority of the miners and a third of the workers in the Baku oil fields. Crucial to the home front, women worked fourteen to eighteen hours a day, often under severe conditions, as in factories hastily evacuated to Siberia with roofs but no walls. Asked if she were tired, a young girl replied: "Tired? Our men are giving their lives for us. How dare I be tired?" Meanwhile, Grandma kept house and minded the children. Women also engaged in actual combat for the Red Army, most often in guerrilla units but also as machine gunners and snipers; no unit lacked women altogether. Women joined the medical and signal corps and several air regiments consisted entirely of women. The unit that captured Hitler's chancellery had a woman major.

After the war, the loss of 20,000,000 men, out of a total population of 170,000,000, severely disrupted the Soviet demographic balance. A woman recalls, "I know of no one—no one—who did not lose a husband, a son, or a lover." Desire to replenish population added to the party's fear of a postwar relaxation of morality and discipline caused a revision of the Family Code in 1944 along still more conservative and pronatalist lines. To prevent wholesale abandonment by returning soldiers in search of younger women, divorce became extremely difficult. As an incentive for the man to stay in the family, other changes made him de facto head of household and favored him in inheritance, which had been gradually reintroduced since the twenties. A reversal of previous policy deprived illegitimate children of inheritance rights and stigmatized them by a line drawn through the space for "father's name" on their identity cards. Women lost their right to file paternity suits. All this was aimed at creating the stable social climate deemed conducive to large families. For women who did not have husbands, however, to stimulate them to bear children and to prevent recourse to illegal abortion, the state assumed direct responsibility for illegitimate children's support at a fixed rate. Two years later, however, the rate was halved, thus shifting the major burden to the mothers. Special honors were provided, including cash subsidies, for large families. Ten children made a woman a Mother Heroine and seven entitled her to an Order of Maternal Glory. The same law introduced family allowances for three or more children and halved their fees for *crèches* (for children under three), nursery schools, and kindergartens, all financed by a new tax levied on single persons and couples with fewer than three children.

After the war, reconstruction absorbed all resources. The industrial heartland of European Russia lay in ruins and huge tracts of formerly fertile farmland had become scorched earth. Much of the existing housing had been destroyed by the war, and both communal facilities and consumer goods remained unavailable. A significant number of women became doctors, engineers, and scientists; indeed, the shortage of men worked to their advantage professionally. Others continued to be skilled workers; the labor shortage prevented their wholesale displacement by returning war veterans. But these women constituted a small proportion of the total female labor force; the overwhelming majority of women remained concentrated in the lower echelons of the economic ladder. They built the roads, dug the ditches, shoveled the snow, labored on the construction sites, and worked in the fields. As late as the 1950s, women made up four-fifths of the unskilled laborers. And the male deficit militated against equality in personal life as women catered to men.

The experience of Soviet women during the Stalin era brings the question of priorities into sharp focus. True, the planners could not create the material conditions for equality overnight. But they had a choice—between forced-draft industrialization (including collectivization) and a slower but more balanced scheme of economic development that included consumer goods. Despite the fact that stinting on consumer goods and communal amenities weighed particularly heavily on women, they chose forced-draft industrialization for military, ideological, and political reasons. Well before the success of Hitler, Stalin aimed to increase the military might of the Soviet Union. Ideologically, gradual economic development (Bukharin's plan) meant continuing the mixed economy that benefited peasants far more than workers. And the political factor, the tremendous power accruing to those who control the economy, must not be discounted as a reason for Stalin's choice. Not only did women's well-being have low priority in the original plan, but as necessity dictated cuts in the budget, women's needs (length of maternity leave, hours of child-care-center operation) were cut first. And there is no evidence that the sexual counterrevolution, which negated so many of the women's gains, was unpopular in the higher echelons of the party; the planners themselves, apparently, were ambivalent about the equality they preached.

5

THE NAZIS

When on January 30, 1933, President Hindenburg named Adolf Hitler head of the German government, the Nazi rank and file rejoiced in their triumph and began an orgy of celebration. Göring proclaimed the rebirth of the Reich, the obliteration of fourteen years of shame, and the founding of a new German state in freedom and honor. That night in Berlin a gigantic torchlight parade of a quarter of a million marched past the führer, while Hindenburg, woodenly expressionless in another window of the chancellery, stood watching the phenomenon to which he had now given his official consecration. The people of Germany watched too, some in fear, some in hope, and all in amazement. Given the horror of the bloodbath into which the regime plunged Europe and the world during its twelve-year existence, historians, political scientists, political sociologists, and others have searched for answers to such questions as how the Nazis came to power, who supported them, and why the German people tolerated their tactics.

What were the reasons for the triumph of Nazism in particular and of fascism in general? Was it the consequence of economic dislocations arising from the depression? If so, why was it not successful in Western Europe as well? Was it rather part of a larger totalitarian movement, an age of dictatorship, which seemed to promise answers to the crises of post–World War I Europe and the depression-ridden 1930s? Can it best be explained in terms of the German historical past? How did Nazi rule affect the lives of women in comparison to those of men? Whatever the reasons for the Nazi triumph in Germany and its consequences in that country, it had ominous implications for the rest of Europe. The selections that follow not only present different views of the Nazis, but may also offer insights into the relationship between the writers and their frameworks of reference.

Women voters by and large continued to support the conservative and religious parties, although many of Hitler's most fanatical followers were women (paradoxically enough in view of what Claudia Koonz was to call the party's "overt misogyny"—its preference for limiting women to traditional roles with *Kinder*, "children," and in *Küche*, "kitchen," if not *Kirche*, "church").[1] In her more general study of women under Nazi rule, Jill Stephenson points out that the call for childbearing nevertheless weakened the stigma attached to unwed motherhood and insists that the retreat from Weimar's commitment to gender equality began before the Nazi accession to power. Indeed, she argues that the attitude toward women in Germany in the 1930s was influenced more by traditional and economic factors than by Nazi ideology, though this might well have been reversed had the Third Reich endured.

Perhaps the chief question raised by any consideration of the Nazi past is whether its acceptance represented a moral surrender of the German people to authoritarianism or whether it reflected the inability of German democracy to meet the economic and political crises that beset the nation in the early 1930s. Purely historical evidence can neither support nor reject the first answer to this question; the excerpts that follow will prove useful in explicating the second.

---

[1]Claudia Koonz, *Mothers in the Fatherland: Women, the Family, and Nazi Politics* (New York: St. Martin, 1987).

The Menace of Fascism

The Marxist View

JOHN STRACHEY

Perhaps the first sustained analysis of fascism in general and Nazism in particular was that of the Marxists, who saw the movement as the result of conscious and calculated planning by the forces of big business. In an early book, British author John Strachey argued that to assure themselves continued control of their property capitalists created a mass organization to do their fighting for them, and their propaganda persuaded the lower middle-class and peasant components "to suppose genuinely that they were part of a progressive movement." But do the financial contributions of some industrialists—and even large estate owners—to the Nazi movement demonstrate that capitalists created and controlled it? Were Strachey's critics nearer the mark when they maintained that nothing supported the theory that Nazism was a capitalist plot except the assertion that there was one?

We must define Fascism as the movement for the preservation by violence, and at all costs, of the private ownership of the means of production. This and nothing else is the real purpose of Fascism. When we understand this, everything else in the apparent madness of Fascism becomes comprehensible. Fascism will try to destroy in war our marvelous powers of production, and to crush democracy, pacifism, and internationalism, because these things are becoming incompatible with Capitalism. Fascism is the enemy of science, of rationalism, of educational progress for the same reason. Fascism kills, tortures and terrorises

From John Strachey, *The Menace of Fascism* (London: Victor Gollancz Ltd., 1933). Reprinted with permission of Charles Strachey, Literary Executor for John Strachey.

in defence of the right of the capitalists to keep the fields, factories and mines of the world as their private property.

Now that we have discovered the purpose of Fascism we must put the question, can Fascism succeed? Can the Fascists successfully defend the private ownership of the means of production? Can they succeed in destroying liberty, democracy, pacifism, the Trade Unions' modern technical progress, everything that threatens it, either directly or indirectly? And, even if they can do this, can they then succeed in setting up a stable and permanent world system of Fascist States?

Now, there is not the slightest doubt that it is possible for a Fascist movement to succeed, in the sense of obtaining all power for itself in a particular State. We do not even need the examples of Germany and Italy to prove that. For in fact a Fascist movement does not really have to conquer power at all. Its struggle with the older forms of the Capitalist State is very much in the nature of a stage battle. For Fascism is merely the militant arm of the largest property owners, who are of course already in power. Its aim is not to seize power, but merely to retain power. This fact is obscured, however, by the composition of the Fascist parties.

The core of these parties always consists of two classes of people, the lower middle class and the peasants. (For no one has hitherto observed a big banker or landowner fighting his own class battles for himself. These gentlemen fight, both at home and abroad, by proxy alone.) Now the shopkeepers and peasants have, of course, by no means the same interests as the great Capitalists. The rank and file of Fascist parties do not realize that they are being used as hired mercenaries for the defence of the ownership of the factories, fields and mines by the great Capitalists. For the Fascists, we must readily admit, are very expert at duping their supporters. Also, they are very frank about it. For example, Hitler, in his autobiography, criticizes the tameness of the propaganda methods of his rivals. "The German," he writes, "has not the slightest notion how a people must be misled if the adherence of the masses is sought." ([This was published in] the first eleven editions of *My Struggle*. The passage was deleted from the twelfth edition.)

Many rank and file Fascists genuinely suppose that their movement is out to accomplish all sorts of progressive things. They are effectively taken in by the façade of the Corporate State; they respond to a more or less idealistic nationalism. They often express the view that Fascism is the "practical" way of accomplishing what Socialism has promised. They genuinely do not see the impossibility of any form of planning while the private ownership of the means of production persists. They sincerely believe, in spite of the fact that each successive Fascist Government when it gets into power does nothing of the sort, that their movement will "nationalize the big banks and trusts," and will discipline the capitalists as well as the workers.

It is of course to cater for the illusions of the lower middle class and the peasant rank and file of the Fascist parties that the elaborate code of economic demagogy was invented. Some observers of Fascism (notably Professor Scott Nearing) have even deduced from the vaguely anti-Capitalist tone which pervades Fascist parties during their early stages, that Fascism is essentially a movement of the lower middle class, the class which stands between the workers and the capitalists, and is primarily directed against both. Such a view, surely, attaches too much importance to Fascist words and too little to Fascist deeds. Professor Scott Nearing agrees, of course, that it is universally observable that when the Fascists come into power they do not support the interests of the lower middle class, but the interests of the biggest bankers and capitalists. ("The Fascist Government frankly champions the cause of big business."—*Fascism,* by Professor Scott Nearing, The Vanguard Press, New York.) He explains this by saying that Fascism, although started as a movement of the middle class, ruined by the Imperialist consolidation of Capitalism, becomes a coalition of all the propertied and privileged classes against the working class.

Is not the truth rather that Fascism is from the very beginning a movement owned and controlled by the very richest and biggest capitalists, who use the lower middle class and the peasants as their indispensable instruments for the destruction of the working class?

Professor Scott Nearing is surely deceived when he speaks of Fascism being a revolutionary force:

> At the centre of the fascist movement is the middle class, seeking to save itself from decimation or annihilation by seizing power and establishing its own political and social institutions. It therefore has the essential characteristics of a social revolutionary movement, since its success means a shift of the centre of power from one social class to another.

This is, we submit, an entire misconception. Fascism is not a movement of the lower middle class seeking to seize power from the capitalist class: its success does not mean the shift of power from one social class to another. On the contrary, it is a movement of the capitalist class using the lower middle class and peasants as its instrument, and its success means merely a consolidation of power in the hands of that same capitalist class which already possesses it. Naturally this fact immensely simplifies the Fascist's task. Indeed, Professor Scott Nearing recognises this in practice, for on p. 17 of his pamphlet he writes:

> The fascist seizure of power was greatly facilitated by the fact that, with minor exceptions, such as Soviet Bavaria and Bolshevik Hungary, much of the

economic and political machinery was already in the hands of fascist supporters, who owned property, held important jobs, dominated, and in many respects controlled, the technical and professional fields. If, as is almost always
the case, these key positions include important posts in the army and navy,
the war and naval ministries, the post, telegraph and other agencies which are
likely to be determining factors in a revolutionary situation, the fascists merely
proclaim the possession of that which they already occupy.

In what sense, then, do the Fascists seize power? Only in the sense that they
seize it from under their own pillows. For power, real power, was always, even in
the States which had maintained democratic forms, in the hands of the capitalists. And the Fascists are only the capitalists and their dupes in fancy dress.

The actual history of the way in which the Fascists have come to power in
Germany and Italy confirms this view. In Germany it must be obvious to all
that Hitler did not seize power. On the contrary, the Nazi movement was during the autumn of 1932 in evident and admitted decline. And then President
von Hindenburg and his advisers suddenly handed over the power of the State
to Hitler—without even the pretence of a struggle. And it was precisely, as we
shall see, *because* German Fascism was in decline; it was *because* there was an evident danger of the blunting of this last remaining weapon of German capitalism that the nervousness of the German ruling classes about handing over the
helm of State to Hitler evaporated in a single day. In Italy, there was more pretence of conflict. But, as a matter of fact, the march on Rome was an exceedingly mild affair. The State forces were never once used against the Fascists, and
Mussolini was given power by the Italian ruling classes for fundamentally the
same reason as was Hitler: viz. that he and his movement represented the best
available means of continuing Italian capitalism.

Fascism, then, is in no sense of the word revolutionary; it is essentially a
movement of counter-revolutionary violence. Fascist violence has never been
turned against the capitalists or their State machine. The dog has never yet bit-
ten its master. (This does not exclude, however, the possibility of sections of a
Fascist movement, which may be imbued with anti-Capitalist ideas, from breaking away and becoming genuinely, although confusedly, revolutionary: this may
well happen in Germany.) Fascist violence is organized for one purpose alone,
and it has never been used for any other. The purpose of Fascism, both before it
has the State power given to it and afterwards, is to smash those institutions
which threaten private ownership—to smash the democratic machinery by
which the workers may obtain a measure of political power; to abolish freedom
of speech, since the worker must not "listen to agitators"; and to withdraw the
right of association, in order to destroy the Trade Unions and Co-operatives,
which are the fundamental forms of working-class organization.

※ ※ ※

The economic crisis, although still mild compared to that which exists in Central Europe, is beginning to be seen, by both the workers and the capitalists, to be incurable by present methods. The Labour party has clearly forfeited the enthusiasm, although not the stubborn support, of the mass of the British workers. The Independent Labour party, an historical and organic part of the British Labour movement, has for the first time in its history split off from the Labour party and clearly contains many workers who are groping their way towards a revolutionary policy. The most advanced workers are turning, under the leadership of the Communist party, towards conscious, revolutionary action. In general, the British workers have begun to doubt the usefulness of that whole policy of progressive gradualism which they have followed for three generations. But they are only beginning to feel their way towards the revolutionary alternative.

Thus the British capitalists' ownership of the factories, fields and mines is threatened, not yet so much by a conscious and clearsighted revolutionary movement of the British workers, as by the spontaneously growing disorder of the British economic and social system. There is a pronounced "lag" between the development of the economic situation and our consciousness of that development. The British workers are still to a large extent dominated by the illusion of the possibility of progress under Capitalism. Yet that possibility has long disappeared, and definite decline has set in.

This is the classic breeding-ground of Fascism. The rise of a Fascist movement, of a movement, that is, for the preservation by violence of the private ownership of the means of production, is an historical certainty in the Britain of today. There is not the slightest doubt that the British capitalists, just so soon as they are thoroughly alarmed, will organize all their forces—their physical forces—in order to attack by violence and terror everything which threatens their position. To suppose anything else is to fall a victim to the most pitiful illusions.

※ ※ ※

Hitler was given power by Hindenburg. Such was the perfect symbol of the duping of the Social Democrats. Hindenburg, who had been put into his supreme office by the massed votes of the German workers, following blindly their blind leaders; Hindenburg, who had been made President by the Social Democrats simply and solely in order to keep out Hitler, nine months later quietly sent for Hitler and made him Dictator of Germany.

The Fascists were given power *precisely because* they were beginning to show signs of disintegration. It was necessary to give Hitler power in the State just because he was losing power with the masses. The Fascists were given power because they were the last possible basis of mass support for German Capitalism; and this basis the German capitalists could not at any price allow to disintegrate.

How different was the conduct of the German capitalists in January 1933 to what the conduct of the Social Democrats had been in 1918, 1923 and 1932. When events forced the Social Democrats to choose between preserving the forms of the Constitution and beginning a struggle to obtain power for their class, they repeatedly chose to abide by the forms of the Constitution. They three times sacrificed the German working class upon the altar of the Constitution.

But what did the capitalists do when in 1933 it became clear that the maintenance of this same Republican Constitution had become incompatible with the maintenance of the economic power of *their* class? Without a second's hesitation they tore the Constitution to shreds. Hindenburg, who had been talking about nothing but his sacred oath to the Constitution for six years past, gave supreme power to Hitler, the man whose whole purpose in life was to destroy that Constitution, and who did at once destroy it. What did a hundred Constitutions, and a thousand sacred oaths to keep it, matter when it was a case of preserving the capitalists' ownership of factories, fields and mines? Oaths and Constitutions were but scraps of paper. Nor will any Capitalist class ever behave in any other way when once its property is threatened.

The Course of German History

A. J. P. TAYLOR

Alan John Percivale Taylor taught for many years at Manchester and Oxford Universities and published extensively in the areas of European diplomatic, German, and Hapsburg history. He also achieved notoriety as a lecturer for the British Broadcasting Corporation (BBC). The following excerpt, from *The Course of German History,* provides a different perspective from that of Strachey. To what extent is Taylor's approach shaped by the period (World War II) in which he wrote? Do you agree that the Nazis were the product of German historical development?

Certain permanent factors have, indeed, influenced German history, since the time when Charlemagne, by establishing the Holy Roman Empire, advanced German history from the stage of tribal legends. First was their geographic position. The Germans are the peoples of the north European plain, the people without a defined natural frontier. Without the sharp limit of mountain ranges, except at the Alps and the Bohemian mountains, the great plain is intersected by four great rivers (Rhine, Elbe, Oder, Vistula) dividing lines sharp enough to split the German people up among themselves, not rigid enough to confine them within settled frontiers. There is no determined geographic point for German expansion, equally none for German contraction; and, in the course of a thousand years, geographic Germany has gone out and in like a concertina. At times Germany has been confined within the Rhine and the Elbe; at others it has blown itself out to the Pyrenees and to the Caucasus. Every German frontier is artificial, therefore impermanent; that is the permanence of German geography.

Reprinted with permission of The Putnam Publishing Group from *The Course of German History* by A. J. P. Taylor. Copyright 1946 by A. J. P. Taylor.

Enduring too for a thousand years has been their ethnographical position. Here too the Germans have been the people of the middle; always they have had two neighbours and have shown two faces. To their west were the Roman Empire and its heir, French civilization; to their east, the Slavs, new barbarians pressing on the Germans as the Germans pressed on Rome. To the west therefore the Germans have always appeared as barbarians, but the most civilized of barbarians, eager to learn, anxious to imitate; and the record of German civilization is a story of sedulous and exaggerated imitation of the established order in the west—an imitation which began with Charlemagne's aping of Caesar and has ended in Hitler's aping of Napoleon. To the Slavs of the east, however, the Germans have made a very different appearance: ostensibly the defenders of civilization, they have defended it as barbarians, employing the technical means of civilization, but not its spirit. For a thousand years, again from Charlemagne to Hitler, the Germans have been "converting" the Slavs from paganism, from Orthodox Christianity, from Bolshevism, or merely from being Slavs; their weapons have varied, their method has always been the same—extermination. Most of the peoples of Europe have, at one time or another, been exterminators. The French exterminated the Albigensians in the thirteenth century and the Huguenots in the seventeenth; the Spaniards exterminated the Moors; the English exterminated the North-American Indians and attempted in the seventeenth century to exterminate the Irish. But no other people has pursued extermination as a permanent policy from generation to generation for a thousand years; and it is foolish to suppose that they have done so without adding something permanent to their national tradition. No one can understand the Germans who does not appreciate their anxiety to learn from, and to imitate, the West; but equally no one can understand Germans who does not appreciate their determination to exterminate the East.

❈ ❈ ❈

The Empire which Charlemagne founded set the tone for German history from the beginning. It was not intended as a German national state; it claimed to be a universal Empire, a revival of the Empire of the Caesars. The revival did not come from the inhabitants of Rome, of Paris, or of Naples; it came from barbarians, whose only connection with the real empire was that their ancestors had helped to destroy it. The history of the Germans as a civilized people thus began with the deliberate, planned imitation of an institution which had never been theirs. The Empire claimed to be universal. Here too the Germans struck the same note from the beginning. Unlike other peoples, they did not start from their own national state and gradually advance claims to domination: they demanded everything from the beginning. Most typical of all, this Empire—ostensibly the bulwark of Christian civilization and often accepted as such by the peoples of the West both then and since—inaugurated at once the policy of exterminating the Slav peoples of the East. Universalism, aping of foreign traditions, ruthlessness towards the Slav peoples, these three things were to form the pattern of the Reich for more than a thousand years, and to compose the "national character" of the German people. There was nothing innate or mysterious in this. The German character was determined by their geographical position: they were the barbarians on the edge of a great civilization. Hence their anxiety both to master this civilization and to imitate it; hence their barbaric ruthlessness towards the peoples who were pressing on them from behind. They were the people of the middle: dualism was dictated to them.

※ ※ ※

In nothing was Luther more typical than in his attitude to the princes. Here, more than in any other aspect, did he represent the despair in themselves which had overcome the German middle classes. When, in 1521, Luther went to the Diet at Worms to defend his doctrines, he went under the protection of and as the spokesman of a united and enthusiastic people; never has there been a more tumultuous journey through Germany. The enthusiasm vanished overnight, and Luther crept under the wing of the princes of northern Germany, who became Protestant not as the most advanced, but as the most backward, section of German society—for them Lutheranism was merely a weapon against the political interference either of the Emperor or of the trading classes. Lutheranism, at first a movement of Reform, became, and remained, the most conservative of religions; though it preached the absolute supremacy of the individual conscience within, it preached an equally absolute supremacy for the territorial power without. Luther gave to Germany a consciousness of national existence and, through his translation of the Bible, a national tongue; but he also gave to Germany the Divine Right of Kings, or rather the Divine Right of any established authority. Obedience was the first, and last, duty of the Christian man. The State can do no wrong; therefore, whatever the State orders, that the Christian man can do without danger to his conscience, and, indeed, the more devout the individual, the more eager he will be to carry out the most violent and unscrupulous orders of the prince, God's mouthpiece. In the general decline which was overcoming Germany, the princes represented the one point of stability and order, and the German middle classes, speaking through Luther, surrendered to the princes without reserve. The movement against Rome which Luther personified had sprung from a national resentment against the Papacy, which, by its co-operation with the great feudatories against the Emperor, had prevented national unity. Lutheranism certainly destroyed Papal influence in north Germany, but, lacking confidence in itself, fell into the arms of the princes and thus actually strengthened, indeed made triumphant, the particularism which it had begun by attacking. So the first great expression of the German national spirit repudiated the universalism of the middle ages, only to fall into a particularism which made German unification impossible for centuries.

※ ※ ※

Such was the strange work of Luther. He made Germany a nation, but a nation divided against itself. He gave the Germans a spiritual individualism and destroyed for centuries their political independence. He broke with the mediaeval dream of universalism, only to lead Germany into the nightmare of particularism. He taught the Germans to believe in liberty, but he taught them also that liberty is to be found only in the service of the prince. He created the German language, and he used his creation for attacking reason, for expressing hysteria. Like the Germans of a thousand years before and of four hundred years later, Luther was the barbarian who looks over the Rhine, at once the most profound expression and the most decisive creator of German dualism.

※ ※ ※

The making of Prussia was the work of the Hohenzollern rulers, almost of one Hohenzollern ruler. Still it could not have been accomplished without the existence of a unique landed class, the Junkers of eastern Germany. No factor is more important in the history of modern Germany, and no factor is less understood. The Junkers were landowners, lords of great estates. But they had nothing else in common with the French nobles or the Whig aristocrats, the landowners of western Europe. The French and English nobles were a leisured class, the French depending on feudal dues, the English on rents from their tenants. Both spent most of their time away from their estates, the French at court, the English in London. The one produced the French civilization of the eighteenth century, the other the British constitution, the greatest political work of man. The Junkers, however, were not a leisured class, drawing tribute from others. They were, for the most part, without tenants and worked their estates themselves, for they were the owners of colonial lands. The landowners of western Europe were part of a settled community, in which even serfs and copyholders had some legal existence, but the Junkers had no obligations to the conquered Slav peoples whose land they owned; these peoples had been utterly expropriated and had been degraded not even into tied serfs, but into landless labourers. The Junker estates were never feudal; they were capitalist undertakings, which closely resembled the great capitalist farms of the American prairie—also the result of a colonial expropriation of the American Indians. The Junkers were hardworking estate managers, thinking of their estates solely in terms of profits and efficiency, neither more nor less than agrarian capitalists.

This economic characteristic had a unique political result. Everywhere in Europe the Crown was striving to make the organization of the State more efficient; therefore, despite the king's personal preference for the manners and culture of the nobility, he had to turn for political backing to the capitalist middle classes, who alone possessed the virtues of efficiency and hard work. But these were the very virtues possessed by the Junkers and not possessed to the same degree by the German burghers of the eighteenth century. The German trading classes had abandoned all attempts to keep up with the capitalist triumphs of England, Holland, or even France. Instead they prided themselves on their civil liberties and on the high level of their culture as citizens of the world. These were not assets likely to appeal to Frederick II. But the Hohenzollerns had long ago stamped out the last flickers of aristocratic liberties; and the Junkers had neither the leisure nor the ability to develop a taste for culture—to go to Berlin was merely to leave the threshing floor for the barrack-room. Thus in Prussia alone in Europe, a reforming Crown could carry out its reforms through the agency of great landowners; and the greater the efficiency of the Prussian State, the more it needed the services of the Prussian Junkers. It was no paradox, but an inevitable development, that Frederick, the most efficient of the Hohenzollerns, first made absolute the Junker monopoly of civilian and military office. The State created by Frederick II combined two qualities which were elsewhere opposites. It had, on the one hand, the unscrupulous authoritarianism, the disregard both of humanity and of principle, everywhere characteristic of rule by a privileged upper class; on the other hand, a striving after efficiency and improvement, a rigid devotion to the balancing of accounts, elsewhere associated with the rule of a reforming middle class. The Prussian Junkers, one might say, were politically in the Stone Age; economically and administratively they looked forward to the age of steel and electricity. They were barbarians who had learnt to handle a rifle and, still more, bookkeeping by double entry. Ruthless exploiters of conquered land, they were untouched by European civilization and yet could master every technical improvement which Europe produced. Of course their achievement was not perfect or unbroken. Just as an individual Junker might neglect his estate for culture, or from laziness, and so paid the penalty in bankruptcy, so the Junker governing class sometimes failed to keep up with the times in organization, in military equipment, or even in political pretence. The great disasters of 1807, of 1848, and of 1918, warned them that the anachronism of their survival could be preserved only by ceaseless efficiency; and in each case the lesson was learnt. If the Junkers had owned fat acres instead of sand, if Prussia had ever enjoyed a long period of secure repose in Europe, the habits of leisure and inefficiency would have been too strong to overcome, and eventually at some crisis both Prussian Junkers and Prussian state would have collapsed. But both lived always on the edge of danger and bankruptcy; this bound them together and preserved them.

❊ ❊ ❊

Eighteen forty-eight was the decisive year of German, and so of European, history: it recapitulated Germany's past and anticipated Germany's future. Echoes of the Holy Roman Empire merged into a prelude of the Nazi "New Order"; the doctrines of Rousseau and the doctrines of Marx, the shade of Luther and the shadow of Hitler, jostled each other in bewildering succession. Never has there been a revolution so inspired by a limitless faith in the power of ideas; never has a revolution so discredited the power of ideas in its result. The success of the revolution discredited conservative ideas; the failure of the revolution discredited liberal ideas. After it, nothing remained but the idea of Force, and this idea stood at the helm of German history from then on. For the first time since 1521, the German people stepped on to the centre of the German stage only to miss their cues once more. German history reached its turning-point and failed to turn. This was the fateful essence of 1848.

❊ ❊ ❊

The refusal of [the] Frankfort [Assembly] to go with the masses, the failure to offer a social programme, was a decisive element in the failure of the German liberals. This refusal and this failure are the theme of *Germany: Revolution and Counter-Revolution,* the pamphlet which Engels wrote for Marx and which is still the best analysis of the events of 1848. But there was another, and even more important cause of failure, a disastrous mistake which Marx, Engels, and most German radicals shared. The National Assembly had come into being when the armed power of Austria and Prussia collapsed; and its prestige waned as Austrian and Prussian armed power revived. These armies won new confidence, no doubt, in the repression of internal disorder. But the prime purpose of armies is foreign war, and it was in foreign war of a sort that Austrian and Prussian absolutism were reborn. Not the social conflict, but the conflict on the national frontiers—in Bohemia, in Poland, and in Slesvig and Holstein—determined the fate of German liberalism. In the struggle against the Czechs, against the Poles, against the Danes, the German liberals unhesitatingly supported the cause of the Prussian and Austrian armies and were then surprised when these weapons were turned against themselves. Liberalism was sacrificed to the national cause.

❊ ❊ ❊

The radicals who did not despair of Germany were few. Far more accomplished their own revolution by emigrating to the freedom of the United States. German emigration had already begun on a big scale, more than a hundred thousand a year, in the early 'forties. It dwindled to fifty thousand in 1848, when it seemed that Germany might be at last a place worth living in. After 1848 it soared once more, running at a steady average of more than a quarter of a million a year throughout the eighteen-fifties. These emigrants were the best of their race—the adventurous, the independent, the men who might have made Germany a free and civilized country. They brought to the United States a contribution of inestimable value, but they were lost to Germany. They, the best Germans, showed their opinion of Germany by leaving it for ever.

Like the radical emigrants, most liberals too were disillusioned by their experience of practical politics. Many withdrew to academic studies or served Germany by applying science to practical needs. Some turned from politics to industry and finance. So Hansemann, most liberal of the Prussian ministers of 1848, founded the Discontogesellschaft, one of the greatest of German banks. The liberal politicians who remained politicians resolved to be more moderate and practical than ever. Their faith in the strength of their idea was destroyed; therefore they believed that liberal Germany must be achieved by subtlety and guile. But it would be wrong to suppose that the liberals of Germany vanished or that liberal convictions counted for nothing in Germany after 1848. The professors, the lawyers, the civil servants of the lesser states, remained predominantly liberal: they were still liberal in 1890 and even, for the most part, in 1930. But in 1848 they were a serious and respected political force. After 1848 they counted for less and less and, at last, for nothing at all.

The real significance of the revolution of 1848 was not so much its failure at the time, but the effect of its failure in the future. After 1850 there began in Germany a period of industrial development, after 1871 an industrial revolution. Economic power passed within a generation into the hands of industrial capitalists. Industrial capitalists, it is commonly held, are in politics liberal; but this view is an abbreviation of the real course of events. Industrial capitalists, like all businessmen, judge everything by the standard of success. A good businessman is one who succeeds; a bad businessman is one who "fails." When industrial capitalists enter politics they apply the same standard and adopt as their own the party and outlook which prevails. In England and the United States the struggle between liberalism and arbitrary power had long been fought out. The execution of Charles I, the overthrow of the army, and the Glorious Revolution in England, the defeat of the redcoats and royal government in America, established the great principles of constitutional freedom and the rule of law. The English and American capitalists found the civilian politicians and lawyers in control. Therefore they too became liberals, advocates of individual freedom and upholders of constitutional government. In France, despite the great revolution, the verdict of success was less clear: therefore the industrial capitalists were confused—some became republicans, some Bonapartists, some corrupt and unprincipled. But in Germany there could be no doubt where success lay. The German capitalists became dependants of Prussian militarism and advocates of arbitrary power as naturally and as inevitably as English or American capitalists became liberals and advocates of constitutional authority. Where Anglo-Saxon capitalists demanded *laissez-faire*, German capitalists sought for state leadership; where Anglo-Saxon capitalists accepted democracy, however grudgingly, German capitalists grudgingly accepted dictatorship. This was the fateful legacy of 1848.

※ ※ ※

There was nothing mysterious in Hitler's victory; the mystery is rather that it had been so long delayed. The delay was caused by the tragic incompatibility of German wishes. The rootless and irresponsible, the young and the violent embraced the opportunity of licensed gangsterdom on a heroic scale; but most Germans wanted the recovery of German power, yet disliked the brutality and lawlessness of the National Socialists, by which alone they could attain their wish. Thus Brüning was the nominee of the Reichswehr and the enemy of the republic, the harbinger both of dictatorship and of German rearmament. Yet he hated the paganism and barbarity of the National Socialists and would have done anything against them—except breaking with the generals. Schleicher, in control of the Reichswehr, was obsessed with German military recovery; yet he contemplated an alliance with the trade unions against the National Socialists and, subsequently, paid for his opposition with his life. The generals, the judges, the civil servants, the professional classes, wanted what only Hitler could offer—German mastery of Europe. But they did not want to pay the price. Hence the delay in the National Socialist rise to power; hence their failure to win a clear majority of votes even at the general election in March 1933. The great majority of German people wanted German domination abroad and the rule of law at home, irreconcilables which they had sought to reconcile ever since 1871, or rather ever since the struggles against Poles, Czechs, and Danes in 1848.

※ ※ ※

This is the explanation of the paradox of the "Third Reich." It was a system founded on terror, unworkable without the secret police and the concentration camp; but it was also a system which represented the deepest wishes of the German people. In fact it was the only system of German government ever created by German initiative. The old empire had been imposed by the arms of Austria and France; the German Confederation by the armies of Austria and Prussia. The Hohenzollern empire was made by the victories of Prussia, the Weimar republic by the victories of the Allies. But the "Third Reich" rested solely on German force and German impulse; it owed nothing to alien forces. It was a tyranny imposed upon the German people by themselves. Every class disliked the barbarism or the tension of National Socialism; yet it was essential to the attainment of their ends. This is most obvious in the case of the old "governing classes." The Junker landowners wished to prevent the expropriation of the great estates and the exposure of the scandals of the *Osthilfe;* the army officers wanted a mass army, heavily equipped; the industrialists needed an economic monopoly of all Europe if their great concerns were to survive. Yet many Junkers had an old-fashioned Lutheran respectability; many army officers knew that world conquest was beyond Germany's strength; many industrialists, such as Thyssen, who had financed the National Socialists, were pious and simple in their private lives. But all were prisoners of the inescapable fact that if the expansion of German power were for a moment arrested, their position would be destroyed.

But the National Socialist dictatorship had a deeper foundation. Many, perhaps most, Germans were reluctant to make the sacrifices demanded by rearmament and total war; but they desired the prize which only total war would give. They desired to undo the verdict of 1918; not merely to end reparations or to cancel the "war guilt" clause, but to repudiate the equality with the peoples of eastern Europe which had then been forced upon them. During the preceding eighty years the Germans had sacrificed to the Reich all their liberties; they demanded as reward the enslavement of others. No German recognized the Czechs or Poles as equals. Therefore every German desired the achievement which only total war could give. By no other means could the Reich be held together. It had been made by conquest and for conquest; if it ever gave up its career of conquest, it would dissolve. Patriotic duty compelled even the best of Germans to support a policy which was leading Germany to disaster.

Totalitarian Dictatorship and Autocracy

CARL J. FRIEDRICH AND
ZBIGNIEW K. BRZEZINSKI

Carl J. Friedrich taught at Harvard University for fifty years, and his publications include studies of the Bronze Age, the philosophy of law, and Kant. He was an adviser to General Clay in Germany after World War II and to the European Constituent Assembly in the early 1950s. Zbigniew K. Brzezinski came to the United States from Poland in 1938 and for many years taught government at Harvard University. He was assistant to the president for National Security Affairs from 1977 to 1981, and is now at the Nitze School of Advanced International Studies of Johns Hopkins University. He has written on the Soviet government and on U.S. foreign policy. Brzezinski and Friedrich collaborated on the study from which this excerpt is taken. What is the larger context into which the authors place the Nazi phenomenon? Do you find any relationship between their approach and the cold war period in which they wrote? How is our understanding of the Nazi phenomenon furthered by focusing on the similarities between Hitler's Germany and Stalin's Russia?

Totalitarian regimes are autocracies. When they are said to be tyrannies, despotisms, or absolutisms, the basic general nature of such regimes is being denounced, for all these words have a strongly pejorative flavor. When they call themselves "democracies," qualifying it by the adjective "popular," they are not contradicting these indictments, except in trying to suggest that they are good or at least praiseworthy. An inspection of the meaning the totalitarians attach to the term "popular democracy" reveals that they mean by it a species of autocracy. The leaders of the people, identified with the leaders of the ruling party, have the last word. Once they have decided and been acclaimed by a party gathering, their decision is final. Whether it be a rule, a judgment, or a measure or any other act of government, they are the *autokrator,* the ruler accountable only to himself. Totalitarian dictatorship, in a sense, is the adaptation of autocracy to twentieth-century industrial society.

Thus, as far as this characteristic absence of accountability is concerned, totalitarian dictatorship resembles earlier forms of autocracy. But it is our contention in this volume that totalitarian dictatorship is historically an innovation and *sui generis.* It is also our conclusion from all the facts available to us that fascist and communist totalitarian dictatorships are basically alike, or at any rate more nearly like each other than like any other system of government, including earlier forms of autocracy. These two theses are closely linked and must be examined together. They are also linked to a third, that totalitarian dictatorship as it actually developed was not intended by those who created it—Mussolini talked of it, though he meant something different—but resulted from the political situations in which the anticonstitutionalist and antidemocratic revolutionary movements and their leaders found themselves.

⌗ ⌗ ⌗

Totalitarian dictatorship then emerges as a system of rule for realizing totalist intentions under modern political and technical conditions, as a novel type of autocracy. The declared intention of creating a "new man," according to numerous reports, has had significant results where the regime has lasted long enough, as in Russia. In the view of one leading authority, "the most appealing traits of the Russians—their naturalness and candor—have suffered most." He considers this a "profound and apparently permanent transformation," and an "astonishing" one. In short, the effort at total control, while not achieving such control, has highly significant human effects.

The fascist and communist systems evolved in response to a series of grave crises—they are forms of crisis government. Even so, there is no reason to conclude that the existing totalitarian systems will disappear as a result of internal evolution, though there can be no doubt that they are undergoing continuous changes. The two totalitarian governments that have perished thus far have done so as the result of wars with outside powers, but this does not mean that the Soviet Union, Communist China, or any of the others necessarily will become involved in war. We do not presuppose that totalitarian societies are fixed and static entities but, on the contrary, that they have undergone and continue to undergo a steady evolution, presumably involving both growth and deterioration. But what about the origins? If it is evident that the regimes came into being because a totalitarian movement achieved dominance over a society and its government, where did the movement come from? The answer to this question remains highly controversial. A great many explanations have been attempted in terms of the various ingredients of these ideologies. Not only Marx and Engels, where the case seems obvious, but Hegel, Luther, and a great many others have come in for their share of blame. Yet none of these thinkers was, of course, a totalitarian at all, and each would have rejected these regimes, if any presumption like that were to be tested in terms of his thought. They were humanists and religious men of intense spirituality of the kind the totalitarians explicitly reject. In short, all such "explanations," while interesting in illuminating particular elements of the totalitarian ideologies, are based on serious invalidating distortions of historical facts. If we leave aside such ideological explanations (and they are linked of course to the "ideological" theory of totalitarian dictatorship as criticized above), we find several other unsatisfactory genetic theories.

The debate about the causes or origins of totalitarianism has run all the way from a primitive bad-man theory to the "moral crisis of our time" kind of argument. A detailed inspection of the available evidence suggests that virtually every one of the factors which has been offered by itself as an explanation of the origin of totalitarian dictatorship has played its role. For example, in the case of Germany, Hitler's moral and personal defects, weaknesses in the German constitutional tradition, certain traits involved in the German "national character," the Versailles Treaty and its aftermath, the economic crisis and the "contradictions" of an aging capitalism, the "threat" of communism, the decline of Christianity and of such other spiritual moorings as the belief in the reason and the reasonableness of man—all have played a role in the total configuration of factors contributing to the over-all result. As in the case of other broad developments in history, only a multiple-factor analysis will yield an adequate account. But at the present time, we cannot fully explain the rise of totalitarian dictatorship. All we can do is to explain it partially by identifying some of the antecedent and concomitant conditions. To repeat: totalitarian dictatorship is a new phenomenon; there has never been anything quite like it before.

The discarding of ideological explanations—highly objectionable to all totalitarians, to be sure—opens up an understanding of and insight into the basic similarity of totalitarian regimes, whether communist or fascist. They are, in terms of organization and procedures—that is to say, in terms of structure, institutions, and processes of rule—*basically alike*. What does this mean? In the first place, it means that they are *not wholly alike*. Popular and journalistic interpretation has oscillated between two extremes; some have said that the communist and fascist dictatorships are wholly alike, others that they are not at all alike. The latter view was the prevailing one during the popular-front days in Europe as well as in liberal circles in the United States. It was even more popular during the Second World War, especially among Allied propagandists. Besides, it was and is the official communist and fascist party line. It is only natural that these regimes, conceiving of themselves as bitter enemies, dedicated to the task of liquidating each other, should take the view that they have nothing in common. This has happened before in history. When the Protestants and Catholics were fighting during the religious wars of the sixteenth and seventeenth centuries, they very commonly denied to one another the name of "Christians," and each argued about the other that it was not a "true church." Actually, and in the perspective of time, both were indeed Christian churches.

The other view, that communist and fascist dictatorships are wholly alike, was during the cold war demonstrably favored in the United States and in Western Europe to an increasing extent. Yet they are demonstrably not wholly alike. For example, they differ in their acknowledged purposes and intentions. Everyone knows that the communists say they seek the world revolution of the proletariat, while the fascists proclaimed their determination to establish the imperial predominance of a particular nation or race, either over the world or over a region. The communist and fascist dictatorships differ also in their historical antecedents: the fascist movements arose in reaction to the communist challenge and offered themselves to a frightened middle class as saviors from the communist danger. The communist movements, on the other hand, presented themselves as the liberators of an oppressed people from an existing autocratic regime, at least in Russia and China. Both claims are not without foundation, and one could perhaps coordinate them by treating the totalitarian movements as consequences of the First World War. "The rise [of totalitarianism] has occurred in the sequel to the first world war and those catastrophies, political and economic, which accompanied it and the feeling of crisis linked thereto." As we shall have occasion to show in the chapters to follow, there are many other differences which do not allow us to speak of the communist and fascist totalitarian dictatorships as wholly alike, but which suggest that they are sufficiently alike to class them together and to contrast them not only with constitutional systems, but also with former types of autocracy.

Before we turn to these common features, however, there is another difference that used to be emphasized by many who wanted "to do business with Hitler" or who admired Mussolini and therefore argued that, far from being wholly like the communist dictatorship, the fascist regimes really had to be seen as merely authoritarian forms of constitutional systems. It is indeed true that more of the institutions of the antecedent liberal and constitutional society survived in the Italian Fascist than in the Russian or Chinese Communist society. But this is due in part to the fact that no liberal constitutional society preceded

Soviet or Chinese Communism. The promising period of the Duma came to naught as a result of the war and the disintegration of tsarism, while the Kerensky interlude was far too brief and too superficial to become meaningful for the future. Similarly in China, the Kuomingtang failed to develop a working constitutional order, though various councils were set up; they merely provided a facade for a military dictatorship disrupted by a great deal of anarchical localism, epitomized in the rule of associated warlords. In the Soviet satellites, on the other hand, numerous survivals of a non-totalitarian past continue to function. In Poland, Czechoslovakia, Hungary, and Yugoslavia we find such institutions as universities, churches, and schools. It is likely that, were a communist dictatorship to be established in Great Britain or France, the situation would be similar, and here even more such institutions of the liberal era would continue to operate, for a considerable initial period at least. Precisely this argument has been advanced by such British radicals as Sidney and Beatrice Webb. The tendency of isolated fragments of the preceding state of society to survive has been a significant source of misinterpretation of the fascist totalitarian society, especially in the case of Italy. In the twenties, Italian totalitarianism was very commonly misinterpreted as being "merely" an authoritarian form of middle-class rule, with the trains running on time and the beggars off the streets. In the case of Germany, this sort of misinterpretation took a slightly different form. In the thirties, various writers tried to interpret German totalitarianism either as "the end phase of capitalism" or as "militarist imperialism." These interpretations stress the continuance of a "capitalist" economy whose leaders are represented as dominating the regime. The facts as we know them do not correspond to this view. For one who sympathized with socialism or communism, it was very tempting to depict the totalitarian dictatorship of Hitler as nothing but a capitalist society and therefore totally at variance with the "new civilization" that was arising in the Soviet Union. These few remarks have suggested, it is hoped, why it may be wrong to consider the totalitarian dictatorships under discussion as either wholly alike or basically different. Why they are basically alike remains to be shown, and to this key argument we now turn.

The basic features or traits that we suggest as generally recognized to be common to totalitarian dictatorships are six in number. The "syndrome," or pattern of interrelated traits, of the totalitarian dictatorship consists of an ideology, a single party typically led by one man, a terroristic police, a communications monopoly, a weapons monopoly, and a centrally directed economy. Of these, the last two are also found in constitutional systems: Socialist Britain had a centrally directed economy, and all modern states possess a weapons monopoly. Whether these latter suggest a "trend" toward totalitarianism is a question that will be discussed in our last chapter. These six basic features, which we think constitute the distinctive pattern or model of totalitarian dictatorship, form a cluster of traits, intertwined and mutually supporting each other, as is usual in "organic" systems. They should therefore not be considered in isolation or be made the focal point of comparisons, such as "Caesar developed a terroristic secret police, therefore he was the first totalitarian dictator," or "the Catholic Church has practiced ideological thought control, therefore . . ." The totalitarian dictatorships all possess the following:

- An elaborate ideology, consisting of an official body of doctrine covering all vital aspects of man's existence to which everyone living in that society is supposed to adhere, at least passively; this ideology is characteristically focused and projected toward a perfect final state of mankind—that is to say, it contains a chiliastic claim, based upon a radical rejection of the existing society with conquest of the world for the new one.

- A single mass party typically led by one man, the "dictator," and consisting of a relatively small percentage of the total population (up to 10 percent) of men and women, a hard core of them passionately and unquestioningly dedicated to the ideology and prepared to assist in every way in promoting its general acceptance, such a party being hierarchically, oligarchically organized and typically either superior to, or completely intertwined with, the governmental bureaucracy.

- A system of terror, whether physical or psychic, effected through party and secret-police control, supporting but also supervising the party for its leaders, and characteristically directed not only against demonstrable "enemies" of the regime, but against more or less arbitrarily selected classes of the population; the terror whether of the secret police or of party-directed social pressure systematically exploits modern science, and more especially scientific psychology.

- A technologically conditioned, near-complete monopoly of control, in the hands of the party and of the government, of all means of effective mass communication, such as the press, radio, and motion pictures.

- A similarly technologically conditioned, near-complete monopoly of the effective use of all weapons of armed combat.

- A central control and direction of the entire economy through the bureaucratic coordination of formerly independent corporate entities, typically including most other associations and group activities.

The enumeration of these six traits or trait clusters is not meant to suggest that there might not be others, now insufficiently recognized. It has more particularly been suggested that the administrative control of justice and the courts is a distinctive trait; but actually the evolution of totalitarianism in recent years suggests that such administrative direction of judicial work may be greatly limited. We shall also discuss the problem of expansionism, which has been urged as a characteristic trait of totalitarianism. The traits here outlined have been generally acknowledged as the features of totalitarian dictatorship, to which the writings of students of the most varied backgrounds, including totalitarian writers, bear witness.

Political Man

The Social Bases of Politics

S E Y M O U R   M A R T I N   L I P S E T

Seymour Martin Lipset, a professor of political science and sociology, has taught at numerous American universities, most recently at Stanford. He has published extensively on the social
origins of political behavior, the American Revolution, the student rebellions in the 1960s, and other subjects. In compiling
this account, he consulted the findings of writers who relied on
German voting records to provide a social and political analysis
of Nazi party supporters in the last elections held in the Weimar
Republic. Who did vote for the Nazis? Why? How do Lipset's
conclusions differ from those of Strachey?

The classic example of a revolutionary fascist party is, of course, the National Socialist Workers' party led by Adolf Hitler. For Marxian analysts, this party represented the last stage of capitalism, winning power in order to maintain
capitalism's tottering institutions. Since the Nazis came to power before the days
of public opinion polls, we have to rely on records of the total votes to locate
their social base. If classic fascism appeals largely to the same elements as those
which back liberalism, then the previous supporters of liberalism should have
provided the backing for the Nazis. A look at the gross election statistics for the
German Reich between 1928 and 1933 would seem to verify this. (See table.)

    Although a table like this conceals changes by individuals which go against
the general statistical trend, some reasonable inferences may be made. As the
Nazis grew, the liberal bourgeois center parties, based on the less traditionalist

From Seymour Martin Lipset, *Political Man: The Social Bases of Politics,* The Johns Hopkins University Press, Baltimore/London, 1981, pp. 138–147.

elements of German society—primarily small business and white-collar workers—completely collapsed. Between 1928 and 1932 these parties lost almost 80 per cent of their vote, and their proportion of the total vote dropped from a quarter to less than 3 per cent. The only center party which maintained its proportionate support was the Catholic Center party whose support was reinforced by religious allegiance. The Marxist parties, the socialists and the Communists, lost about a tenth of their percentage support, although their total vote dropped only slightly. The proportionate support of the conservatives dropped about 40 per cent, much less than that of the more liberal middle-class parties.

PERCENTAGES OF TOTAL VOTE RECEIVED BY VARIOUS GERMAN PARTIES, 1928–1933, AND THE PERCENTAGE OF THE 1928 VOTE RETAINED IN THE LAST FREE ELECTION, 1932[*]

Party	Percentage of Total Vote					Ratio of 1928 to Second 1932 Election Expressed as Percentage
	1928	1930	1932	1932	1933	
Conservative Party						
DNVP	14.2	7.0	5.9	8.5	8.0	60
Middle-class Parties						
DVP (right liberals)	8.7	4.85	1.2	1.8	1.1	21
DDP (left liberals)	4.8	3.45	1.0	0.95	0.8	20
Wirtschaftspartei (small business)	4.5	3.9	0.4	0.3	[†]	7
Others	9.5	10.1	2.6	2.8	0.6	29
Total proportion of middle-class vote maintained						21
Center (Catholic)	15.4	17.6	16.7	16.2	15.0	105
Workers' Parties						
SPD (Socialist)	29.8	24.5	21.6	20.4	18.3	69
KPD (Communist)	10.6	13.1	14.3	16.85	12.3	159
Total proportion of working-class vote maintained						92
Fascist Party						
NSDAP	2.6	18.3	37.3	33.1	43.9	1277
Total proportion of increase in Fascist party vote						1277

[*] The basic data are presented in Samuel Pratt, *The Social Basis of Nazism and Communism in Urban Germany* (M.A. thesis, Dept. of Sociology, Michigan State University, 1948), pp. 29, 30. The same data are presented and analyzed in Karl D. Bracher, *Die Auflösung der Weimarer Republik* (Stuttgart und Düsseldorf: Ring Verlag, 1954), pp. 86–106. The 1933 election was held after Hitler had been chancellor for more than a month.

[†]The *Wirtschaftspartei* did not run any candidates in the 1933 elections.

An inspection of the shifts among the non-Marxist and non-Catholic parties suggests that the Nazis gained most heavily among the liberal middle-class parties, the former bulwarks of the Weimar Republic. Among these parties, the one which lost most heavily was the *Wirtschaftspartei*, which represented primarily small businessmen and artisans. The right-wing nationalist opponent of Weimar, the German National People's party (DNVP), was the only one of the non-Marxist and non-Catholic parties to retain over half of its 1928 proportion of the total vote.

The largest drop-off in the conservative vote lay mainly in the election districts on the eastern border of Germany. The proportion of the vote obtained by the German National People's party declined by 50 per cent or more between 1928 and 1932 in ten of the thirty-five election districts in Germany. Seven of these ten were border areas, including every region which fronted on the Polish corridor, and Schleswig-Holstein, fronting on the northern border. Since the party was both the most conservative and the most nationalist pre-Nazi opponent of the Versailles Treaty, these data suggest that the Nazis most severely weakened the conservatives in those areas where nationalism was their greatest source of strength, while the conservatives retained most of their voters in regions which had not suffered as directly from the annexations imposed by Versailles and in which, it may be argued, the party's basic appeal was more conservative than nationalist. The German-American sociologist Rudolf Heberle has demonstrated in a detailed study of voting patterns in Schleswig-Holstein that the conservatives lost the backing of the small property owners, both urban and rural, whose counterparts in nonborder areas were most commonly liberals, while they retained the backing of the upper-strata conservatives.

Some further indirect evidence that the Nazis did not appeal to the same sources as the traditional German right may be found in the data on the voting of men and women. In the 1920s and 1930s the more conservative or religious a party, the higher, in general, its feminine support. The German National People's party had more female backing than any party except the Catholic Center party. The Nazis, together with the more liberal middle-class parties and Marxist parties, received disproportionate support from men.

More direct evidence for the thesis is given in Heberle's study of Schleswig-Holstein, the state in which the Nazis were strongest. In 1932 *"the Conservatives were weakest where the Nazis were strongest and the Nazis were relatively weak where the Conservatives were strong.* The correlation in 18 predominantly rural election districts between percentages of votes obtained by the NSDAP [Nazis] and by the DNVP [Conservatives] is negative (minus .89). . . . It appears that the Nazis had in 1932 really succeeded the former liberal parties, like the *Landespartei* and Democratic party, as the preferred party among the small farmers . . . while the landlords and big farmers were more reluctant to cast their vote for Hitler."

A more recent analysis by a German political scientist, Günther Franz, identifying voting trends in another state in which the Nazis were very strong— Lower Saxony—reported similar patterns. Franz concluded:

> The majority of the National Socialist voters came from the bourgeois center parties. The DNVP [conservatives] had also lost votes, but in 1932, they held the votes which they received in 1930, and increased their total vote in the next two elections. They were (except for the Catholic Center) the only bourgeois party, which had not simply collapsed before the NSDAP....

This situation in Schleswig-Holstein and Lower Saxony also existed in Germany as a whole. Among the thirty-five electoral districts, the rank-order correlation of the proportionate Nazi gain with the liberal parties' loss was greater (.48) than with the conservatives' loss (.25).

Besides the liberal parties, there was one other group of German parties, based on the *Mittel-stand,* whose supporters seem to have gone over almost en masse to the Nazis—the so-called "federalist" or regional autonomy parties. These parties objected either to the unification of Germany or to the specific annexation of various provinces like Hesse, Lower Saxony, and Schleswig-Holstein to Prussia. In large measure they gave voice to the objections felt by the rural and urban middle classes of provincial areas to the increasing bureaucratization of modern industrial society and sought to turn the clock back by decentralizing government authority. At first glance, the decentralist aspirations of the regional autonomy parties and the glorification of the state inherent in fascism or Nazism seem to reflect totally dissimilar needs and sentiments. But in fact both the "state's rights" ideology of the regionalists and the Nazis' ideological antagonism to the "big" forces of industrial society appealed to those who felt uprooted or challenged. In their economic ideology, the regional parties expressed sentiments similar to those voiced by the Nazis before the latter were strong. Thus the *Schleswig-Holsteinische Landespartei,* which demanded "regional and cultural autonomy for Schleswig-Holstein within Germany," wrote in an early program:

> The craftsman [artisan] has to be protected on the one hand against capitalism, which crushes him by means of its factories, and on the other hand against socialism, which aims at making him a proletarian wage-laborer. At the same time the merchant has to be protected against capitalism in the form of the great department stores, and the whole retail trade against the danger of socialism.

The link between regionalism as an ideology protesting bigness and centralization, and the direct expression of the economic self-interest of the small businessmen may be seen in the joining of the two largest of the regional parties, the Lower Saxon *Deutsch-Hanoverischen Partei* and the Bavarian *Bauern und Mittelstandsbund*, into one parliamentary faction with the *Wirtschaftspartei*, the party which explicitly defined itself as representing the small entrepreneurs. In the 1924 elections the Bavarian regionalists and the small businessmen's party actually presented a joint electoral ticket. As Heberle points out about these parties: "The criticism of Prussian policy . . . the demand for native civil servants, the refusal to accept Berlin as the general center of culture, were all outlets for a disposition which had been formed a long time before the war. . . . At bottom the criticism against Prussia was merely an expression of a general antipathy against the social system of industrial capitalism. . . ."

The appeal of the Nazis to those elements in German society which resented the power and culture of the large cities is also reflected in the Nazis' success in small communities. A detailed ecological analysis of voting in German cities with 25,000 or more population, in 1932, indicates that *the larger the city, the smaller the Nazi vote*. The Nazis secured less of their total vote in cities over 25,000 in size than did any of the other five major parties, including the Catholic Center and the conservative DNVP. And Berlin, the great metropolis, was the only predominantly Protestant election district in which the Nazis received under 25 per cent of the vote in July 1932. These facts sharply challenge the various interpretations of Nazism as the product of the growth of anomie and the general rootlessness of modern urban industrial society.

Examination of the shifts in patterns of German voting between 1928 and 1932 among the non-Marxist and non-Catholic parties indicates, as we have seen, that the Nazis gained disproportionately from the ranks of the center and liberal parties rather than from the conservatives, thus validating one aspect of the thesis that classic fascism appeals to the same strata as liberalism. The second part of the argument, that fascism appeals predominantly to the self-employed among the middle strata, has been supported by three separate ecological studies of German voting between 1928 and 1932. Two American sociologists, Charles Loomis and J. Allen Beegle, correlated the percentage of the Nazi vote in 1932 in communities under 10,000 in population in three states with the percentage of the labor force in specific socioeconomic classes and found that "areas in which the middle classes prevailed [as indicated by the proportion of proprietors in the population and the ratio of proprietors to laborers and salaried employees] gave increasingly larger votes to the Nazis as the economic and social crises settled on Germany."

This high correlation between Nazi vote and proprietorship holds for farm owners as well as owners of small business and industry in Schleswig-Holstein and Hanover, but not in Bavaria, a strongly Catholic area where the Nazis were relatively weak. Heberle's study of Schleswig-Holstein, which analyzed all of the elections under Weimar, concluded that "the classes particularly susceptible to Nazism were neither the rural nobility and the big farmers nor the rural proletariat, but rather the small farm proprietors, very much the rural equivalent of the lower middle class or petty bourgeoisie *(Kleinbuergertum)* which formed the backbone of the NSDAP in the cities."

The sociologist Samuel Pratt's excellent study of urban voting prior to the Nazi victory related the Nazi vote in July 1932 to the proportion of the population in the "upper middle class," defined as "proprietors of small and large establishments and executives," and to the proportion in the "lower middle class," composed of "civil servants and white-collar employees." The Nazi vote correlated highly with the proportion in both middle-class groups in different-size cities and in different areas of the country, but the correlations with the "lower middle class" were not as consistently high and positive as those with the "upper middle." As Pratt put it: "Of the two elements of the middle class, the upper seemed to be the more thoroughly pro-Nazi." The so-called upper class, however, was predominantly composed of small businessmen, so that the correlation reported is largely that of self-employed economic status with Nazi voting. This interpretation is enhanced by Pratt's finding that the Nazi vote also correlated (+.6) with the proportion of business establishments with only one employee—in other words, self-employment. "This would be expected, for plants of one employee are another measure of the proprietorship class which was used in measuring the upper middle class."

The occupational distribution of the membership of the Nazi party in 1933 indicates that it was largely drawn from the various urban middle-class strata, with the self-employed again being the most overrepresented. (See table.) The

---

THE RATIO OF THE PERCENTAGE OF MEN IN THE NAZI PARTY TO THE PERCENTAGE IN THE GENERAL POPULATION FROM VARIOUS OCCUPATIONS, 1933*

Occupational Category	1933
Manual workers	68%
White-collar workers	169
Independents[†]	187
Officials (civil servants)	146
Peasants	60
Domestic servants and nonagricultural family helpers	178

*Computed from a table in Hans Gerth, "The Nazi Party: Its Leadership and Composition," in Robert K. Merton, et al., eds., *Reader in Bureaucracy* (Glencoe: The Free Press, 1952), p. 106.

[†]Includes self-employed businessmen, artisans, and free professionals.

second most overrepresented category—domestic servants and nonagricultural family helpers—also bears witness to the party's appeal to small business, since this category is primarily composed of helpers in family-owned small businesses.

The relation of German big business to the Nazis has been a matter of considerable controversy, particularly since various Marxists have attempted to demonstrate that the movement was from the outset "fostered, nourished, maintained and subsidized by the big *bourgeoisie,* by the big landlords, financiers, and industrialists." The most recent studies suggest that the opposite is true. With the exception of a few isolated individuals, German big business gave Nazism little financial support or other encouragement *until* it had risen to the status of a major party. The Nazis did begin to pick up financial backing in 1932, but in large part this backing was a result of many businesses' policy of giving money to all major parties except the Communists in order to be in their good graces. Some German industrialists probably hoped to tame the Nazis by giving them funds. On the whole, however, this group remained loyal to the conservative parties, and many gave no money to the Nazis until after the party won power.

Women in Nazi Society

JILL STEPHENSON

Jill Stephenson's thoroughly researched study of women in Nazi society was first presented as a thesis to the University of Edinburgh. She has also written a book on women's organizations associated with the Nazi party. The following excerpt reveals the Nazi emphasis on domestic roles for women, but also some less well-known aspects of Nazi policy in this area. What accounts for the inconsistencies in Nazi attitudes toward the roles assigned to German women in the "thousand-year Reich"?

It can only be surmised what the position of women in a 'thousand-year Reich' would have been. Clearly, the Nazis' chief concern with women was for their capacity as childbearers. Women with a full-time job might be reluctant to start or add to a family, and so women were to be encouraged to give up work to spend their time in the home, and to have many children in order to fill this time. Girls with an academic education might be reluctant to forego the opportunity of an interesting, responsible, and possibly well-paid career, even if they were married; accordingly, the emphasis was to be shifted away from the study of academic subjects, and where a preponderance of these remained in a curriculum, girls were also to be reminded of their maternal role at every opportunity, by taking compulsory courses in domestic science and by mixing socially in the organisations and usefully in the Labour Service with girls and women from different backgrounds, who would be more interested in human relationships than in physics or foreign languages. Above all, women were to be kept physically healthy for childbearing, and had therefore to be removed from work that was actually or potentially damaging to their reproductive capacity.

The motive was world domination; one of the means to this was to be a dramatic increase in the population, by means of creating an atmosphere in which procreation was considered natural and was rewarded in both material and psychological terms, and by attempting to make any means of conception control beyond total abstinence from sexual intercourse unavailable. But some of the side effects were desirable. For example, the Nazis were considered puritanical in their condemnation of tobacco and alcohol—no doubt partly influenced by Hitler's abstinence from and aversion to them—but they were medically correct in urging pregnant women not to smoke or to drink alcohol. While the Nazis claimed to advocate temperance rather than abstinence with regard to alcohol, they were uncompromising in their opposition to cigarette smoking, at a time when it was accepted as fashionable among women as well as men, and before the health hazards directly connected with it were widely accepted. Foreigners were mildly amused by the zeal of some of the Party faithful in encouraging cafes to hang notices prominently on their premises bearing the legend 'The German woman does not smoke,' but it was the Rector of Erlangen University, whose own field was medicine, who stated unequivocally that 'For a woman, smoking is without doubt a vice.'

Another aspect of social mores which seemed to the Nazis to have implications for the birth rate was women's clothing. They condemned the foreign influences—of Paris and the United States—which, they claimed, had encouraged German women to adopt a style of dressing that was either frivolous or else an imitation of men's clothes, and was in any case decadent and not conducive to a healthy rate of population growth (*fortpflanzungsfeindlich*); the reasoning behind this assertion was not explained. To give guidance about the kind of clothing that was considered desirable in the Nazi State, the German Fashion Bureau was opened in Berlin in the spring of 1933, under the honorary presidency of Magda Goebbels, who claimed that she was 'trying to make the German woman more beautiful.' At first, there was emphasis on the creation of a 'German style' for German women, but the women's magazines continued to carry fashion articles featuring clothes which were considered fashionable in Paris and London, and eventually in 1937 the DFW denied that there had been, or should be, attempts to devise a 'German style.' These ideas, however, were not new in the 1930s; during the Great War there had been criticism of the 'improper' clothes that some women and girls were wearing, and the call went out for the creation of a 'German style.' The objections were against something which was clearly too terrible to be described explicitly, but the implication was that new styles were being adopted which were at once unpatriotic—presumably imported from enemy countries—and morally risky.

The ideal type of woman in Nazi theory was the peasant wife, whose peaceful, wholesome life was devoted to her work on the land and, above all, her family. The picture of this woman at her spinning wheel was offered as the alternative to the city bred chic sophisticates of the decadent 1920s. To encourage the simple perfection embodied—it was quite unrealistically believed—in this rural figure, edicts were issued castigating and ridiculing women who 'shave their eyebrows, use rouge, dye their hair' in an altogether foreign manner. The Party's puritans conducted a vigorous campaign against cosmetics, although Hitler was apparently not averse to women's using them. Himmler, however, maintained a strict attitude, giving instructions that the mothers in the SS's *Lebensborn* homes should not be permitted to use lipstick, to paint their nails, or to shave their eyebrows. It was further made clear that the SS expected the future wives of its members to demonstrate their wholesomeness by achieving the Reich Sport Medal, since the kind of woman who was suitable for the nation's elite to marry was not the one 'who can dance nicely through five-o'clock teas, but who has proved her fitness by sports activity. For good health, the javelin or the pole-vault are of more value than the lipstick.' This motif ran throughout Nazi speeches about women—naturally enough, since it was directly relevant to the function regarded as most important, childbearing, the function to which all Nazi thought about women was ultimately related.

It is this consistent obsession that renders comprehensible some of the apparent inconsistencies in Nazi thought and practice; for example, while some Nazis undoubtedly took a more puritanical view of social and sexual life than others, there was general acceptance that the family was the essential basic unit of society, to be maintained and protected by every possible means. But the very existence of the family was an obstacle to the Nazis' attempt at totalitarian control, and so the Nazi organisations had to try to exert some influence over individual members of the family in the hope that the family unit as a whole would be permeated by National Socialist ideas and would grow in corporate loyalty to the Nazi regime. A strict line of demarcation was, however, to be drawn between business and pleasure: Hess repeatedly reminded Party members that they were not allowed to wear Party uniform when out on social occasions with women, unless the function was an official one to which wives were invited. Hess particularly condemned those who wore Party uniform when taking their wives for a ride in a car, and ordered that on no account was a woman to be driven in an open car with her husband when he was in uniform. This potential source of petty family friction was, however, trivial compared with the apparent threat to the family unit by some Nazi social policies.

The more tolerant attitude towards unmarried motherhood and the introduction of 'irretrievable breakdown' as a ground for divorce in the Third Reich alarmed some of those who had believed Nazi promises of restoring respectability to German life after the permissiveness of the Weimar Republic. They were, in fact, policies which were more similar to those of liberals and even Communists than to the standard Christian morality of conservatives who had supported Hitler in preference to socialists of any colour. No doubt Himmler and the SS and Hess were in a small minority in the NSDAP in positively encouraging unmarried motherhood, but the Party clearly, after some initial hesitation, moved to a position where it accepted that motherhood was desirable, therefore those women who became mothers out of wedlock should not be discriminated against, even if they should equally not be acclaimed as examples worthy of imitation. The result was more humane treatment of unmarried mothers, of the kind advocated particularly by radical feminists both before and after the Great War and by Communists, in imitation of the Soviet Russian example. On the whole, the Nazis recognised that there was an implicit contradiction in their claim to be upholding the family unit and their attempt to diminish prejudice against the unmarried mother; but their overriding desire for children led them to welcome any 'racially valuable' child, regardless of the marital status of its parents, and therefore to value the parents themselves.

Population policy, again, underlay the peculiar situation which arose from the Nazis' being more concerned with the health and welfare of women workers than some of the avowed champions of women's rights. While the Communists and the Socialists were, like the Nazis, anxious to develop schemes of labour protection for women, particularly for pregnant women and nursing mothers, the radical feminists of the Open Door International, who were the first to claim that the Nazis had no regard for women and aimed to subject them fully to male domination, denied that special provision for women's welfare was anything other than a device for discriminating against women. Thus, the most militant feminists were prepared to countenance a situation where women and girls were free to work during the day or at night for as many hours as they chose, regardless of the damage they might do to their health. Indeed, they, along with the Communists, demanded equal pay for equal work, which might have discouraged employers from using women for heavy work since men were more obviously fitted for it; but it was the Nazis who actually introduced equal pay in some cases for this very purpose. And the radical feminists never suggested that their aim in agitating for equal pay was to discourage employers from using female labour on the same terms as male. In the end—always for the natalist motive—the Nazis showed more concern for the physical well-being of women.

Perhaps this helps to account for the acceptance of the Nazis by women generally, and even by some of those who had been opposed to the Nazis in the pre-1933 period.

❇ ❇ ❇

It is one of the many ironies of National Socialism that its policies and its defeat created a situation in which discrimination against women in many areas, particularly in employment, was not a practical proposition. The need for many women to assume the role of breadwinner after the Second World War, in the absence of men who were dead, incapacitated, or in prison, led to the opening up of new opportunities for women in the Federal Republic. In the Democratic Republic, that which so many of the Nazis' supporters had feared above all, and which the Nazis had been pledged to prevent, the victory of Communism, has meant that there has been a much more decisive change of policy, so that women have—within the limits of a new dictatorship—equal rights and equality of opportunity. The Nazis, then, unwittingly acted as the agents of the kind of changes they had aimed to prevent or reverse, and women became more self-reliant and were accorded a greater degree of legal and social equality. But the Nazis had certainly given the impression of arresting developments in the direction of greater equality for women; it remains to decide how far this was true.

In the first place, progress was made in improving opportunities for women even before 1914, notably in education; 'emancipation' did not suddenly begin in 1918. After the Great War far less progress was made than feminists had hoped for and conservatives had feared. Indeed, certain areas of activity were opened to women for the first time, including full participation in politics and entry to the legal profession. But the progress made in winning real influence for women in politics and significant representation for them in professions other than teaching, where they were already well-established, was slow and gradual, as it was bound to be, while the provisions of the Imperial Civil Code continued to affirm the superiority of the male sex in society, and especially in marriage. In addition, no sooner were modest reforms introduced after the Great War than the forces of reaction asserted themselves, so that German women—insofar as they were interested—were, like the nation as a whole, bitterly divided between those who resented even cautious change, associating it with 'Bolshevism,' and those who poured contempt on the small improvements that were effected. Even moderate feminists, who accepted that evolution was the best course, but a slow one, began to be disillusioned by the later 1920s, and to be alarmed in the early 1930s when the effects of the depression seemed to many justification—or excuse—for a retreat from the Weimar Constitution's commitment to equal rights for members of both sexes. The conservatives, the Churches, and even some trade unionists were very ready to see in, for example, the deliberate discrimination against the employed married woman the solution to Germany's problems which were, in the view of the Churches and the conservatives, at least, not merely of an economic nature but political and moral as well.

Thus, the clock was stopped not in 1933 but in 1930. The Nazis, with their weird, backward looking philosophy, benefited from attitudes which had already developed and hardened, and found at least tacit—and often open—support for their promised policy of restoring women to a position of security, decency and domesticity. But it was not their intention, they repeatedly asserted, to restrict women to the traditional 'three K's'—*Kinder, Küche, Kirche* (nursery, kitchen, church)—as conservatives hoped. Once again, German conservatives had mistaken the Nazis for old style, nationalist reactionaries like themselves, failing to comprehend the essentially revolutionary nature of Nazism. Certainly, in the Nazi State women were to concern themselves to a considerable degree with children and with household matters; but a regime which aspired to totalitarian control had to urge all its citizens to look outward from their private lives, to surrender their privacy and allow themselves to be imbued with the Nazi *Weltanschauung*, and to accept the primacy of the needs of the State as interpreted by the Nazi leadership. Thus, German women were to be less 'requisites of German men' than—like German men—agents at the disposal of the Nazi regime. It was crucial to women's position that the needs of the regime became such that women could be discriminated against to only a very limited extent.

In the Third Reich, men were, after all, controlled and confined to the same extent as women, and often, given the relative immunity of the housewife from official surveillance, even more. If men monopolised positions of power in the Nazi State, only a minority of men exercised power, and the great mass of men were excluded in the same way as women. Male and female opponents and victims of Nazi racist policies were discriminated against and persecuted on an equal basis. Certainly the Nazis were determined to persuade as many women as possible, in the early years, at least, that their natural sphere of activity was the home and family; but it is often overlooked that the majority of women choose to marry and have children in the absence of official pressure to do so. The Nazis were starting their campaign with the advantage of women's biological character and natural disposition on their side. Their aim was to reverse the evident trend towards contempt for the *nur-Hausfrau* (the woman who is 'only a housewife'), which was a side effect of the provision of more opportunities for women outside the home. In this, they to some extent succeeded; where they were wrong was in trying to coerce women into complying with their policy, by limiting opportunities outside the home and by trying to remove all means of birth control.

Attempts to limit opportunities for women outside the home were made, at a time when the massive unemployment problem made them doubly attractive. But the change which came in the economic situation in the mid-1930s made even the campaign against employed married women first redundant and then positively harmful. Similarly, the steps taken to reduce the academic content of girls' school curricula—a reaction against the strong emphasis there had been on academic ability after the Great War—proved to be damaging even before the Second World War gave rise to an urgent demand for girl students in all disciplines. In the later 1930s, women were not only to be given the opportunity to work and to study, whether they were married or single, but were to be positively encouraged to do these things. The motive was, as ever, the serving of the needs of the Nazi State at the time, not the improvement of opportunities for women; but such an improvement was in fact a result. The unrealistic and ideologically motivated barriers raised against women's advancement in the highest echelons of the civil service and to the practice of law by women were indeed indicative of what was, in the Nazi view, ideal, and of what would no doubt have been their aim in the 'thousand-year Reich,' if other policies had permitted it. But these instances were exceptions, and the result of the abnormal 1930s—abnormal in political and economic terms and culminating in war—was that women's position in employment outside the home, including the professions as a whole, was consolidated, not eroded, while, in addition, the status of the housewife and mother was raised.

6

APPEASEMENT

The Munich Pact

The Munich Conference of September 29–30, 1938, included Germany, Italy, France, and Great Britain, represented respectively by Hitler, Mussolini, Daladier, and Chamberlain. It called for the annexation by Germany of the Sudetenland, the western end of Czechoslovakia, whose population contained a majority of German-speaking people. After signing the agreement, Daladier and Chamberlain told the Czech representatives, who had been left waiting in a hotel room, that their country had been partitioned. Signed later by Chamberlain and Hitler, the official statement, which saw the agreement "as symbolic of the desire of our two peoples never to go to war with one another again," marked the touchstone of the appeasement policy pursued by Britain and France during much of the decade. On their return to London and Paris, Chamberlain and Daladier were cheered by huge crowds for having prevented war. "No conqueror returning from a victory on the battlefield," said the London *Times* on October 1, "has come home adorned with nobler laurels than Mr. Chamberlain from Munich yesterday," and most newspapers published that day on both sides of the English Channel shared the sentiment. Only a few agreed with Winston Churchill when he told the House of Commons that "we have suffered a total and unmitigated defeat. All is over. Silent, mournful, abandoned, broken Czechoslovakia recedes into the darkness." Indeed, for that country, which had remained faithful to her democratic belief and had relied on her friends in the West, the betrayal was a cruel one. Unconsulted, ignored, she lost her fortifications, three-quarters of her heavy industry, much of her vital transportation, and, of course, what remained of the morale of her people. The German press exulted in the gains made: a dangerous enemy neutralized, the Versailles monstrosity removed, the Reich's power revealed, quantities of men and material added to her military—all accomplished without bloodshed. In the future, the word "appeasement," once a wholly honorable diplomatic alternative designed to minimize the risk of armed conflict, became a term of opprobrium and conjured up a hateful and despicable policy. The "Munich analogy" would be made countless times in the years to come to show the consequences of yielding to a dictator.

Should the British and the French have realized that Hitler's demands on Czechoslovakia presaged his ultimate goal of European conquest? Or did the two democracies act in the most appropriate manner given existing circumstances? The four excerpts that follow provide four different views. While not defending appeasement in theory, two support the Munich Accord, although for different reasons. The other two see the policy as wrong from beginning to end but do not question the appeasers' sincerity or honesty, only their policy and their wisdom.

What, then, are the "lessons" of Munich? That nations must behave honorably and fulfill commitments (Churchill)? That to be effective, statesmen must have an understanding of history (Rowse)? That to have freedom of action a great power must support a sufficient defense establishment (Butler)? That democracies cannot enter wars without full public support (Weinberg)? Politicians and the public at large have concluded that Munich teaches us that dictators cannot be appeased. But the most important lesson may well be that historical lessons themselves, rather than historical realities, influence events— and that their consequences can be more unpleasant historical lessons.

The Gathering Storm

WINSTON S. CHURCHILL

Sir Winston Churchill, active for many years in British politics, led his country in war from 1940 to 1945. A noted historian, he published extensively, and his multivolume memoirs of World Wars I and II constitute invaluable sources. The following is drawn from the first volume of the latter. On what grounds does Churchill condemn Chamberlain? What are his arguments for calling a halt to appeasement in 1938?

Chamberlain returned to England. At Heston where he landed, he waved the joint declaration which he had got Hitler to sign, and read it to the crowd of notables and others who welcomed him. As his car drove through cheering crowds from the airport, he said to Halifax, sitting beside him, "All this will be over in three months"; but from the windows of Downing Street he waved his piece of paper again and used these words, "This is the second time there has come back from Germany to Downing Street peace with honour. I believe it is peace in our time."

⊠ ⊠ ⊠

We have now also Marshal Keitel's answer to the specific question put to him by the Czech representative at the Nuremberg Trials:

Colonel Eger, representing Czechoslovakia, asked Marshal Keitel: "Would the Reich have attacked Czechoslovakia in 1938 if the Western Powers had stood by Prague?"

Marshal Keitel answered: "Certainly not. We were not strong enough militarily. The object of Munich [i.e., reaching an agreement at Munich] was to get Russia out of Europe, to gain time, and to complete the German armaments."

❊ ❊ ❊

Hitler's judgment had been once more decisively vindicated. The German General Staff was utterly abashed. Once again the Fuehrer had been right, after all. He with his genius and intuition alone had truly measured all the circumstances, military and political. Once again, as in the Rhineland, the Fuehrer's leadership had triumphed over the obstruction of the German military chiefs. All these generals were patriotic men. They longed to see the Fatherland regain its position in the world. They were devoting themselves night and day to every process that could strengthen the German forces. They, therefore, felt smitten in their hearts at having been found so much below the level of the event, and in many cases their dislike and their distrust of Hitler were overpowered by admiration for his commanding gifts and miraculous luck. Surely here was a star to follow, surely here was a guide to obey. Thus did Hitler finally become the undisputed master of Germany, and the path was clear for the great design. The conspirators lay low, and were not betrayed by their military comrades.

❊ ❊ ❊

It may be well here to set down some principles of morals and action which may be a guide in the future. No case of this kind can be judged apart from its circumstances. The facts may be unknown at the time, and estimates of them must be largely guesswork, coloured by the general feelings and aims of whoever is trying to pronounce. Those who are prone by temperament and character to seek sharp and clear-cut solutions of difficult and obscure problems, who are ready to fight whenever some challenge comes from a foreign Power, have not always been right. On the other hand, those whose inclination is to bow their heads, to seek patiently and faithfully for peaceful compromise, are not always wrong. On the contrary, in the majority of instances they may be right, not only morally but from a practical standpoint. How many wars have been averted by patience and persisting good will! Religion and virtue alike lend their sanctions to meekness and humility, not only between men but between nations. How many wars have been precipitated by firebrands! How many misunderstandings which led to wars could have been removed by temporising! How often have countries fought cruel wars and then after a few years of peace found themselves not only friends but allies!

The Sermon on the Mount is the last word in Christian ethics. Everyone respects the Quakers. Still, it is not on these terms that Ministers assume their responsibilities of guiding states. Their duty is first so to deal with other nations as to avoid strife and war and to eschew aggression in all its forms, whether for nationalistic or ideological objects. But the safety of the State, the lives and freedom of their own fellow countrymen, to whom they owe their position, make it right and imperative in the last resort, or when a final and definite conviction has been reached, that the use of force should not be excluded. If the circumstances are such as to warrant it, force may be used. And if this be so, it should be used under the conditions which are most favourable. There is no merit in putting off a war for a year if, when it comes, it is a far worse war or one much harder to win. These are the tormenting dilemmas upon which mankind has throughout its history been so frequently impaled. Final judgment upon them can only be recorded by history in relation to the facts of the case as known to the parties at the time, and also as subsequently proved.

There is, however, one helpful guide, namely, for a nation to keep its word and to act in accordance with its treaty obligations to allies. This guide is called *honour*. It is baffling to reflect that what men call honour does not correspond always to Christian ethics. Honour is often influenced by that element of pride which plays so large a part in its inspiration. An exaggerated code of honour leading to the performance of utterly vain and unreasonable deeds could not be defended, however fine it might look. Here, however, the moment came when Honour pointed the path of Duty, and when also the right judgment of the facts at that time would have reinforced its dictates.

For the French Government to leave her faithful ally, Czechoslovakia, to her fate was a melancholy lapse from which flowed terrible consequences. Not only wise and fair policy, but chivalry, honour, and sympathy for a small threatened people made an overwhelming concentration. Great Britain, who would certainly have fought if bound by treaty obligations, was nevertheless now deeply involved, and it must be recorded with regret that the British Government not only acquiesced but encouraged the French Government in a fatal course.

Appeasement

The Art of the Possible

R. A. BUTLER

Richard Austen Butler was born in India in 1902 and served as undersecretary for India in the Conservative government of 1932–1937 and as undersecretary for foreign affairs from 1938 to 1941. He was accordingly very much involved in the appeasement policy practiced during the pre–World War II period. He was minister of education during the war, and afterward he was a candidate for, but never attained, the leadership of the Conservative party. Why does Butler believe that at the time there was no real alternative to appeasement? What advantages does he say were gained by Britain as a result of postponing the outbreak of war?

Within a few days of my going to the Foreign Office, Hitler had given us one more indication of the shape of things to come by his forcible incorporation of Austria into Germany. The *Anschluss*, I told the assembly at Chatham House, had increased my conviction that 'This country must be strong, strong of purpose and strong in arms. We are living in critical times and it is therefore no more than the plain duty of the government to press ahead with our rearmament programme so that we may have the strength to back our policy and so that in case of need we shall be able to defend ourselves.' Churchill had at last been listened to with rapt attention and respect when he warned the House of Commons that we were confronted with a nicely calculated and carefully timed programme of aggression, unfolding stage by stage. There was general agreement

R. A. Butler, *The Art of the Possible: The Memoirs of Lord Butler* (Hamish Hamilton, 1971) copyright © R. A. Butler 1971. Reprinted by permission.

and apprehension that the next stage would involve Czechoslovakia. Accordingly the Prime Minister asked the Chiefs of Staff for a report on the new military situation following the *Anschluss*. They specified that the Czechoslovak frontier of 2,500 miles could not be protected from a German attack, thus confirming Austen Chamberlain's warning in 1936 that 'If Austria goes, Czechoslovakia is indefensible.' They also advised that Britain was not in a position to wage war, particularly in view of our unreadiness in the air. Later in the summer they reported to the Committee of Imperial Defence that it was of vital importance for us to gain time for the completion of the defence programme. The government was therefore faced with a categorical warning that the country was not ready for war, especially if this involved (as was expected or feared) not only a German front, but conflict in the Mediterranean with Italy and trouble in the Far East with Japan.

This was the unpalatable military appreciation which Chamberlain and Halifax gave to the representatives of France—who alone had a direct treaty obligation to the Czechs—when they came to London at the end of April. The main result of these Anglo-French conversations was therefore a decision to make a joint *démarche* in Prague to secure the maximum concessions from President Beneš. It has been wrongly assumed that Chamberlain believed such concessions would inevitably forestall a German military invasion of Czechoslovakia. On the contrary, he was fully aware, as were all the best of our diplomatic advisers, that the Sudeten problem might not be the real issue and that Hitler might have ambitions far beyond the restoration of Sudeten rights. Chamberlain felt that this was a situation which would have to be faced if it came, but that a world war could not be fought to maintain inviolate the ascendancy of seven million Czechs over an almost equal multitude of discontented minorities. The boundaries of Czechoslovakia had been drawn, as Churchill himself testified, in flagrant defiance of the doctrine of self-determination. There is no doubt that the government of the new State kept the three million Germans in a position of political, educational and cultural inferiority, and that bitterness was exacerbated by the economic depression of the 'thirties which hit the German industrialized areas (the Sudetenland) more severely than elsewhere. These grievances were outrageously exploited by the Nazis and their Sudeten puppet, Henlein; but the grievances were real. In the week of the *Anschluss*, Basil Newton, our Ambassador in Prague, advised us (correctly, as was seen in 1945) that the *status quo* in Czechoslovakia could not be perpetuated even after a victorious war. On 22nd March I wrote to Lord Brabourne in India questioning whether we could defend by force a feature of the Peace Treaties which was in fact indefensible. I indicated that I had tried to get the Cabinet Committee involved to issue a statement saying that we were prepared to seek revision of the Treaties. I also said, 'To summon the League, talk to Litvinov [the Soviet Foreign Minister], or act as mediator between Germans and Czechs, is likely to bring down on our heads more trouble than standing aloof.' This letter proved, alas, to be prophetic.

I was not myself a prime mover in the complex and dramatic events of the succeeding months. As a junior Minister I was little consulted about their cause or course. My role was sometimes that of a sceptical spectator, as when I stood in the Foreign Secretary's room in July studying the glass-fronted bookcase and heard Lord Runciman accept his impossible mediating mission to Prague with the words, 'I am being cut off like a small rowing boat from a great liner.' Throughout the fateful weeks of September I was off-stage in Geneva where, however, I conducted two important interviews with the Foreign Ministers of the Soviet Union and of France. The former convinced me that Russia had no intention of coming to the help of the Czechs, even if the Czechs had wanted this, which they didn't; the latter gave me the measure of France's political unreliability. These two factors were interrelated, since a French declaration of war was stipulated by the Russians to be a condition of their own intervention. I am thus convinced that Sir John Wheeler-Bennett's conclusion about the inevitability of the Munich agreement was correct and, in view of his own vehement and sustained reaction to appeasement, all the more creditable to his historical mastery. 'Let us say of the Munich Settlement,' he wrote, 'that it was inescapable; that, faced with the lack of preparedness in Britain's armaments and defences, with the lack of unity at home and in the Commonwealth, with the collapse of French morale, and with the uncertainty of Russia to fight, Mr. Chamberlain had no alternative to do other than he did; let us pay tribute to his persistence in carrying out a policy which he honestly believed to be right. Let us accept and admit all these things, but in so doing let us not omit the shame and humiliation that were ours; let us not forget that, in order to save our own skins— that because we were too weak to protect ourselves—we were forced to sacrifice a small Power to slavery.' In the light of the events of March 1939 the defenders of Munich, of whom I have always been one, cannot be morally blind to the savage impeachment of those concluding words; but in the light of the political and strategic realities of 1938 the critics of Munich, though deserving all respect, persevere in passion by denying its historical inevitability.

❋ ❋ ❋

I was left in no doubt that the Russians themselves did not mean business. Litvinov had been deliberately evasive and vague, except when he had said that if France acted the Soviet would act too. Since his conversations with his opposite number had been far more numerous and dispiriting than mine, this was tantamount to saying that if Bonnet threw himself off the Eiffel Tower Litvinov would be there to catch him. It seemed to me preposterous for him to pretend ignorance of Soviet military preparations. He was, and gave the clear impression of being, much nearer the centre of power than any other Russian Foreign Minister with whom I have had dealings, and he had been at his desk in the Kremlin in the first week of September. He was perfectly well aware that, in the absence of a common frontier between Russia and Czechoslovakia, the 'barrier' policy of Poland and Roumania would limit Soviet aid to modest air support. Nor is there any evidence that if the railways through the Carpathian Mountains had been available to Russian forces, they would have been capable of rendering effective aid. Appreciations arriving at the Foreign Office from our Embassy in Moscow warned that the great purges of 1937 had had a disastrous effect on the morale and efficiency of the Red Army which, 'though no doubt equal to a defensive war within the frontiers of the Soviet Union, is not capable of carrying the war into the enemy's territory with any hope of ultimate success or without thereby running the risk of endangering the régime.' We now know that precisely similar appreciations were reaching Berlin from the German Ambassador.

Nevertheless, the theory that we deliberately 'excluded Russia from Europe' and that this played a decisive part in the ultimate tragedy was widely held by political opinion at home. It was endorsed after the war by Churchill who, advancing a somewhat medieval interpretation of history, argued that Stalin wanted to help Beneš because in 1936 the latter had revealed a plot against his life. The murders and massacres of his régime hardly reveal Stalin as so warm-hearted a man even in matters concerning his own family. Nor was this hypothetical affection and affinity reciprocal. As Beneš told the French Ambassador in Prague, and as Litvinov admitted more or less explicitly to the League, the Czechs did not wish to accept Soviet intervention unless France acted first. Many Czechs had fought against the Bolsheviks in 1918 and feared Soviet domination. General Jan Syrovy is on record as saying, 'We don't want the Russians in here as we shall never get them out.' Though, in the light of subsequent history, no sentiment compels readier or sadder assent, it was of secondary significance to the British in 1938. For us the criterion was whether Russia intended to oppose the German army, whether indeed she could afford to fight. My interview with Litvinov only confirmed our conclusion that, both on political and military grounds, the U.S.S.R. could not be trusted to wage war in defence of interests that were not bound up with her own security.

It is true that none of the diplomatic negatives I have exhibited were to be any less in evidence in 1939 than they were in 1938. In neither year could any reliance have been placed on the League of Nations to deter aggression. In either year the worm-eaten fabric of French political society and the self-seeking duplicity of the Soviet régime would have combined to leave us alone to face at close quarters the onslaught of the Luftwaffe. But the crucial change that came about as a result of the year's delay was in our preparedness to meet this onslaught. The 'special importance of preparation in the air and of developing the passive resistance of our population,' which had been my theme at Chatham

House in April 1938, proved indeed to be the key factors. In September 1938 the R.A.F. had only one operational fighter squadron equipped with Spitfires and five in process of being equipped with Hurricanes; by the summer of 1939, thanks to Lord Swinton's earlier tenure of the Air Ministry, it had twenty-six squadrons of modern eight-gun fighters, and a year later forty-seven. Our ground defences against air attack were also substantially strengthened in this period. The provision of anti-aircraft guns was increased fourfold to 1,653, of which more than half were the newer 3.7- and 4.5-inch guns, and barrage balloon defence was completed in London and extended outside. More important was the fact that, by the time war broke out, the chain of radar stations, which during the Munich crisis had been in operation only in the Thames estuary, guarded the whole of Britain from the Orkneys to the Isle of Wight. Meanwhile, the administrative talents of John Anderson had wrought corresponding transformations in civilian A.R.P., and plans for evacuating schoolchildren and finding emergency hospital beds were completed.

These preparations extended to the pace and scope of British rearmament generally, as Professor Postan has described in his official history of British war production. But I stress them here both because they undoubtedly constituted the most important defence achievement between Munich and the outbreak of war and because, though we now know that the figures of German strength quoted by our professional advisers and our critics alike to have been greatly exaggerated, they did provide the indispensable means by which we won the Battle of Britain. On this reckoning Munich was not, in Wheeler-Bennett's phrase, a 'prologue to tragedy,' but the pause, however inglorious, which enabled Churchill when his time came to lead the nation through the valley of the shadow to victory. Nor was the military breathing-space the only gain. There were subtler but equally significant changes of opinion at home and abroad. During 1938 it had been possible to argue, and I argued myself, that the principles of self-determination for which the previous war had ostensibly been fought could not be denied to the Sudetens simply because they were Germans or even because they were supported by Nazis. The Treaty of Versailles still weighed heavily. By 1939 the morality was quite clearly all on one side. There could no longer be any doubt in any mind that the ambitions of Germany stretched far beyond its ethnic frontiers and that it had indeed, in Chamberlain's phrase, 'made up its mind to dominate the world by fear of its force.' These considerations affected not only the will and conscience of our own people but the attitudes of Commonwealth governments and of enlightened leaders in foreign countries, most notably in the U.S.A.

Appeasement

A Study in Political Decline

A. L. ROWSE

Alfred Leslie Rowse, noted British historian and writer, has
published extensively on Elizabethan England, on Shakespeare,
and on other historical and cultural subjects including his Cor-
nish childhood. His account of Britain's appeasement policy
has been praised for its intensity and sense of personal commitment. Unlike other critics, Rowse is especially interested in the
appeasers themselves. Why, in his view, did they behave the
way they did?

What was characteristic of this inner group, especially of Chamberlain, Simon
and Hoare, but of the egregious Runciman, Kingsley Wood and Ernest Brown
too—the Chamberlainites as such? There were several things that united them.
They were 'men of peace,' *i.e.* no use for confronting force, or guile, or wicked-
ness. That they did not know what they were dealing with is the most charita-
ble explanation of their failure; but they might at least have taken the trouble to
inform themselves. There were plenty of people to tell them, but they would
not listen. They all shared a Nonconformist origin, and its characteristic self-
righteousness—all the more intolerable in the palpably wrong. These things are
more important than people realise; to the historian they are significant elements. One way or another they had none of the old 18th-century aristocracy's
guts—they were middle-class men with pacifist backgrounds and no knowledge
of Europe, its history or its languages, or of diplomacy, let alone of strategy or
war. Of the most ennobled of them, also middle-class on his paternal side,

Churchill has a verbal comment; 'Grovel, grovel, grovel! First grovel to the Indians, then grovel to the Germans; next grovel to the Americans, then it's grovel to the Russians.' The plain truth is that their deepest instinct was defeatist, their highest wisdom surrender.

※ ※ ※

All the same people were shocked when on 7 September 1938 *The Times* came out with Dawson's notorious leader—Amery describes it as 'mischievous'—advocating the cession of the Sudeten areas: at that juncture a plain invitation to Hitler to take them. John Walter, of the old *Times* tradition, wrote a formal protest to Dawson: 'I felt that our leader on Czechoslovakia yesterday must have come as a shock to many readers of *The Times*, advocating as it did the cause of the Wolf against the Lamb, on the ground of Justice. No wonder there is rejoicing in Berlin.' He received a pretty disingenuous reply—and Dawson could be pretty disingenuous (like Simon) when he tried. After expressing surprise that there was not more criticism of the leader—actually the press rocked with it, 'but personally I think the leader was right. My own impression is that neither Hitler nor Henlein wants a revision of frontiers!' What was the value of Dawson's 'impression' any way? All that we wanted from him was that he should stand for the urgent interests of this country, which were one with the interests of Europe and civilisation. In truth, Hitler wanted not a mere revision of frontiers: he wanted the lot. These people were bent on helping him to it, and nothing could stop them. *The Times History* says that John Walter's 'remonstrance had no effect on their policy'; and anyway they had all the Astors with them all the time.

The Times History admits the sensation the leader caused in Europe—taken everywhere as evidence of retreat beforehand. The Foreign Office had to put out an assurance that no such cession was contemplated; but who would believe its assurance now? Dawson assured B.-W. that Halifax 'does not dissent privately from the suggestion that any solution, even the secession of the German minorities, should be brought into free negotiations at Prague.' More humbug: anyone might know that there could be no free negotiation in these circumstances. The only step that could strengthen our hands in the negotiation would be to call in Russia, and that these people would never do. Dawson's biographer says, 'Geoffrey was certainly influenced too by the thought that Nazi Germany served as a barrier to the spread of Communism in the West.'

This was what was so short-sighted and confused their minds. The immediate and overwhelming danger to Britain was Hitler's Germany. To call Russia into the balance was the only way to contain him, perhaps overthrow him. Amery noted at the time, 'A really definite declaration from the British and French governments any time in the last three weeks might have saved the situation. German generals have actually risked their lives secretly sending word to us that we should make such a declaration in order to stop Hitler in his wild career.' If a break had come inside Germany, as it still could have been forced by resisting Hitler, it is true that the German Army, the generals and conservative forces would have come out on top. Such a Germany, retaining the decencies of civilisation though conservative and resting on the Army, would have been a strong counterpoise to Russia. It was letting Hitler get away with it, until nothing would stop him except war, that let the Russians into the centre of Europe.

These people had no sense of strategy any more than they had of history. Their very pursuit of peace at any price brought the war down on them. Amery noted of Chamberlain's craven speech at the time, harping on the horror of war 'because of a quarrel in a far-away country between people of whom we know nothing': 'Poor Neville. He described himself as a man of peace to the inmost of his being, and that he assuredly is. If ever there was an essential civilian, a citizen accustomed to deal with fellow citizens on City Council or in Cabinet, and a man quite incapable of thinking in terms of force, or strategy or diplomacy, it is Neville. If he survives his efforts as a Foreign Minister I wonder how long he can survive as a war leader.'

※ ※ ※

Considerations on the other side were totally ignored. Amery tells us that 'the heads of the German Army were convinced that they could not possibly have faced a war at that time. General Beck considered it hopeless, as Marshal von Keitel also declared in his evidence at the Nuremberg trial.' The group of generals at this time planned Hitler's arrest; 'at the same time they sent a succession of envoys, more particularly a German Conservative leader, Herr von Kleist, who came over in August "with a rope round his neck" and saw Vansittart and Churchill to tell them that the German Army and people were unanimous against war, but could only stop Hitler if we made our attitude quite clear.' So far from attaching any importance to such information, Chamberlain's environment preferred Lindbergh's. 'The only result was to encourage Chamberlain in his determination to see Hitler personally. This entirely disorganised the generals' coup, which had actually been planned for the very day when Chamberlain flew to Berchtesgaden.' The Mayor of Leipzig, Goerdeler, who was to have been Chancellor in Hitler's place could only comment 'by refusing to take a small risk Chamberlain has made war inevitable.'

These were the circumstances in which Chamberlain was fool enough to go to the footstool, with nothing to negotiate with, never even considering the only possible counterpoise to bring into the balance. Nothing could be more condemnatory than his friend Amery's summing up of it all. 'Inflexibly dedicated to his self-imposed mission, he ignored the warnings of the Foreign Office, dominated his colleagues, overrode wavering French Ministers, brushing aside their moral compunctions as lacking realism, and, to the last moment, refused to acknowledge failure. It was only in that fixed determination that he could persuade himself, in spite of all evidence to the contrary, that Hitler's pledges were sincere, or shut his eyes to the dishonourable aspect of his treatment of the Czechs or to the worthlessness of the guarantees which he persuaded himself at the time he had secured for their future independence and which he afterwards cynically repudiated. . . . Russia's attitude throughout the crisis was perfectly clear. Litvinov had consistently backed the conception of collective security—in effect an alliance between Russia and the Western Powers to meet the growing danger from Germany. . . . Only sheer infatuation with appeasement at almost any price can explain the cold shouldering of Russian offers of help when things were already on the eve of war.'

But Chamberlain was bent on going. He wrote to his sister, 'Afterwards I heard from Hitler himself, and it was confirmed by others who were with him, that he was struck all of a heap, and exclaimed, "I can't possibly let a man of his age come all this way; I must go to London." Of course, when he considered it further, he saw that wouldn't do, and indeed it would not have suited me, for it would have deprived my coup of much of its dramatic force. But it shows a side of Hitler that would surprise many people in this country.' No wonder Hitler used to call him, so Adam von Trott told me, *der Arschloch* [the arsehole]. It was this kind of smug vanity that made us hate him, apart from the mortal danger he was to his country. His biographer, Feiling, can do no better for him than to say, 'simple he was, as his letters show, and obstinately sanguine in that he was bent on finding decency even in dictators.' He reported himself of his first meeting with Hitler, 'I had established a certain confidence, which was my aim, and on my side, in spite of the hardness and ruthlessness I thought I saw in his face, I got the impression that here was a man who could be relied upon when he had given his word.' Vain old fool—his *impression* against all the evidence of perjury, torture, murder, thuggery that had accumulated since 1933, and was there before!

Those of us who understood knew that so far from being 'Peace for our time,' Munich made war certain and in the worst possible conditions—minus thirty-five Czech divisions and without an ally, save a France utterly unnerved and divided within. *The Times* thought that Chamberlain had done better than Sir Edward Grey in 1914; even Halifax repeats this piece of Tory meanness about the Liberal government of 1914. Apropos of the guarantee to Poland in 1939 he says, 'There was in that no room for misunderstanding of the British position as there had been in 1914.' All the historian needs to observe is that in 1914, under a Liberal government, this country entered the war with both France and Russia as allies and shortly gained Italy too to our side; after twenty years of Tory domination and virtually unbroken Tory government—smart they were at elections—this country was on the verge of war with both Germany and Italy, alone save for a France that *we* had broken, only half at our side.

❊ ❊ ❊

How to account for this prolonged aberration of the most eminent?

It is indeed a strange case, and takes some explaining: yet it has its histori-cal significance, and was something of a symptom, a pointer to the future too. These men came at the end of an age; they were late Victorians by birth and upbringing, sharing to the full the standards of that era, with all their limita-tions, public-spirited and respectable, conventional and unimaginative. Indeed, they distrusted imagination and intellectualism; it was not good form to ham-mer things out in discussion, perhaps even to think things out. The contrast here with Churchill is very marked. *The Times History* bears this out in Daw-son, the most powerful man of them all. 'His remarkable capacity to decide quickly the innumerable questions that present themselves every day was ac-companied by a strong reluctance to discuss in detail the serious questions of the time. In conversation it was imperative that such questions be handled lightly. If anyone attempted to entrap him in discussion, or hold forth to him, he was swift in closing the interview. Those in professional contact with him were soon made conscious of particular forms of Dawsonian disapproval. Those lacking a hereditary sense of social tact were briefly dealt with. It was a serious obstacle to a man's progress in the office if he were so unfortunate as to qualify for the description of "Bore."'

That is completely accurate. As I observed Dawson, I regarded him as an empiricist, with no principles, properly speaking, to guide him in a world pro-foundly changing, where the Victorian landmarks were toppling over, their val-ues inapplicable. What was the point of attaching so much importance to social convention? (He used to observe of one Cabinet, half-humorously, that it had all too few Etonians, and not one 'wet-bob' among them—but it was only *half* humorously.)

G. M. Trevelyan has several times suggested one line of explanation for them—there is no excuse—and that perhaps the fairest and best. These decent good men did not know what kind of men they were dealing with in Hitler and his kind. I dare say that is true. But they were told often enough: why would they not take telling?

This leads us nearer the heart of the problem.

As I have said, they were ignorant of Europe and European history; they had read Greats at Oxford, then Dawson went to South Africa and Simon to the Bar. All this group knew more about the Empire than they did about Europe, or the world. In addition, some of them were much influenced by Cecil Rhodes's insistent (and ignorant) pro-Germanism.

There is a further consideration of some interest for political thought—or for those who are interested in English processes of political thought. In this story we see the decadence of British empiricism, empiricism carried beyond all rhyme or reason. In general I am in sympathy with empiricism in politics;

I much prefer it to doctrinairism. The practical way of looking at things, not looking too far in advance (*pace* Amery), not rocking the boat, and other clichés that do duty for thinking ahead, may serve well enough in ordinary, normal times. But our times are not 'normal' in the good old Victorian sense, and never will be again. And this habit of mind in politics will certainly not serve in times of revolution, perpetual stress and conflict, war, the reshaping of the world. This conventional British way of looking at things was simply not equal to the times, and it caught these men out badly.

Even so, the empirical habit of mind, that considered itself so much more practical—E. H. Carr in his writings at the time thought these people more 're-alist' in their estimate of Hitler!—need not have equated itself with ignorance. Not one of these men in high place in those years ever so much as read *Mein Kampf,* or would listen to anybody who had. They really did not know what they were dealing with, or the nature and degree of the evil thing they were up against. To be so uninstructed—a condition that arose in part from a certain superciliousness, a lofty smugness, as well as superficiality of mind—was in itself a kind of dereliction of duty.

They would not listen to warnings, because they did not wish to hear. And they did not think things out, because there was a fatal confusion in their minds between the interests of their social order and the interests of their country. They did not say much about it, since that would have given the game away, and anyway it was a thought they did not wish to be too explicit about even to themselves, but they were anti-Red and that hamstrung them in dealing with the greater immediate danger to their country, Hitler's Germany.

There is a rider to add to this point about class. These men, even Halifax, were essentially middle-class, not aristocrats. They did not have the hereditary sense of the security of the state, unlike Churchill, Eden, the Cecils. Nor did they have the toughness of the 18th-century aristocracy. They came at the end of the ascendancy of the Victorian middle-class, deeply affected as that was by high-mindedness and humbug. They all talked, in one form or another, the language of disingenuousness and cant: it was second nature to them—so different from Churchill. This, and the essential pettiness of the National Government, all flocking together to keep Labour out, was deeply corrupting, both to them and the nation. It meant that they failed to see what was true, until too late, when it was simply a question of survival.

What I had under observation, then, in all those years was a class in decadence. These eminent specimens of it, be-ribboned and be-coroneted—all except Dawson, who, as editor of *The Times,* was above such things—with the best will in the world well-nigh ruined their country and reduced it to a second-rate place in the world.

The total upshot of their efforts was to aid Nazi-Germany to achieve a position of brutal ascendancy, a threat to everybody else's security or even existence, which only a war could end. This had the very result of letting the

Russians into the centre of Europe which the appeasers—so far as they had any clear idea of policy—wished to prevent. Of course their responsibility was a secondary one. The primary responsibility was all along that of the Germans: the people in the strongest strategic position in Europe, the keystone of the whole European system, but who never knew how to behave, whether up or down, in the ascendant arrogant and brutal, in defeat base and grovelling.

These men had no real conception of Germany's character or malign record in modern history. Quite simply, we owe the wreck of Europe's position in the world to Germany's total inability to play her proper rôle in it.

That was no reason why these Englishmen should—largely out of ignorance and confusion of mind—have done everything to aid the process; in the event bringing down the British Empire with it too, for which they cared infinitely more than ever they did for Europe or Europe's place in the world.

Munich after Fifty Years

GERHARD L. WEINBERG

⊠

Gerhard L. Weinberg was born in Germany and educated in the
United States. He has taught at the Universities of Chicago and
Michigan and is currently on the faculty of the University of
North Carolina, where he specializes in modern German and
diplomatic history. He is best known for his two-volume study
of the foreign policy of Nazi Germany and the history of World
War II. The article in the respected journal *Foreign Affairs*, from
which the following is taken, was written on the fiftieth anniversary of the Munich Accord. How does Weinberg challenge the
traditional conception of the pact? Why was Hitler disappointed
in the diplomatic settlement reached? Is Weinberg defending
the decision taken by Chamberlain and Daladier?

Half a century after the Munich conference, that event lives in the public memory as a series of interrelated myths. For most people, Munich represents the
abandonment of a small country, Czechoslovakia, to the unjust demands of a
bullying and powerful neighbor by those who would have done better to defend
it. It is believed that the Allies, by the sacrifice of one country, only whetted the
appetite of the bully whom they had to fight anyway, later and under more difficult circumstances. The "lesson" derived from this widely held view is that it
makes far more sense to take action to stop aggression at the first opportunity.

⊠ ⊠ ⊠

Three aspects of the Munich conference that developed more fully afterward, or on which we are now better informed, suggest that this traditional interpretation warrants a closer look.

In the first place, it was after all the same two Allied leaders who went to Munich, Chamberlain of Great Britain and Edouard Daladier of France, who one year later led their countries into war against Adolf Hitler's Germany, something no other leader of a major power did before his own country was attacked. The Italians, who under Benito Mussolini thought of themselves as a great power, joined with Hitler in June 1940 in what Mussolini saw as an opportunity to share the spoils of victory. Joseph Stalin was sending the Nazis essential war supplies until a few hours before the German invasion of June 1941 awoke the Kremlin from its confidence in an alignment with Hitler. Franklin D. Roosevelt, who had repeatedly but vainly warned the Soviet leader of the German threat, had worked hard to rouse the American people to the dangers facing them; but until confronted by a Japanese surprise attack and by German and Italian declarations of war, he had hoped that Americans might be spared the ordeal of war.

Only Britain and France went to war with Germany out of calculations of broader national interest instead of waiting to be attacked; and it is perhaps safe to argue that without the lead from London, the French government would have backed off in 1939 and awaited a German invasion of its own territory. It is rather ungracious, especially for Americans whose country would not take action to defend either Czechoslovakia or Poland, and which had provided by law that it would not help anyone who did, to condemn as weaklings the only leaders of major powers who mustered up the courage to confront Hitler on behalf of another country.

A second factor that prompts us to take a new look at the 1938 crisis is the view that Hitler, the man usually thought to have triumphed at Munich, is now known to have held of it. The opening of German archives and the new availability of important private papers provide a picture rather different from the one commonly held.

We now know that Hitler had never been particularly interested in helping the over three million people of German descent living inside Czechoslovakia, but only in the ways they might help him in his project to isolate Czechoslovakia from outside support, create incidents that would provide a pretext for the invasion and destruction of that country, and thereafter provide manpower for additional army divisions. The new divisions, in turn, he considered useful for the great war he planned to wage against the powers of Western Europe as the prerequisite for the quick and far easier seizure of enormous territories in Eastern Europe.

Hitler believed that German rearmament was far enough advanced by late 1937 and early 1938 to make this first little war against Czechoslovakia possible. While spreading propaganda on behalf of the ethnic Germans of Czechoslovakia, Hitler was counting on the threat of Japan's advance in East Asia and Italy's support in Europe, and the reluctance of France and England to fight another great war, to isolate Czechoslovakia from outside support. It is understandable in this context that the successful and peaceful annexation of Austria in March 1938 (which left Czechoslovakia even more vulnerable than before), followed by a dramatic reaffirmation of Germany's alignment with Italy during Hitler's visit to Rome, produced Hitler's decision in the second week of May 1938 to go to war that year. We are not ever likely to know whether his belief that he was suffering from throat cancer contributed to his haste; he was certainly a man with a mission in a hurry who would explain later in 1938 that he preferred to go to war at the age of 49 so that he could see the whole issue through to resolution!

But there proved to be inner flaws in his strategy. The prospective allies he had selected turned out to be reluctant. The Japanese at that time wanted an alliance against the Soviet Union, not against the Western powers. Poland and Hungary both hoped to obtain pieces of Czechoslovakia but wanted them without a general European war. The Italians, furthermore, were not as enthusiastic as Hitler thought. Mussolini had given a hostage to fortune by committing large forces to the support of Francisco Franco in the Spanish Civil War, forces certain to be lost in a general war in which they would be cut off from their homeland.

The basic miscalculation of the German government was, however, of a different type: it was integrally related to the issue that Hitler deliberately placed at the center of public attention, the Sudeten Germans living in Czechoslovakia. The purpose of this focus was obvious. The constant attention in both publicity and diplomacy to the allegedly mistreated millions of Germans living in Czechoslovakia was designed to make it politically difficult, if not impossible, for Britain and France to come to Czechoslovakia's assistance when it was eventually attacked. How could democracies contest the principle of self-determination that they had themselves proclaimed? Would they act to turn a small war into a huge one on the unproven assumption that a big war inevitably would come anyway?

But there were aspects of this program that might, from Hitler's perspective, cause problems. One was that the continued diplomatic focus on the Sudeten Germans, which was needed to assure the isolation of Czechoslovakia, might eventually make the transition from diplomacy to war more difficult. The other was that, despite the number and significance of the Germans inside the Czechoslovak state, there were obviously far more Czechs and Slovaks. If ever the real as opposed to the pretended aim of German policy became clear, the very same concept of self-determination that worked against support of Czechoslovakia as long as its German-inhabited rim was under discussion would shift in favor of Prague once the undoubtedly non-German core came into question. It was in this regard that the crisis of the end of September 1938 came to be so dramatic and its resolution, in Hitler's eyes, so faulty.

We now know that Hitler had originally planned to stage an incident inside Czechoslovakia to provide Germany with a pretext for invading that country with the objective of destroying it all rather than merely annexing the German-inhabited fringe. He was influenced by the experience of 1914, when Austria-Hungary had taken the assassination of the Archduke Francis Ferdinand as an excuse to attack Serbia.

※ ※ ※

What, then, went wrong? Why was there no transition from propaganda and diplomacy to war?

The constant emphasis on the Sudeten Germans in Nazi propaganda brought too late a response from the government in Prague, which until August left the initiative to Berlin. And this in spite of a formal and explicit, but confidential, warning to Prague from the French government in July that under practically no circumstances would it come to the defense of its Czechoslovak ally. Keeping this message undisclosed—and it was one of the few secrets that did not leak out in the Paris of the 1930s—was of course essential to the official French pretense that it was the British who were holding them back from full support of Prague, a pretense that turned to panic when the British position hardened and could no longer provide a fig leaf for French unwillingness to act.

The centrality of the nationality issue also created a terrible dilemma for London. Canada, Australia and the Union of South Africa (as it was then known) all made it absolutely clear to the British government that they would not go to war alongside Britain over the Sudeten German question. The British chiefs of staff strongly argued against the risk of military action. If war were to come, it would have to come under circumstances that made the issues clear to the public in Britain and the dominions, and, as the British learned in September 1938, to the French.

It was under these circumstances that on September 13 Neville Chamberlain decided to fly to Germany, originally planning not even to tell Berlin that he was coming until after his plane had taken off. The Germans were startled enough even when notified in advance, and they were trapped by their own propaganda that there were nationality issues to discuss. Moreover, those who genuinely believed in the fairy tale of the "stab in the back"—that Germany had not been beaten at the front in World War I, but had instead lost the war because of the collapse of the German home front—could not risk starting a second war unless German public opinion could be convinced that such a war, with all its costs in lives and treasure, was everybody else's fault.

So the British prime minister had to be received at Berchtesgaden. All he could be told, of course, was the official public line that something had to be done for the poor Sudeten Germans. While Chamberlain set about getting the agreement of France and Czechoslovakia to having the German-inhabited portions of Czechoslovakia ceded to Germany, Hitler began plotting other ways to arrange for war in spite of the meddlesome Englishman. When at their second meeting, on September 22 at Bad Godesberg, Chamberlain offered Hitler an Allied capitulation to his ostensible demands—the French, Czechoslovak and British governments had all agreed to the transfer of the Sudeten territory—the German dictator was dumbfounded and raised new and obviously preposterous conditions for a peaceful settlement.

It was at this point that the issue shifted conspicuously from the fate of the Sudeten Germans to that of the Czechs and Slovaks. Here Hitler was indeed trapped by his own strategy. He now had either to risk a war with Britain and France as well as Czechoslovakia or pull back, call off the planned invasion, and settle for what Prague, London and Paris had already agreed to.

It was not only Germany's military and diplomatic leaders who urged caution on the Nazi dictator. Troubled by the prospect of a general war when the German people gave every sign of being unenthusiastic about it, Hitler's closest political associates, Hermann Göring and Joseph Goebbels, argued for a peaceful settlement. The prospective allies of Germany in this crisis were hesitant, now that war was a real and not merely a theoretical possibility. The Poles certainly wanted a piece of Czechoslovakia, but not at the risk of breaking completely with their French ally and Great Britain. The Hungarians were watering at the mouth over the possibility of realizing their extensive territorial demands: all of the Slovak and Carpatho-Ukrainian portions of the Czechoslovak state and a few additional pieces if they could get them. The authorities in Budapest, however, were very conscious of having only recently begun their own rearmament; they were also fairly certain that Britain and France would go to war over a German invasion of Czechoslovakia and that such a general war would end in a German defeat.

Hitler never forgave the Hungarians, whose resolution, in his eyes, was not commensurate with their appetite, but he was even more astonished by the defection of his most important ally, Italy. Mussolini's urging him to settle for the German-inhabited fringe of Czechoslovakia instead of attacking that country as a whole—when Hitler had expected encouragement to go forward, along with a full promise of support—appears to have played a major part in his decision to recall the orders for war, already issued, and instead agree to a settlement by conference at Munich.

Precisely because he had not tested the predictions of those who had warned against an attack on Czechoslovakia, Hitler was then and ever after angry over having pulled back. He projected his own reticence onto others, denouncing as cowards those whose advice he had followed instead of testing his own concept in action, and despising the British and French leaders before whose last-minute firmness he had himself backed down.

If the Munich agreement, which others then and since have regarded as a great triumph for Germany, appeared to Hitler then and in retrospect as the greatest setback of his career, it was because he had been unwilling or unable, or both, to make the shift from propaganda and diplomacy to war as he had always intended. He had been trapped in a diplomatic maze of his own construction and could not find the exit to the war that he sought. In the last months of his life, in 1945, as he reviewed what had gone wrong and caused the dramatic descent from Germany's earlier heights of victory, he appears to have asserted that his failure to begin the war in 1938 was his greatest error, contributing to the eventual collapse of all his hopes and prospects.

In the intervening years he was most careful not to repeat what he considered were the great errors of 1938. A massive campaign was begun to rally the German people for war. As Hitler put it on November 10, 1938, meeting with the German press, the peace propaganda designed to fool others had carried in it the risk of misleading his own people into thinking that peace, not war, was intended. Thereafter, Hitler would sometimes postpone but would never again call off an attack on another country once ordered, and he would never again allow himself to be trapped in diplomatic negotiations.

In 1939 German ambassadors were kept away from London and Warsaw; they were in fact forbidden to return to their posts. The incident the Nazis had planned as the pretext for war against Poland—an assault on a radio station inside Germany—would be organized and managed directly from Berlin. Furthermore, as Hitler explained to his military leaders on August 22, 1939, he had things organized so well that his only worry was that at the last minute some *Schweinehund* would come along with a compromise and again cheat him of war. The allusion to Chamberlain and Munich was unmistakable. And it ought to be noted that this "lesson" of Munich remained with him. When the Soviet Union made desperate efforts in 1941 to avert war with Germany, by volunteering the most extensive concessions, by offering to join the Tripartite Pact and by soliciting diplomatic approaches from Berlin, Hitler once again claimed to be worried about only one thing: a last-minute compromise offer that would make it difficult for him to continue on the road to yet another extension of the war.

As for the remainder of Czechoslovakia, he was even more determined that it be destroyed. The German government devoted itself in the months after Munich to accomplishing that objective, never realizing that, in the face of universal relief over the avoidance of war, the violation of the agreement just signed would make any further step by Germany the occasion for war. In 1939 no one listened to Nazi tales of persecuted Germans in Poland; the Germans themselves had demonstrated to everyone that such propaganda was merely a pretext for actions with entirely different objectives. And when soundings were taken in London before the invasion of Poland, the answer was that Czechoslovakia must have its independence back first before any negotiations; similar soundings after the German conquest of Poland were answered with the demand that both Czechoslovakia and Poland be restored to independence. Since Hitler and his associates had not been interested in the fate of those who had been used as propaganda instruments, they never could understand that others had taken the issue seriously—but only once.

A third facet of the Munich agreement as we look back on it from the perspective of fifty years is the light shed on events by the opening of wartime archives and the progress of research. The account of German policy presented here is in large part based on materials that became available after World War II. The British archives have also been opened and show a government hoping against hope for a peaceful settlement, but prepared to go to war if there were an invasion of Czechoslovakia in spite of all efforts at accommodating what were perceived as extreme but not entirely unreasonable demands. We now know that Chamberlain was correctly reported as willing to contemplate the territorial cession of the German-inhabited portions of Czechoslovakia in early May 1938, and that the British knew that there was no serious French military plan to assist Czechoslovakia—the only offensive operation planned by the French if war broke out was into Libya from Tunisia. It is now also known that in June 1938 Winston Churchill explained to a Czechoslovak official that it was essential for Czechoslovakia to work out an agreement with Konrad Henlein, the leader of the Sudeten Germans, and that although he, Churchill, was criticizing Chamberlain, he might well have followed the same policy if he had held the responsibilities of power.

It is also clear that there were serious doubts within the British government—which may or may have not been justified—about the ability of Britain and France to defeat Germany, and a determination that if war came and victory were attained, the German-inhabited portions of Czechoslovakia would *not* be returned to Prague's control.

The question of whether or not Britain and France would have been militarily better off had they gone to war in 1938 will remain a subject for debate for historians. Most would agree that the defenses of Czechoslovakia would have proved more formidable in 1938 than those of Poland in 1939, but then the question remains whether, since there was to be no attack by the French in the west in 1938, a somewhat longer Czechoslovak resistance would have made any significant difference. It can be argued that the Germans used the last year of peace more effectively than the British and the French, but it must also be recalled that new British fighter planes and radar defenses would not in any case have been available to meet a German onslaught in 1939 as they were for the Battle of Britain in 1940. And the excellent Czechoslovak tanks Germany acquired must be weighed against Poland's essential 1939 contribution to breaking the German Enigma-machine code.

7

RESISTANCE OR COLLABORATION?

The Example of Vichy France

In one sense Vichy stands as a classic example of collaboration in World War II; in another it is unique, for no lawfully constituted government of any other occupied country chose to cooperate with the victorious enemy. France fell a scant six weeks after the German attack that began May 10, 1940. Fearful that a continuation in North Africa of what appeared to be a hopeless struggle might provoke civil unrest, Marshal Philippe Pétain, the hero of the Battle of Verdun in World War I, formed a government and negotiated an armistice. On July 10, at the resort town of Vichy in unoccupied France, a remnant of the French legislature by a large majority voted Pétain full power to issue a new constitution. The next day he took the title chief of state, repealed the Constitutional Laws of 1875, and indefinitely adjourned the Chamber of Deputies and the Senate. On the initiative of Pierre Laval, who had been appointed vice premier, Pétain met with Hitler at Montoire on October 24. The Vichy regime, as it became known, attempted to replace France's Third Republic with a new order, the "National Revolution," and unhappiness with the prewar Popular Front electoral coalition of Socialists, Communists, and Liberals induced many Conservatives to follow Pétain in his quest. The motto "Work, Family, Country" replaced the revolutionary slogan of "Liberty, Equality, Fraternity," and "The French State" (L'Etat français) superseded "The Republic." Anti-Semitic and anti-Communist decrees were passed, as were laws establishing rigid censorship and vast increases in state power.

Pétain's appeal defies simple explanation. His supporters assert that at times he tried to resist the harshest forms of Nazi pressure and intimidation, for example, by dismissing Laval in December 1940 and by writing to Hitler defining the limits of collaboration. (However, under German threats, Laval was replaced by men whose willingness to collaborate was beyond doubt, and Laval himself was subsequently reappointed.) There are still people in France, like the concierge Madame Lucie, who praise Pétain for having saved her sons: "While de Gaulle left us, the Marshal stayed with us, though he was an old man."[1]

Others, however, opposed Pétain and chose to resist, aware that any amount of collaboration, though it might seem a lesser evil than the "Polandization" of France, must lead the French down a slippery moral slope and result in Vichy France becoming Germany's most important supplier of both goods and labor during the war years.

The story of the Resistance fell subject to mythology in the decades after the war, when apparently nearly everyone had been a resister. Then in the 1970s came demythologizing with a vengeance, as highlighted by such films as Marcel Ophuls' *The Sorrow and the Pity* and Robert O. Paxton's history of Vichy, which revealed the extent to which so many of the French collaborated, or supported collaboration. Most recently, some historians have rejected the belief that Vichy enjoyed wide support; they consider misleading both the Gaullist view of France as a nation of resisters and the revisionist view of a nation of collaborators.

What is one to conclude from these samples, drawn over a thirty-five-year span, from the histories of the Vichy experience? That much depends on how one defines collaboration and resistance? That history may be distorted because it is written by those on the winning side, in this case the Gaullists who created the myth of a nation of resisters? That revisionists may sometimes distort history as well? That if there were minorities committed to Vichy or the Resistance, a majority of the French was motivated by self-interest, which would explain the growth of resistance movements as Allied victory became more probable? Although there were collaborators in all the occupied countries, why was Vichy the only example of official government collaboration? To what extent was Vichy a reflection of an indigenous fascism? Finally, what should be said about the moral dilemma confronted by the French? Does not the dramatic historical situation represented by Vichy reinforce the validity of Sartre's existential interpretation: that every person has the freedom to choose a course of action, but what is not possible is not to choose, for this too is a choice?

---

[1] Bonnie Smith, *Confessions of a Concierge: Madame Lucie's History of Twentieth Century France* (New Haven: Yale University Press, 1985), p. 64.

The Vichy Regime

ROBERT ARON

🏵

Robert Aron participated in both the rival Giraud and de Gaulle movements in Algiers during World War II. He published many works of history, including material on Vichy and on the liberation of France. He also wrote studies of Jesus, Waterloo, and French Socialism. How legitimate is it to present French collaborationists and particularly Pétain as victims of circumstance doing their best to shield France from Nazi tyranny? How does Aron distinguish between Pétain and Laval, and how does he explain the Marshal's willingness to face his accusers as the war drew to an end?

Very early, on Thursday 24th October (1940), the Head of the State left Vichy. He did not conceal his great satisfaction at meeting the Führer.

🏵 🏵 🏵

The conversation that followed bore little relation to that between Hitler and Laval. A difference which, with an interval of only two days, was due to three causes.

In the first place, Hitler had returned weary and disappointed from his interview with Franco. For nine hours, the two men had discussed the conditions for Spain's entry into the war. Franco, forewarned by Pétain, and determined not to yield, put forward demands which made agreement impossible. He asked for the whole of French Morocco and part of Algeria. For all their polite words, Franco inflicted a complete defeat on Hitler on the 23rd

From Robert Aron, *The Vichy Regime, 1940–1944,* pp. 216, 218–221, 224–225, 310–311, 460–463, 514–515, 517. Permission granted by The Bodley Head, publishers.

October. On the 24th, when he met Pétain, the Führer was still suffering from his disappointment: he had none of that dynamism which, two days before, had so impressed Laval.

A second difference between the interview of the 22nd and 24th was that the principal negotiator with the Chancellor had changed. Instead of it being Laval, whose attitude was precise and who was ready to take his stand at the side of Germany, it was now the Marshal who, having decided to refuse military collaboration with the Reich, avoided making any precise promises.

Resolved not to yield on the essential points, Pétain was led to make a concession on a matter which he judged to be of secondary importance, without realising its gravity. It consisted, on Hitler's demand, of making a broadcast extolling collaboration.

Hitler opened the interview with one of his customary monologues.

"I am certain of winning the war, but I must finish it as soon as possible, for nothing is more ruinous than war. England will have to pay the greater part of the cost. But every European country will suffer from its prolongation.

"It is therefore in their interest to form a continental community with the object of shortening the duration of hostilities.

"What position does the French Government propose to adopt?"

Pétain saw in this an excellent opportunity for replying vaguely: certainly, he was prepared to accept collaboration in principle, but he could not immediately specify to what extent France could participate; ways and means must be studied by his Government.

▨ ▨ ▨

Pétain cleverly took the opportunity of making a diversion: since the Führer had spoken of peace, would he state in what terms he envisaged the final treaty, "in order that France might know her fate and the two million prisoners return as soon as possible to their families?"

As, no doubt, the Marshal expected, Hitler avoided answering: the final treaty could only be considered after the ultimate defeat of England. Pétain then observed that, while waiting upon events, measures must be taken to assure the early return of the prisoners at least, to ameliorate the situation with regard to the demarcation line, which was creating an intolerable situation, and to reduce the indemnity for the occupation.

To these questions, which for Pétain were the real object of the interview, Hitler did not reply with an immediate refusal: he agreed to study them.

The fate of the prisoners was, he knew, one of the means of exerting pressure to which Pétain was most sensitive. Hitler, also, by this shift, re-introduced the problem of collaboration and put the deal squarely before the Marshal: "If France and Germany achieve an agreement on collaboration, France may expect concessions on all the points the Marshal has mentioned."

At this point, Laval intervened: "Thanks to the Führer's offer, France is no longer face to face with a blank wall. . . . However, in spite of my own personal desire to do so, I recognise that there are difficulties in declaring war on England. . . . Public opinion must grow accustomed to the idea and then, in accordance with constitutional law, we need the consent of the National Assembly."

There followed a long speech by Laval, who repeated almost word for word his declarations of two days before and reaffirmed his desire to collaborate. Pétain listened without saying a word and only spoke again to demand the return to France of the departments in the north which had been attached to the military government in Belgium; he was less precise over Alsace-Lorraine.

Hitler finally promised to make known in writing his position on the various points raised; the Marshal, for lack of any more concrete promises, would make a radio appeal inviting the French to collaborate with Germany and thus, for lack of the reality, content himself with words. So the interview came to an end. Pétain, throughout, had been extremely reticent. Having obtained from Marshal Keitel the freeing of General Laure and an authorisation to visit a Prisoners' Camp near Amboise, the Marshal left for Vichy, where he arrived on the evening of the 25th and, on the 26th October, informed the Council of Ministers of the results of the interview. The impression he gave them was very different from that given by Laval in the Council of the 23rd after the first meeting at Montoire.

For Pétain, there was no question of military collaboration with Germany: Montoire had merely been an opportunity to make contact. The Marshal had not gone beyond the limits he had set himself.

※ ※ ※

Thus, the Montoire interview aggravated and lent precision to the initial disagreements which, since the 25th June, 1940, had separated Pétain and Laval.

For the Marshal, the armistice was not and could not be more than a pause, which allowed France to exist provisionally, while awaiting the outcome of the war between England and the Axis; Montoire, looked at from his point of view, was but an episode and made no change in his policy towards Germany.

For Laval, on the other hand, the armistice permitted of a reversal of alliances, of which Montoire, in the most definite way, was to mark the beginning.

It is clear that Montoire was the origin of a triple misunderstanding whose consequences were to weigh heavily upon the whole Vichy drama.

Misunderstandings between Pétain and Laval, which were soon to come to a head in the clash of the 13th December; misunderstandings between Hitler and the Marshal on the exact meanings of "collaboration" and Franco-German relations, which would bring in their train the occupation of the free zone in November, 1942, the scuttling of the Fleet and, in August, 1944, the removal of Pétain by the Germans.

But there was also another misunderstanding, more grievous and more eventful in its dramatic and long term consequences for France, more complex and profound, though perhaps involuntary, between Pétain and public opinion. The majority of Frenchmen did not and could not understand what Pétain's real attitude, after Montoire, was towards the occupying power.

They did not know that by his secret message to Franco, Pétain had tried to torpedo the interview before even going to it.

They did not know that at Montoire he had not agreed to the proposals put forward by Hitler and Laval.

They did not know that, at the same time, he was carrying on negotiations with London.

They only knew of his spectacular statements on the French radio in which he extolled in words the collaboration he had been constrained to accept, but which he had decided never to allow to become military engagements.

Certain words have a terrifying and injurious power, when the head of a vanquished State, after an interview with the conqueror, expresses himself as did Pétain on the 30th October:

"It is in all honour and in order to maintain the unity of France—a unity of ten centuries within the framework of the constructive activity of the new European Order—that I am today pursuing the path of collaboration. . . . This collaboration must be sincere. It must bring with it patient and confident effort. An armistice, after all, is not peace. France is constrained by the many engagements she has taken towards the conqueror. At least, she remains sovereign. This sovereignty imposes upon her the duty of defending her soil, to extinguish divergency of opinion and to diminish the number of dissidents in her colonies. This policy is mine. The Ministers are only responsible to me. It is I alone whom history will judge.

"Until today I have spoken to you the language of a father. Today I speak to you in the language of a leader. Follow me. Put your faith in France eternal."

These words, even admitting that they were only words, were fateful in their consequences.

Montoire is perhaps the principal cause of the appalling crises of conscience that Vichy imposes on public opinion.

It explains why, for instance, certain patriots, who were originally loyal to Pétain, now tore up their photographs of the Marshal, who had, during the first months, been the object of their veneration and in whom they had placed their hopes. At Vichy itself, it brought about the resignation of the Secretary-General of the Ministry of Foreign Affairs, François Charles-Roux.

Conversely, it justified to some extent the actions of all those who believed that, by collaborating, they were obeying the Marshal and serving the country. This speech of the 30th October incited many Frenchmen to take a path that was to be fatal to them.

❈ ❈ ❈

Pétain and Darlan tried to negotiate, each on his own level, as Pétain and Laval had done after the armistice.

Darlan used Benoist-Méchin as intermediary to establish contact with Ribbentrop and Keitel. But Keitel said to the French emissary:

"If France does not give Germany the control she demands in North Africa, she will be treated like Yugoslavia."

And, a fortnight before, between the 6th and 8th April, the Luftwaffe had bombed Belgrade, even though the capital of Yugoslavia had been declared an open town; it had caused 12,000 casualties.

Pétain had recourse to the good offices of a certain German art historian, Erckmann, a confidant of Hitler's, in order to get a letter to the Führer in which he complained in violent terms of the German proceedings in France. This letter remained unanswered.

At the same time, Pétain made a speech over the radio in which he was categorical: "Honour," he said on the 11th April, "demands that we should not undertake anything against our old allies."

Similarly, on the 14th February, he had assured the Caudillo, during the course of an interview at Montpellier, that he would never let the Germans enter North Africa.

❈ ❈ ❈

On the 4th December, Otto Abetz reappeared on the scene, having been recalled from disgrace by Ribbentrop.

❈ ❈ ❈

In an interview which lasted half an hour, the Ambassador gave the Marshal a letter from Ribbentrop dated 29th November. It was a long document, which took the Marshal to task for his permanent resistance to the occupying power.

Ribbentrop began by recapitulating the crisis of the 13th November: it denoted a state of mind "in open contradiction to the policy of collaboration between France and Germany." Then he transmitted, on behalf of the Führer, an ultimatum containing five points:

1. The Chancellor opposed all remitting of power to the National Assembly "which, in September, 1939, had declared war on Germany without any cause whatever, and of which a not negligible proportion of members are again fighting against Germany."

2. Since no election could take place in time of war, there existed, and could exist, "no legal body capable of exercising the functions which the proposed

broadcast wished to confer on it, and which, for this purpose, could be recognised by Germany."

3. The Führer took the opportunity of declaring that the Marshal had not remained loyal to the spirit of collaboration envisaged at Montoire, but had on the contrary shown "permanent resistance." "The policy of the supreme controllers of the French State at Vichy has pursued a direction which the Government of the Reich cannot approve and which it will not accept in the future in its capacity as occupying power, in view of the fact that it is responsible for the maintenance of order and public calm in France."

After these threats, here are the terms of the ultimatum:

4. "The Government of the Reich is compelled to demand that the supreme direction of the French State should in future submit all proposed modifications of laws to the agreement of the Government of the Reich [a statute for a Protectorate]; that, moreover, Monsieur Laval, should be charged with re-organising the French Cabinet without delay in a manner acceptable to the German Government as a guarantee of collaboration. This Cabinet must thereafter enjoy the unreserved support of the supreme directorate of the State.

"Finally, the supreme direction of the French State will be responsible for taking measures to eliminate immediately all elements obstructive to the important work of recovery in the influential posts of the administration and also for appointing persons worthy of confidence to these posts."

After this ultimatum, clause 5 was an insolent piece of blackmail.

5. "Today, the one and only guarantee for the maintenance of public calm and order in the interior of France and thereby the security of the French people and its regime against revolution and Bolshevik chaos is the German Wehrmacht . . . I pray you to take such action that Germany will be able to safeguard these interests in all circumstances by one means or another."

In conclusion, there was a formal recognition of the "freedom" left to the Marshal: "If however you do not consider that you are in a position to respond favourably to the German demands mentioned above, or if our rejection of your proposed law, directed against German interests, should decide you to consider yourself afterwards as before prevented from exercising your functions, I am to inform you, in the name of the Führer, that he leaves you entirely free to draw what conclusions you please. . . ."

It was an invitation, couched in barely diplomatic terms, to submit or resign.

Pétain's reaction was dignified. With his hands clasped, he replied: "I perfectly understand the meaning of this letter and as a soldier I cannot admit what you say. But it has taken three weeks to give me this answer. It raises extremely delicate questions which I want to consider. I would like to see you again to-morrow morning to give you my reply."

Abetz agreed to the delay, but not without inflicting two somewhat spe-cious arguments on the Marshal. If Pétain refused, he was playing the game of the Communists. While the summoning of the National Assembly in the case of the Marshal's death placed a premium upon it. The "British Intelligence Ser-vice" would not fail to make use of it. "Do you think so?" said the Marshal.

"Yes, Monsieur le Maréchal, and we wish to preserve you."

All this did not unduly alarm the Head of the State; hardly had Abetz left when he openly took Romier for a little walk and confided in him as follows:

"Really the Germans are not clever politicians and Monsieur Laval is ab-surd to hang on to them. If he thinks that Churchill and the Americans will sit down at the same table as himself, he's making a big mistake. He'll prevent my welcoming them, and that's all he'll succeed in doing. If he was really intelli-gent, he would have taken the opportunity I gave him of flying to the Argen-tine or elsewhere."

✖ ✖ ✖

Alone of all the survivors of Vichy, Pétain wished at all costs to return to France. The Marshal, while still at Sigmaringen, had learned on 5th April, by the radio, that his trial would begin in Paris on the 24th April. Far from wish-ing to avoid appearing, he desired to reply personally to the accusations.

"Monsieur le Chef de l'Etat Grand Allemand," he immediately wrote to Hitler, "I have just learned that the French authorities propose to put me on trial in my absence before the High Court of Justice. The trial will begin on the 24th April. This news imposes an obligation on me which I look on as impera-tive and I ask your Excellency to facilitate my accomplishing my duty.

"I received on the 10th July, 1940, from the National Assembly, a mandate which I have fulfilled to the best of my ability in the circumstances. As Head of the Government in June, 1940, at Bordeaux, I refused to leave France. As Head of the State, when grave hours once more faced my country, I decided to re-main at my post in Vichy. The Government of the Reich compelled me to leave on the 20th August, 1944.

"I cannot, without forfeiting my honour, allow it to be believed, as some tendentious propaganda is insinuating, that I sought refuge in a foreign country in order to evade my responsibilities. It is only in France that I can answer for my actions and I am the only judge of the risks that this attitude may entail.

"I therefore have the honour of earnestly asking your Excellency to give me this opportunity. You will naturally understand the decision I have reached of defending my honour as Head of the State and of protecting by my presence all those who have followed me. It is my only object. No argument can make me abandon this decision.

"At my age, there is only one thing one still fears: it is not to have done all one's duty, and I wish to do mine."

✠ ✠ ✠

At the agreed hour, a leading French official, the Commissaire de la République of Dijon, entered Swiss territory to meet Pétain and inform him that a warrant had been issued against him: the Marshal was to be placed under surveillance.

At the Frontier, the barrier rose; the cars entered France and stopped.

A few soldiers and policemen hesitated, uncertain whether they should present arms or not. A General came forward and asked the Marshal to get out of his car: it was General Koenig, whom Pétain did not know.

Having placed his foot to earth, the Marshal extended his hand. Koenig refused to take it.

Vichy France

Old Guard and New Order

ROBERT O. PAXTON

Robert O. Paxton, professor emeritus at Columbia University, has published three books on Vichy France. The book from which the following excerpts are drawn has had considerable impact both in the English original and in the French translation, and, unlike earlier works on the Vichy government, it has made extensive use of German archival material. How does Paxton attempt to debunk the myth that France was a nation of resisters? In what way does his view of Pétain differ from Aron's? How, specifically, does he treat the rationales for collaboration made by Vichyites? In his opinion, what was the real explanation for their decision to collaborate?

The prospect of liberation by the sword, under the auspices of "brigands," was anything but alluring to many Frenchmen. Some 45,000 volunteered for the infamous Milice in 1944, partly, perhaps, to escape from labor service, partly for fanaticism, but at least in part to help defend "law and order." Counting police and military guard units as well, it is likely that as many Frenchmen participated in 1943–44 in putting down "disorder" as participated in active Resistance. Almost every Frenchman wanted to be out from under Germany, but not at the price of revolution.

Under these conditions, the number of active Résistants was never very great, even at the climactic moment of the Liberation. After the war, some 300,000 Frenchmen received official veterans' status for active Resistance service: 130,000 as deportees and another 170,000 as "Resistance volunteers." Another 100,000 had lost their lives in Resistance activity. This brings the total of active Resistance participation at its peak, at least as officially recognized after the war, to about 2 percent of the adult French population. There were no doubt wider complicities. But even if one adds those willing to read underground newspapers, some two million persons, or around ten percent of the adult population, seem to have been willing to take even that lesser risk. Let nothing said here detract from the moral significance of those who knew what they had to do. But the overwhelming majority of Frenchmen, however they longed to lift the German yoke, did not want to lift it by fire and sword.

⌧ ⌧ ⌧

In the end, one must make some overall judgment of the immediate results of collaboration for Frenchmen. With all its one-sided social favors and with all its complicity in the brutal last stages of nazism's paroxysm, did it not save many Frenchmen from still worse direct German administration? Was it not better to have Frenchmen administering Frenchmen than the tender ministrations of a gauleiter? Did not the Vichy regime save France from "Polandization"? Did it not "éviter le pire"?

⌧ ⌧ ⌧

Pierre Laval, in his turn before the High Court, claimed that his government had managed to "éviter le pire," to act as a "screen" between the conqueror and the French population. The refrain was taken up by succeeding defendants before the High Court and by a stream of self-exculpating memoirs.

Despite these partisan origins, the material advantage theory has been quite widely accepted. Robert Aron, trying to strike a reasonable balance on the basis of the trial records, the only sources available in 1954, argued that life was easier, statistically speaking, for Frenchmen than for others in occupied Europe. The reproaches against Vichy, he said, are moral rather than material.

In its most widespread form, the material advantage thesis argues that Vichy kept France from "Polandization," and everyone knows that the Poles suffered more in World War II than the French. Nazi contempt for Slavic Untermenschen makes Poland an invalid comparison with France, however. Nazi purists might well cast aspersions upon French "mongrelization" and lack of racial self-consciousness, but they did not contemplate French extinction. The shield theory must be understood in terms of actual German demands, rather than in terms of vaguely infinite possibilities of evil. It can be validly tested only in comparison with fully occupied Western countries like Belgium, Holland, or Denmark, or other collaborating regimes like Quisling's Norway. If incomplete occupation or the existence of a quasiautonomous indigenous administration spared France any of the rigors of direct German rule, those favors should show up in comparison with fully occupied Western countries without an indigenous collaborationist regime.

One can suppose two ways in which Vichy France could have suffered less than France under a gauleiter. The German occupation authorities might have asked for less in order to reward and solidify a useful collaborationist regime. Or if the German occupation authorities asked no less of France than of fully occupied Western nations, the Vichy regime might have been better able or more willing to refuse excessive demands than would a gauleiter. A hard comparative look at the material conditions of life in Western occupied countries fails to show any important advantage for France, either granted by or extorted from Berlin.

Frenchmen were no better nourished than other Western occupied countries. Comparison of caloric intakes in France and fully occupied Western nations is, of course, treacherous ground, for access to food depended greatly on one's location, ready cash for the black market, or connections—and a cousin on the farm might be more useful in that respect than a cabinet minister. Average figures mean even less in this case than in most, and agricultural statistics are certainly less reliable for French *paysans* than for Danish dairy farmers. Nevertheless, it appears that French caloric intake was the lowest in Western Europe, with the exception of Italy, which is astonishing for so rich an agricultural country. Furthermore, in Eastern Europe, Rumania, Bulgaria, Hungary, and the Protectorate of Bohemia-Moravia seem to have eaten better than France. French caloric intake is estimated to have descended under the occupation as low as 1,500 calories a day where there was access to black market supplies and even lower for city populations where there was not.

Not all the French hunger can be attributed directly to German occupation policy, of course. With much food production in the hands of a notoriously small, independent, and secretive peasantry, France suffered as much from maldistribution as from genuine shortages. Moreover, France had depended before the war upon imports of some staples, such as vegetable oils, so that Allied blockade and shipping shortages made matters worse.

There is no sign, however, that Vichy managed to win significant concessions in those areas where German policy added to French hunger. The armistice provision (copied from that of 1918) that French prisoners of war should not be repatriated until the peace produced a serious labor shortage in agriculture, keeping French agricultural production from ever returning to prewar figures. The petroleum shortage prevented the replacement of farm laborers with machines. Moreover, the gigantic German requisitions of French foodstuffs, for the occupying army and for export to the Reich, were among Germany's most important single sources of nourishment. France supplied more foodstuffs to Germany, both absolutely and relatively, than did even Poland.

It was indeed explicit German policy that the French should have a lower standard of living than the Germans. Both Goering and Abetz, as we have seen, thought that Frenchmen should have less to eat than Germans. Abetz stated early in July 1942 that French wages must remain lower than those in Germany (which had been the lowest in industrial Europe in the 1930s) so that French workmen would go to work in Germany.

It begins to look as if material conditions of life in occupied Europe depended less upon avoiding total occupation and having an indigenous regime than upon Germany's ethnic feelings about the occupied power and upon simple opportunity. Bargaining by Vichy was quite incapable of preventing increases in Germany's food delivery quotas in France in the summer of 1942 and in early 1943 or of preventing France, the richest agricultural producer of the occupied nations, from experiencing localized malnutrition.

❀ ❀ ❀

There remains the somber business of the Jewish Final Solution. It is true, as Xavier Vallat claimed, that a larger proportion of the Jewish populations of totally occupied Holland, Belgium, Norway, and Italy (totally occupied after 1943) perished than that of France, even taking refugees and citizens together. The real question, however, is not whether fewer Jews were deported from France than from the totally occupied countries, but whether more Jews were deported from France because of Vichy preparations and assistance than would have been the case if the Germans had had to do it all alone. Vichy bears a heavy burden of responsibility, seen in these terms.

It is true that the unoccupied zone of France provided a refuge of sorts for tens of thousands of Jewish refugees from Germany and Eastern Europe for the first two years. Republican France having taken over from England the role of Europe's refugee haven in the late nineteenth century, German Jews and then, after September 1939, Polish Jews, followed a well-worn path to the west. The fact that the armistice and the division of France into two zones kept many of these refugees one jump ahead of the German armies was not the result of any Vichy sentimentality about the refugees. In fact, Vichy objected vigorously when the Germans delivered more expatriate Jews into the unoccupied zone in the fall of 1940. After protest, Vichy acquiesced in Article 19 of the armistice, which empowered Germany to demand the extradition of German citizens who had sought refuge in France. Under this provision, such prominent figures as Herschel Grynspan (who had assassinated a German diplomat in Paris in 1938) and the socialist economist and Weimar minister Rudolf Hilferding were delivered back into German hands—an ominous first warning about the precariousness of asylum in Vichy France. Moreover, Vichy did everything possible to encourage the further emigration of Jewish refugees. At a time when French Jews were being uprooted from the economy, there was no possibility of foreigners settling. Vichy also revoked some recent citizenships, enlarging the number of Jews in France without the protection of citizenship. Finally, Vichy gathered destitute Jewish refugees into work camps. Although Pétain spared them the yellow star, thousands were waiting behind barbed wire when the Germans came into the unoccupied zone in November 1942. Only those with money had managed to use southern France as a springboard for safer havens. For the rest, the French tradition of refuge made the unoccupied zone a trap.

The possibilities of sheltering Jews in southern France were far greater, say, than in the ghetto of Amsterdam. Furthermore, by the time the Germans actually arrived in southern France, in November 1942, there had been ample time for emergency arrangements. The final irony is that Italian-occupied Alpine France provided the cover in 1943 that Vichy refused. Many French citizens did the same, but the Vichy authorities deserve none of their credit. Vichy bears the guilt for not having used its opportunity for the kind of escape operation that the totally occupied Danes managed to carry out by moving almost the entire Jewish population by small boat to Sweden in September 1943.

This survey suggests that the shield theory hardly bears close examination. The armistice and the unoccupied zone seemed at first a cheap way out, but they could have bought some material ease for the French population only if the war had soon ended. As the war dragged on, German authorities asked no less of France than of the totally occupied countries. In the long run, Hitler's victims suffered in proportion to his need for their goods or his ethnic feelings about them, not in proportion to their eagerness to please. Vichy managed to win only paltry concessions: a few months of the *relève* instead of a labor draft, exemption from the yellow star for Jews in the unoccupied zone, slightly lower occupation costs between May 1941 and November 1942, more weapons in exchange for keeping the Allies out of the empire. Judged by its fruits, Vichy negotiation was barren.

In the last analysis, fruitful negotiation depends upon some comparable capacity of each party to threaten the other with damage if acceptable compromises are not made and to withhold that damage if acceptable compromises are made. Vichy's one serious threat—to take fleet and empire over to the Allied side—lacked credibility. Vichy leaders could not exercise it without suffering more than the Germans. To be sure, the Germans did not want the effort and expense of a total occupation of France. Vichy leaders could delude themselves for the first months that France had found a cheap way out of the war. Even after the sufferings increased, however, they could not flee abroad without sacrificing the National Revolution, their commitment to internal order, and, after the Gaullists took over the empire from the Giraudists, their personal liberty and even life.

❋ ❋ ❋

There is, finally, a grave moral case to be made against the Vichy elite. There is, first of all, the charge of using the defeat of 1940 for narrowly sectarian purposes, to seek revenge upon the Popular Front and to remake France along new lines, no less partisan than the old and in the service of narrower interests. This does not mean that they had plotted the defeat of France in advance. But their domestic enmities were so all-consuming, after four years of the Popular Front and its successors, that they committed the most elementary of political errors. They wrote new laws under an armed foreign occupation.

There is also the charge of abetting the further internal division of France. No other major occupied country entered the war so torn; no other major occupied country used the occupation as the occasion for such a substantial restructuring of domestic institutions. When biographies of Marshal Pétain began to appear in 1966, it became regular practice to blame the poisons of division attending the Liberation upon de Gaulle's rigorous sectarianism and the upwelling of revenge encouraged by Resistance lawlessness. A will to healing reconciliation coexisted within the Liberation forces alongside a well-justified determination to purge and punish the collaborators, however. It was most visible in the Liberation army, a successful amalgam of Armistice Army, Free French, and Forces Françaises Libres under two ex-Pétainiste officers (Marshals de Lattre de Tassigny and Juin) and one Gaullist officer (Marshal Leclerc de Hauteclocque). If that will to reconciliation did not prevail over the will to revenge in 1944, it was very largely because the Vichy regime had not been the mere caretaker regime in 1940–44 that its defenders claim. Vichy waged another round in the virtual French civil war of the 1930s. Then, its geopolitical gamble having failed and war having ended neither in German victory nor in a French-mediated compromise but in total Allied victory, Vichy reaped the winds of sectarian passion that it had sown.

There is, finally, the issue of complicity. Continually repurchasing its shadow sovereignty at a higher and higher price, the Vichy regime made many Frenchmen accomplices in acts and policies that they would not normally have condoned. Marshal Pétain, in particular, was a figure to whom millions of Frenchmen looked with more than usual confidence. After the total occupation of France in November 1942, or at least after the constitutional crisis of November–December 1943, it was time to cease lending the stamp of one's approval to an enterprise that no longer worked. "Old age is a shipwreck," as de Gaulle observed, but Germans who met Pétain in 1943 still found him fresh and alert. Moreover, he was surrounded by men whose brilliance of preparation and of administrative career made them superior to the Third Republic leadership of the late 1930s. These able and intelligent men led other Frenchmen deeper into complicity with the besieged Third Reich's last desperate paroxysms:

the Final Solution, forced labor, reprisals against a growing resistance. What can explain such egregious choices?

Tactical motives, the hope of saving France from worse, can not explain that complicity after November 1942. Of the four elements composing the Vichy bargaining position—military defeat, continuation of others in the war, the stranglehold of German occupation upon the richest two-thirds of France, and the exclusion from German grasp of the French fleet and empire—only the last one was ever within Vichy's control. After the total occupation of France, the scuttling of the French fleet, and the return of French North Africa to war in November 1942, Vichy no longer had even that leverage. Life was clearly no easier for Frenchmen by then than for the totally occupied Western European countries.

Clearly other motives led Frenchmen deeper into that final complicity. Bureaucratic inertia and blindness to considerations beyond the efficiency of the state were among them. Beyond that was the attraction of the National Revolution for its partisans.

At bottom, however, lay a more subtle intellectual culprit: fear of social disorder as the highest evil. Some of France's best skill and talent went into a formidable effort to keep the French state afloat under increasingly questionable circumstances. Who would keep order, they asked, if the state lost authority? By saving the state, however, they were losing the nation. Those who cling to the social order above all may do so by self-interest or merely by inertia. In either case, they know more clearly what they are against than what they are for. So blinded, they perform jobs that may be admirable in themselves but are tinctured with evil by the overall effects of the system. Even Frenchmen of the best intentions, faced with the harsh alternative of doing one's job, whose risks were moral and abstract, or practicing civil disobedience, whose risks were material and immediate, went on doing the job. The same may be said of the German occupiers. Many of them were "good Germans," men of cultivation, confident that their country's success outweighed a few moral blemishes, dutifully fulfilling some minor blameless function in a regime whose cumulative effect was brutish.

Readers will prefer, like the writer, to recognize themselves in neither of these types. It is tempting to identify with Resistance and to say, "That is what I would have done." Alas, we are far more likely to act, in parallel situations, like the Vichy majority. Indeed, it may be the German occupiers rather than the Vichy majority whom Americans, as residents of the most powerful state on earth, should scrutinize most unblinkingly. The deeds of occupier and occupied alike suggest that there come cruel times when to save a nation's deepest values one must disobey the state. France after 1940 was one of those times.

Choices in Vichy France

JOHN F. SWEETS

John F. Sweets received two graduate degrees from Duke University and since 1977 has been teaching at the University of Kansas. How can his view of the Vichy regime be compared to that of Aron? What is the nature of his disagreement with Paxton and how does the question of defining a resister help explain this disagreement?

In describing their eventual fate and by treating them apart from the earlier discussion of the National Revolution, I do not wish to imply that the SOL [Service d'Ordre Légionnaire, which became the Milice Française, collaborationist groups] or the Milice—nor, for that matter, the Parisian collaborationists—were somehow foreign to the true French experience, or mere creatures of the occupation, unrelated to the French past. The best of recent scholarship has demonstrated conclusively that the history of Vichy is best understood as a whole. There was not a "Vichy of Pétain" in contrast to a "Vichy of Laval," but a regime that evolved over time in an increasingly authoritarian direction within a framework of changing conditions. The growing literature on the phenomenon of collaboration has established beyond question that these movements, representing to varying degrees a French form of fascism, although drawing special advantages from the occupation era, were firmly rooted in the French past. On the other hand, I do hope readers will see that these collaborationist organizations represented a very small minority of the French population. Most French people were unwilling to accept the ideology and programs associated with Vichy's National Revolution. A still greater number, indeed an overwhelming majority, rejected the more aggressive and violent designs of the collaborationist parties and the

Milice, who, for themselves, rarely had any illusions about their unpopularity and isolation within the national community.

As often occurs with problems of historical interpretation, in recent years there has been a shift away from an earlier, particularly Gaullist perspective, which had portrayed France during the occupation as a nation of resisters with only a handful of rascally collaborators to mar the nation's behavior during this tragic era. A wave of films in the 1960s and 1970s—notably *The Sorrow and the Pity,* which purported to re-create the experience of Clermont-Ferrand during the war and occupation—and several important studies of collaborationist movements and individual collaborationist leaders have focused much more attention on those aspects of the era that were considered less pleasant, perhaps even better forgotten. We should not ignore the fascism, anti-Semitism, and other disreputable phenomena that rose to the surface in occupied France with generic French origins; but these should be placed in proper perspective. In otherwise excellent accounts, some of the authors of this recent literature on the collaborationists have exaggerated the strength of collaborationism, sometimes subtly by implication, or more directly by a questionable interpretation of statistics concerning membership in collaborationist groups. Although no serious study of which I am aware argues that collaborationists were more than a tiny minority of the population, we are led to believe that there were roughly as many collaborationists as resisters in France. As the liberation approached, the feud between these two extremist minorities erupted in a bloody civil war. Reaching this point, the pendulum of historical interpretation has swung far beyond a version that can be supported by a careful scrutiny of the evidence. If one were forced to choose a myth, the Gaullist version of a "nation of resisters" would be far more accurate than the new myth of a "nation of collaborators." Although there was a great deal of excitement and some violence, there was no "Franco-French civil war" at the liberation for the very good reason that there was virtually no one around anxious to fight for Vichy's New Order, much less for the more extreme visions of the ultracollaborationists. The tremendous surge of enthusiasm for the resistance was almost universal and represented a genuine following out of all proportion to the small comfort the population had afforded the collaborationist groups in their prime.

The status of the extreme right in France, at least as measured by the size of its constituency, *fell* during the German occupation, even though some of their ideas were incorporated into governmental policy, public activity on the part of their prewar rivals to the left was dissolved and prohibited, and they received some support from the Germans. In the 1930s Doriot's PPF [Parti Populaire Français] and Colonel de la Rocque's Parti Social Français (PSF) each attracted far more adherents than all of the wartime collaborationist groups combined. The PPF and the other collaborationist organizations were much less popular under the occupation, no doubt because they were linked so closely to the German conquerors in the popular mind. That so many people considered the collaborationists creatures of the Germans during the occupation helps to explain how they were so easily dismissed as "un-French" after the liberation. A brief discussion of the membership, motivations, and activities of the collaborationist groups at Clermont-Ferrand will suggest a theme of some continuity of leadership with past extremist organizations and demonstrate the futility of efforts by these groups to obtain popular support. Although the relative strength of these movements was undoubtedly greater in other parts of the country, local studies of collaborationist groups elsewhere indicate that the feeble response to collaborationist organizations at Clermont-Ferrand was not inconsistent with the general pattern for France.

❖ ❖ ❖

In order to successfully convey the atmosphere or reconstitute the history of France under the German occupation, a reformulation of the definition of resistance is required. The notion of a small band of activist conspirators must be made to square with, or be incorporated into, a broader perspective that will account for the existence of an atmosphere in 1943–1944 in which resistance was nurtured by massive and widespread popular complicity, while collaboration, its polar opposite, was discouraged, and collaborators were made to feel like outcasts in their own land. The existence of an extensive network of sympathizers and accomplices beyond the framework of the organized resistance has sometimes been overlooked or underestimated in scholarly accounts of the Vichy period. The problem at one level is simply one of counting, where documentation is incomplete and often unreliable. Beyond that basic consideration are problems of definition and interpretation. We know that many individuals who were not members of resistance movements committed acts of opposition to the Vichy regime or to the Germans. How many such actions were necessary for one to be considered a resister? Or was membership in an organized group required before acts of opposition could be described as resistance? A definition that is limited to active members of organized groups has the advantage of greater precision, but such a limitation may prohibit an adequate appreciation of the *phenomenon of resistance*. A broader construction of the term *resistance,* involving a concept of *active opposition* to the Vichy regime and the Germans, is admittedly unwieldy. But it is also truer to the complex reality of the resistance in France.

To illustrate the methodological and interpretative issues involved, let us consider the conclusions of one of the most objective and fair-minded general histories of the Vichy period. Starting with what seems to be an unchallengeable proposition that most people in France were neither active resisters nor active collaborators, and repeating an earlier scholarly estimate that perhaps 400,000 persons, or 2 percent, of the adult population of France belonged to the resistance, Robert Paxton has written that if one lumps together volunteers for the Milice, regular police, and French guard units, "it is likely that *as many Frenchmen participated in 1943–44 in putting down 'disorder' as participated in active Resistance*," adding that "the overwhelming majority of Frenchmen, however they longed to lift the German yoke, did not want to lift it by fire and sword." Other authors, taking their cue from Paxton, or following a similar logic, have posited the concept of a "Franco-French" civil war at the liberation. According to this scenario, extremists on either side fought it out, while the vast majority of the population stood aside, uncommitted and uninvolved. Insofar as these perspectives have served to revise an earlier viewpoint—the myth that all the French were resisters during the Nazi occupation of France—they have served a useful purpose. Our study of Clermont-Ferrand and the Auvergne suggests that the revision has been overdrawn, that the idea of a "nation of resisters," while unquestionably an exaggeration, cannot be dismissed out of hand.

※ ※ ※

Consider, for example, that at least 543 persons, not included in the preceding figures [for members of resistance organizations], were executed *(fusillés)* "for acts of resistance" in the Auvergne (238 in the Puy-de-Dôme, 120 in the Cantal, 27 in the Haute-Loire, and 158 in the Allier); more than 1000 persons were arrested by the Germans in the Puy-de-Dôme in 1943 and 1944; and at least 1171 were deported from the Puy-de-Dôme to concentration camps in Germany or central Europe for political motives or resistance, as were hundreds of other suspected resisters in the other three departments of the region. If one adds several hundred persons the French police arrested on suspicion of Communist propaganda or "antinational" activity, many of whom were sent to internment camps, and recalls the massive opposition to the forced labor draft from which several thousand Auvergnats escaped by direct acts of disobedience, the total numbers of individuals *actively involved* in opposition to Vichy and the German occupation, although still a minority, becomes a substantial minority. Moreover, to this point we have dealt only with individuals who, after a great deal of painstaking research, could be identified and counted individually. What of those men and women who, while not found on the membership lists of a resistance formation, nor on the lists of deported, executed, or outlawed, contributed in a meaningful way to the resistance? Can one omit the doctors in the Puy-de-Dôme, who although not usually members of resistance movements, sabotaged the operation of the STO [Service du Travail Obligatoire] and the attempted requisition of men for railroad guard duty by signing hundreds of certificates of physical incapacity for individuals who the police complained continued "to pursue as usual their occupations"? What of the village priests who were credited by the resisters with numerous acts of bravery in sheltering those sought by French and German authorities, or those men and women who gave work, food, and shelter to maquis groups or individuals forced to live off of the land?

On Armistice Day 1943, in response to tracts signed by the CGT [Confédération Général du Travail, the largest trade union federation], MUR [Mouvements Unis de la Résistance, a major national resistance group], the Front National, and the Socialist Party, hundreds of workers at Ollier, Bergougnan, Michelin, and the other major factories at Clermont-Ferrand stopped working for ten or fifteen minutes at 11:00 A.M. in a symbolic protest, and even the thirty saleswomen at Prisunic joined them by crossing their arms in silence. Several months before that, when Marcel Michelin had been arrested by the Germans, all 7000 employees of the Michelin firm were preparing to go out on strike until the management convinced them that such an action might bring further harm to Monsieur Michelin. Beyond such specific incidents, of which there are other examples, how can one quantify the amount of passive resistance involved in high worker absence from the workplace? Especially during the last months of the occupation, absence rates were 20 percent or more above normal in the mines and factories of the Puy-de-Dôme. Although loud explosions were more likely to draw attention to resistance sabotage, some resisters believed that much had been accomplished by workers in silent, but more subtle actions, such as faulty wiring of precision parts for airplane motors that were machined ever so slightly under specifications. Interestingly, at Clermont-Ferrand's most important industrial center, the Michelin works, management insisted that there be no sabotage in terms of inferior workmanship. The company was very concerned that Michelin uphold its reputation for making only "the best tires." On the other hand, the company produced far fewer tires than it was capable of manufacturing and was able to hide fairly significant quantities of material from German overseers. And, of course, the resistance movements had contacts in the factory who informed them when shipments of tires were scheduled for delivery, so that large quantities of "the best tires" would not arrive in Germany.

One could continue to enumerate an impressive array of individuals responsible for actions not attributable to the organized resistance—the fifteen-year-old girl who on her own initiative burned the records of hundreds of young men scheduled to be drafted for the STO, public employees charged with collecting and melting down metal statues who saved them from destruction by delays and falsification of records, directors and staff at Clermont-Ferrand's central hospital who were suspected by police of "a tacit connivance" with the resisters and political prisoners who seemed to escape with a remarkable frequency when in treatment there, or numerous PTT [Postes Télégraphes et Téléphones] agents singled out for particular praise by resistance leaders because of their courageous and timely warnings concerning military or police movements by German or French forces. A comprehensive listing would be at least as impressive as those more spectacular sabotage or guerilla actions of the organized resistance formations.

What was the cumulative impact of all of these isolated acts of opposition to the Vichy regime and the German occupation? In terms of "effectiveness" in hindering the German war machine, the value of such actions is impossible to calculate. Who knows how many, if any, airplane motors failed in flight or tanks broke down on the eastern front as a result of the sabotage of workers in factories at Clermont-Ferrand? We do know that factories in the city producing goods for Germany were constantly behind schedule in filling orders, despite the careful supervision of German officials. No one would claim that the hundreds of thousands of French men and women who listened to the BBC or read and passed on to friends copies of underground newspapers were great heroes, no more than were those who participated in symbolic strikes of short duration or mingled anonymously among crowds that gathered in city squares for fleeting demonstrations on May Day or Bastille Day. Yet these actions were illegal under Vichy France, and they signified a choice consciously made, and never entirely without risk.

Eugène Martres has concluded that one in six persons in the Cantal was associated with the resistance in one way or another as a sympathizer or active participant, suggesting that there were perhaps ten sympathizers for every resister. I have been unable to arrive at a satisfactory estimate of that kind for the Puy-de-Dôme, although resistance membership and the range of its activity was certainly higher there than in the Cantal. After more than fifteen years of research into the matter, I have become convinced that (short of a roll call in the hereafter) we will never have an entirely satisfactory statistical description of the French resistance. Even the rosters of FFI [Forces Françaises de l'Intérieur, resistance movement] and lists of the various resistance medals awarded after the liberation are highly untrustworthy gauges for minimum calculations. For example, at Clermont-Ferrand when Alphonse Rozier was asked by the prefect of the Puy-de-Dôme to suggest members of the Front National who had been particularly distinguished in their service to the resistance, Rozier suggested the name of a young woman, killed by the Germans, who had been an intelligence informant for his organization, and was a prostitute. The prefect apparently felt that there was something undignified or improper about awarding a resistance medal to a prostitute, and consequently Rozier refused to submit other names or accept a commendation himself. Therefore, the numbers of people active in the Front National are understated in "official" records of resistance membership. The problem, really, is not to add some names to one roster or subtract others where claims of resistance derring-do have been exaggerated. One must go beyond the ultimately insoluble issue of precise head counts to an appreciation of the general atmosphere, the climate in which resistance operated in the last two years of the German occupation.

Earlier chapters of this study have demonstrated the relatively rapid disenchantment of the Auvergnat population with Vichy's New Order and the patent failure of most of the regime's policies, the increasingly hostile reaction to German troops and occupation policies, the overwhelmingly negative response to genuine collaborationist groups, and the evolution of public opinion toward enthusiasm for a Gaullist political alternative. Therefore, it was not surprising that disgruntled police officers reported time after time that they were unable to obtain help from the local population in their efforts to fight resistance in the Auvergne. Gendarmes in the countryside cited "enormous difficulty in the search for information about the terrorists," and referred to "a veritable conspiracy of silence and a pretense of ignorance." Their colleagues in the cities remarked that witnesses to robberies or sabotage never seemed to remember license numbers and were never able to describe vehicles used by resisters, and they noted "a tacit complicity on the part of the population." Numerous documents originating from central police headquarters at Vichy indicated that this situation was not peculiar to the Auvergne—that "the individuals being sought often benefit from the sympathy of the population and start off with numerous accomplices."

If one is looking for heroes, a choice to remain silent was certainly not comparable to full-time commitment to resistance activism. Still, in the conditions of occupied France, the cumulative weight of such decisions was significant. Moreover, when one considers the other side of the coin, the climate in which the "forces of order" were operating, the difference was striking. As surely as a simple enumeration of membership in the FFI understates the size of the resistance in France, calculations of the total number of Milice, GMR [Gardes Mobiles de Réserve, an antiresistance organization], and French police overstate the number of those *actively opposing* the resistance. First, effective Milice membership has often been greatly exaggerated. Instead of the more than 1000 adherents suggested by some accounts, no more than 250 men actually fought resisters in Milice formations drawn from the Puy-de-Dôme. According to the careful records of the officer in charge of all uniformed security forces for the Puy-de-Dôme, with headquarters at Clermont-Ferrand, 2237 men and officers were available for duty in the summer of 1944. Not only was this number well below the number of armed resisters in the department, but, for reasons that were discussed earlier in this chapter, these men were by no means reliable upholders of public order.

Not without reason had the Vichy regime begun to threaten its own servants with harsher and harsher penalties for failure to carry out the government's orders. In addition to the desertions on D-Day of large numbers of police and gendarmerie units surrendering their arms to maquis units, the verdicts of postliberation purge committees for the police and gendarmerie offer another indication of how little substantial support the Vichy regime enjoyed in its last months. Since the commission included a significant number of resisters, lenient treatment of officers who had actively fought the resistance was unlikely. Individual notations concerning those police examined by the purge commission suggest that it was almost impossible to be maintained on the police force if one had fired a weapon in operations against the maquis. Officers who had participated in such operations, but had shown no zeal in action versus the resistance, were not usually penalized. Under that sort of careful scrutiny, only 244 policemen in the Auvergne were sanctioned by loss of their job, transfer to another region, or some other form of punishment. In other words, aside from the Milice and a few GMR units, in the last months of the occupation resisters in the Auvergne did not find Vichy's "forces of order" to be serious threats, except, of course, when they operated in conjunction with German troops or the Gestapo.

No "Franco-French" civil war took place at the liberation in the Auvergne (nor for that matter elsewhere in France) because no one was left to fight for Vichy once the German troops had departed, taking with them the last diehard supporters of a French and European New Order. The liberation of France brought the establishment of the government of Charles de Gaulle without the widespread disorder and even chaos that some had predicted. No one should have been surprised. What a minority of French men and women had fought for during four long years was what almost everyone wanted—the Germans driven out of their country and freedom to choose their own way in the future. They had given scant aid and comfort to the enemy and little more to the government of Pétain and Laval. And when a skeptic asked, "What did you do when the Germans were there?" and thought that many seemed to embrace too eagerly the myth of a nation of resisters, most French people could answer honestly: "Our hearts were in the right place."

8

THE HOLOCAUST

One would think that unlike other topics in this anthology the Holocaust does not lend itself to varying and conflicting interpretations. Except to a handful of perverse or anti-Semitic writers who deny it occurred, the facts seem clear. Nazi racial policy was described by Hitler in *Mein Kampf,* in which he stated his belief in Aryan racial supremacy and his contempt for "lesser" peoples. At the bottom rank, below that occupied by Slavs, were Jews and gypsies, as well as gay men and lesbians[1] from all racial and religious groups. In the 1930s, legislation was enacted to exclude German Jews from public life and to try to force them to emigrate. There is evidence that in conversations, in a speech, and in a memorandum dated January 25, 1939, Hitler spoke of his intention to destroy the Jews. After World War II began and millions of Jews were brought under German control, thousands were murdered by SS troops.[2] A "final solution," that is, the annihilation of the Jews, was ordered in the summer of 1941. It soon became clear, however, that such methods as machine-gun fire presented technical obstacles to genocide because of the large number of victims involved. In early 1942, at a conference in Wannsee, a Berlin suburb, plans were formulated by high-ranking Nazis for assembly-line destruction of the Jews by gassing. Six centers were established, the largest at a Polish rail center near the village of Auschwitz where an average of twelve to fifteen thousand deaths per day could be managed. From roundup points, Jews from everywhere in conquered Europe

---

[1] Paragraph 175, which outlawed homosexuality in 1871, applied only to males. There are, however, a few documented cases of lesbians being removed to concentration camps solely on the basis of their sexual orientation.

[2] The SS stands for "Schutzstaffel," translated as "protection force." Created in the early 1920s, the original purpose of the SS was to protect Nazi party leaders. After Heinrich Himmler assumed leadership of the SS in the late 1920s, however, the organization grew from an elite group to a massive police force designed to promote Nazi terrorism. During World War II, the SS set up Einsatzgruppen, or action groups, which rounded up and massacred two million Jews in Nazi-occupied territories.

were dispatched by trains, and with horrible efficiency about six million were killed, approximately two-thirds of the previous Jewish population of Europe and about two-fifths of all the Jews in the world. Most came from Poland (three million) and the Soviet Union (one-and-a-half million), but with some exceptions, such as Denmark, Jews in other countries died in proportionate numbers. How mass extermination was carried out with ruthless efficiency is the subject of Raul Hilberg's meticulous and authoritative investigation.

Questions can nevertheless be raised. How did Nazi anti-Semitism evolve into mass murder? Hitler's racial ideology notwithstanding, was the Nazi leadership influenced by the additional millions of Jews in the newly conquered lands and by the imperatives of an inefficient bureaucracy? Exactly how important was Hitler's own role? Persecution could not have been effective without the participation—or acquiescence—of ordinary German men and women. These issues are explored by a controversial scholar of the subject, Daniel Jonah Goldhagen. The debate between "intentionalists," convinced that mass destruction was decided on from the outset, and "functionalists," who see it as the end of an evolutionary process, is discussed by Michael Marrus. Of equal concern is the reaction, or lack of it, by the Allies, even when confronted with evidence that mass murder was taking place. Why did the Allies not aggressively try to save Jews before the war's end? Why did they refuse, for example, to bomb the rail facilities at Auschwitz? Historians Walter Laqueur and David S. Wyman analyze these questions and arrive at different conclusions.

The Destruction of the European Jews

RAUL HILBERG

Raul Hilberg came to the United States from Vienna, served in
the U.S. Army, and, as a member of the War Documentation
Project, examined masses of German records. He began work
on *The Destruction of the European Jews* in 1948 and has published several studies concerning the fate of European Jews. He
served as a member of the U.S. Holocaust Memorial Council,
and he testified for the Department of Justice in cases against
individuals implicated in the killings. The following excerpt
comes from the revised edition of *The Destruction of the European Jews*, a book concerned with the *process* by which the Holocaust took place. The "machinery" of destruction is recounted
in sequential steps: first the definition of who were Jews, then
their expropriation, their deportation, and, finally, their annihilation. The excerpt that follows describes the clearing of the
ghettos that the Jews were forced to inhabit and their subsequent removal to extermination centers.

In the Reich-Protektorat area [most of Czechoslovakia], considerable difficulties
were caused by privileged or semi-privileged categories of Jews. No such en-
cumbrances hindered the deportations in Poland. There was no Mischling [half-
Jew, of which there were different categories] problem, no mixed-marriage
problem, no old-Jews problem, no war-veterans problem. There were only a
handful of foreign Jews in Poland, some of whom were pulled out of the ghettos at the very last minute and some of whom were shipped to killing centers by
mistake. Only one major difficulty arose in connection with any particular

group of Jews, and that problem did not become acute until the end of 1942: the labor shortage. Arrangements had to be made to keep a few skilled laborers alive a little longer. These arrangements, which were concluded at the close rather than at the beginning of the deportations, will be discussed later.

As the ghetto-clearing operations began, notice of roundups would sometimes be given to the Polish population in announcements posted a day or so in advance. The Poles were told that any ghetto passes in their possession were canceled, and they were warned against lingering in the streets or opening windows while the evacuation was in progress. Anyone interfering with the operation or giving shelter to Jews was going to be punished by death, and any unauthorized presence in a Jewish apartment was going to be construed as pillage.

Inside the ghettos, the policemen and their helpers had to cope with another problem: filth, sewage, and vermin. In the words of the Gettoverwaltung, the work was "nauseous in the extreme [*im äussersten Grade ekeleregend*]." In the Galician ghettos the police were confronted by vast epidemics. In the ghetto of Rawa Ruska, the Jewish population had concealed its sick in holes in the hope of saving them from deportation. Before the Rawa Ruska Aktion was over, the SS and Police had dragged 3,000 sick and dying Jews out of their hiding places. We have no overall figures for German losses incurred by reason of the epidemics, but in Galicia alone SS and Police Leader Katzmann reported that one of his men had died of spotted fever and that another 120 had fallen ill with the disease.

After a ghetto was cleared of Jews, the police and municipal officials had to reenter the Jewish quarter and clean it up. Although Poles and Jews could be used for some of the dirtiest labor, the job was still far from pleasant. A large ghetto could be emptied in two or three days, but the cleanup operation required weeks or even months. Thus the Lublin ghetto was disbanded and its inhabitants deported April 17–20, 1942, but the cleanup action (*Säuberungsaktion*) was still in progress two months later.

The operation was carried out in stages. First, a demolition Kommando entered the ghetto and blew up all uninhabitable buildings. Next came the salvage crew (*die Lumpensammelkolonne*), which collected all sorts of junk left behind by the deportees. This detachment was followed by a clearing Kommando (*die Aufräumungskolonne*), which had to do the hardest work: the cleaning of the latrines. In some latrines the feces were piled up to a height of three feet. The Aufräumungskolonne had to use hoses to clean up the mess. The fourth crew consisted of carpenters and glass workers who sealed hermetically all doors and windows in order to enable the gas column (*Vergasungskolonne*) to kill all vermin in the apartments. Finally, the cleanup column (*Reinmachungskolonne*) was called up to remove the dead rats, mice, flies, and bugs, and to tidy up the place.

Still, the dilapidation in the ghettos was a comparatively minor annoyance in the total picture, and the bureaucrats were not much concerned with it. Their primary worry was the progress of the deportations, the rate at which Jewry was disappearing. The top men were interested only in speed. As early as June 18, 1942, Staatssekretär Dr. Bühler asked Higher SS and Police Leader Krüger when he would finish. Krüger replied that in August he would be able to "survey" the situation.

Krüger was a bit cautious because just then he was experiencing his first *Transportsperre*, a complete shutdown of traffic in deportation trains. The *Transportsperre* was instituted for only two weeks, and Krüger managed even then to wangle a few trains from Präsident Gerteis of the Ostbahn. Moreover, after the lifting of the restrictions, Krüger expected to resume the deportations with redoubled effort. Then, in July, another hitch occurred when the railway line to the killing center of Sobibór, on the Bug, broke down and had to be repaired. The SS and Police had hoped to deport several hundred thousand Jews to Sobibór.

On July 16, 1942, Obergruppenführer Wolff, chief of Himmler's Personal Staff, telephoned Staatssekretär Dr. Ganzenmüller of the Transport Ministry for help. Ganzenmüller looked into the situation and found that the matter had already been settled locally. Three hundred thousand Warsaw ghetto Jews had been diverted from Sobibór to Treblinka. Beginning on July 22, 1942, a daily train crammed with not fewer than 5,000 Jews per run was to leave Warsaw for Treblinka, while twice weekly another train carrying 5,000 Jews was to run from Przemyśl to Bełżec. When Wolff received this news, he wrote the following letter of thanks:

Dear Party Member Ganzenmüller:
For your letter of July 28, 1942, I thank you—also in the name of the Reichsführer-SS—sincerely [*herzlich*]. With particular joy [*mit besonderer Freude*] I noted your assurance that for two weeks now a train has been carrying, every day, 5,000 members of the chosen people to Treblinka, so that we are now in a position to carry through this population movement [*Bevölkerungsbewegung*] at an accelerated tempo. I, for my part, have contacted the participating agencies to assure the implementation of the process without friction. I thank you again for your efforts in this matter and, at the same time, I would be grateful if you would give to these things your continued personal attention.
   With best regards and

Heil Hitler!
Your devoted
W.

At the end of 1942, when the deportations were already two-thirds over, the SS and Police offices were confronted by another breakdown. Urgently, Krüger wrote to Himmler:

SS and Police Leaders today report unanimously that by reason of Transportsperre every possibility of transport for Jewish resettlement is cut off from December 15, 1942, to January 15, 1943. Because of this measure, our master plan for Jewish resettlement is severely jeopardized.

Obediently request that you negotiate with central offices of Armed Forces High Command and Transport Ministry for allocation of at least three pairs of trains for this urgent task [*dass mindestens 3 Zugpaare für die vordringliche Aufgabe zur Verfügung stehen*].

Apparently the negotiations were not very successful this time, for on January 20, 1943, Himmler wrote to Ganzenmüller for more trains. The Reichsführer pointed out that he knew under what strain the railway network was operating but that the allocation of the trains was, in the last analysis, in Ganzenmüller's own interest. The Jews, said Himmler, were responsible for all the railway sabotage in the Generalgouvernement, the Białystok district, and the occupied eastern territories. Hence the sooner the Jews were "cleared out," the better for the railways. While writing about the eastern Jews, Himmler also took occasion to remind Ganzenmüller that unless trains were made available for the Jews of the western occupied areas, sabotage would break out there too.

While the shortage of transport was a particularly pressing problem in the planning of the whole operation, a host of complications was to arise after the organizational problems were solved. These ramifications developed like shock waves from a single point of impact: the discovery by outsiders of the true nature of the "resettlements."

If concealment was difficult within the German-Czech area, it was doubly difficult in Poland. The Reich-Protektorat area had no death camps and most Reich transports were moving out to the east. Poland, on the other hand, was the home of all six killing centers and Polish transports were moving in short hauls of not more than 200 miles in all directions. Many eyes were fixed on those transports and followed them to their destinations. The deputy chief of the Polish Home Army (London-directed underground force), General Tadeusz Bor-Komorowski, reports that in the spring of 1942 he had complete information about the Kulmhof (Chełmno) killing center in the Warthegau. When the Germans cleared the Lublin ghetto, the Polish underground traced the transports to Bełżec. The underground command could not find out what was going on inside Bełżec, but, estimating that 130,000 Jews had been shoved into the camp, the Poles concluded that it "was not big enough to accommodate such a large number of people." In July 1942 the Home Army collected reports from railroad workers that several hundred thousand Jews had disappeared in Treblinka without a trace.

Sometimes the information spilling out of the camps was quite specific. In the Lublin district the council chairman of the Zamość ghetto, Mieczysław

Garfinkiel, was a recipient of such news. During the early spring of 1942 he heard that the Jews of Lublin were being transported in crowded trains to Bełżec and that the empty cars were being returned after each trip for more victims. He was asked to obtain some additional facts and, after contacting the nearby Jewish communities of Tomaszów and Bełżec, was given to understand that 10,000 to 12,000 Jews were arriving daily in a strongly guarded compound located on a special railroad spur and surrounded by barbed wire. The Jews were being killed there in a "puzzling manner." Garfinkiel, an attorney, did not give credence to these reports. After a few more days, two or three Jewish strangers who had escaped from Bełżec told him about gassings in barracks. Still he did not believe what he heard. On April 11, 1942, however, there was a major roundup in Zamość itself. Counting the remaining population of his ghetto, Garfinkiel calculated a deficit of 3,150 persons. The next day, the thirteen-year-old son of one of the council functionaries (Wolsztayn) came back from the camp. The boy had seen the naked people and had heard an SS man make a speech to them. Hiding, still clothed, in a ditch, the young Wolsztayn had crawled out under the barbed wire with the secret of Bełżec.

What the Home Army had found out through its investigations, and what Garfinkiel had discovered almost unwittingly, ordinary people were suspecting without much proof. The population drew its conclusions quickly and spread them as rumors throughout the occupied Polish territory. By late summer of 1942 almost every inhabitant of Poland, whether outside or inside a ghetto, had some inkling of what was going on. In the end even children knew the purpose of the deportations. When, during the summer of 1944 in the Łódź ghetto, the children of an orphanage were piled on trucks, they cried, "*Mir viln nisht shtarbn!* [We don't want to die!]"

❄ ❄ ❄

The Jewish leadership in the Polish ghettos stood at the helm of the compliance movement, and ghetto chiefs were the implementors of the surrender. Always they delivered up some Jews to save the other Jews. Having "stabilized" the situation, the ghetto administration would bisect the remaining community. And so on. Moses Merin, president of the Central Council of Elders for Eastern Upper Silesia, presided over such a shrinking process. On the eve of the first deportations, Merin made his first decision. "I will not be afraid," he said, to "sacrifice 50,000 of our community in order to save the other 50,000." During the summer of 1942 the other 50,000 Jews were lined up in a mass review, from which half were sent to Auschwitz. Merin commented after that deportation: "I feel like a captain whose ship was about to sink and who succeeded in bringing it safe to port by casting overboard a great part of his precious cargo." By 1943 there were only a few survivors. Merin addressed them in the following words: "I stand in a cage before a hungry and angry tiger. I stuff his mouth with meat, the flesh of my brothers and sisters, to keep him in his cage lest he break loose and tear us all to bits."

Throughout Poland the great bulk of the Jews presented themselves voluntarily at the collecting points and boarded the trains for transport to killing centers. Like blood gushing out of an open wound, the exodus from the ghettos quickly drained the Polish Jewish community of its centuries-old life.

However, in an operation of such dimensions not everybody could be deported so smoothly. As the circle of Jewish survivors shrank, the awareness of death increased, and the psychological burden of complying with German "evacuation" orders became heavier and heavier. Toward the end of the operations increasing numbers of Jews hesitated to move out, while others fled from the ghettos or jumped from trains to find refuge in the woods. In the Warsaw ghetto a few of the surviving Jews rallied in a last-minute stand against the Germans.

The Germans reacted to the recalcitrant Jews with utmost brutality. Howling raiders descended upon the ghettos with hatchets and bayonets. In the Warthegau the police were sent into such actions in a half-drunken stupor. Every Gestapo man assigned to ghetto-clearing duty received daily an extra ration of a little over half a pint of brandy. The Gettoverwaltung in Łódź demanded a brandy allocation for its employees, too, on the ground that employment without such brandy was "irresponsible." In Galicia the Jews were particularly aware of their fate because they had already witnessed the mobile killing operations in 1941. In the words of the SS and Police report, they "tried every means in order to dodge evacuation." They concealed themselves "in every imaginable corner, in pipes, chimneys, even in sewers." They "built barricades in passages of catacombs, in cellars enlarged to dugouts, in underground holes, in cunningly contrived hiding places in attics and sheds, within furniture, etc."

In the Galician operations massacres were interspersed with deportations, particularly during the *Transportsperren* in the early summer of 1942 and in December–January 1942–43. Often, the old and infirm Jews were not transported at all, but shot in the course of the roundup. The general mode of procedure in Galicia may be illustrated by events in three towns.

In Stanisławow, about 10,000 Jews had been gathered at a cemetery and shot on October 12, 1941. Another shooting took place in March 1942, followed by a ghetto fire lasting for three weeks. A transport was sent to Bełżec in April, and more shooting operations were launched in the summer, in the course of which Jewish council members and Order Service men were hanged from lampposts. Large transports moved out to Bełżec in September and October, an occasion marked by the bloody clearing of a hospital and (according to reports heard by a German agricultural official) a procession of Jews moving to the train station on their knees.

The Galician town of Rawa Ruska, only about twenty miles from Bełżec, was a railway junction through which deportation trains passed frequently. A survivor, Wolf Sambol, recalling scenes of shootings in the town, quotes a drunken Gendarmerie man shouting at the victims: "You are not Jews anymore, you are the chosen. I am your Moses and I will lead you through the Red Sea." He then opened fire at the victims with an automatic weapon. The same survivor remembers a little girl under the corpses, pushing herself out covered with blood, and looking carefully to the right and left, running away. Transports moved out of Rawa Ruska as soon as the *Sperre* [blockade] was lifted in July 1942. Although the nature of Bełżec was no longer a secret that summer, the Rawa Ruska Jewish Council pursued a cooperative course, and large numbers of Jews gathered at the collecting point for transport. Their wish, said Sambol, was to live half an hour longer *(Ihr Wunsch ist es, eine halbe Stunde älter zu sein)*. Several thousand others, however, sought to hide, and many jumped from trains.

One transport pulled out from the southern Galician town of Kołomyja on September 10, 1942. In its fifty cars it carried 8,205 deportees. Some of the victims had been driven to the train on foot from villages in the area, while others had been waiting in the town itself. Neither group had had much to eat for days before departure. The slowness of the train, pulled by an under-powered locomotive that periodically had to stop, contributed to the agony of the Jews inside. They stripped off their clothes in the heat, ripped off the barbed wire at the aperture near the ceiling of the car, and tried to squeeze through and jump out. The Order Police Kommando, consisting of one officer and fifteen men, shot all of its ammunition, obtained more rounds from army personnel along the way, and finally hurled stones at escapees. When the train arrived in Bełżec, 200 of those aboard were dead.

Such scenes aroused people in the entire district. Once a Polish policeman related his experiences freely to an ethnic German woman who then wrote anonymously to Berlin. Her letter reached the *Reichskanzlei.* The Polish policeman, she wrote, had asked her whether she was not finally ashamed of being an ethnic German. He had now become acquainted with German culture. During the dissolution of the ghettos, children had been thrown on the floor and their heads trampled with boots. Many Jews whose bones had been broken by rifle butts were thrown into graves and covered with calcium flour. When the calcium began to boil in the blood, one could still hear the crying of the wounded.

The Holocaust in History

MICHAEL MARRUS

Michael Marrus teaches at the University of Toronto. He has
published a book on the assimilation of the French Jews at the
time of the Dreyfus Affair and has coauthored an acclaimed
study of the Jews and Vichy France. The work from which the
following is taken, *The Holocaust in History,* received widespread
applause for its assessment of scholarly knowledge on the Holocaust. Do the arguments of the "intentionalists" or those of the
"functionalists" seem the more persuasive? Why? What appears
to be Marrus' view?

For an important body of historical opinion, the questions asked about the
emergence of the Final Solution can be answered easily with reference to Hitler's
anti-Jewish rhetoric, drawn from various points in his career but seen to reflect
a consistent murderous objective. In this view, Hitler is seen as the driving force
of Nazi anti-semitic policy, whose views indicate a coherent line of thought
from a very early point. Hitler is also seen as the sole strategist with the authority and the determination to begin the implementation of the Final Solution.
In what is probably the most widely read work on this subject, Lucy Dawidowicz argues that the Führer set the stage for mass murder in September 1939,
with the attack on Poland. "War and the annihilation of the Jews were interdependent," she writes. "The disorder of war would provide Hitler with the cover
for the unchecked commission of murder. He needed an arena for his operations where the restraints of common codes of morality and accepted rules of
warfare would not extend." September 1939, therefore, saw the beginning of

"a twofold war": on the one hand there was the war of conquest for traditional goals such as raw materials and empire; on the other there was the "war against the Jews," the decisive confrontation with the greatest enemy of the Third Reich. Orders to begin Europe-wide mass murder, issued in the late spring or summer of 1941, are seen as flowing directly from Hitler's idea on Jews, expressed as early as 1919. On various occasions his "program of annihilation" may have been camouflaged or downplayed. But Dawidowicz insists that it was always his intention: "Once Hitler adopted an ideological position, even a strategic one, he adhered to it with limpetlike fixity, fearful lest he be accused, if he changed his mind, of incertitude, of capriciousness on 'essential questions.' He had long-range plans to realize his ideological goals, and the destruction of the Jews was at their center."

Borrowing from the British historian Tim Mason, Christopher Browning was the first to dub this interpretation "intentionalist," linking it to other historiographical themes in the history of the Third Reich. This line of thought accents the role of Hitler in initiating the murder of European Jewry, seeing a high degree of persistence, consistency, and orderly sequence in Nazi anti-Jewish policy, directed from a very early point to the goal of mass murder. Like much of the interpretative literature on Nazism, this explanation of the Final Solution rests on quotations and depends, in the final analysis, on the notion of a Hitlerian "blueprint" for future policies, set forth in *Mein Kampf* and other writings and speeches. Critics of this approach, referred to as "functionalists," are rather impressed with the evolution of Nazi goals, with the sometimes haphazard course of German policies, and with the way that these are related to the internal mechanisms of the Third Reich.

Intentionalism, it may be supposed, was born at Nuremberg in 1945, when American prosecutors first presented Nazi crimes as a carefully orchestrated conspiracy, launched together with the war itself. At that time American legal experts hoped to prove that there had been a deliberate plan to commit horrendous atrocities as well as other breaches of international law; in this way they expected to designate certain German organizations and institutions as part of a criminal conspiracy, vastly simplifying the work of future prosecutions. Years later, after much historical analysis, many historians still accept the notion of an unfolding Hitlerian plan. In his detailed critique of David Irving, for example, Gerald Fleming sees an "unbroken continuity of specific utterances" leading from Hitler's first manifestations of anti-semitism "to the liquidation orders that Hitler personally issued during the war." A major task of Fleming's work is the collection of such utterances, which the author hopes will tear away the camouflage covering Hitler's primary responsibility.

One can sympathize with an effort to remind a sometimes negligent audience of Hitler's incessant, raving hatred of Jews. And it is similarly valuable to expose the Nazis' linguistic perversions—distortions intended to conceal the killing process from the victims, from the Allies, and from the German public as well. Nevertheless, the problem of interpreting Hitlerian rhetoric still remains. For the fact is that Hitler was forever calling for the most ruthless action; for sudden, crushing blows; for the complete annihilation of his foes; or evoking his irrevocable, ironlike determination to do this or that. We cannot ignore Hitler's amply demonstrated blood lust, and there is no doubt that the contemplation of mass killing inspired him on more than one occasion. In retrospect, historians have little difficulty in tracing "direct lines," but it is much more problematic to ascertain what Hitler actually intended and how he acted on such expressions at specific moments. In May 1938, for example, Hitler told his generals of his "unalterable decision to destroy Czechoslovakia by military action in the foreseeable future." According to Gerhard Weinberg, the Nazi leader indeed wanted military action, but believed he could avoid a general war. When he learned in September, on the eve of his attack, that a general war threatened, that neither Mussolini nor the German public were likely to follow him, and that he could achieve a stunning success peacefully, he changed his mind. So "unalterable decisions" could be altered. The implication is that Hitler's words should indeed be taken seriously, but that they must also be seen in the context of his actions and the concrete situations he faced.

This is a reasonable reply to the use made of Hitler's famous speech of 30 January 1939 by intentionalist historians such as Dawidowicz and Fleming. Adopting a characteristically "prophetic" tone in his address to the Reichstag, Hitler issued a terrible warning: "One thing I should like to say on this day which may be memorable for others as well as for us Germans: In the course of my life I have very often been a prophet, and I have usually been ridiculed for it. During the time of my struggle for power it was in the first instance the Jewish race which only received my prophecies with laughter when I said that I would one day take over the leadership of the State, and with it that of the whole nation, and that I would then among many other things settle the Jewish problem. Their laughter was uproarious, but I think that for some time now they have been laughing on the other side of their face. Today I will once more be a prophet. If the international Jewish financiers outside Europe should succeed in plunging the nations once more into a world war, then the result will not be the bolshevization of the earth, and thus the victory of Jewry, but the annihilation of the Jewish race in Europe."

Fleming is certainly right to stress the importance of Hitler's self-portrayal as a "fighting prophet," and Hitler's subsequent references to this speech in the middle of the war indicate a conscious desire, once the Final Solution was under way, to assert a continuity of actions against the Jews. This is but one of many pieces of evidence that suggest Hitler insisted on a definitive solution to the Jewish question, and in this sense the speech is an important measure of his priorities. Less clear, however, is what the January speech tells us about Hitler's objectives at the time. A look at his words in context shows that Hitler spoke for several hours, but devoted only a few minutes to the Jews. Speaking in the wake of the Munich conference, Hitler focused mainly on economic matters, in an address judged by the British ambassador to be relatively conciliatory. One of the purposes of Hitler's address was likely to sow confusion and division among the Western powers. He probably did envisage war in Europe as his "prophecy" suggested; but this was likely not a world war, but rather a fight over Poland, which would be over quickly. As Uwe Dietrich Adam points out, Hitler and other Nazi leaders looked to an even more ruthless crackdown on Jews in the event of war. We shall never know for certain precisely what plans lurked in Hitler's consciousness and whether his reference to "annihilation" at that particular time should be taken literally. But it is not at all plain that he had fixed upon mass murder, which presumably would have to begin once the short Polish campaign was over. And it is even less likely that Hitler thought concretely about Europe-wide killings, which he was not in a position to undertake until his stunning military successes in 1940–41.

⚝ ⚝ ⚝

Against this interpretation, so-called functionalist historians present a picture of the Third Reich as a maze of competing power groups, rival bureaucracies, forceful personalities, and diametrically opposed interests engaged in ceaseless clashes with each other. They see Hitler as a brooding and sometimes distant leader, who intervened only spasmodically, sending orders crashing through the system like bolts of lightning. While in theory the power of the Führer was without limit, in practice he preferred the role of arbiter, according legitimacy to one or another favorite or line of conduct. Add to this Hitler's curious leadership style—his inability to mount a sustained effort, his procrastination, his frequent hesitation—and one can understand the reluctance of many to accept the idea of a far-reaching scheme or ideological imperative necessitating the Final Solution. Few historians of this school doubt that Hitler was murderously obsessed with Jews; they question, however, whether he was capable of long-term planning on this or any other matter, and they tend to look within the chaotic system itself for at least some of the explanation for the killing of European Jews.

Reflecting this perspective, Martin Broszat's 1977 critique of David Irving's *Hitler's War* presented to a wide public a serious interpretation of the origins of the Final Solution in which Hitler did not have full operational responsibility. Broszat's approach was hardly an exculpation of the Nazi leader. On the contrary, he took Irving to task for his "normalization" of Hitler and pointed to dangerous forces within the German Federal Republic that utilized the apologetic drift in the British historian's work. Broszat reasserted Hitler's "fanatical, destructive will to annihilate" that traditional historiography has always seen at the core of the Führer's personality. He stressed Hitler's "totally irresponsible, self-deceiving, destructive and evilly misanthropic egocentricity and his lunatic fanaticism." As the author of a 1969 work, *Der Staat Hitlers*, Broszat had no doubt about who was in charge and what kind of a person he was.

Nevertheless, the heart of Broszat's argument was that the Final Solution was not begun after a single Hitlerian decision, but arose "bit by bit." He suggested that deportations and systematic killings outside the sphere of the Einsatzgruppen[1] in Russia started through local Nazi initiatives, rather than a directive from the Führer. According to this view, Hitler set the objective of Nazism: "to get rid of the Jews, and above all to make the territory of the Reich *judenfrei*, i.e., clear of Jews"—but without specifying how this was to be achieved. In a vague way, the top Nazi leadership hoped to see the Jews pushed off to the east, and uprooted large masses of people with this in mind. Top Nazi officials had "no clear aims . . . with respect to the subsequent fate of the deportees," however. Their policy was "governed by the concept that the enormous spaces to be occupied in the Soviet Union would . . . offer a possibility for getting rid of the Jews of Germany and of the allied and occupied countries," but they also toyed with other schemes, such as the Madagascar Plan, to achieve their objectives. Expectations of an early resolution heightened during the Russian campaign, which was supposed to finish in a matter of weeks. Deportation trains carrying Jews from the Reich began to roll eastward. Yet by the autumn these plans were upset. Military operations slowed, and then came to a standstill. Transportation facilities were overloaded. Nazi officers in the occupied east, receiving shipments of Jews from the Reich, now complained that they had no more room in the teeming, disease-ridden ghettos. It was then, in Broszat's view, that Nazi officials on the spot started sporadically to murder the Jews who arrived from the west. Killing, therefore, "began not solely as the result of an ostensible will for extermination but also as a 'way out' of a blind alley into which the Nazis had manoeuvered themselves." In its early stages, annihilation was improvised, and its execution was marked by confusion and misunderstanding. Only gradually, in early 1942, did Himmler and the SS establish the coherent structures of the Final Solution, coordinated on a Europe-wide basis.

Among functionalists, Hans Mommsen has presented the most forceful case for a Führer uninvolved in and perhaps incapable of administration, concerned rather with his personal standing and striking propaganda postures. Mommsen goes even further than Broszat in suggesting that Hitler had little directly to do with anti-Jewish policy. While not denying the Führer's intense hatred of Jews, Mommsen sees the Nazi leader as thinking about the Jews mainly

---

[1] Special killing squads that accompanied the German army.—Eds.

in propagandistic terms, without bothering to chart a course of action. The Final Solution, he observes, resulted from the interaction of this fanatical but distant leader with the chaotic structure of the Nazi regime. In the Third Reich, office was piled upon office, and underlings were left to find their way in a bureaucratic and administrative jungle. The only guide to success, and a compelling one, was fidelity to the Hitlerian vision. Underlings competed for the favor of this ideologically obsessed, but essentially lazy leader. Given the Führer's mad compulsions, this competition programmed the regime for "cumulative radicalization," a process that ended ultimately, of course, in its self-destruction. Hitler's heightened rhetoric prompted others to realize his "utopian" ravings about Jews and undoubtedly stimulated murderous excesses. But he issued no order for the Final Solution and had nothing to do with its implementation.

❊ ❊ ❊

The crisis came with Barbarossa, not only because of the apocalyptic character of the campaign, but also because it promised to bring hundreds of thousands more Jews within the hegemony of the Reich. What were the Germans to do with them? During the early course of the campaign Hitler tipped the scales for mass murder. The decision to massacre the Soviet Jews was probably taken in March, as part of the Barbarossa planning process. Before the end of July, Hitler, buoyed up by the spectacular successes of the Wehrmacht in the early part of the Russian campaign, probably issued his order for Europe-wide mass murder. At that point, the Führer likely felt, everything was possible. On 31 July, Göring authorized Heydrich to prepare a "total solution" *(Gesamtlösung)* of the Jewish question in the territories under the Nazis' control. Before long, work began on the first two death camps—at Bełżec and Chełmno, where construction started in the autumn. On 23 October, Himmler issued a fateful order that passed along the Nazi chain of command: henceforth there would be no Jewish emigration permitted anywhere from German-held territory. On 29 November, invitations went out to the Wannsee Conference, intended to coordinate deportations from across Europe. The Final Solution was about to begin.

Browning and others have criticized the work of various functionalists on three grounds. First, they challenge Adam's notion that pushing great masses of Jews off "to the east" was still an option for the Nazis in the summer of 1941. No concrete preparations for such a massive deportation have ever been discovered, and it is unlikely that serious planning for it could have been under way without leaving a trace in the historical record. Göring's authorization to Heydrich on 31 July to prepare a "total solution" could hardly have referred to such expulsions, they say, since Heydrich already had such authority and had been expelling Jews on a smaller scale since the beginning of 1939. Seen in the context of the furious killings then under way by the Einsatzgruppen, Göring's communication appears rather like a warrant for genocide. Like many, Klaus Hildebrand finds it difficult to distinguish between the gigantic operations of the killing teams in Russia and the other aspects of the Final Solution. "In qualitative terms the executions by shooting were no different from the technically more efficient accomplishment of the 'physical final solution' by gassing, of which they were a prelude." Second, historians have challenged Broszat's idea of locally initiated mass murders. Not only does it seem unlikely that the systematic killing of Jews from the Reich, for example, could have been undertaken without the Führer's agreement, there is also too little evidence of local initiatives with which to sustain this theory. As Eberhard Jäckel noted recently, there is rather "a great deal of evidence that some [local officials] were shocked or even appalled when the final solution came into effect. To be sure, they did not disagree with it. But they agreed only reluctantly, referring again to an order given by Hitler. This is a strong indication that the idea did not originate with them."

Third, Browning contends that the decision for Europe-wide mass murder was taken in the summer of 1941, in the euphoria of the first victories in the Barbarossa campaign, and not a few months later. He draws upon postwar evidence from Rudolf Höss, the commandant of Auschwitz, and Adolf Eichmann, from the start a key official in the bureaucracy of the Final Solution, to the effect that the Führer's mind was made up during the summer. This sense of timing differs notably from functionalists who conclude that the Final Solution arose from disappointment with the outcome of the fighting in Russia. Adam, for example, sees the Nazis depressed by the prospect of having to spend another winter with the Jews; the journalist Sebastian Haffner imagines, much less plausibly, that Hitler saw as early as the end of 1941 that the European war could not be won and that the other contest, "the war against the Jews," could at least be pursued to its final conclusion.

Outsiders to these disputes may well suspect that some of the sharp edges of the controversy are wearing off and that there is more agreement among these historians than meets the eye. Opinion is widespread that there was some Hitlerian decision to initiate Europe-wide killing. The range of difference over timing extends across only a few months, with intentionalists positing a Führer order sometime in March 1941, with Browning and others opting for the summer, and with a few, such as Adam, looking toward the early autumn. What finally precipitated this decision, however, is likely to remain a mystery. Military historians tell us that, despite the extraordinary successes of the Wehrmacht in the first weeks of the Barbarossa campaign, the Germans found the going difficult as early as mid-July 1941. Although their forces advanced great distances and destroyed much of their opposition, they were surprised at the extent and efficacy of Soviet resistance and were greatly slowed by faulty intelligence, poor roads and bridges, and marshes. Chief of the army general staff Franz Halder portrayed an exasperated Führer after only six weeks of fighting, and it seems likely that by late August Hitler already knew that the war would continue well into 1942. This was a major setback, even though the Germans did not taste real defeat until December. Whether euphoria or disappointment prompted the decision is therefore difficult to say. On the other hand, the idea of Hitler breaking the logjam caused by an ill-defined policy rings true, given what we know of his leadership style. Students of Hitler's behavior in other areas have been struck by his preference for sudden, unexpected, spectacular coups. His was the method of the supreme gambler, "forever looking for short cuts." For someone as ruthless and fanatical as Hitler, a decision for the Final Solution can well be imagined in the apocalyptic atmosphere of Barbarossa, the war to settle once and for all the fate of the thousand-year Reich.

"La guerre révolutionna la Révolution," French historian Marcel Reinhard once wrote about the revolutionary impact of the war of 1792 on the revolutionaries in Paris. So it has been observed that the war against the Soviet Union revolutionized the Third Reich, and it is not surprising that this campaign transformed Nazi Jewish policy as well. It is difficult to follow the process of political and ideological radicalization in detail, for this was a period of extensive fluidity—even for a regime that, as Karl Dietrich Bracher has said, "remained in a state of permanent improvisation." Ian Kershaw observes that "the summer and autumn of 1941 were characterized by a high degree of confusion and contradictory interpretations of the aims of anti-Jewish policy by the Nazi authorities." It seems useful, however, to understand Jewish policy in this period as evolving within a genocidal framework—extending beyond Jews to include the incurably ill, Soviet intelligentsia, prisoners of war, and others as well. In this fevered atmosphere, incredible as it may seem, an "order" to send millions of people to their deaths may have been no more than a "nod" from Hitler to one of his lieutenants.

Hitler's Willing Executioners

DANIEL JONAH GOLDHAGEN

What motivated the perpetrators of the Holocaust to commit unspeakable crimes against the Jews? Most historians believe that the Nazis either blindly obeyed orders or adopted a different personality in order to kill Jews. Daniel Jonah Goldhagen, an associate professor of government at Harvard University, came to a much more controversial conclusion. He argues anti-Semitism had so permeated the German population by the 1940s that the perpetrators desperately *wanted* to kill the Jews. Goldhagen's critics seriously question his conclusions. If the Holocaust, as Goldhagen charges, was primarily motivated by "exterminationist antisemitism," why did the Nazis expend so much time and effort murdering non-Jews such as the Gypsies and members of other groups? Critics have also charged that he disregarded evidence contrary to his thesis, such as the role of non-German perpetrators of the Holocaust. Others charge that Goldhagen ignores the degree of Nazi control over the German population and how most feared punishment in the event that they aided the Jews in any way. Taking these criticisms into consideration, how tenable are Goldhagen's arguments?

Not only was German antisemitism in this historical instance a sufficient cause, but it was also a *necessary* cause for such broad German participation in the persecution and mass slaughter of Jews, *and* for Germans to have treated Jews in all the heartless, harsh, and cruel ways that they did. Had ordinary Germans not shared their leadership's eliminationist ideals, then they would have reacted to the ever-intensifying assault on their Jewish countrymen and brethren with at least as much opposition and non-cooperation as they did to their government's attacks on Christianity and to the so-called Euthanasia program. As has already been discussed, especially with regard to religious policies, the Nazis backed down when faced with serious, widespread popular opposition. Had the Nazis been faced with a German populace who saw Jews as ordinary human beings, and German Jews as their brothers and sisters, then it is hard to imagine that the Nazis would have proceeded, or would have been able to proceed, with the extermination of the Jews. If they somehow had been able to go forward, then the probability that the assault would have unfolded as it did, and that Germans would have killed so many Jews, is extremely low. The probability that it would have produced so much German cruelty and exterminatory zeal is zero. A German population roused against the elimination and extermination of the Jews most likely would have stayed the regime's hand.

❈ ❈ ❈

The Nazi leadership, like other genocidal elites, never applied, and most likely would not have been willing to apply, the vast amount of coercion that it would have needed to move tens of thousands of non-antisemitic Germans to kill millions of Jews. The Nazis, knowing that ordinary Germans shared their convictions, had no need to do so.

The Holocaust was a *sui generis*[1] event that has a historically specific explanation. The explanation specifies the enabling conditions created by the long-incubating, pervasive, virulent, racist, eliminationist antisemitism of German culture, which was mobilized by a criminal regime beholden to an elimination-ist, genocidal ideology, and which was given shape and energized by a leader, Hitler, who was adored by the vast majority of the German people, a leader who was known to be committed wholeheartedly to the unfolding, brutal elim-inationist program. During the Nazi period, the eliminationist antisemitism provided the motivational source for the German leadership and for rank-and-file Germans to kill the Jews. It also was the motivational source of the other non-killing actions of the perpetrators that were integral to the Holocaust.

❈ ❈ ❈

. . . Even if, for explanatory purposes, it is not essential to discuss German antisemitism comparatively, it is still worth stating that the antisemitism of no

---

[1] *Sui generis*: Being unique of its kind.—Eds.

other European country came close to combining *all* of the following features of German antisemitism (indeed, virtually every other country fell short on *each* dimension). No other country's antisemitism was at once so widespread as to have been a cultural axiom, was so firmly wedded to racism, had as its foundation such a pernicious image of Jews that deemed them to be a mortal threat to the *Volk*, and was so deadly in content, producing, even in the nineteenth century, such frequent and explicit calls for the extermination of the Jews, calls which expressed the logic of the racist eliminationist antisemitism that prevailed in Germany. The unmatched volume and the vitriolic and murderous substance of German antisemitic literature of the nineteenth and twentieth centuries alone indicate that German antisemitism was *sui generis*.

❊ ❊ ❊

Indeed, the German's anti-Jewish policy evolved in a logical manner—always flowing from the eliminationist ideology—in consonance with the creation of new eliminationist opportunities, opportunities which Hitler was happy to exploit, promptly and eagerly, to their limits. . . .

In no sense was Hitler's monumental, indeed world-historical, decision—driven as it was by his fervent hatred of Jews—to exterminate European Jewry an historical accident, as some have argued, that took place because other options were closed off to him or because of something as ephemeral as Hitler's moods. Killing was not undertaken by Hitler reluctantly. Killing, biological purgation, was for Hitler a natural, preferred method of solving problems. Indeed, killing was Hitler's reflex. He slaughtered those in his own movement whom he saw as a challenge. He killed his political enemies. He killed Germany's mentally ill. . . . Already in 1929, he publicly toyed with the idea of killing all German children born with physical defects, which he numbered in a murderously megalomaniacal moment of fantasy at 700,000 to 800,000 a year. Surely, death was the most fitting penalty for the Jews. A demonic nation deserves nothing less than death.

Indeed, it is hard to imagine Hitler and the German leadership having settled for any other "solution" once they attacked the Soviet Union. The argument that only circumstances of one sort or another *created* Hitler's and the Germans' *motive* to opt for a genocidal "solution" ignores, for no good reason, Hitler's oft-stated and self-understood intention to exterminate the Jews. This argument also implies, counterfactually, that had these putative motivation-engendering circumstances not been brought about—had Hitler's allegedly volatile moods not allegedly swung, had the Germans been able to "resettle" millions of Jews—then Hitler and the others would have survived the war.

❊ ❊ ❊

The idea that death and death alone is the only fitting punishment for Jews was publicly articulated by Hitler at the beginning of his political career on August 13, 1920, in a speech entirely devoted to antisemitism, "Why Are We Antisemites?" In the middle of that speech, the still politically obscure Hitler suddenly digressed to the subject of the death sentence and why it ought to be applied to the Jews. Healthy elements of a nation, he declared, know that "criminals guilty of crimes against the nation, i.e., parasites on the national community," cannot be tolerated, that under certain circumstances they must be punished only with death, since imprisonment lacks the quality of irrevocableness.

❊ ❊ ❊

. . . Mere imprisonment would be clement a penalty for such world-historical criminals and one, moreover, fraught with danger, since the Jews could one day emerge from their prisons and resume their evil ways. Hitler's maniacal conception of the Jews, his consuming hatred of them, and his natural murderous propensity rendered him incapable of becoming reconciled permanently to any "solution of the Jewish Problem" save that of extinction.

The road to Auschwitz was not twisted. Conceived by Hitler's apocalyptically bent mind as an urgent, though future, project, its completion had to wait until conditions were right. The instant that they were, Hitler commissioned his architects, Himmler and Heydrich, to work from his vague blueprint in designing and engineering the road. They, in turn, easily enlisted ordinary Germans by the tens of thousands, who built and paved it with an immense dedication born of great hatred for the Jews whom they drove down that road. When the road's construction was completed, Hitler, the architects, and their willing helpers looked upon it not as an undesirable construction, but with satisfaction. In no sense did they regard it as a road chosen only because other, preferable venues had proven to be dead ends. They held it to be the best, safest, and speediest of all possible roads, the only one that led to a destination from which the satanic Jews are absolutely sure never to return.

The Terrible Secret

WALTER LAQUEUR

Walter Laqueur was born in Germany but left in 1938. A distinguished professor of history, he is an eminent commentator and an expert in international affairs. He chairs the International Research Council of the Center for Strategic and International Studies at Georgetown University and edits the *Washington Quarterly*, a review of strategic and international issues. He also directs the Institute of Contemporary History and the Wiener Library in London, coedits the *Journal of Contemporary History*, and teaches contemporary history at Tel Aviv University. His books include studies on European history, the Middle East, guerrilla movements, Zionism, terrorism, fascism, nationalism, and human rights. Do all of Laqueur's answers appear equally valid, or are some more credible than others?

The evidence gathered so far shows that news of the 'final solution' had been received in 1942 all over Europe, even though all the details were not known. If so, why were the signals so frequently misunderstood and the message rejected?

The fact that Hitler had given an explicit order to kill all Jews was not known for a long time. His decision was taken soon after he had made up his mind to invade Russia. Victor Brack, who worked at the time in Hitler's Chancellery, said in evidence at Nuremberg that it was no secret in higher party circles by March 1941 that the Jews were to be exterminated. But 'higher party circles' may have meant at the time no more than a dozen people. In March 1941, even Eichmann did not know, for the preparations for the deportations and the camps had not yet been made. First instructions to this effect were given in Goering's letter to Heydrich of 31 July 1941. The fact that an order had been given by Hitler became known outside Germany only in July 1942 and even then in a distorted form: Hitler (it was then claimed) had ordered that no Jew should be left in Germany by the end of 1942. But there is no evidence that such a time limit had ever been set. It would not have been difficult, for instance, to deport all Jews from Berlin in 1942, but in fact the city was declared empty of Jews by Goebbels only in August 1943. Witnesses claimed to have seen the order, but it is doubtful whether there ever was a written order. This has given rise to endless speculation and inspired a whole 'revisionist' literature—quite needlessly, because Hitler, whatever his other vices, was not a bureaucrat. He was not in the habit of giving written orders on all occasions: there were no written orders for the murderous 'purge' of June 1934, for the killing of gypsies, the so-called euthanasia action (T4) and on other such occasions. The more abominable the crime, the less likely that there would be a written 'Führer-order.' If Himmler, Heydrich or even Eichmann said that there was such an order, no one would question or insist on seeing it.

The order had practical consequences, it affected the lives or, to be precise, the deaths of millions of people. For this reason details about the 'final solution' seeped out virtually as soon as the mass slaughter started.

The systematic massacres of the *Einsatzgruppen* [mobile killing units] in Eastern Galicia, White Russia, the Ukraine and the Baltic countries became known in Germany almost immediately. True, the scene of the slaughter was distant and it took place in territories in which at the time civilians and foreigners were not freely permitted to travel. But many thousands of German officers and soldiers witnessed these scenes and later reported them and the same is true of Italian, Hungarian and Romanian military personnel. The German Foreign Ministry was officially informed about the details of the massacres; there was much less secrecy about the *Einsatzgruppen* than later on about the extermination camps. The Soviet Government must have learned about the massacres within a few days; after several weeks the news became known in Western capitals too, well before the Wannsee Conference. The slaughter at Kiev (Babi Yar) took place on 29–30 September 1941. Foreign journalists knew about it within a few days; within less than two months it had been reported in the Western press. The massacres in Transniestria became known almost immediately. Chelmno, the first extermination camp, was opened on 8 December 1941; the news was received in Warsaw within less than four weeks and published soon afterwards in the underground press. The existence and the function of Belzec and Treblinka were known in Warsaw among Jews and non-Jews within two weeks after the gas chambers had started operating. The news about the suicide of Czerniakow, the head of the Warsaw *Judenrat*, reached the Jewish press abroad within a short time. The deportations from Warsaw were known in London after four days. There were some exceptions: the true character of Auschwitz did not become known among Jews and Poles alike for several months after the camp had been turned into an extermination centre. At the time in Poland it was believed that there were only two types of camps, labour camps and extermination camps, and the fact that Auschwitz was a 'mixed camp' seems to have baffled many.

If so much was known so quickly among the Jews of Eastern Europe and if the information was circulated through illegal newspapers and by other means—there were wireless sets in all major ghettos—why was it not believed? In the beginning Russian and Polish Jewry were genuinely unprepared, and the reasons have been stated: Soviet Jews had been kept uninformed about Nazi intentions and practices, Polish Jews believed that the massacres would be limited to the former Soviet territories. At first there was the tendency to interpret these events in the light of the past: persecution and pogroms. The Jewish leaders in Warsaw who learned about events in Lithuania and Latvia in early 1942 should have realized that these were not 'pogroms' in the traditional sense, spontaneous mob actions, nor excesses committed by local commanders. There are few arbitrary actions in a totalitarian regime. The *Einsatzgruppen* acted methodically and in cold blood. The majority of Jewish leaders in Eastern Europe did not yet realize that this was the beginning of a systematic campaign of destruction. The whole scheme was beyond human imagination; they thought the Nazis incapable of the murder of millions. Communication between some of the ghettos was irregular; Lodz ghetto, the second largest, was more or less isolated. But rumours, on the other hand, still travelled fast. If the information about the 'final solution' had been believed it would have reached every corner of Poland within a few days. But it was not believed and when the 'deportations' from Polish ghettos began in March 1942 it was still generally thought that the Jews would be transported to places further East.

※ ※ ※

Jewish leaders and the public abroad (Britain, America and Palestine) found it exceedingly difficult in their great majority to accept the ample evidence about the 'final solution' and did so only with considerable delay. They too thought in categories of persecution and pogroms at a time when a clear pattern had already emerged which pointed in a different direction. It was a failure of intelligence and imagination caused on one hand by a misjudgment of the murderous nature of Nazism, and on the other hand by a false optimism. Other factors may have played a certain role: the feeling of impotence ('we can do very little, so let us hope for the best'), the military dangers facing the Jewish community in Palestine in 1942. If the evidence was played down by many Jewish leaders and the Jewish press, it was not out of the desire to keep the community in a state of ignorance, but because there were genuine doubts. As the worst fears were confirmed, there was confusion among the leaders as to what course of action to choose. This was true especially in the U.S. and caused further delay in making the news public. In Jerusalem the turning point came with the arrival of a group of Palestinian citizens who had been repatriated from Europe in November 1942. The leaders of the Jewish Agency, who had been unwilling to accept the written evidence gathered by experienced observers, were ready to believe the accounts delivered by chance arrivals in face-to-face meetings.

※ ※ ※

Millions of Germans knew by late 1942 that the Jews had disappeared. Rumours about their fate reached Germany mainly through officers and soldiers returning from the eastern front but also through other channels. There were clear indications in the wartime speeches of the Nazi leaders that something more drastic than resettlement had happened. Knowledge about the exact manner in which they had been killed was restricted to a very few. It is, in fact, quite likely that while many Germans thought that the Jews were no longer alive, they did not necessarily believe that they were dead. Such belief, needless to say, is logically inconsistent, but a great many logical inconsistencies are accepted in wartime. Very few people had an interest in the fate of the Jews. Most individuals faced a great many more important problems. It was an unpleasant topic, speculations were unprofitable, discussions of the fate of the Jews were discouraged. Consideration of this question was pushed aside, blotted out for the duration.

Neutrals and international organizations such as the Vatican and the Red Cross knew the truth at an early stage. Not perhaps the whole truth, but enough to understand that few, if any, Jews would survive the war. The Vatican had an unrivalled net of informants all over Europe. It tried to intervene on some occasions on behalf of the Jews but had no wish to give publicity to the issue. For this would have exposed it to German attacks on one hand and pressure to do more from the Jews and the Allies. Jews, after all, were not Catholics. In normal times their persecution would have evoked expressions of genuine regret. But these were not normal times and since the Holy See could do little—or thought it could do little—even for the faithful Poles, it thought it could do even less for the Jews. This fear of the consequences of helping the Jews influenced its whole policy.

※ ※ ※

Neither the United States Government, nor Britain, nor Stalin showed any pronounced interest in the fate of the Jews. They were kept informed through Jewish organizations and through their own channels. From an early date the

Soviet press published much general information about Nazi atrocities in the occupied areas but only rarely revealed that Jews were singled out for extermination.
To this day the Soviet Communist party line has not changed in this respect: it
has not admitted that any mistakes were made, that the Jewish population was
quite unprepared for the *Einsatzgruppen*. It is not conceded even now that if specific warnings had been given by the Soviet media in 1941 (which were informed
about events behind the German lines) lives might have been saved. As far as the
Soviet publications are concerned the Government and the Communist Party
acted correctly—Soviet citizens of Jewish origin did not fare differently from the
rest under Nazi rule, and if they did, it is thought inadvisable to mention this.
The only mildly critical voices that have been heard can be found in a few literary
works describing the events of 1941–42. Some Western observers have argued
that the (infrequent) early Soviet news about anti-Jewish massacres committed
were sometimes dismissed as 'Communist propaganda' in the West and that for
this reason the Soviet leaders decided no longer to emphasize the specific anti-
Jewish character of the extermination campaign. This explanation is not at all
convincing because Soviet policy at home was hardly influenced by the *Catholic
Times*, and it should be stressed that domestically even less publicity than abroad
was given to the Jewish victims from the very beginning.

In London and Washington the facts about the 'final solution' were known
from an early date and reached the chiefs of intelligence, the secretaries of foreign affairs and defence. But the facts were not considered to be of great interest
or importance and at least some of the officials either did not believe them, or
at least thought them exaggerated. There was no deliberate attempt to stop the
flow of information on the mass killings (except for a while on the part of officials in the State Department), but mainly lack of interest and disbelief. This
disbelief can be explained against the background of Anglo-American lack of
knowledge of European affairs in general and Nazism in particular. Although it
was generally accepted that the Nazis behaved in a less gentlemanly way than
the German armies in 1914–18, the idea of genocide nevertheless seemed far
fetched. Neither the *Luftwaffe* nor the German navy nor the Afrika Korps had
committed such acts of atrocities, and these were the only sections of the German armed forces which Allied soldiers encountered prior to 1944. The
Gestapo was known from not very credible B-grade movies. Barbaric fanaticism
was unacceptable to people thinking on pragmatic lines, who believed that slave
labour rather than annihilation was the fate of the Jews in Europe. The evil nature of Nazism was beyond their comprehension.

But even if the realities of the 'final solution' had been accepted in London
and Washington the issue would still have figured very low on the scale of Allied
priorities. Nineteen forty-two was a critical year in the course of the war, strategists
and bureaucrats were not to be deflected in the pursuit of victory by considerations
not directly connected with the war effort. Thus too much publicity about the

mass murder seemed undesirable, for it was bound to generate demands to help the Jews and this was thought to be detrimental to the war effort. Even in later years when victory was already assured there was little willingness to help. Churchill showed more interest in the Jewish tragedy than Roosevelt and also more compassion but even he was not willing to devote much thought to the subject. Public opinion in Britain, the United States and elsewhere was kept informed through the press from an early date about the progress of the 'final solution.' But the impact of the news was small or at most shortlived. The fact that millions were killed was more or less meaningless. People could identify perhaps with the fate of a single individual or a family but not with the fate of millions. The statistics of murder were either disbelieved or dismissed from consciousness. Hence the surprise and shock at the end of the war when the reports about a 'transit camp' such as Bergen-Belsen came in: 'No one had known, no one had been prepared for this.'

※ ※ ※

One of the questions initially asked was whether it would have made any difference if the information about the mass murder had been believed right from the beginning. It seems quite likely that relatively few people might have been saved as a result and even this is not absolutely certain. But this is hardly the right way of posing the question, for the misjudgment of Hitler and Nazism did not begin in June 1941 nor did it end in December 1942. The ideal time to stop Hitler was not when he was at the height of his strength. If the democracies had shown greater foresight, solidarity and resolution, Nazism could have been stopped at the beginning of its campaign of aggression. No power could have saved the majority of the Jews of the Reich and of Eastern Europe in the summer of 1942. Some more would have tried to escape their fate if the information had been made widely known. Some could have been saved if Hitler's satellites had been threatened and if the peoples of Europe had been called to extend help to the Jews. After the winter of 1942 the situation rapidly changed: the satellite leaders and even some of the German officials were no longer eager to be accessories to mass murder. Some, at least, would have responded to Allied pressure, but such pressure was never exerted. Many Jews could certainly have been saved in 1944 by bombing the railway lines leading to the extermination centres, and of course, the centres themselves. This could have been done without deflecting any major resources from the general war effort. It has been argued that the Jews could not have escaped in any case but this is not correct: the Russians were no longer far away, the German forces in Poland were concentrated in some of the bigger towns, and even there their sway ran only in daytime—they no longer had the manpower to round up escaped Jews. In short, hundreds of thousands could have been saved. But this discussion belongs to a later period. The failure to read correctly the signs in 1941–42 was only one link in a chain of failures.

There was not one reason for this overall failure but many different ones: paralyzing fear on one hand and, on the contrary, reckless optimism on the other; disbelief stemming from a lack of experience or imagination or genuine ignorance or a mixture of some or all of these things. In some cases the motives were creditable, in others damnable. In some instances moral categories are simply not applicable, and there were also cases which defy understanding to this day.

The Abandonment of the Jews

DAVID S. WYMAN

David S. Wyman received his Ph.D. in history from Harvard University in 1966 and is a professor of history (emeritus) at the University of Massachusetts at Amherst. His work on the Holocaust has been regarded as controversial. He not only accuses American leaders of ignoring strong evidence of atrocities against the Jews, but he also asserts that the American State Department and British Foreign Office actually stymied efforts to save thousands of Jews from extermination. How do his views compare with those expressed by Walter Laqueur in the previous selection?

Why did America fail to carry out the kind of rescue effort that it could have?

In summary form, these are the findings that I regard as most significant:

1. The American State Department and the British Foreign Office had no intention of rescuing large numbers of European Jews. On the contrary, they continually feared that Germany or other Axis nations might release tens of thousands of Jews into Allied hands. Any such exodus would have placed intense pressure on Britain to open Palestine and on the United States to take in more Jewish refugees, a situation the two great powers did not want to face. Consequently, their policies aimed at obstructing rescue possibilities and dampening public pressures for government action.

2. Authenticated information that the Nazis were systematically exterminating European Jewry was made public in the United States in November 1942. President Roosevelt did nothing about the mass murder for fourteen

months, then moved only because he was confronted with political pressures he could not avoid and because his administration stood on the brink of a nasty scandal over its rescue policies.

3. The War Refugee Board, which the President then established to save Jews and other victims of the Nazis, received little power, almost no cooperation from Roosevelt or his administration, and grossly inadequate government funding. (Contributions from Jewish organizations, which were necessarily limited, covered 90 percent of the WRB's costs.) Through dedicated work by a relatively small number of people, the WRB managed to help save approximately 200,000 Jews and at least 20,000 non-Jews.

4. Because of State Department administrative policies, only 21,000 refugees were allowed to enter the United States during the three and one-half years the nation was at war with Germany. That amounted to 10 percent of the number who could have been legally admitted under the immigration quotas during that period.

5. Strong popular pressure for action would have brought a much fuller government commitment to rescue and would have produced it sooner. Several factors hampered the growth of public pressure. Among them were anti-Semitism and anti-immigration attitudes, both widespread in American society in that era and both entrenched in Congress; the mass media's failure to publicize Holocaust news, even though the wire services and other news sources made most of the information available to them; the near silence of the Christian churches and almost all of their leadership; the indifference of most of the nation's political and intellectual leaders; the President's failure to speak out on the issue.

6. American Jewish leaders worked to publicize the European Jewish situation and pressed for government rescue steps. But their effectiveness was importantly diminished by their inability to mount a sustained or unified drive for government action, by diversion of energies into fighting among the several organizations, and by failure to assign top priority to the rescue issue.

7. In 1944 the United States War Department rejected several appeals to bomb the Auschwitz gas chambers and the railroads leading to Auschwitz, claiming that such actions would divert essential air power from decisive operations elsewhere. Yet in the very months that it was turning down the pleas, numerous massive American bombing raids were taking place within fifty miles of Auschwitz. Twice during that time large fleets of American heavy bombers struck industrial targets in the Auschwitz complex itself, not five miles from the gas chambers.

8. Analysis of the main rescue proposals put forward at the time, but brushed aside by government officials, yields convincing evidence that much more

could have been done to rescue Jews, if a real effort had been made. The record also reveals that the reasons repeatedly invoked by government officials for not being able to rescue Jews could be put aside when it came to other Europeans who needed help.

9. Franklin Roosevelt's indifference to so momentous an historical event as the systematic annihilation of European Jewry emerges as the worst failure of his presidency.

10. Poor though it was, the American rescue record was better than that of Great Britain, Russia, or the other Allied nations. This was the case because of the work of the War Refugee Board, the fact that American Jewish organizations were willing to provide most of the WRB's funding, and the overseas rescue operations of several Jewish organizations.

※ ※ ※

America's response to the Holocaust was the result of action and inaction on the part of many people. In the forefront was Franklin D. Roosevelt, whose steps to aid Europe's Jews were very limited. . . .

In December 1942, the President reluctantly agreed to talk with Jewish leaders about the recently confirmed news of extermination. Thereafter, he refused Jewish requests to discuss the problem; he even left the White House to avoid the Orthodox rabbis' pilgrimage of October 1943. . . .

It appears that Roosevelt's overall response to the Holocaust was deeply affected by political expediency. Most Jews supported him unwaveringly, so an active rescue policy offered little political advantage. A pro-Jewish stance, however, could lose votes. . . .

The main justification for Roosevelt's conduct in the face of the Holocaust is that he was absorbed in waging a global war. He lived in a maelstrom of overpowering events that gripped his attention, to the exclusion of most other matters. Decades later, Dean Alfange doubted that he actually realized what the abandonment of the European Jews meant: "He may not have weighed the implications of it to human values, to history, to a moral climate without which a democracy can't really thrive."

Roosevelt's personal feelings about the Holocaust cannot be determined. He seldom committed his inner thoughts to paper. And he did not confide in anyone concerning the plight of Europe's Jews except, infrequently, Henry Morgenthau. There are indications that he was concerned about Jewish problems. But he gave little attention to them, did not keep informed about them, and instructed his staff to divert Jewish questions to the State Department. Years later, Emanuel Celler charged that Roosevelt, instead of providing even "some spark of courageous leadership," had been "silent, indifferent, and insensitive to the plight of the Jews."

※ ※ ※

. . . [T]he Roosevelt administration turned aside most rescue proposals. In the process, government officials developed four main rationalizations for inaction. The most frequent excuse, the unavailability of shipping, was a fraud. When the Allies wanted to find ships for nonmilitary projects, they located them. In 1943, American naval vessels carried 1,400 non-Jewish Polish refugees from India to the American West Coast. The State and War departments arranged to move 2,000 Spanish Loyalist refugees to Mexico using military shipping.

※ ※ ※

When it was a matter of transporting Jews, ships could almost never be found. This was not because shipping was unavailable but because the Allies were unwilling to take the Jews in. In November 1943, Breckinridge Long told the House Foreign Affairs Committee that lack of transportation was the reason the State Department was issuing so few visas. "In December 1941," he explained, "most neutral shipping disappeared from the seas. . . . There just is not any transportation." In reality, ample shipping existed. Neutral vessels crossed the Atlantic throughout the war. Three Portuguese liners, with a combined capacity of 2,000 passengers, sailed regularly between Lisbon and U.S. ports. Each ship made the trip about every six weeks. Most of the time, because of the tight American visa policy, they carried only small fractions of their potential loads. Two dozen other Portuguese and Spanish passenger ships crossed the Atlantic less frequently but were available for fuller service.

※ ※ ※

Another stock excuse for inaction was the claim that Axis governments planted agents among the refugees. Although this possibility needed to be watched carefully, the problem was vastly overemphasized and could have been handled through reasonable security screening. It was significant that Army intelligence found not one suspicious person when it checked the 982 refugees who arrived at Fort Ontario. Nevertheless, potential subversion was continually used as a reason for keeping immigration to the United States very tightly restricted.

※ ※ ※

A third rationalization for failing to aid European Jews took the high ground of nondiscrimination. It asserted that helping Jews would improperly single out one group for assistance when many peoples were suffering under Nazi brutality.

❇ ❇ ❇

The Roosevelt administration, the British government, and the Inter-governmental Committee on Refugees regularly refused to acknowledge that the Jews faced a special situation. One reason for this was to avoid responsibility for taking special steps to save them. Such steps, if successful, would have confronted the Allies with the difficult problem of finding places to put the rescued Jews. Another reason was the fear that special action for the Jews would stir up anti-Semitism. Some asserted that such action would even invite charges that the war was being fought for the Jews. Emanuel Celler declared years later that Roosevelt did nearly nothing for rescue because he was afraid of the label "Jew Deal"; he feared the political effects of the accusation that he was pro-Jewish. The Jews, according to artist Arthur Szyk, were a skeleton in the democracies' political closet, a matter they would rather not mention.

❇ ❇ ❇

The fourth well-worn excuse for rejecting rescue proposals was the claim that they would detract from the military effort and thus prolong the war. That argument, entirely valid with regard to projects that actually would have hurt the war effort, was used almost automatically to justify inaction. Virtually none of the rescue proposals involved enough infringement on the war effort to lengthen the conflict at all or to increase the number of casualties, military or civilian.

Actually, the war effort was bent from time to time to meet pressing humanitarian needs. In most of these instances, it was non-Jews who were helped. During 1942, 1943, and 1944, the Allies evacuated large numbers of non-Jewish Yugoslavs, Poles, and Greeks to safety in the Middle East, Africa, and elsewhere. Difficulties that constantly ruled out the rescue of Jews dissolved. Transportation somehow materialized to move 100,000 people to dozens of refugee camps that sprang into existence. The British furnished transport, supplies, much of the camp staffing, and many of the campsites.

❇ ❇ ❇

It was not a lack of workable plans that stood in the way of saving many thousands more European Jews. Nor was it insufficient shipping, the threat of infiltration by subversive agents, or the possibility that rescue projects would hamper the war effort. The real obstacle was the absence of a strong desire to rescue Jews.

9

THE OUTBREAK
OF THE COLD WAR

If the controversies of the cold war show signs of receding into the "historical" past, historians remain divided with regard to its origins and—as time will doubtless reveal—its impact. Even its chronological outbreak remains a subject of contention, although most will agree that the seeds of confrontation were sown in the years following the Bolshevik Revolution. Certainly Stalin's Russia had less in common with the Western capitalist democracies than with Hitler's Germany, and it may well be that what requires explanation is not how the wartime Allies fell apart but how such an uneasy alliance could have been maintained. With the disappearance of the wartime necessity to maintain the alliance, and with the West and the Soviet Union for all practical purposes sharing a common border soon after the German surrender, was it understandable, if not inevitable, that old tensions and antagonisms would resurface?

From Stalin's point of view and based on his experiences with the West, he had little reason to trust their intentions vis-à-vis the Soviet Union—hence his determination to secure his borders with friendly buffer states. The "atomic diplomacy" practiced by the United States beginning in the summer of 1945 and President Truman's staunch anti-Communism reinforced these suspicions. From the standpoint of the Western Allies, the absorption of the Eastern European states into the Russian empire and their transformation into Soviet satellites attested to Stalin's imperialist ambitions and his drive for European—if not world—hegemony. Given this mutual distrust and the personalities involved with decision making on both sides, conflict becomes more comprehensible, and this should be kept in mind when approaching the historical interpretations that follow.

Regardless of whether one believes that a U.S.–USSR confrontation was inevitable, historians stress that the last year of World War II and the two or three years immediately afterward were crucial in determining subsequent relations between the two superpowers. Prior to the Yalta Conference in February 1945, the Western Allies emphasized military considerations in their relations with the Soviet Union. By July of that year, however, at the time of the Potsdam Conference, the situation had changed and "immediate decisions on the future of Europe could no longer be set aside in favor of more congenial discussions of military progress."[1] It was these decisions that began to make the cold war a visible reality.

If the atmosphere had changed, historians disagree as to whether American policy had. More or less reflecting the views of the American government,[2] "orthodox" historians also maintain that while the successful testing of an atomic bomb strengthened Truman's resolve at Potsdam, American policy was defined by officials who, having given little consideration to the bomb until it was exploded on Hiroshima, remained consistent. Gar Alperovitz, on the other hand, states unequivocally that the bomb changed American foreign policy and even suggests that it was dropped on Japan not so much for the military purpose of ending the Pacific war as quickly as possible but to bring political pressure on Russia. The elaboration and defense of both positions are found in the first two readings.

A larger perspective is taken in the two that follow, in which the writers attempt to assess responsibility for the cold war. Reflecting the views of revisionist historians such as William Appleman Williams and Gabriel Kolko, Ronald Steel points to U.S. policy (especially as formulated by Dean Acheson) as seeing the world in ideological terms, and specifically the Truman Doctrine and the decision to create a new state in West Germany as hardening existing mistrust and hastening the division of Europe. Finally, the distinguished historian of U.S. diplomacy, John L. Gaddis, has described what he sees as a "post-revisionist" synthesis on the origins of the cold war.

Rather than encourage the student to take sides in regard to the outbreak of the cold war, these readings should raise larger questions about the subject and also about the process of writing history. For example, how inevitable was the cold war? Were there identifiable turning points which transformed suspicions into confrontations? What motivated each side to take the stand it did, and were these motives ideological biases or more traditional power politics? Or were miscalculations to blame? Should the purpose of sorting through piles of evidence be simply to prove a historical point, as Alperovitz was one of the first to attempt to do so for the atomic bomb, or rather to seek understanding of the

---

[1] Robert O. Paxton, *Europe in the Twentieth Century*, 3rd ed. (Fort Worth: Harcourt Brace, 1997), p. 497.

[2] Vojtech Mastny blames Stalin and the Soviet system (of which Stalin was a product) for the wish to build an empire, which understandably provoked a Western response.

larger process at work—that is, of why things happen? It may well be that the major question here is why a decision was never taken to prevent use of the bomb; diplomatic considerations alone are too limiting to provide an answer.[3] Perhaps we must investigate not only the political but the personal context (for example, Stalin's paranoia and the differences between Roosevelt and Truman), not only the scientific but also the institutional forces at work, and in so doing change the nature of diplomatic history itself.

[3] Martin J. Sherwin, "Old Issues in New Editions," *Bulletin of the Atomic Scientist* 41 (December 1985), p. 44.

Russia's Road to the Cold War

VOJTECH MASTNY

Vojtech Mastny was born in Prague and later became an American citizen. He did graduate work at Columbia University and taught at the University of Illinois and the U.S. Naval War College. A Guggenheim and Danforth Fellow, he directs the Institute for East Central Europe. He has published works on the Czechs under Nazi rule and on the Benes-Stalin-Molotov conversations of 1943. In *Russia's Road to the Cold War*, he focuses on Soviet wartime aims and policies in Eastern Europe. To what extent does Mastny see the cold war as an inevitable result of leadership and policies (especially Soviet leadership and policies) as early as the 1941–1945 period? How sensitive is he to the realities of a coalition war when he condemns the United States and Great Britain for failing to challenge Soviet territorial demands in the last years of World War II?

The crucial years of the Stalin–Hitler pact left a durable imprint on both the content and the style of Soviet foreign policy. It was in collusion and competition with his congenial Nazi rival that Stalin had formulated the main objectives of that policy in Europe and had developed the means for their attainment as well. Those objectives had not proved very different from the traditional goals of Russian imperialism. Nor had the principal means—the pursuit of a balance of power, with a special predilection for the time-honored device of spheres of influence—been unknown in the arsenal of the "old diplomacy." Nonetheless, in pursuing his goals Stalin had added and perfected a blend of opportunism and savagery that was peculiarly his own. He did not regard it as his fault that the mixture had failed to protect him from Hitler; therefore neither his aims nor his methods were likely to alter in the future—provided, that is, that he could survive the catastrophe he had been so instrumental in bringing on the heads of his people.

❋ ❋ ❋

Of the new perspectives that the Red Army's ascendancy had opened to Stalin in 1943, a separate peace leading to a Soviet–German condominium over Europe had been of interest to him only during the brief span of time between Stalingrad and Kursk. The alternative possibility of using that ascendancy to advance the cause of Communism also did not appeal to the cautious dictator. Thus a gradual and "orderly" growth of Soviet strength from an eastern European base—perhaps with the help of his Communist followers in different countries but not at the cost of a confrontation with his powerful Western allies—emerged as the most desirable goal. The ever more accommodating Western attitude toward a possible division of the continent into spheres of influence abetted Stalin's quest for power and influence. Yet what exactly was worth striving for, in the wide range between his minimum aims and the enticing prospect of Russia's possible hegemony over a prostrate Europe, still remained undecided. The many unanswered questions were to be clarified at the great Allied conferences scheduled in Moscow and in Teheran later that year.

❋ ❋ ❋

The flurry of diplomatic activities at the end of 1943 had shaped Stalin's outlook in a curious way. There was an irony in the relationship between his original expectations and the results of Moscow and Teheran. He had sought, above all, Western military commitments that would shorten the war, and only secondarily looked for political gains to facilitate the growth of Soviet power and influence in postwar Europe. On his first priority he believed he had accomplished less, and on his second priority more, than he had been bargaining for. In reality, his gains were the opposite: the promise of the Second Front was definite whereas the Anglo-American recognition of his freedom of action in eastern Europe was not. Nor could Czechoslovakia's willing subordination, a windfall rather than a viable precedent, provide the desired model for other countries. Nonetheless, Stalin's peculiar illusions and misperceptions continued to shape his view of the relationship between military and political affairs for several more months.

❋ ❋ ❋

Stalin's grasping for a unilateral solution to the Polish question highlighted the profound change in his outlook that had been brought about by the advent of the Second Front. In shaping his long-term aims, the Normandy landings proved an even greater landmark than Stalingrad. After the elaborate Soviet blandishments to induce the enemy to surrender had come to naught, the compelling Anglo-American commitment to further struggle at last prompted Stalin to order his armies beyond the frontier of June 1941 and conquer the lands that would eventually become components of his new empire. With the Rubicon crossed, any premature end to hostilities now would only serve to reduce the potential rewards of the conquest. For the first time since the war began, concern for those rewards started to outweigh Soviet military considerations. It was at this moment that the uprising in Warsaw posed starkly the dilemma between political and military imperatives, with all its grave implications for Stalin's nascent empire.

❀ ❀ ❀

The empire that Nazi folly and Western forbearance had prompted Stalin to seek was his triumph and his nemesis. By military action and inaction, he had by the fall of 1944 secured Russia's supremacy in all the countries he regarded as vital for its security, and beyond. However, on the issue of how the West could be persuaded to sanction that supremacy permanently, the Soviet ruler showed a disturbing reluctance to define the extent of his inflated security needs. Nor did the Western powers act with the necessary determination to clarify the extent of their tolerance, Churchill's elusive percentages deal notwithstanding. They would all have a further chance at another summit meeting, on whose success the future of the alliance now hinged.

❀ ❀ ❀

If we may draw an analogy with Germany's responsibility for World War I, the Soviet Union "willed" the post-Yalta crisis, much though the West helped to "cause" it. The conflict would not have arisen if Stalin had not all along regarded the suppression of majority will in the neighboring countries as indispensable for the pursuit of what he defined as the Russian national interest. Nor would the situation have deteriorated so precipitously if, once the sham of Yalta had been exposed, Stalin had chosen the path of conciliation rather than confrontation. Even so, the process he had set in motion was not yet irreversible; the impending common victory over Nazism had many dangers but also many opportunities for continued, though strictly limited, collaboration. In determining which trend would prevail, the remaining weeks of the war were crucial.

❀ ❀ ❀

In guiding Russia on its road to the Cold War, Stalin was both a victim and an accomplice. He was a victim in the sense that his 1945 military triumph fell short of his hopes—inflated hopes, to be sure, because of his exaggerated

and quixotic notion of security. But he was also an accomplice, for he had provoked the adverse Western reaction which, contrary to his expectations, had
frustrated those hopes. He might have acted with more restraint if, as Litvinov
noted, the Western powers had taken a firm and unequivocal stand early
enough. By not doing so, they too had become both accomplices and victims,
for their own pious hopes for a stable relationship with Moscow had likewise
been frustrated. There was an element of predestination in all this: Stalin could
have taken a more enlightened view of what security means—but only if he had
not been Stalin. And the Western statesmen could have acted with fewer scru-
ples—but then *they* would have had to be akin to Stalin. Wielding so much
greater control over Russian policies than they did over theirs, the dictator may
still seem to have been capable of steering away from confrontations more easily. But in the last analysis, his hands were tied by the Soviet system which had
bred him and which he felt compelled to perpetuate by his execrable methods;
that system was the true cause of the Cold War.

What are the lessons of the Cold War? For better or for worse, they are
lessons of an irrevocable past; it is remarkable how much those events, hardly
more than thirty years old, already have the unmistakable air of another era. In
pondering the thoughts and actions of the statesmen of the time, one cannot
help noticing how small and simple their world was in comparison with ours.
How modest were their tools, how rudimentary their perceptions. Certainly the
Americans and Russians have since learned a great deal about one another. It is
this sense of a distance traveled that makes irresistible a broad appraisal of the
perspectives lost and found.

The longer the perspectives, the more does June 1941 appear as one of the
great turning points in history. Not only did Hitler's gratuitous aggression open
the door through which the Soviet Union eventually stepped out to become the
world's mightiest and perhaps last imperial power; it also provided the dubious
justification for Stalin's imperialism. The humiliation of his life, the Nazi treach-
ery imbued Stalin with an extraordinary drive to justify in retrospect the wisdom
of the expansionistic policies he had initiated during his abortive association
with the German dictator. The experience thus perpetuated rather than discredited the mixture of cynical opportunism and ruthless power politics, disregarding the interests of other nations, that had been the hallmark of the association.
Neither Stalin nor his successors have ever repudiated this legacy.

The enduring memory of a narrow escape from catastrophic defeat in 1941
nurtured a cult of military strength in the Soviet Union. The cult has since bur-
geoned into a militarism so pervasive that critics have sometimes wondered
whether it may have acquired a momentum beyond the leaders' ability to control. Having created the biggest war machine the world has ever seen, the Russians have far exceeded any reasonable security requirements. Whether their

feeling of security has increased proportionately is doubtful; that such a feeling among other nations has diminished as a consequence is certain.

In bringing the war against Nazi Germany to a victorious end, Stalin created the Soviet empire as a by-product. He had not originally sought a military conquest of the whole area he won. He would have preferred to advance his power and influence there, as elsewhere, by less risky and more subtle means, although he never ruled out resorting to force if the conditions were right; in this respect, his approach differed from that of his successors less than it may seem. But Stalin was unable (contrary to his hopes) to satisfactorily project his power abroad except by force of arms and to maintain it except by putting in charge vassal Communist regimes; as a result, he saddled his country with a cluster of sullen dependencies whose possession proved a mixed blessing in the long run.

Far from providing the ultimate protective shield, the empire enlarged the area whose integrity the Russians had to uphold and also diluted its internal cohesion. In coping with the ensuing challenges, the Soviet leaders since Stalin had greatly refined the art of penetrating other countries without outright conquest and of controlling those previously conquered without excessive resort to force. Despite the refinements, however, the fundamental dilemmas of imperialism they inherited from him are still very much with them, with no resolution in sight. The recurrent Soviet setbacks in uncommitted countries and the smoldering discontent throughout eastern Europe suggest a disconcerting lack of alternatives to force.

In masterminding Russia's ascent during World War II and its aftermath, Stalin proved an accomplished practitioner of the strategy of minimum and maximum aims, a strategy his heirs then continued to pursue with variable success. Apt at both exploiting the existing opportunities and creating new ones, he let his aspirations grow until he realized that he had misjudged the complacency of his Anglo-American partners—as they had misjudged his moderation. So he plunged his country into a confrontation with the West that he had neither desired nor thought inevitable. Not without reason were tributes to his diplomatic proficiency conspicuously missing among the accolades that he afterward stage-managed to impress his subjects by the multiple facets of his presumed genius.

Since Stalin, in pursuing his rising aspirations, took into close account the actual and anticipated Western attitudes, his coalition partners contributed their inseparable share to a development that they soon judged was detrimental to their own vital interests. If the Soviet ruler did not rate nearly so high as a diplomat as his reputation suggested, his American and British opposite numbers surely rated even lower. The great war leaders, Roosevelt and Churchill, failed not so much in their perceptions as in their negligence to prepare themselves and their peoples for the disheartening likelihood of a breakdown of the wartime alliance. The British Prime Minister, whose perceptions were keener, is that much more open to criticism than the American President. In any case, by their reluctance (however understandable) to anticipate worse things to come, the Western statesmen let matters worsen until the hour of reckoning was at hand.

The undistinguished performance of Britain's World War II diplomacy is perhaps the main revelation so far to come out from the recently opened London government archives. Quite apart from the substance of policies, the striking decline of professionalism makes the preceding blunders of appeasement appear less as temporary aberrations than as symptoms of the same unsurmounted crisis of adjustment to the eclipse of power. Nor, to be sure, did the American diplomacy of those days exactly shine. Its shortcomings were largely those of innocence and inexperience, as its subsequent coming of age demonstrated. Since then the United States foreign policy has, for all its persisting deficiencies, drawn on an expertise beyond any comparison with that available thirty years ago—surely one of the most encouraging differences between then and now.

It has been a commonplace to observe that nothing could have prevented the Russians from overrunning the countries they did and installing there regimes of their choice. Indeed, compelling reasons can be cited to explain why the development was inevitable. But this "realistic" argument, which overlooks the difference between Soviet capability and Soviet aims, is a poor guide to both understanding history and inspiring action.

Atomic Diplomacy

GAR ALPEROVITZ

Gar Alperovitz is the Lionel R. Bauman Professor of Political
Economy at the University of Maryland at College Park. In his
controversial *Atomic Diplomacy*, a scrutiny of a critical four-
month period in the closing days of World War II from spring
to September 1945, he tries to show that the atomic bomb
played a major role in the formation of a tougher American policy toward Russia, pointing out Truman's new confidence when
he met with Stalin at Potsdam. Alperovitz was criticized for
making an unobjective evaluation of the records and for taking
remarks out of context. It was to counter these criticisms that in
1985 he published a revised edition of his book that generally
reinforces the author's original account. Does the evidence presented fully support the interpretation offered? Because his book
begins with Roosevelt's death, does Alperovitz's omission of the
original assumption that the bomb would be used in wartime
weaken his argument?

The political developments after August 1945, like the later (mid-1946), ill-
fated attempts to control atomic energy, cannot here be analyzed. And, unfortunately, Admiral Leahy's summary judgment that the Cold War began in the
Balkans can only be tested with further research. However, at this point the
major conclusions to be drawn from a study of American policy during the first
five months of the Truman administration can be briefly summarized. It is also
possible to attempt to define certain other problems which, with presently available materials, can be stated but cannot be conclusively resolved.

The most important point is the most general: Contrary to a commonly held view, it is abundantly clear that the atomic bomb profoundly influenced the way American policy makers viewed political problems. Or, as Admiral Leahy has neatly summarized the point, "One factor that was to change a lot of ideas, including my own, was the atom bomb. . . ." The change caused by the new weapon was quite specific. It did not produce American opposition to Soviet policies in Eastern Europe and Manchuria. Rather, since a consensus had already been reached on the need to take a firm stand against the Soviet Union in both areas, the atomic bomb *confirmed* American leaders in their judgment that they had sufficient power to affect developments in the border regions of the Soviet Union. There is both truth and precision in Truman's statement to Stimson that the weapon "gave him an entirely new feeling of confidence."

This effect was a profoundly important one. Before the atomic bomb was tested, despite their desire to oppose Soviet policies, Western policy makers harbored very grave doubts that Britain and America could challenge Soviet predominance in Eastern Europe. Neither Roosevelt nor Truman could have confidence that the American public would permit the retention of large numbers of conventional troops in Europe after the war. (And Congressional rejection of Truman's military-training program later confirmed the pessimistic wartime predictions.) Thus, at the time of the Yalta Conference, as Assistant Secretary of State William L. Clayton advised Secretary Stettinius, "a large credit . . . appear[ed] to be the only concrete bargaining lever for use in connection with the many other political and economic problems which will arise between our two countries."

That this lever of diplomacy was not sufficiently powerful to force Soviet acceptance of American proposals was amply demonstrated during the late-April and early-May crisis over Poland. Despite Truman's judgment that "the Russians needed us more than we needed them," Stalin did not yield to the firm approach. Hence, without the atomic bomb it seemed exceedingly doubtful that American policy makers would be able substantially to affect events within the Soviet-occupied zone of Europe. It may well be that, had there been no atomic bomb, Truman would have been forced to reconsider the basic direction of his policy as Churchill had done some months earlier.

Indeed, Churchill's 1944 estimate of the power realities usefully illuminates the problems faced by Western policy makers as they attempted to judge their relative strength vis-à-vis the Soviet Union. As soon as Roosevelt rejected Churchill's desperate pleas for an invasion through the Balkans, the Prime Minister understood that he would have little power in Southeastern Europe, and that, indeed, the British position in Greece was seriously threatened. As he told Roosevelt, "the only way I can prevent [utter anarchy] is by persuading the Russians to quit boosting [the Communist-oriented] E.A.M." Again, there was overwhelming logic in his parallel 1944 argument: "It seems to me, considering the Russians are about to invade Rumania in great force . . . it would be a good thing to follow the Soviet leadership, considering that neither you nor we have any troops there at all and that they will probably do what they like anyhow." As he later recalled, before the atomic test, "the arrangements made about the Balkans were, I was sure, the best possible."

As I have attempted to show, by the time of the Yalta Conference, somewhat reluctantly, and against the wishes of the State Department, Roosevelt came to the same conclusion. Even the State Department was forced to adopt the official view that "this Government probably would not oppose predominant Soviet influence in [Poland and the Balkans]." And one high-ranking official went beyond this judgment; substituting his concern for Western Europe for the Prime Minister's specific fears about Greece, he stated: "I am willing to sponsor and support the Soviet arguments if it will save . . . the rest of Europe from the diplomacy of the jungle which is almost certain to ensue otherwise." As Truman's Balkan representative recalled the Yalta Conference, it was "fateful that these discussions should have been held at a time when Soviet bargaining power in eastern Europe was so much stronger than that of the western allies." But it remained for Byrnes to summarize the early-1945 relative strengths of the powers: "It was not a question of what we would *let* the Russians do, but what we could *get* them to do."

As I have shown, this appraisal was radically changed by the summer of 1945. Since Byrnes advised Truman on both the atomic bomb and the need for strong opposition to the Russians in Eastern Europe before the President's first confrontation with Molotov, the new weapon's first impact possibly can be seen as early as the April showdown. However, no final judgment can be rendered on this point, using the evidence presently available. But there is no question that by the middle of July leading American policy makers were convinced that the atomic bomb would permit the United States to take a "firm" stand in subsequent negotiations. In fact, American leaders felt able to demand *more* at Potsdam than they had asked at Yalta. Again, Churchill's post-atomic appraisal is in striking contrast to his view of the pre-atomic realities: "We now had something in our hands which would redress the balance with the Russians." And Byrnes's new advice to Truman was quite straightforward: "The bomb might well put us in a position to dictate our own terms. . . ."

⬚ ⬚ ⬚

To recall the judgments of Stimson and Eisenhower in the autumn of 1945 is to state the ultimate question of to what extent the atomic bomb affected the entire structure of postwar American-Soviet relations. But it is not possible at this juncture to test Secretary Stimson's September view that "the problem of our satisfactory relations with Russia [was] not merely connected with but [was] virtually dominated by the problem of the atomic bomb." Nor can the issue of why the atomic bomb was used be conclusively resolved.

This essay has attempted to describe the influence of the atomic bomb on certain questions of diplomacy. I do not believe that the reverse question—the influence of diplomacy upon the decision to use the atomic bomb—can be answered on the basis of the presently available evidence. However, it is possible to define the nature of the problem which new materials and further research may be able to solve.

A fruitful way to begin is to note General Eisenhower's recollection of the Potsdam discussion at which Stimson told him the weapon would be used against Japan:

> During his recitation of the relevant facts, I had been conscious of a feeling of depression and so I voiced to him my grave misgivings, first on the basis of my belief that Japan was already defeated and that dropping the bomb was completely unnecessary, and secondly because I thought that our country should avoid shocking world opinion by the use of a weapon whose employment was, I thought, no longer mandatory as a measure to save American lives. It was my belief that Japan was, at that very moment, seeking some way to surrender with a minimum loss of "face."

"It wasn't necessary to hit them with that awful thing," Eisenhower concluded.

Perhaps the most remarkable aspect of the decision to use the atomic bomb is that the President and his senior political advisers do not seem ever to have shared Eisenhower's "grave misgivings." As we have seen, they simply assumed that they would use the bomb, never really giving serious consideration to not using it. Hence, to state in a precise way the question "Why was the atomic bomb used?" is to ask why senior political officials did *not* seriously question its use as Eisenhower did.

The first point to note is that the decision to use the weapon did not derive from overriding military considerations. Despite Truman's subsequent statement that the weapon "saved millions of lives," Eisenhower's judgment that it was "completely unnecessary" as a measure to save lives was almost certainly correct. This is not a matter of hindsight; *before the atomic bomb was dropped each of the Joint Chiefs of Staff advised that it was highly likely that Japan could be forced to surrender "unconditionally," without use of the bomb and without an invasion.* Indeed, this characterization of the position taken by the senior military advisers is a conservative one.

General Marshall's June 18 appraisal was the most cautiously phrased advice offered by any of the Joint Chiefs: "The impact of Russian entry on the already hopeless Japanese may well be the decisive action levering them into capitulation. . . ." Admiral Leahy was absolutely certain there was no need for the bombing to obviate the necessity of an invasion. His judgment after the fact was the same as his view before the bombing: "It is my opinion that the use of this barbarous weapon at Hiroshima and Nagasaki was of no material assistance in our war against Japan. The Japanese were already defeated and ready to surrender. . . ." Similarly, through most of 1945 Admiral King believed the bomb unnecessary, and Generals Arnold and LeMay defined the official Air Force position in this way: Whether or not the atomic bomb should be dropped was not for the Air Force to decide, but explosion of the bomb was not necessary to win the war or make an invasion unnecessary.

Similar views prevailed in Britain long before the bombs were used. General Ismay recalls that by the time of Potsdam, "for some time past it had been firmly fixed in my mind that the Japanese were tottering." Ismay's reaction to the suggestion of the bombing was, like Eisenhower's and Leahy's, one of "revulsion." And Churchill, who as early as September 1944, felt that Russian entry was likely to force capitulation, has written: "It would be a mistake to suppose that the fate of Japan was settled by the atomic bomb. Her defeat was certain before the first bomb fell. . . ."

The military appraisals made before the weapons were used have been confirmed by numerous postsurrender studies. The best known is that of the United States Strategic Bombing Survey. The Survey's conclusion is unequivocal: "Japan would have surrendered even if the atomic bombs had not been dropped, even if Russia had not entered the war, and even if no invasion had been planned or contemplated."

That military considerations were not decisive is confirmed—and illuminated—by the fact that the President did not even ask the opinion of the military adviser most directly concerned. General MacArthur, Supreme Commander of Allied Forces in the Pacific, was simply informed of the weapon shortly before it was used at Hiroshima. Before his death he stated on numerous occasions that, like Eisenhower, he believed the atomic bomb was completely unnecessary from a military point of view.

Although military considerations were not primary, as we have seen, unquestionably political considerations related to Russia played a major role in the decision; from at least mid-May American policy makers hoped to end the hostilities before the Red Army entered Manchuria. For this reason they had no wish to test whether Russian entry into the war would force capitulation—as most thought likely—long before the scheduled November invasion. Indeed, they actively attempted to delay Stalin's declaration of war.

Nevertheless, it would be wrong to conclude that the atomic bomb was used simply to keep the Red Army out of Manchuria. Given the desperate efforts of the Japanese to surrender, and Truman's willingness to offer assurances to the Emperor, it is entirely possible that the war could have been ended by negotiation before the Red Army had begun its attack. But, again, as we have seen, after Alamogordo neither the President nor his senior advisers were interested in exploring this possibility.

One reason may have been their fear that if time-consuming negotiations were once initiated, the Red Army might attack in order to seize Manchurian objectives. But, if this explanation is accepted, once more one must conclude that the bomb was used primarily because it was felt to be politically important to prevent Soviet domination of the area.

Such a conclusion is very difficult to accept, for American interests in Manchuria, although historically important to the State Department, were not of great significance. The further question therefore arises: Were there other political reasons for using the atomic bomb? In approaching this question, it is important to note that most of the men involved at the time who since have made their views public always mention *two* considerations which dominated discussions. The first was the desire to end the Japanese war quickly, which, as we have seen, was not primarily a military consideration, but a political one. The second is always referred to indirectly.

In June, for example, a leading member of the Interim Committee's scientific panel, A. H. Compton, advised against the Franck report's suggestion of a technical demonstration of the new weapon: Not only was there a possibility that this might not end the war promptly, but failure to make a combat demonstration would mean the "loss of the opportunity to impress the world with the national sacrifices that enduring security demanded." The general phrasing that the bomb was needed "to impress the world" has been made more specific by J. Robert Oppenheimer. Testifying on this matter some years later he stated that the second of the two "overriding considerations" in discussions regarding the bomb was "the effect of our actions on the stability, on our strength, and the stability of the postwar world." And the problem of postwar stability was inevitably the problem of Russia. Oppenheimer has put it this way: "Much of the discussion revolved around the question raised by Secretary Stimson as to whether there was any hope at all of using this development to get less barbarous relations with the Russians."

Vannevar Bush, Stimson's chief aide for atomic matters, has been quite explicit: "That bomb was developed on time. . . ." Not only did it mean a quick end to the Japanese war, but "it was also delivered on time so that there was no necessity for any concessions to Russia at the end of the war."

In essence, the second of the two overriding considerations seems to have been that a combat demonstration was needed to convince the Russians to accept the American plan for a stable peace. And the crucial point of this effort was the need to force agreement on the main questions in dispute: the American proposals for Central and Eastern Europe. President Truman may well have expressed the key consideration in October 1945; publicly urging the necessity of a more conventional form of military power (his proposal for universal military training), in a personal appearance before Congress the President declared: "It is only by strength that we can impress the fact upon possible future aggressors that we will tolerate no threat to peace. . . ."

If indeed the "second consideration" involved in the bombing of Hiroshima and Nagasaki was the desire to impress the Russians, it might explain the strangely ambiguous statement by Truman that not only did the bomb end the war, but it gave the world "a chance to face the facts." It would also accord with Stimson's private advice to McCloy: "We have got to regain the lead and perhaps do it in a pretty rough and realistic way. . . . We have coming into action a weapon which will be unique. Now the thing [to do is] . . . let our actions speak for themselves." Again, it would accord with Stimson's statement to Truman that the "greatest complication" would occur if the President negotiated with Stalin before the bomb had been "laid on Japan." It would tie in with the fact that from mid-May strategy toward all major diplomatic problems was based upon the assumption the bomb would be demonstrated. Finally, it might explain why none of the highest civilian officials seriously questioned the use of the bomb as Eisenhower did; for, having reversed the basic direction of diplomatic strategy *because* of the atomic bomb, it would have been very difficult indeed for anyone subsequently to challenge an idea which had come to dominate all calculations of high policy.

At present no final conclusion can be reached on this question. But the problem can be defined with some precision: Why did the American government refuse to attempt to exploit Japanese efforts to surrender? Or, alternatively, why did they refuse to test whether a Russian declaration of war would force capitulation? Were Hiroshima and Nagasaki bombed primarily to impress the world with the need to accept America's plan for a stable and lasting peace— that is, primarily, America's plan for Europe? The evidence strongly suggests that the view which the President's personal representative offered to one of the atomic scientists in May 1945 was an accurate statement of policy: "Mr. Byrnes did not argue that it was necessary to use the bomb against the cities of Japan in order to win the war . . . Mr. Byrnes's . . . view [was] that our possessing and demonstrating the bomb would make Russia more manageable in Europe. . . ."

Commissar of the Cold War

RONALD STEEL

Ronald Steel has written extensively on American politics and foreign policy. His books include *Pax Americana* and the award-winning biography *Walter Lippman and the American Century.* Educated at Northwestern and Harvard Universities, he has been a visiting professor at several U.S. universities. The following is taken from his lengthy review of Dean Acheson's memoirs, *Present at the Creation.* Insofar as Steel's account touches on such pivotal episodes in the cold war as the Truman Doctrine, the Marshall Plan, and the Berlin Blockade, it offers a useful and concise summary of how revisionist historians interpret these events. How do Steel's analyses of the Truman Doctrine and the Marshall Plan compare with those of Gaddis in the reading that follows?

The first testing of the new diplomacy came early in 1947 when the British informed Washington that they could no longer afford the cost of supporting the Greek royalist government against communist insurgents. Acheson, substituting for Secretary Marshall, convinced Truman of the need to preserve the Western sphere of influence in the eastern Mediterranean. Congress was asked to provide $400 million for emergency aid to Greece, with Turkey thrown in for good measure. During the initial briefing, the Congressmen were skeptical about providing help for Britain's client state. Instead of arguing that the balance of power required US intervention, an argument which he evidently assumed his audience would not understand, Acheson chose to scare them with the specter of communism running rampant. "Like the apples in a barrel infected by one rotten one," he told the skeptical legislators,

> the corruption of Greece would infect Iran and all to the East. It would also carry infection to Africa through Asia Minor and Egypt, and to Europe through Italy and France, already threatened by the strongest domestic communist parties in Western Europe. The Soviet Union was playing one of the greatest gambles in history at minimal cost. It did not need to win all the possibilities. Even one or two offered immense gains. We and we alone were in a position to break up the play. These were the stakes that British withdrawal from the eastern Mediterranean offered to an eager and ruthless opponent.

Of course, as Milovan Djilas later pointed out, not only was Stalin not instigating the communist uprising in Greece, but he was actually trying to discourage it and told the Yugoslavs to stop supporting it. "What do you think," Djilas quotes Stalin as saying in February 1948, "that Great Britain and the United States—the United States, the most powerful state in the world—will permit you to break their line of communication in the Mediterranean? Nonsense. And we have no navy. The uprising in Greece must be stopped, and as quickly as possible."

But Acheson was not interested in such subtleties at the time, nor is he now. His lurid analysis scared the legislators, and the Greek-Turkish aid bill was sent to Congress on March 12, 1947, encapsuled in the message that came to be known as the Truman Doctrine. In his pride over the doctrine, Acheson neglects to mention what one learns from Charles Bohlen's recently published *The Transformation of American Foreign Policy*—that General Marshall, who was at the time en route to Moscow with Bohlen, thought the message unduly severe and asked Truman to change it:

> When we received the text of the President's message, we were somewhat startled to see the extent to which the anti-communist element of this speech was stressed. Marshall sent back a message to President Truman questioning the wisdom of this presentation, saying he thought that Truman was overstating the case a bit. The reply came back that from all his contacts with the Senate, it was clear that this was the only way in which the measure could be passed.

In assessing the Truman Doctrine it is important to remember that in the spring of 1947 the discord between Russia and the West had not yet hardened into the confrontation of the Cold War. The division of Europe was not yet completed, and at the time many believed that the Truman Doctrine was hastening it. Walter Lippmann asked whether the President had laid down a policy or was launching a crusade, and scored what he called "big hot generalities." What particularly troubled him was the sentence, which later came to be considered the key part of the Doctrine, in which Truman declared:

> I believe that it must be the policy of the United States to support free peoples who are resisting attempted subjugation by armed minorities or by outside pressures.

In this seemingly innocuous sentence Lippmann saw what others later discovered: a formula for the repression of revolutionary movements. Gradually the American people became convinced, above all by the propaganda of their own government, that they were involved in a life-or-death struggle with an ideology. Communism, whatever its form, became equated with a threat to America's survival.

The fault lies with the Cold War liberals such as Acheson. They treated the American people cynically, thinking they could be manipulated, giving them injections of anti-communism in order to get through military appropriations they felt inadequate to explain otherwise. Acheson is not the only offender, but he is among the worst, for he was intelligent enough to know what he was doing. With a distaste for public opinion bordering on contempt, he did not tell the truth to Congress and he did not tell the truth to the people. The wave of anti-communism Acheson helped to unleash proved far too powerful for him to handle, especially after McCarthy appeared on the scene. It paralyzed him as Secretary of State, discredited the office he held, justly drove the Democrats from office, and made it virtually impossible for the nation to follow a rational foreign policy. Treat the people with contempt, and you will be treated contemptuously in return. That is the lesson of Dean Acheson's presence at the creation, and the greater misfortune is that we have all been paying for it ever since.

In selling the Truman Doctrine to a skeptical Congress, Acheson laid down the basic tenets of American post-war foreign policy: the ideological division of the world, the equation of "freedom" with American strategic and political interests, the belief that every outpost of the empire (the "free world"), however unimportant it might be in itself, must be prevented from falling under communist control lest the entire structure be threatened (collective security). These were Acheson's justifications for Korea, as they are for Vietnam.

⊠ ⊠ ⊠

The Marshall Plan is, of course, considered an unprovocative act of enlightened self-interest that saved Western Europe from falling into the communist orbit. But at the time many Europeans, despite the economic crisis they were facing, feared American assistance presented in a form that might antagonize Moscow. As Louis Halle has observed, "When the offer of rescue came at last, in the form of the Marshall Plan, it undoubtedly did contribute to the final fall of Czechoslovakia and its incorporation in the Russian empire." To Stalin's mind the Marshall Plan, coming hot on the heels of the Truman Doctrine, was a design for an anti-communist Western Europe backed up by American military power. This, one recalls, was at a moment when the United States still had an atomic monopoly, and when certain high officials in the government were calling for a "preventive" nuclear strike against the Soviet Union. We cannot know what effect a different American posture would have had on Stalin's plans. But from the record available to us it seems clear that the hardening American attitude reinforced traditional Russian fears of isolation by hostile forces and led the Kremlin to tighten its grip on the territories already under its control. The Russians rejected Washington's call to cooperate in the European Recovery Program and forbade their satellites from participating—just as Washington expected they would. As Charles Bohlen further notes in *Transformation:*

> Kennan and I . . . said we were convinced that the Soviet Union could not accept the plan if it retained its original form, because the basis of self-help and the fact that the United States was to have a voice with the receiving country as to how the aid was used would make it quite impossible for the Soviet Union to accept . . .

Russia's rejection was greeted with relief in Washington and saved the Marshall Plan from almost certain Congressional dismemberment. The breach was widened.

The division of Europe was sealed in the winter of 1948 by the coup in Czechoslovakia and the blockade of Berlin. Today it is assumed that the blockade was an unprovoked act of Soviet aggression to push the Western allies out of Berlin. But it was not that clear-cut. In retrospect, the Russian aim was to prevent the United States, together with Britain and France, from establishing an independent, anti-communist West German state. Nothing that happened during this or any other period can excuse the ruthlessness with which Soviet puppet regimes treated the peoples of Eastern Europe and East Germany. For the most part, however, Russia's diplomatic moves were made in response to Western initiatives, as the sequence of events reveals: In May 1947 the US and Britain fused their occupation zones into an economic union. The next month General Marshall proposed the European Recovery Program in his speech at Harvard, and a month later Washington announced that the German economy was to be self-sustaining. In August the Germans were allowed to increase production to the 1936 level, and at this point the French agreed to fuse their zone with the other two. "By November," Acheson reports, "the three allies were able to present a solid front to the Russians."

The inability of the Western allies to work together with Russia in governing Germany led to discussions in London in February and March 1948 toward the creation of an independent German state in the Western zones: the so-called "London Program." That same February the Russians gave the go-ahead for the coup in Czechoslovakia, and, upon the allies' signing the Brussels Defense Pact, walked out of the Allied Control Council in Berlin. The US, Britain, and France proceeded with the integration of their zones, and in June announced they would proceed to form a West German government with "the minimum requirements of occupation and control." As a first step they set up a separate currency for West Germany.

This, in Acheson's words, "triggered the final break with the Soviet Union in Germany." Five days after the announcement of the Western currency reform, the Russians set up their own currency system for East Germany and all Berlin. The Allies responded by extending the West German currency reform to Berlin (still under four-power control). The next day the Russians imposed a full blockade on Berlin.

For Acheson, this sequence of events, culminating in a separate West German state, was a triumph of US diplomacy. But it solidified the division of Europe. Was it entirely the fault of the Russians, or was Moscow reacting defensively? According to George Kennan, chief of the policy planning staff of the State Department at the time,

> There can be no doubt that, coming as it did on top of the European recovery program and the final elaboration and acceptance of the Atlantic alliance, the move toward establishment of a separate government in Western Germany aroused keen alarm among the Soviet leaders. It was no less than natural that they should do all in their power to frustrate this undertaking and to bring the three Western powers back to the negotiating table in order that Russia might continue to have a voice in all-German affairs.

Kennan feared that the "London Program," providing for a separate West German state, would induce the Russians to set up a rival government in the East, and "the fight would be on for fair; the division of Germany, and with it the division of Europe itself, would tend to congeal." Instead of a separate arrangement for Berlin, he favored a settlement for Germany as a whole involving the withdrawal of Russian troops. In November 1948 the Planning Staff presented a package entitled "Plan A," which provided for a new provisional German government under international supervision, withdrawal of allied forces to garrisons on the periphery of Germany, and complete demilitarization of the country. Kennan says the plan was never seriously considered. "Mr. Acheson, if I read his mind correctly in retrospect, regarded it as no more than a curious . . . aberration," while "the London Program . . . was being rushed frantically to completion with the scarcely concealed intention that it should stand as a *fait accompli* before the Big Four foreign ministers."

Acheson's formula for German reunification, expressed at the foreign ministers' meeting in Paris in May 1949, was "to extend the Bonn constitution to the whole country." This would, of course, not only have eliminated the pro-Soviet regime in the eastern zone, but have brought a unified Germany into the Western camp. As Acheson was no doubt aware, this possibility was anathema not only to the Russians but to the East (and even West) Europeans who had twice been invaded by Germany in this century and were opposed to reunification under any conditions.

Of course Acheson did not seriously expect the Russians to accept. He wanted to anchor West Germany firmly to NATO and feared that unification through neutrality would lead to European neutrality, if not communization. In his eyes there was nothing to negotiate, other than a Russian withdrawal from Eastern Europe—for which he was willing to give up nothing in return. He believed the United States must stand firm everywhere the status quo was tested, such as Berlin, and later in such places as Korea and Vietnam, lest the Soviets be tempted to make even greater incursions elsewhere.

Like his followers Rusk and Rostow, Acheson saw every situation as a global confrontation. There were no local contests, but only localized testing of America's will to resist Soviet (or Chinese, or simply "communist") aggression. As part of his policy of creating situations of strength, Acheson was engaged in a race against time to build up German and European military power before the participants lost interest, "to achieve the European Defense Community and end the occupation in Germany before ebb tide in Europe and America lowered the level of will too far."

A momentary threat to these plans came in March 1952 when Stalin sought four-power talks on a German peace treaty. Stalin's proposal differed from previous ones in calling for a reunified Germany free of foreign troops, neutralized, demilitarized, and with the boundaries agreed upon at Potsdam. Acheson surmised, quite correctly, that this was designed to prevent the further integration of Germany into the West. It was, in his words, "a spoiling operation." Rather than a unified neutral Germany, Acheson, like Adenauer, wanted a divided Germany with the strongest segment linked to the West. If Stalin were really serious, German unification would have meant abandoning NATO. The price was too high.

Although he knew better, Acheson persisted in equating communism with Soviet imperialism even in cases where it obviously did not apply. This helped him to squeeze foreign and military aid out of a recalcitrant Congress and to justify policies which might otherwise have seemed unjustifiable. "Of course we opposed the spread of communism," he writes of US policy in Asia with the marvelous assurance of one whose hypocrisy has moved on to the higher plane of self-congratulation. "It was the subtle, powerful instrument of Russian imperialism, designed and used to defeat the very interests we shared with the Asian peoples, the interest in their own autonomous development uncontrolled from abroad."

To show our concern for the interests of the Asians, Acheson in May 1950 called for American military and economic aid to France to help put down Ho Chi Minh's independence movement. This was justified under the catch-all strategy of blocking Soviet imperialism. "The United States government," the official State Department document declared,

> convinced that neither national independence nor democratic evolution can exist in any area dominated by Soviet imperialism, considers the situation to be such as to warrant its according economic aid and military equipment to the Associated States of Indochina and to France in order to assist them in restoring stability and permitting these states to pursue their peaceful and democratic development.

Helping French colonialism caused him no moral pain, although he continually griped about the stubbornness of the French in wanting to run their colony themselves rather than turn it over to American "advisers." His sympathies naturally seem to lie with the colonizers rather than with those being colonized. By the time Acheson left office, the United States was paying nearly half of France's military bill in Indochina. "I could not then or later," he explains of this policy, "think of a better course." After all that has happened there since, he still cannot.

The Emerging Post-Revisionist Synthesis on the Origins of the Cold War

JOHN L. GADDIS

John L. Gaddis is a professor of history at Ohio University and has published extensively on cold war diplomacy. In a paper first presented at the 1983 meeting of the Organization of American Historians and subsequently published, he argues that a "post-revisionist consensus" has emerged on the origins of the cold war, one that reflects new research, more sober analyses, and the absence of a Vietnam War to attract nonspecialists to the debate. On which points does Gaddis find that agreement has been reached? Does his synthesis seem more sympathetic to the "orthodox" school or to the "revisionist" school? How does he insist that postrevisionism is not "simply orthodoxy plus archives"?

It is no secret that there was once a certain amount of disagreement among American historians about the origins of the Cold War. A decade ago this subject was capable of eliciting torrents of impassioned prose, of inducing normally placid professors to behave like gladiators at scholarly meetings, of provoking calls for the suppression of unpopular points of view, threats of lawsuits, and, most shocking of all, the checking of footnotes. Today, in contrast, the field is very much quieter, its occupants are much more polite to one another, and talk of consensus is heard throughout the land. It may be that we are all getting older and have not the stomach for combat any longer. But I prefer to think that what is happening is the emergence of a genuine synthesis of previously antagonistic viewpoints, based upon an impressive amount of new research.

John Gaddis, "The Emerging Post-Revisionist Synthesis on the Origins of the Cold War," *Diplomatic History*, Vol. 7, pp. 171–190, 1983. Copyright The Society for Historians of American Foreign Relations.

There is no question that this research is taking place. The recent Society for Historians of American Foreign Relations *Guide to Diplomatic History Since 1700* devotes no less than 42 percent of its pages (514 out of 1213) to the period since 1945. One out of every five doctoral dissertations on U.S. foreign relations completed during the past four years dealt with some aspect of the 1945–50 period. The first six volumes of *Diplomatic History* contained 130 articles, of which 47 (36 percent) focused just on the years between the end of World War II and the onset of the Korean War.

Despite this volume of work, and despite the array of newly declassified sources upon which most of it is based, the recent literature on Cold War origins has not attracted the same attention New Left historiography was receiving in the late 1960s and early 1970s. In part, this is because the revisionism of that period coincided with the growth of public opposition to the Vietnam War; no comparable contemporary issue has drawn the interest of nonspecialists to the more recent literature. In part, as well, one must acknowledge that much of the new writing is sober stuff: it lacks the pungency of the earlier revisionist accounts; its conclusions, most of the time, are less than spectacular. Nevertheless, the new literature is making some fundamental changes in our understanding of the early Cold War, to such an extent that it is now generally acknowledged that we have reached a third stage, beyond both orthodoxy and revisionism, in the historiography of that period.

Various labels have been proposed to characterize this new school—"neoorthodoxy," "eclecticism," "postrevisionism"—the latter term seems to have caught on more than the others and is the one that will be used here. In the best assessment of it we have had to date, J. Samuel Walker describes postrevisionism as a "new consensus" which "draws from both traditional and revisionist interpretations to present a more balanced explanation of the beginning of the cold war." What follows is an attempt to examine some of the elements of that consensus, to indicate where they differ from both orthodox and revisionist accounts, and to suggest some of the implications they may pose for future research.

As its name implies, the postrevisionist literature on Cold War origins cannot be understood apart from the "revisionism" that preceded it. A useful starting point, therefore, might [be] a brief review of the fundamental propositions of New Left historiography, with a view to clarifying how postrevisionism differs from them. It should be emphasized at the outset that the New Left perspective on the origins of the Cold War was never monolithic. No one revisionist would have accepted all lines of argument associated with that school of thought; differences among New Left scholars at times rivaled in intensity those with more "orthodox" colleagues. Nevertheless, and allowing for these differences, there would appear to have been four interlocking propositions upon which the New Left view rested:

1. That postwar American foreign policy approximated the classical Leninist model of imperialism—that is, that an unwillingness or inability to redistribute wealth at home produced an aggressive search for markets and investment opportunities overseas, without which, it was thought, the capitalist system in the United States could not survive.

2. That this internally motivated drive for empire left little room for accommodating the legitimate security interests of the Soviet Union, thereby ensuring the breakdown of wartime cooperation.

3. That the United States imposed its empire on a mostly unwilling world, recruiting it into military alliances, forcing it into positions of economic dependency, maintaining its imperial authority against growing opposition by means that included bribery, intimidation, and covert intervention.

4. That all of this took place against the will of the people of the United States, who were tricked by cynical but skillful leaders into supporting this policy of imperialism through the propagation of the myth that monolithic communism threatened the survival of the nation.

With regard to the first assertion—that postwar American foreign policy fits the Leninist model of imperialism—postrevisionists have pointed out several problems:

1. If we can accept the testimony, both public and private, of the policymakers themselves, there is little evidence that they saw a crisis of capitalism as the most pressing issue facing the country at the end of World War II. There was concern about a postwar depression, to be sure, but that concern was only one aspect of a more general preoccupation with what was now coming to be called "national security." As Michael Sherry and Daniel Yergin have pointed out, the experience of war had sensitized American leaders to the possibilities of future external threats even before the Soviet Union had emerged as the most obvious postwar adversary. This sense of vulnerability reflected not so much fears of an economic collapse at home as it did a new awareness of the global balance of power and the effect recent developments in the technology of warfare might have on it. Although it does not totally dismiss concerns about the future of the domestic economy, this emphasis on national security does assign them a considerably lower priority than was characteristic of most New Left accounts.

2. Even if the fate of capitalism had been primary in the minds of American leaders at the time, the policies they actually followed did less than one might think to advance it. The concept of multilateralism, upon which postwar economic security was thought to rest, quickly took a back seat to containment, which to a considerable extent [involved] preserving rather

than breaking down regional economic blocs. It also is becoming clear that the United States made no systematic effort to suppress socialism within its sphere of influence, despite the fact that one might have expected a militantly capitalist nation to promote free enterprise wherever possible. We are coming to understand as well that domestic economic interests themselves were not monolithic and hardly could have provided precise guidance to policymakers had they been inclined to give primacy to them.

3. All of which is not to say that the United States was bashful about using the very considerable economic power that it did possess. Here, postrevisionists generally have accepted revisionist arguments that the United States did in fact employ Lend Lease, prospects of reparations shipments from Germany, postwar credits, and Marshall Plan aid to achieve certain political objectives. But that is just the point: economic instruments were used to serve political ends, not the other way around as the Leninist model of imperialism would seem to imply. American economic strength was a potent weapon that could be used—and indeed, in the early days of the Cold War, was the primary weapon used—to help redress the political-military balance of power. But that is very different from saying that U.S. political-military power was used to stave off what was seen as an otherwise inevitable collapse of the capitalist order.

The second major proposition upon which the New Left account of the origins of the Cold War rested was that the American drive for world empire, motivated primarily by the requirements of capitalism, left no room for accommodating the legitimate security interests of the Soviet Union and therefore made the Cold War unavoidable. The main point to note about this argument is that it was based upon faith, not research. However great their energies in mining the American archives, not one of the New Left revisionists was a Soviet specialist; few, if any, knew Russian. They simply assumed a willingness to cooperate on the part of Stalin's Russia that was frustrated by American intransigence. Soviet specialists in the United States and elsewhere were skeptical of this argument, but few of them had mastered the American archives, so their efforts to refute the revisionists were not very convincing.

⊠ ⊠ ⊠

The third New Left argument was that the United States imposed its empire on unwilling clients, forcing them into military alliances and into positions of economic dependency against their will. This, too, was an argument derived more from intuition than research: familiarity with the concerns of third parties in the Cold War was no more a strong point of revisionist literature than was consideration of the Soviet Union's role in that conflict. Postrevisionist scholarship, to some extent, has corrected that deficiency by giving attention to the domestic background of decisions that caused countries in Western Europe, the Mediterranean, and the Near East to align themselves with the United States after World War II.

Two fine regional studies, Lundestad's *American, Scandinavia, and the Cold War* and Bruce Kuniholm's *The Origins of the Cold War in the Near East*, show that as far as those parts of the world were concerned, the American sphere of influence arose as much by invitation as by imposition. In Greece, Turkey, and even Iran, Kuniholm shows, American influence was welcomed after the war as a counterweight to the Russians. To be sure, there was U.S. intervention in the internal affairs of those countries. But Kuniholm suggests that that was what leaders in those countries wanted: American intervention against the Left was preferable, from their point of view, to Soviet intervention on behalf of it. Similarly, Lundestad has shown that the alignment of Norway and Denmark with NATO could not have happened without significant support inside those countries; that the United States did not use all means available to it to recruit members—witness Washington's eventual acceptance of Sweden's decision to stay out; and that the United States probably would have gone along with a less formal security arrangement had the Scandinavians been able to agree on one.

This same pattern of invitation rather than imposition shows up in the recently opened records of the British Foreign Office, as the work of Terry Anderson and Robert Hathaway makes clear. In London, the concern was not that the United States would be too aggressive but that it would be too passive. The fear was not of American expansionism but of American isolationism, and much time was spent considering how such expansionist tendencies could be reinforced.

What these postrevisionist arguments seem to show, then, is that the United States was not alone in perceiving the Soviet Union as a threat after World War II. Other countries shared this impression and sought to bring in the United States to redress the balance. It remains to be seen whether this same pattern will hold up in parts of the world that have not yet been studied in the same detail as Britain, Scandinavia, or the Near East—or whether these generalizations can be projected forward into the 1950s, when the American presence became far more overbearing than it was in the late 1940s. Revisionists might legitimately ask, as well, who was doing the inviting in each of these cases—the government elite, or the "masses"? Still, enough work has been done to make it clear that the revisionist view of an American empire imposed upon unwilling subjects is in some need of revision itself.

The fourth argument made by the New Left was that the policy of containment evolved against the will of the American people, who had to be tricked into supporting imperialism by the government, using the imaginary threat of an international Communist monolith. Postrevisionists have not dealt extensively with the interaction between domestic influences and foreign policy, although the logic of their analysis, which stresses the extent to which Soviet policies alarmed other countries, would seem to suggest that policymakers would not have had to work very hard to convince the public to support containment. Indeed, some postrevisionists have suggested that public and congressional opinion moved in this direction before the policymakers did. Other postrevisionists have stressed the capacity of policymakers to shape public opinion in predetermined directions. The two viewpoints may not be as contradictory as they might seem: it is possible that policymakers sought to move public opinion in anti-Soviet directions at a time when it was shifting in that direction of its own accord. Still, this is one area where postrevisionists remain divided.

Furnishing the means to support a "get tough" policy was something else again. Here revisionist charges that the government found it necessary to manipulate public opinion have found support among postrevisionists, whether one is looking at the effort to sell aid to Greece and Turkey, the Marshall Plan, the Military Assistance Program, or, had the Korean War not intervened, the massive increases in the defense budget called for in NSC-68. Perhaps the explanation for this campaign is consistent with what we know to be true of human nature—people find it easy to view with alarm, but more difficult to accept without some persuasion the sacrifices necessary to do something about it.

Two variations of this argument about administrations manipulating public opinion should be mentioned here. One is the assertion that something like a "military-industrial complex" came to dominate the making of foreign policy during the early Cold War years. It is true that World War II had brought about close cooperation between defense contractors and the government. It is true, as Yergin has pointed out, that expenditures for research and development in the military sphere increased impressively during the early Cold War period. But, significantly, overall military spending did not. The era of budgetary plenty for the military did not come until the Korean War had legitimized the conclusions of NSC-68. Prior to that time, defense spending was kept under such tight control that the Joint Chiefs of Staff despaired of meeting the obligations to which political leaders had committed them. There was, as well, as Lawrence S. Kaplan has pointed out, a curious passivity among military leaders of that day, who seemed content to leave key decisions, even on significant military matters, up to civilians in the State Department. This is hardly the pattern one would expect if a military-industrial complex had been operating at that time.

❈ ❈ ❈

One might well ask, at this stage, just how postrevisionism differs from traditional accounts of the origins of the Cold War written before New Left revisionism came into fashion. What is new, after all, about the view that American officials worried more about the Soviet Union than about the fate of capitalism in designing the policy of containment, about the assertion that Soviet expansionism was the primary cause of the Cold War, about the argument that American allies welcomed the expansion of U.S. influence as a counterweight to the Russians, about the charge that the government responded to as well as manipulated public opinion? Were not all of these things said years ago?

The answer is yes, but they were said more on the basis of political conviction or personal experience than systematic archival research. What the postrevisionists have done is to confirm, on the basis of the documents, several of the key arguments of the old orthodox position, and that in itself is a significant development. But postrevisionism should not be thought of as simply orthodoxy plus archives. On several major points, revisionism has had a significant impact on postrevisionist historiography. This coincidence of viewpoints between the revisionists and their successors needs to be emphasized, if only to make the point that postrevisionism is something new, not merely a return to old arguments.

1. Postrevisionist accounts pay full attention to the use by the United States of economic instruments to achieve political ends. This dimension of American diplomacy was given short shrift in orthodox accounts; it was as if to mention economics was to call into question the aura of innocence and naiveté that somehow was supposed to distinguish Washington's policies from those of other countries. The revisionists have made it emphatically clear that when it came to the use of economic power, the United States was neither naive nor innocent. It was, as Truman once said, the "economic giant" of the world, and most postrevisionists now accept that it was determined to make thorough use of this unique strength to promote specific political ends.

2. Postrevisionism tends to stress the absence of any ideological blueprint for world revolution in Stalin's mind; this is another point at which revisionism and postrevisionism are closer to each other than to orthodoxy. Stalin is now seen as a cagey but insecure opportunist, taking advantage of such tactical openings as arose to expand Soviet influence, but without any long-term strategy for or even very much interest in promoting the spread of communism beyond the Soviet sphere.

3. Postrevisionist analyses differ from their orthodox predecessors in confirming revisionist assertions that the government, from time to time, did exaggerate external dangers for the purpose of achieving certain internal goals. Attempts to manage public and congressional opinion were not wholly products of a later generation.

4. But the aspect of New Left historiography that postrevisionists are likely to find most useful—and the point upon which their work will depart most noticeably from orthodox accounts—is the argument that there was in fact an American "empire." I should like to develop this line of thought at greater length because it not only illustrates the most important line of continuity between revisionist and postrevisionist scholarship; it also provides some interesting opportunities for future research.

One curiosity of New Left scholarship on the Cold War is that although it assumed the existence of an American empire, it made no effort to compare that empire with those that have existed at other times and in other places. And yet, Washington's experience in projecting first its interests and then its power on a global scale does bear a striking resemblance to the experiences of other great imperial powers in history; from these resemblances, it would seem, revealing comparative insights might be derived.

For example, the New Left seemed to find it difficult to understand how an empire could arise for what its leaders perceived to be defensive reasons. Surely, they insisted, there must have been sinister forces—for which read economic forces, because they always seem more sinister than others—operating behind the scenes. Policymakers either refused to acknowledge them or were unaware of their existence.

But the history of other empires suggests that they can as often arise from perceptions of external as well as from internal insecurity: it is one of the characteristics of great powers that they often do offensive things for defensive reasons. Empires can arise at the invitation of those seeking security as well as by the impositions of those who would deny it. They can develop as unexpected responses to unforeseen circumstances as well as by crafty and farsighted design. They can vary considerably in the extent to which they tolerate diversity within their boundaries.

What the postrevisionists are showing, it would seem, is that the American empire fits more closely the model of defensive rather than offensive expansion, of invitation rather than imposition, of improvisation rather than careful planning. That it was an empire, subject to patterns of development and decay that have affected other empires in the past, can hardly be denied. That it expanded more rapidly and more widely than its Soviet counterpart must be admitted, though that is not too surprising given the facts of geography and the extent of American power in the postwar era. But, as Lundestad has pointed out, this was expansion with limitations; it was an empire operated, at least initially, along defensive lines, and with some sense of restraint.

One can argue at length about the reasons for this restraint: did it reflect the basic decency and good will of the American people, or did the Americans hold back simply because they lacked the manpower and the expertise to remake other societies in their image? Answering this question should provide broad opportunities for future research, as will the question, discussed earlier, of how and by whom the Americans were invited to expand their influence in the first place. It seems beyond argument, though, that there was an American empire, and that a surprising number of governments around the world wanted to be associated with it, given the alternative.

❊ ❊ ❊

We owe a considerable debt to the New Left for forcing us to think about the Cold War in these "imperial" terms. To the extent that we can move beyond revisionism's dependence on the inadequate Leninist explanation of imperialism, and beyond the parochialism that sees only the American experience as relevant, then we may in fact be approaching a basis upon which the long sought-after synthesis of orthodox and revisionist viewpoints can be constructed.

10

THE END OF EUROPEAN EMPIRE

Decolonization refers to the "process by which the peoples of the Third World gained their independence from their colonial rulers"[1] and in so doing brought an end to almost five hundred years of European empire. Nearly all of it took place in the decade or two after the end of World War II, although its origins may be found well before that time. An age of colonization was over, one that despite the brutalities of imperialism had placed its stamp on Western civilization as the first to relate all the peoples of the globe. Whether independence was achieved by the willingness of the European powers to grant it, or whether it was forced upon the powers by national movements (Third World countries prefer the term "national liberation" to "decolonization"), remains a subject of controversy. In any case, as shown by Henri Grimal, World War II provided the colonies with their opportunity. The devastating setbacks incurred by Britain, France, and the Netherlands in the early years of the war shattered the myth of Western invincibility, and if many colonials once more sided with their "mother countries," after 1945 the latter faced a choice between providing concrete reforms or promising future independence.

Was the age of imperialism in fact over, or has the dominance of the Western nations over their former colonies continued under other forms? "Neocolonialism"—that is, continued economic domination or control by foreigners—may be more invidious than direct colonization in that a colony at least had an opportunity to seek redress for its grievances. Certainly the colonial power that had exercised direct rule assumed that the newly sovereign state would maintain the strong political and economic ties established during the period of colonial rule. Even when these ties were severed with the former

---

[1]M. E. Chamberlain, *Decolonization: The Fall of the European Powers* (Oxford: Blackwell, 1985), p. 1.

mother country, direct rule by colonial powers was often replaced by the indirect rule of the post–World War II superpowers. Resentment against any kind of foreign involvement was particularly strong in the cases of former colonial governments taken over by new leaders who had not been associated with the "colonial tradition" and who in many cases rejected Western culture and Western political forms.

Developing countries have claimed that their relationships with the superpowers are at best uneven and that economic control, whether practiced by foreign nations or multinational corporations, is even more damaging than political control because it perpetuates dependency. The former president of Ghana, Kwame Nkrumah, was an articulate and forceful spokesman for an African view of Third World problems.

To what extent does either the colonial legacy or neocolonialism explain the precarious economic position of many Third World countries? Can their economic—and perhaps also political—problems be explained, as sociologist Immanuel Wallerstein has argued, by the impossibility of all states developing simultaneously, a theory that has won favor with some Marxists?[2] Other developmental economists have argued that "periphery countries" have failed to develop because they produce largely for export and have neglected the growth of a home market. Or was it imperialist control that destroyed indigenous industry and brought a halt to domestic agricultural production for home consumption? Could these economies have been sufficiently protected from international competition or exploitation, or both, to develop a sound economic footing? In view of a mounting awareness of global interrelatedness in a rapidly shrinking world, such questions are of primary concern.

---

[2] Immanuel Wallerstein, *The Modern World System: Capitalist Agriculture and the Origins of the European World Economy in the Sixteenth Century* (New York: Academic Press, 1974). Briefly, Wallerstein points to the historical division of the world into core, periphery, and semiperiphery states that possess unequal political and military power and consequently engage in unequal exchange relationships. Two other volumes, published in 1980 and 1989, carry the story through the 1840s.

Patterns in the Transfer of Power

French and British Decolonization Compared

TONY SMITH

Tony Smith is the editor of *The End of European Empire* (1975) and the author of several studies of imperialism. This article appeared in a collection of essays on the transfer of power in Africa. Although he argues that an understanding of the end— as well as the beginning—of European empire requires that emphasis be placed on "the actions of the industrial powers," he insists that the role of Africans and Asians in making their own history cannot be minimized.

Although definite political options were open to Britain and France in imperial policy after 1945, the historically conditioned realm of the possible precluded the adoption of certain courses of action. The material hardships following the havoc of World War II combined with the clear ascendance of the two "anti-imperial" powers, the United States and the Soviet Union, and with the increased maturity of nationalist elites throughout Africa and Asia, to force a decided retrenchment of Europe overseas. In retrospect, we can see that the truly important political decisions that had to be made by Paris and London after 1945 concerned, not whether the colonies would be free, but, rather, which local nationalist factions they would favor with their support and over what piece of territory these new political elites would be permitted to rule. What would be federated, what partitioned, who should govern and according to what procedures constituted decisive issues where the Europeans continued

From Tony Smith, "Patterns in the Transfer of Power: A Comparative Study of French and British Decolonization," in Gifford and Lewis, eds., *The Transfer of Power in Africa* (New Haven: Yale University Press, 1982), pp. 87–89, 97–98, 100–102, 114–115. Reprinted with permission.

to exercise a significant degree of control. When the Europeans did not respect the historically imposed limits of their power, however, their policies were destined to meet with defeat. Thus, although the Suez invasion of October– November 1956 constituted a political crisis of the first order in Britain, it was the only occasion when colonial matters occupied such a prominent position. In France, by contrast, the interminable wars in Indochina and Algeria cost not only the lives of hundreds of thousands of Asians and Africans but eventually brought about the collapse of the Fourth Republic as well.

A comparative analysis of British and French abilities to withdraw from their empires after 1945 suggests four respects in which the British were favored. First, there was the legacy of the past in terms of ideas and procedures on imperial matters, precedents built up over the decades before the Second World War which served to orient European leaders and organize their responses to the pressures for decolonization. On this score, the British proved to be temperamentally, and especially institutionally, more fit than the French to cope with overseas challenges to their rule. Second, there was the international "place" of Britain and France and especially the different relations with the United States maintained by the two countries. Third, there was the question of the domestic political institutions of France and Britain, with their very unequal capacities to deal with a problem of the magnitude of decolonization. The French multiparty system with its weak governing consensus clearly was not the equivalent of the two-party system in Britain. Even had the French system been stronger, however, it is not evident it would have dealt more effectively with decolonization; for national opinion, and especially the "collective conscience" of the political elite in France, was significantly different from that in Britain. The fourth variable to be analyzed directs attention from Paris and London to the character of the nationalist elites with whom the Europeans had to deal. Here, it will be argued that the situations in Indochina and Algeria presented France with serious problems that Britain was simply fortunate enough to escape (at least until Suez).

So the comparative study of European decolonization depends in important measure on the comparative study of colonial nationalism. These four factors correspond to the three analytical "levels" proposed by Wm. Roger Louis and Ronald Robinson in their chapter in this volume, with the category of "imperial traditions" warranting special attention, in my view, as a bridge between the colonial and the metropolitan spheres of action.

With respect to prewar preparations for the transfer of power, the Government of India Act of 1935 must appear as the first major step in the decolonization process which began in earnest after 1945. For although the act itself fell far short indeed of according independence to India, it was not undeniable that the "white" Dominions would eventually be joined in their informal alliance by peoples of other racial stock. To the Indians, of course, this was scant satisfaction, because not only the time of their independence but, more importantly, the politically most crucial features of their emerging state seemed to be outside their ability to control. But in London the act was in many ways decisive. It reconciled the majority of popular and elite opinion to the eventual independence of this "crowning jewel" of empire, considered along with the British Isles themselves to be the other "twin pillar" of Britain's international rank.

Of course, there is the mistake, encountered in the works of British writers especially, of seeing in retrospect a grand design for decolonization which in fact did not exist. Closer inspection commonly reveals the British to have been following Burke's sage counsel to reform in order to preserve: London made concessions more usually to subvert opposition to British rule than to prepare for its demise. So, for example, to see Indian independence in 1947 as necessarily following from the Government of India Act of 1935, which in turn unerringly confirmed the intentions of the Government of India Act of 1919 (itself the natural product of the Morley-Minto reforms of 1909), assumes belief in a British gift for foresight which a detailed examination of the historical record makes it difficult to sustain. What is lacking in these accounts is a sense of the conflicts, hesitations, and uncertainties of the past and of the attempts to reinterpret or renege on the promise of eventual independence for India.

Nonetheless, the British *did* establish a tradition of meeting colonial discontent by reforms which associated the subject peoples more closely with their own governing. The prior evolution of the Dominion system *did* exert an important influence on the style of British policy toward India. And the ultimate decision to grant India independence and to permit her to withdraw from the Commonwealth if she wished *did* constitute a momentous precedent for British policy toward the rest of the colonies. The chapters in this volume by John Hargreaves and Cranford Pratt offer additional documentation that, however shortsighted London may have been about the eventual speed of decolonization, British foresight was remarkable indeed relative to that of the French (not to speak of the Belgians or Portuguese).

How limited, by contrast, was the French experience in handling political change within their empire. When, in January–February 1944, a group of colonial civil servants met in Brazzaville, capital of French Equatorial Africa, to draw up proposals for imperial reorganization in the aftermath of the war, the many worthwhile recommendations they made—the end of forced labor and special native legal codes, the creation of territorial assemblies and their coordination in a "French Federation," the representation of colonial peoples at the future French Constituent Assembly—failed to deal with the truly central problem, the possibility of a colonial evolution toward independence. That is, the French are not to be criticized for failing to provide complete and immediate independence to their colonies, but rather for their steadfast refusal to consider even eventual separation as a viable political option. As the conference report preamble put it:

> The ends of the civilizing work accomplished by France in the colonies exclude any idea of autonomy, all possibility of evolution outside the French bloc of the Empire: the eventual constitution, even in the future, of self-government in the colonies is denied.

❊ ❊ ❊

Time and again throughout the history of the Fourth Republic, beneath the invective of political division one finds a shared anguish at the passing of national greatness, a shared humiliation at three generations of defeat, a shared nationalistic determination that France retain her independence in a hostile world—all brought to rest on the conviction that in the empire they would *maintenir.* Thus the Socialists shared with most of their fellow-countrymen an image of France, a kind of collective conscience, born of the political paralysis of the 1930s, the shame of the Occupation, the stern prophecies of General de Gaulle, the fear of domestic communism, and the initial expectations and ensuing disappointments of the Resistance. With most of their fellow-country-men, they, too, experienced the loss of Indochina as the failure, not of a histori-cally absurd colonial policy first launched by de Gaulle, but as the failure of a regime. They feared, then, that the decline of France to second-power status marked not so much an inevitable phase of world history as the inner failing of a people. The charges of being a *bradeur d'empire* raised much more profound self-doubt in the National Assembly than did charges of "scuttle" at Westminster.

Therefore, not only the political institutions of France and Great Britain were dissimilar but, perhaps more importantly, there were great contrasts be-tween the national moods or psychologies of the political elites in these two countries. Where, for example, does one find in the annals of French leaders anything equivalent to the entry in the journal of Hugh Dalton, who closely followed Lord Mountbatten's handling of the independence of India, dated February 24, 1947?

> If you are in a place where you are not wanted and where you have not got the force, or perhaps the will, to squash those who don't want you, the only thing to do is to come out. This very simple truth will have to be applied to other places too, e.g., Palestine.

One may object that this analysis fails to disaggregate sufficiently the con-stituent forces in each country. How important was it, for example, that Labour was in power immediately after the war and so could set an example in Britain of how to deal with colonial nationalism? Doubtless the influence of the Fabian colonial bureau and the work of Arthur Creech Jones as colonial secretary from late 1946 until 1950 had their positive impact. But it should be recalled that Socialists led the government in France as well in the crucial years 1946–47, when the decision to fight nationalism in Southeast Asia was made. Thus, at the very time when the British Socialists were deciding to hasten the withdrawal from India, the French Socialists were staging emotional appeals in the National Assembly in favor of supporting military action in Indochina. The leaders of both parties wore socialist labels, but they were more clearly to be recognized by their national than by their party memberships.

In France there was one place where a realistic colonial policy was held. Despite the usually prejudiced attacks on the French Communist party's colonial stand, it was the PCF alone of the major parties in France which respected the historical limits of the moment and recognized very early the kind of flexibility a successful postwar imperial policy must possess. Thus, while the Party did tend to discourage independence movements in the empire, it preferred to work with them rather than repress them, seeking to ensure that, should separation become inevitable, it would occur under the auspices of a nationalist elite best able to represent the interests of the local population and preserve the area from the encroachments of foreign powers other than France. In these respects, the PCF compares well with the Labourites.

❊ ❊ ❊

However thorough a comparison might be made between the policies of Paris and London, such an approach focuses the study of decolonization too narrowly on the imperial capitals, neglecting the decisive role played by the peoples of Asia and Africa in their own liberation. For it is possible to trace the history of decolonization not in terms of European, but of Asian and African developments. The victory of Japan over Russia in 1904; Lenin's rise to power in 1917 and his subsequent aid to national elites striving to reduce European influence in their countries; the triumph of Mustafa Kemal in Turkey after World War I; the rise of Gandhi to leadership of the National Congress Party of India in 1920; the increasing importance of Cairo in Arab affairs following the defeat of efforts at Arab unity in World War I and the emergence of modern Egyptian nationalism under Saad Zaghlul Pasha; the rapid growth of colonial economies during the interwar period, with corresponding shifts in local social and political structures; the Japanese conquest of European colonies east of India and the hardships suffered by colonial peoples in all other parts of the globe during World War II; Kwame Nkrumah's return to the Gold Coast in December 1947; Mao Tse-tung's entry into Peking in January 1949—all these

developments offer an alternative way of charting the course of history and analyzing its decisive movements.

From this perspective, concentration on the formal boundaries of empire
or on events deemed significant in European capitals at the time risks obstructing our vision of those determining processes of history which occurred silently
within colonial territories giving a local pedigree to nationalism, or which took
place regionally without respect for imperial frontiers on the basis of communication among Asians or Africans. Looked at from this angle, history ran by
other clocks, whose timing mechanisms synchronized only occasionally with
the pacing of events in Europe. In order to form a just appreciation of the colonial problems facing Paris and London, our attention must turn from these
capitals to Hanoi and Delhi, to Cairo and Algiers, to Accra and Abidjan.

Whatever their political values, what Bourguiba, Ataturk, Sukarno,
Nkrumah, Nyerere, Ho Chi Minh, Gandhi, and Houphouët-Boigny all shared,
was their leadership at the moment of national independence over groupings,
both traditional and modern in values and structure, with a scope so broad that
the split between the countryside and the city was overcome. Obviously such
nationalist alliances varied enormously among themselves, depending on the
interests represented, the solidity of the party apparatus aggregating anticolo-
nial forces, the relative power of local groups outside the nationalist fold, and
the international dangers which a young independence movement had to face.
But it is, I believe, through an analysis of these forces that we can best elaborate
a typology of colonial nationalism and so understand the contribution of the
peoples of Asia and Africa to the character of the decolonization process. In a
word, *who mobilized, or could claim to mobilize, the peasantry?*

❊ ❊ ❊

A comparison of reactions in black Africa and Madagascar to postwar
French colonial policy with those of nationalists in Algeria and Indochina offers
a good illustration of the importance of local conditions in determining this
historical movement. For it is important to emphasize that *French policy was essentially the same throughout the empire:* political reforms were granted only so
long as they could be seen tending to preserve French rule. Demands for change
which might ultimately destroy the French presence were immediately to be
squelched. De Gaulle was the chief architect of this plan, and he made its terms
clear to the Vietnamese by his Declaration of March 25, 1945, which his successors in power reaffirmed in their negotiations with Ho Chi Minh at
Fontainebleau in the summer of 1946. The Second Constituent Assembly
adopted the same stand with the Algerians, and the first legislature of the Fourth
Republic confirmed it in the terms of the Statute of Algeria voted in the summer of 1947. General Juin took the message to Morocco after having delivered

it in Tunis. Marius Moutet, the Socialist colonial minister, was relying on the same view when he called for a boycott of the extraordinary conference called at Bamako, Soudan, by the black Africans under French rule in October 1946. The French subsequently demonstrated the seriousness of their resolve. In November 1946 they shelled the port of Haiphong, taking the lives of several thousand Vietnamese in their determination to rid the city of the Vietminh. In March–April 1947, they responded to a nationalist raid on an army base on Madagascar with a repression which by official estimates killed 86,000. Since the Sétif repression of May 1945 had momentarily cowed the Algerians, rigged elections commencing in the spring of 1948 kept the peace in North Africa. But shortly thereafter, the French felt obliged to launch a concerted repression south of the Sahara against the Africans of the Rassemblement Démocratique Africain (RDA).

If the policy was the same, the results were not. Within a month of the French attack on Haiphong, the Vietminh had responded with a coup attempt in Hanoi. While the Sétif repression effectively fragmented the Algerian political elite for a time, a revolution willing to give no quarter finally broke out in 1954. But in black Africa the policy succeeded. A closer analysis of the situation there may suggest why by reviewing the variables mentioned earlier: the ability of a nationalist party to harness the forces it represents; the relative strength (actual or potential) of the party's local opponents; the degree of need of such a party for aid from the international system in order to maintain its local predominance. Thus, to understand the process of European decolonization means to perceive some particulars of the variety of colonial situations, as a French policy that was anachronistic in certain areas proved well suited to master the events in others. For instance, why did French policy succeed so well in Africa when it so totally failed elsewhere?

⊠ ⊠ ⊠

The foregoing case studies offer examples of a spectrum of colonial responses to the maintenance of European rule after 1945, ranging from militant revolutionary opposition to the call for independence within the framework of a continuing European presence. They are not intended to establish rigid, predictive models for the likelihood of colonial uprisings, but to establish instead a heuristic typology. The factor which this study suggests should be most closely analyzed is the place the momentarily predominant elite occupies in respect to the double challenge it faces: that from the international system and that from local rivals. Import–export elites and traditional rulers are threatened in both respects and are well-advised to moderate their nationalist demands in order to assure continued foreign support for their regimes. On the other hand, a national manufacturing elite allied with rural forces representing more than a handful of great landlords is clearly more able to press its autonomous claims. But it must avoid if possible the radical suggestion to push for an all-out war of national liberation, as it should recognize that the radicals intend to take advantage of popular mobilization, not only to oust the foreigners, but to create a revolution from below and be done with them as well. By this same token, the most militant elite will be one which fears no local rivals—since none exists to any politically significant degree—and at the same time sees the outsiders with whom it must deal as the inveterate enemy of its most essential demands.

In these respects, Algeria and Indochina were idiosyncratic in the challenge they posed to France. These two colonies simply had no genuine parallels in the British experience. Kenya might be thought comparable to Algeria, but in essential respects this was not the case. For how could this relatively insignificant East African land be the equivalent to the British of what Algeria meant to France: the home of more than 2 percent of the national population; the location of badly needed petroleum resources; and a strategic outpost of France whose capital, Algiers, was only 500 miles southwest of Marseille? It was largely because Kenya was so unimportant that the British could arrange for the sale of the European farms to the Africans at full value and so create, virtually overnight, an export elite on whom they could base their postindependence relations. In Algeria, to the contrary, the incomparably more powerful settler presence negated any attempt to create a politically important Muslim bourgeoisie. Nor could the French copy the example of the Republic of South Africa and cut themselves off from their North African territory. This was not because of "centralizing traditions," but because, unlike South Africa, Algeria was far too poor for a small minority of the population to maintain its rule without constant aid from the outside. For these reasons—which had to do with Algeria and not with France—withdrawal was especially difficult. Had the French had the experiences and institutions of the British it is not evident that they would have responded more ably to the crisis.

This chapter has reviewed a range of factors determining the character of the process of European decolonization, with special emphasis on Africa. I have attempted to stress the distinctive contribution to this great historical movement of the colonial peoples themselves: the character of their economic, social, and political organization. At the same time, I should emphasize that I am not at all persuaded that the history of the expansion and contraction of European empire is best understood by giving primary emphasis to the study of the "periphery" or colonial areas, in the manner of John Gallagher, Ronald Robinson, and D. K. Fieldhouse, or of Henri Brunschwig in his chapter in this volume. In my opinion, the decisive events in world history continue to be determined by the actions of the industrial powers. Thus the study of decolonization must reflect centrally the impact of the Second World War, the relations of the European countries with the United States, and the formative impact of France and

Britain (as well as Portugal and Belgium) on their colonial possessions. Africans have nonetheless had an important hand in the making of their history, and one can hope that this will increasingly be the case, without at the same time supposing that the power of industrial Europe was, or is today, without critical importance to the character of modern Africa.

The Trauma of Decolonization

The Dutch and West New Guinea

AREND LIJPHART

In contrast to Tony Smith, Arend Lijphart, a political scientist at the University of California, San Diego, focuses on decision making in the Netherlands in a case study of the Dutch withdrawal (or, more precisely, reluctance to withdraw) from West New Guinea. Relying on extensive use of Dutch sources and interviews, Lijphart rejects arguments that colonialism necessarily has an economic base. He rather points to subjective psychological reasons, not the least of which is national pride, and his book provides a superb analysis of the formation of public opinion and actual policy making at the top. Even so, to what extent does the omission of indigenous currents of opinion constitute a shortcoming—or would the Dutch realization of the imposition of Indonesian "guided democracy" (authoritarian rule) limit the political rights of the Papuan population?

The agonies of the decolonization process are well exemplified by the painful and reluctant withdrawal of the Netherlands from its colonies. It did not grant independence to Indonesia until after more than four years of bitter conflict. Then another twelve and a half years were spent in a vain attempt to hang on to West New Guinea, the last remnant of its colonial empire. These experiences were extremely traumatic. Holland acted with an intense emotional commitment, manifested in pathological feelings of self-righteousness, resentment, and pseudo-moral convictions. These emotions started to decrease in intensity in

From Arend Lijphart, *The Trauma of Decolonization: The Dutch and West New Guinea* (New Haven: Yale University Press, 1966), pp. 285–289. Reprinted with permission.

the late 1950s, but protracted and ultimately unsuccessful resistance to decolonization still left the country internally divided, frustrated, and humiliated. In addition to these psychological wounds, Holland was physically hurt. Investment and trade opportunities in Indonesia, the livelihood of thousands of Dutchmen in Indonesia, and the lives of Dutch soldiers who died in the defense of New Guinea were sacrificed in the useless and futile struggle to resist colonial disengagement. This last colonialist effort damaged Holland's well being even more seriously by dominating its foreign policy and diverting its energies away from more vital pursuits.

Undoubtedly the psychological and physical wounds account for Dutch feelings on the New Guinea issue since Holland's departure from the territory in 1962. Almost immediately after decolonization the New Guinea issue disappeared from the Dutch scene. Concern for the future of New Guinea and the Papuans, which ostensibly motivated the Dutch before 1962, are hardly voiced any longer. This is not merely indifference; rather, the deep trauma attending the fruitless struggle for New Guinea has caused a compulsive urge to forget. The Dutch now anxiously and guiltily want to banish New Guinea from their range of attention. In fact this reorientation has been of metamorphic proportions: diplomatic relations with Indonesia have been restored, and exchanges of amicable and cordial visits by high government officials took place less than two years after the two countries were at war in New Guinea.

What were the causes of the passionate attachment of the Dutch to their colonial empire, and especially to West New Guinea? The Dutch themselves justified their continued presence in New Guinea with a whole series of historical, geographical, ethnological, legal, and ethical arguments. They were far from convincing. Holland assumed the "white man's burden" to promote the economic welfare and political development of the Papuans, but its paternalistic guardianship was not in the best interests of the native population, especially because Holland was too weak to execute its designs in the long run. Furthermore, Holland's insistence on keeping *exclusive* responsibility for the Papuans revealed how the Dutch concern for New Guinea was overlaid with selfish motives. Holland's altruism was strongly egocentric. The Dutch themselves were not entirely unaware of their ambivalence toward the Papuans. For instance, the important Call to Reflection issued by the General Synod of the Dutch Reformed Church forcefully called attention to the "selfishness which is not focused on material gain, but on the pursuit of high ideals." The ultimate shallowness of Dutch altruism is also demonstrated by its sudden disappearance after the departure from New Guinea.

Many observers, both Communist and non-Communist, interpreted the New Guinea issue in economic terms and asserted that Holland wanted to keep possession of the territory because of its material wealth, especially its rich natural resources and immigration possibilities. This image of West New Guinea played a very important role on the Dutch domestic political scene, too. In particular, the Eurasian minority and its interest groups regarded New Guinea as an area suitable for settlement and assumed that it had the economic potential to sustain a large population. West New Guinea was often compared with the rich Belgian Congo and with the prosperous former Dutch colony in the Gold Coast. These attractive images of New Guinea were prevalent among some Cabinet members, many legislators, right-wing politicians, high bureaucrats in the Ministry of Overseas Territories, and various nationalistic and colonialistic groups.

The view of New Guinea as an economically advantageous area was completely false. New Guinea was a liability rather than an asset to the Dutch treasury: it offered no rich source of raw materials, no trade advantages, no investment opportunities, and no possibilities for immigration either by Eurasians or by white Dutchmen. On balance, Holland's national economic interests suffered as a result of the New Guinea issue, for it contributed to the loss of Holland's economic interests in Indonesia. The same can be said of Dutch special interests in New Guinea. Some Dutch firms made profits there, but these were offset by greater losses in Indonesia. Therefore Holland's refusal to decolonize can certainly not be explained on the basis of economics.

Another explanation of Holland's motivation emphasizes the strategic significance of New Guinea. It was argued that Holland served the cause of the Western alliances by refusing to hand the territory over to the Indonesians. Outside Holland only Communist spokesmen and commentators used this argument. Few of Holland's allies were sufficiently impressed by it to give meaningful support to the Dutch. On the Dutch domestic political scene this image of Holland's role as the guardian of the free world's military interests was widespread. Various right-wing, nationalistic, veterans', and militaristic groups were insistent advocates of Holland's retention of New Guinea for military-strategic reasons, but in the 1950s it also struck a responsive chord among more moderate groups and even among the Socialists. Again, this view was utterly false. Holland had neither a direct nor an indirect strategic interest in New Guinea. Similarly, the idea that Holland's prestige in world politics could be maintained by remaining a colonial power was incorrect. New Guinea only contributed to a misplaced self-esteem for the Dutch.

Objective interests cannot explain Holland's reluctance to decolonize. Holland was, in fact, hurt rather than helped by its last efforts to remain a colonial power. When objective interests did begin to play a major role in the New Guinea issue, their influence was exerted in the direction of disengagement rather than continued colonialism. In the late 1950s and early 60s the Dutch were shocked into realizing the futility of their policies by outside military and diplomatic pressures, as well as domestic pressures of the Dutch Reformed Church, the increasingly oppositional Labor Party, business groups with interests in Indonesia, and the press. The actions of the Dutch Reformed Church were prompted at least partly by its missionary interests, and the business lobby hoped to restore cordial economic relations with Indonesia. The growing Socialist opposition and the radical change in press opinion occurred primarily in response to very real military dangers to which Holland was exposing itself. In short, analysis of the reasons behind Holland's policies toward New Guinea does reveal the presence of certain objective interests, but these played a role in the process of decolonization only, *not* in the policies of retaining colonial control.

The real motives behind Holland's reluctance to decolonize were entirely subjective and psychological: the search for national self-esteem, feelings of moral superiority, egocentric altruism, and deep resentment against Indonesia. The common denominator was the sense of frustrated nationalism. To the Dutch, New Guinea became the symbol of Holland's continued national grandeur, power, and moral worth. The attachment to New Guinea was definitely pathological: it was a symptom of a serious and protracted inferiority complex, which healed only very slowly. The symbolic value of New Guinea overshadowed all other considerations. This accounts for the totally unrealistic appraisals of the objective economic, strategic, and political importance of the territory. Because New Guinea symbolized Holland's political and moral strength, it *had* to be rich and potentially prosperous and a vital strategic bastion, with a population yearning for benevolent Dutch tutelage. In other words, the expectations of economic and other benefits from New Guinea were mere appendages and subjective conditions of the psychological symbolism of New Guinea.

The sense of frustrated nationalism that was the fundamental causative factor in Dutch policies toward New Guinea was felt with particular intensity by a number of special groups, such as the Eurasians, veterans' groups, and the whole array of right-wing extremist and superpatriotic associations. They played an important role in Dutch politics and were able to exert considerable influence. Nevertheless, it would be wrong to blame the New Guinea problem exclusively on these relatively small and weak groups. The Dutch people and their political leaders could easily have ignored their pleas. These groups were extreme and vocal, but they represented ideas that permeated the entire nation. It should be remembered that the responsibility for retaining Dutch control over New Guinea in 1949 lay with the center groups and in particular the Liberal Party. By the middle of the 1950s the Dutch were virtually unanimous in their opposition to colonial disengagement, and dissenting voices were almost completely stifled.

The conclusion that Holland's stubborn refusal to abandon New Guinea was motivated exclusively by subjective and irrational factors gives the New Guinea problem a special significance in the context of theories of imperialism and colonialism. As indicated in the introductory chapter, many of these theories attribute some importance to subjective forces but generally emphasize the role of objective factors. The case of New Guinea clearly disproves the contention that colonialism is solely motivated by objective interests. But this is only a negative conclusion. Unfortunately, the study of one case cannot lead to the formulation of a positive general proposition; no case study can ever prove anything. A case study can, however, exemplify, indicate significant problems for further analysis, or suggest the need for reappraisal of well-established and accepted theories.

The case of New Guinea cannot and does not prove that colonialism is caused by subjective forces to the exclusion of all objective forces. It merely shows that, in one instance, subjective forces alone were sufficiently powerful to keep colonialism alive. This strongly suggests that subjective forces should not be underestimated, even in cases where objective interests also play a major role. A brief glance at the history of colonialism and decolonization since the Second World War reveals the prominent role of nationalistic pride and self-righteousness in the refusal to decolonize, not only in the case of the Netherlands, but also in many other instances, especially French and Portuguese colonialism. Another aspect of the New Guinea case that suggests a conclusion of wider applicability is the influence exerted by white settler groups identified with the colonial ruler and motivated by totally unrealistic expectations of continued supremacy: the Eurasians in the case of New Guinea; the *colons* of Algeria; the white settlers of the Congo, Kenya, and Southern Rhodesia; the American "Zonians" of the Panama Canal Zone. Other parallels between New Guinea and other cases of colonialism suggest themselves when the roles of various right-wing groups, the military, the bureaucracy, etc., are investigated.

Decolonization

HENRI GRIMAL

Although the process of decolonization was not quite over when Henri Grimal, a specialist in colonial history, completed the book from which the following excerpts are taken, the major empires had been dismantled, and patterns had been established. Why does Grimal identify the period between the two world wars as a turning point, with World War II accelerating the movement? His emphasis on colonial nationalism as a precipitator appears to match that of Tony Smith. Where do they seem to differ?

While the colonial powers were set on perpetuating the past, a new mood was building up in the colonies themselves. During the years immediately following the First World War, the desire for independence was barely perceptible, but this period was in fact a turning-point. The idea of striving for independence, while not yet widespread, began to take hold in a number of the more advanced territories, and the forces which would eventually lead to the day of reckoning began to gather momentum. Europe herself was contributing to this development by accepting the colonial 'élite' in her schools and universities, where they learned to appreciate the value of freedom. One amongst them observed: 'The Western Powers themselves, by teaching their own history to the peoples they colonized, have shown them how to throw off the yoke of foreign domination.' This new attitude, although not yet widely held or expressed, did not escape the notice of experienced observers. Gabriel Hanotaux, a former minister, wrote in 1928:

Who would have said to the founders of the colonial empire, the pride of the Third Republic, that even before the last one among them had disappeared, the principles and the value of their enterprise would be subjected to the judgment and the scrutiny of those very people they pretended to rule!

The Second World War greatly accelerated developments. Its consequences were in certain ways similar to those of the 1789 Revolution in Europe. It gave currency to ideas which, though not novel, had never before been so widely grasped. The 'right to self-determination', expressed in the Atlantic Charter and the San Francisco Charter, excited considerable interest in the colonies. It was taken up by sections of the population in Asia and Africa who, aware that their countries had not always been 'dependent', idealized their pre-colonial freedom. This period of their history was often obscure, but from it they drew the inspiration to fight against their present subservience. The idea of self-determination was also taken up by Africans in territories where nationalism was a comparatively new phenomenon, for whom colour, race, tribe or even allegiance to their colonial rulers had previously had more significance than the concept of nationhood. The right to self-determination meant the right to reject the state of dependence to which they ascribed their impoverished condition and the injustice of their destiny. New thinking developed, influenced by local factors, leading either to the formulation of precise proposals or merely to a statement of ultimate objectives. The options regarding their political future, as they saw it, were either total independence and the severance by force of all links with the colonial power, or autonomy within a political framework (a commonwealth or federation) of which the former colonial power would be but one constituent member. The old concept of assimilation, whereby the colonial territories were completely integrated with the home country although with equal rights, was no longer regarded as acceptable. In fact this formula was raised again from time to time, but was generally recognized as being unworkable. In the home countries (France especially) it was put forward without due consideration of the consequences and obligations that would follow from taking responsibility for native peoples whose customs and way of life were vastly different from those practised in Europe. The idea of assimilation was more often than not put forward as a cover for a course of action meant to perpetuate the domination and leadership of the minority. The peoples of the colonial territories, who had earlier sought full assimilation and been refused it, now in turn rejected this formula under the influence of a nationalist drive for complete independence.

On the whole, the home countries were not prepared to acknowledge the right to independence claimed by the colonies. Only Britain, following the end of the Second World War, had successfully applied the 'commonwealth principle' with regard to India and Ceylon, and then reluctantly and under more difficult conditions to her West African possessions. The other colonial powers refused to recognize that the process of decolonization was inevitable. They could not accept that the independence movements which had gathered force among the Asian and African peoples now had the momentum of an irresistible tidal wave. Their desire to dominate the colonies was reinforced by their awareness of the temporary weakness of their position: the slightest surrender of their political supremacy appeared to them to be the possible beginning of a total loss of power. They saw the continuation of their authority as essential to the continuation of their economic links and interests, which guaranteed their future power. Dialogue was difficult between partners with totally different points of view, whose reasoning led them to opposite conclusions. Unable to halt the rapid development of the independence movement throughout the non-European world, each colonial power none the less tried to counter it within its own territories. They hastily prepared constitutional frameworks which, intended as they were to prevent the further advance of nationalism, were doomed from the outset. They worked out long-term economic and social aid programmes for people whose aspirations for freedom took precedence over such aid. Force, the *ultima ratio*, was urged in the guise of 'pacification' or of 'police action' and legitimized by the affirmation that the existing order, which the population as a whole accepted, was threatened only by a minority of agitators inspired by subversive theories or foreign powers.

After many bitter experiences and repeated failures, the colonial powers finally acknowledged the situation for what it was and sought to evolve new forms of relationship where the free acquiescence of the colonies would be the only guarantee of continued links. The initiative was now with the colonies. The days of classic colonialism were over.

🞘 🞘 🞘

In 1919, P. Leroy-Beaulieu wrote: 'Whereas the nineteenth century was the heroic age of colonial history, the twentieth century may be its critical age.' This remark, made by one of the leading French theoreticians of colonial expansion, was totally out of keeping with current opinion at the time. The great conflict which had come to an end with the victory of the Western Powers, had shaken the world. But the colonial empires acquired over several centuries, and chiefly during the fifty years immediately preceding the war, had held together. Not one subject territory had caused its rulers serious difficulties, even during the critical stages of the war. An outbreak of mutiny in Indochina (1916) had quickly proved abortive. The Indian Congress party, the only nationalist party of any real consequence, had confirmed its loyalty to the Crown and expressed the wish that India be kept within the British Empire. The rule which 200 million Europeans exercised over 700 million subjects seemed undisputed.

Germany and Turkey had been thoroughly vanquished with the aid of troops levied in the colonies. The Allies proceeded to divide the spoils of war, the former colonial possessions of the two defeated powers, among themselves. In doing so they settled a number of long standing disputes (for example the question of the Congo) to their mutual satisfaction, and increased their spheres of influence in the Middle East.

For the first time the colonial territories had been called upon to aid their rulers on a massive scale, in a conflict which was not really their concern. The material resources, the manpower and the troops drawn from Asia and Africa had considerably influenced the outcome of the war. The general public in Europe did not suspect that this participation on the part of the colonies was less than spontaneous. It accepted wholeheartedly the official version of events, which was that the colonial peoples had come enthusiastically to the aid of the mother country in its hour of need. Practical aid received from the colonies, far more than any propaganda in favour of empire building, served to increase the popularity of the colonies and to create the notion of an imperial community. Much of the scepticism which had been felt regarding colonial policies faded: colonialism was bearing fruit, justifying both the efforts made in the past to spread the light of European civilization throughout the world, and also future efforts. However despite the war, the home countries had gained little knowledge of the peoples living in the various colonies: the gap between them was still as wide. The difference in standard of living was sufficient to convince the rulers of their superiority over the ruled. The Europeans were convinced that their own type of civilization was the only valid one. The indigenous population attached very little importance to the amenities of white life, which they did not as yet desire for themselves. On the other hand, the fact that the European powers had fought each other mercilessly, while still claiming to be the defenders of humanitarian principles, had caused the prestige of Europe to drop considerably in the eyes of the colonies. Those who had been sent to fight or work for the mother country had developed opinions which contrasted sharply with those they held before; the miseries and ills of Europe at war had given them a less elevated image of their masters' existence. But neither this more realistic view of Europe, nor the ideals of 'right' and 'democracy' in whose name they had been called to fight, were yet sufficient to provoke demands for independence.

The 'rising tide of the coloured races' was still to come. The colonies began to feel, however, that their masters were indebted to them.

※ ※ ※

As early as 1940, the temporary eclipse of most of the colonial powers and the partial or total severance of relations with their overseas possessions, destroyed the political balance which had been maintained up to 1939. Furthermore, it was impossible to contain the consequences of the struggle between freedom and totalitarianism to Europe when the European powers had enlisted the support of the peoples in the dependencies. Finally, the dominating forces in world politics were no longer to be found in Europe but in those countries which were resolutely opposed to the colonial system. All these factors created a new climate of opinion which had to be taken into account by the home countries. In any case 'the relationship between home country and colony after the great upheaval could no longer be what it was before'.

As close observers of this new world conflict, the colonial peoples had been astounded by the disasters of 1940: the collapse of Belgium and the Netherlands, the elimination of the French army in a matter of weeks, the hurried retreat to her island of a Britain threatened with invasion or devastation by bombs. At a stroke, Europe lost the immense, long-standing respect which for a century its might had built up in the eyes of the overseas peoples; its subsequent victories proved inadequate to restore the respect it had lost, for in the meantime the nationalist forces had drawn renewed vigour from this loss of prestige.

It was above all in Japanese-occupied South-east Asia that this phenomenon was apparent. The ease with which the Japanese took possession of Malaysia, Indonesia, Indochina, etc., and demolished European authority, revealed to the colonies the weakness of their former white masters. The myth of the latters' racial superiority, still present in the minds of the Asian masses, was exploded. The Japanese victory was proof that the West no longer enjoyed a monopoly in terms of technological and military potential from which it had derived its superiority; that victory was a decisive blow to the spread of European ideas.

Is one therefore to conclude, as does Gerbrandy *(Indonesia)*, that 'by a clever and insidious type of propaganda, they [the Japanese] managed to instil into the minds of the people a violent hatred of the West'? A reply is given by the author himself and others following him, for whom the justification of the subsequent attempts to reconquer those territories resided precisely in the friendship and the loyalty those peoples had retained towards their former masters. In fact, if those peoples sometimes welcomed their 'Asian liberators' with alacrity, if they viewed the humiliating conditions to which the whites were reduced without displeasure, it was because they saw it as a possibility of freedom and emancipation. But when the occupiers, soon after their arrival, had shown the extent of their greed and harshness, their anti-Western propaganda fell upon deaf ears; their efforts to start pro-Japanese movements and engage the population in the war against the Allies was, for the most part, ineffective. The organizations, including the military brigades, set up for that purpose were quickly infiltrated by nationalists and turned out to be of little help. On the other hand, resistance movements led by nationalists and Communists were springing up everywhere with the support of the people.

The share the Japanese had in the destruction of the colonial structures was, however, very considerable. Not only did they eliminate physically the European administrative and economic personnel, they also systematically destroyed the existing institutions, which they replaced by others, according to the needs of the moment. The staff available was inadequate to administer the vast regions they had conquered; they were therefore forced either to set up puppet governments or to entrust the high administrative responsibilities to the local élite, whom the former colonial authorities had always systematically kept in lower grade jobs. These local administrators, whom the European considered as enemy 'collaborators', were viewed by their compatriots as defenders of a national cause. Their authority was a greater help towards preparations for independence than towards encouraging a Japanese victory. The Japanese for their part, being anxious to preserve their hegemony regarding 'the Greater East Asian Co-prosperity Sphere', did not consider it beneficial to their interests to encourage nationalist aspirations towards autonomy. This is why none of the territories they occupied became a sovereign state, with the exception of Burma where the Ba Maw government was recognised as an independent government by Germany's friends and the Vatican (1 August 1943). In the other territories, with a view to rallying the population behind its war effort, Japan made more or less vague promises, none of which had been carried out at the time of Japan's capitulation. The nationalists took advantage of the period of chaos which immediately followed the sudden collapse of Japan. Before the Allies had had time to disembark, the nationalists had taken over the ammunition stocks of the vanquished, proclaimed the independence of their country (Republic of Indonesia, 17 August 1945; Democratic Republic of Vietnam, 3 September) and put their own men in charge of all administration. This *fait accompli* was bound to make a simple return o the pre-war *status quo* difficult. The former rulers would have to make concessions or fight.

❊ ❊ ❊

At the end of this necessarily short and incomplete survey of the irresistible movement which, in less than two decades, has transformed the world map and the political relationship between the continents, some facts stand out.

The decolonization process was not the result of chance or circumstances, though the latter undeniably were favourable to its development. Just as colonization, at the end of the nineteenth century, had found its roots in the upsurge of nationalist fever which had affected Europe, the decolonization process originated in the growth of colonial nationalism which was often bred in Western thinking. The distortion between the ideas of freedom, equality and justice proclaimed as the foundations of political morality and ordinary conduct gave rise, among the élites, to a desire for change.

First colonial nationalism was essentially nourished by the idea of inequality and the wish to put an end to it. 'The most besotted and the basest of drunkards was (in white colonial society) superior to the most distinguished of men to be found among the subjugated races, in the field of science, culture and industry' (Carlo Romulo). Access to equality seemed to be linked above all to severing the links of dependence:

> I saw [wrote Nkrumah] that the only solution to this problem lay in political freedom for our people, because it is only when a people is politically free that the other races show it the respect it deserves. It is impossible to talk about equality in any other terms. No people without its own government can deal with sovereign peoples on an equal footing. A race, a people, a nation cannot exist freely, or be respected either at home or abroad, without political independence.

In order to prolong their rule, the Europeans relied on the slow pace of progress among the native masses: peoples devoid of any political awareness could not be allowed to rule themselves, it was argued. Yet this awareness developed at a surprising speed, under the influence of the élites who directed it towards fulfilling the aspirations of freedom. The argument was put forward that, in a world where interdependence tended to predominate, nationalism was out of place and the pursuit of national sovereignty a dangerous anachronism. The French Socialist party put forward as their own the doctrine of 'individual liberation of each man, each woman; an economic and social liberation which would free them from poverty and free them politically by putting them in a situation where they could express their opinions freely' (speech by G. Mollet in New York, 28 February 1957). The colonial peoples were the less satisfied with all these good intentions in that the Western powers seemed reluctant to abandon their sovereignty; moreover the colonial peoples discovered that they were faced with an attitude which was expressed baldly, to say the least, by a leading French journalist:

> Nowadays [wrote R. Cartier] the European living in Africa uses all his skill in justifying his presence. He describes himself as a trustee whose mission will end when the peoples he rules come of age. . . . The remedy against this is to declare calmly that the white man is in Africa to stay because his interest urges him to be there and to stay there. The benefits which colonization brought to primitive African civilizations are incalculable but they are not the main reason for colonization and they have far too often been used as a smokescreen or a justification. Without Africa, Europe is only a small overpopulated and

dependent peninsula; it is a clear and sufficient reason not to get rid of Africa even if it means fighting to keep her. (Special Report, *Paris-Match*, October–November–December 1953.)

The colonial leaders knew that independence was not a magic panacea which would cure all the ills of their countries; they also knew that independence would not by itself give them the means to build a modern economy capable of quickly raising their standards of living. But they preferred 'poverty in freedom to wealth in slavery' (Sekou Touré). For them, however, prosperity was not a condition of autonomy but, on the other hand, the development of their prosperity depended on their autonomy.

Colonial nationalism was the driving force in the 'acceleration of history'. Not only did it provoke the rapid disappearance of the old type of imperialism, it also gave to these territorial units autonomous political life, for which role nothing seemed to have prepared them. From the moment the emancipation movement achieved some importance, the objections about the political and economic maturity which for many years the colonial powers had used as an argument, disappeared. 'The New Zealand government,' noted *The Economist* (6 January 1962), not without humour, 'has accepted the demand for independence of Western Samoa on a vote of its inhabitants (113,000); few Samoans had any idea what the written constitution was all about, and although most of them wanted independence some time, they do not feel that their leaders are yet ready for it; but there was no opportunity to express this point of view on the voting paper. Thus the average Samoan simply felt that since he did not want to be a slave, he had better vote Yes to both questions.'

Nationalism based itself on the historical past of the peoples, if they possessed one; the absence of a written history did not harm the nationalist cause. 'Perhaps there are no African nations as such in history. But then nations are not always a heritage or a resurrection; they grow and develop as much on the future as on the past.' (A. Charton, *Le Pluralisme ethnique et culturel en AOF.*) Those Africans, and they were the majority, who did not have the memory of a sovereign state in their past history, settled within the 'colonial plots' which the Europeans had arbitrarily cut out when they came to Africa. For them, colonialism was the cradle of nationalism by giving it a geographical framework which, without the intervention of colonialism, would probably have taken a long time to establish itself. Nationalism would no doubt have grown within limits more in accordance with geographical and, above all, ethnic realities, but certainly at the price of prolonged conflicts. The confines of tribes and groups has been superseded; the regrouping took place in relation to the problems and the interests of the territory in particular. The struggle for independence engendered a genuine form of patriotism.

Neo-Colonialism

The Last Stage of Imperialism

KWAME NKRUMAH

Kwame Nkrumah published several books but is best known for his role in Ghana's struggle for independence and as that country's first president. A spokesman for African unity, he insisted that socialism constituted the most valid expression of the African conscience and denied that a state subject to neocolonialism is independent. Moreover, he argued that, despite appearances to the contrary, African neocolonialism was in reality economically and politically directed "from the outside" and that U.S. capital provided it with critical support. His book *Neo-Colonialism: The Last Stage of Imperialism,* the conclusion of which is presented here, attempted to document these charges by providing detailed information on firms, consortia, and directors, and it caused Washington to turn down a three-million-dollar loan to Ghana and to send a sharp note of protest to Nkrumah. The book is clearly modeled on Lenin's *Imperialism: The Last Stage of Capitalism.* If it can be criticized for being an impassioned political argument rather than a dispassionate economic analysis, it still constitutes a powerful influence on African intellectuals.

The neo-colonialism of today represents imperialism in its final and perhaps its most dangerous stage. In the past it was possible to convert a country upon which a neo-colonial regime had been imposed—Egypt in the nineteenth

From Kwame Nkrumah, *Neo-Colonialism: The Last Stage of Imperialism,* New York, 1966, pp. ix–xvi. Reprinted by permission of International Publishers Co., Inc.

century is an example—into a colonial territory. Today this process is no longer feasible. Old-fashioned colonialism is by no means entirely abolished. It still constitutes an African problem, but it is everywhere on the retreat. Once a territory has become nominally independent it is no longer possible, as it was in the last century, to reverse the process. Existing colonies may linger on, but no new colonies will be created. In place of colonialism as the main instrument of imperialism we have today neo-colonialism.

The essence of neo-colonialism is that the State which is subject to it is, in theory, independent and has all the outward trappings of international sovereignty. In reality its economic system and thus its political policy is directed from outside.

The methods and form of this direction can take various shapes. For example, in an extreme case the troops of the imperial power may garrison the territory of the neo-colonial State and control the government of it. More often, however, neo-colonialist control is exercised through economic or monetary means. The neo-colonial State may be obliged to take the manufactured products of the imperialist power to the exclusion of competing products from elsewhere. Control over government policy in the neo-colonial State may be secured by payments towards the cost of running the State, by the provision of civil servants in positions where they can dictate policy, and by monetary control over foreign exchange through the imposition of a banking system controlled by the imperial power.

Where neo-colonialism exists the power exercising control is often the State which formerly ruled the territory in question, but this is not necessarily so. For example, in the case of South Vietnam the former imperial power was France, but neo-colonial control of the State has now gone to the United States. It is possible that neo-colonial control may be exercised by a consortium of financial interests which are not specifically identifiable with any particular State. The control of the Congo by great international financial concerns is a case in point.

The result of neo-colonialism is that foreign capital is used for the exploitation rather than for the development of the less developed parts of the world. Investment under neo-colonialism increases rather than decreases the gap between the rich and the poor countries of the world.

The struggle against neo-colonialism is not aimed at excluding the capital of the developed world from operating in less developed countries. It is aimed at preventing the financial power of the developed countries being used in such a way as to impoverish the less developed.

Non-alignment, as practised by Ghana and many other countries, is based on co-operation with all States whether they be capitalist, socialist or have a mixed economy. Such a policy, therefore, involves foreign investment from capitalist countries, but it must be invested in accordance with a national plan drawn up by the government of the non-aligned State with its own interests in mind. The issue is not what return the foreign investor receives on his investments. He may, in fact, do better for himself if he invests in a non-aligned country than if he invests in a neo-colonial one. The question is one of power. A State in the grip of neo-colonialism is not master of its own destiny. It is this factor which makes neo-colonialism such a serious threat to world peace. The growth of nuclear weapons has made out of date the old-fashioned balance of power which rested upon the ultimate sanction of a major war. Certainty of mutual mass destruction effectively prevents either of the great power blocs from threatening the other with the possibility of a world-wide war, and military conflict has thus become confined to 'limited wars.' For these neo-colonialism is the breeding ground.

Such wars can, of course, take place in countries which are not neo-colonialist controlled. Indeed their object may be to establish in a small but independent country a neo-colonialist regime. The evil of neo-colonialism is that it prevents the formation of those large units which would make impossible 'limited war.' To give one example: if Africa was united, no major power bloc would attempt to subdue it by limited war because from the very nature of limited war, what can be achieved by it is itself limited. It is only where small States exist that it is possible, by landing a few thousand marines or by financing a mercenary force, to secure a decisive result.

The restriction of military action of 'limited wars' is, however, no guarantee of world peace and is likely to be the factor which will ultimately involve the great power blocs in a world war, however much both are determined to avoid it.

※ ※ ※

Neo-colonialism is also the worst form of imperialism. For those who practise it, it means power without responsibility and for those who suffer from it, it means exploitation without redress. In the days of old-fashioned colonialism the imperial power had at least to explain and justify at home the actions it was taking abroad. In the colony those who served the ruling imperial power could at least look to its protection against any violent move by their opponents. With neo-colonialism neither is the case.

Above all, neo-colonialism, like colonialism before it, postpones the facing of the social issues which will have to be faced by the fully developed sector of the world before the danger of world war can be eliminated or the problem of world poverty resolved.

Neo-colonialism, like colonialism, is an attempt to export the social conflicts of the capitalist countries. The temporary success of this policy can be seen in the ever widening gap between the richer and the poorer nations of the world. But the internal contradictions and conflicts of neo-colonialism make it certain that it cannot endure as a permanent world policy. How it should be brought to an end is a problem that should be studied, above all, by the developed nations of the world, because it is they who will feel the full impact of the ultimate failure. The longer it continues the more certain it is that its inevitable collapse will destroy the social system of which they have made it a foundation.

The reason for its development in the post-war period can be briefly summarised. The problem which faced the wealthy nations of the world at the end of the second world war was the impossibility of returning to the pre-war situation in which there was a great gulf between the few rich and the many poor. Irrespective of what particular political party was in power, the internal pressures in the rich countries of the world were such that no post-war capitalist country could survive unless it became a 'Welfare State.' There might be differences in degree in the extent of the social benefits given to the industrial and agricultural workers, but what was everywhere impossible was a return to the mass unemployment and to the low level of living of the pre-war years.

From the end of the nineteenth century onwards, colonies had been regarded as a source of wealth which could be used to mitigate the class conflicts in the capitalist States and, as will be explained later, this policy had some success. But it failed in its ultimate object because the pre-war capitalist States were so organised internally that the bulk of the profit made from colonial possessions found its way into the pockets of the capitalist class and not into those of the workers. Far from achieving the object intended, the working-class parties at times tended to identify their interests with those of the colonial peoples and the imperialist powers found themselves engaged upon a conflict on two fronts, at home with their own workers and abroad against the growing forces of colonial liberation.

The post-war period inaugurated a very different colonial policy. A deliberate attempt was made to divert colonial earnings from the wealthy class and use them instead generally to finance the 'Welfare State.' As will be seen from the examples given later, this was the method consciously adopted even by those working-class leaders who had before the war regarded the colonial peoples as their natural allies against their capitalist enemies at home.

At first it was presumed that this object could be achieved by maintaining the pre-war colonial system. Experience soon proved that attempts to do so would be disastrous and would only provoke colonial wars, thus dissipating the anticipated gains from the continuance of the colonial regime. Britain, in particular, realised this at an early stage and the correctness of the British judgement at the time has subsequently been demonstrated by the defeat of French colonialism in the Far East and Algeria and the failure of the Dutch to retain any of their former colonial empire.

The system of neo-colonialism was therefore instituted and in the short run it has served the developed powers admirably. It is in the long run that its consequences are likely to be catastrophic for them.

Neo-colonialism is based upon the principle of breaking up former large united colonial territories into a number of small non-viable States which are incapable of independent development and must rely upon the former imperial power for defence and even internal security. Their economic and financial systems are linked, as in colonial days, with those of the former colonial ruler.

At first sight the scheme would appear to have many advantages for the developed countries of the world. All the profits of neo-colonialism can be secured if, in any given area, a reasonable proportion of the States have a neo-colonialist system. It is not necessary that they *all* should have one. Unless small States can combine they must be compelled to sell their primary products at prices dictated by the developed nations and buy their manufactured goods at the prices fixed by them. So long as neo-colonialism can prevent political and economic conditions for optimum development, the developing countries, whether they are under neo-colonialist control or not, will be unable to create a large enough market to support industrialisation. In the same way they will lack the financial strength to force the developed countries to accept their primary products at a fair price.

In the neo-colonialist territories, since the former colonial power has in theory relinquished political control, if the social conditions occasioned by neo-colonialism cause a revolt the local neo-colonialist government can be sacrificed and another equally subservient one substituted in its place. On the other hand, in any continent where neo-colonialism exists on a wide scale the same social pressures which can produce revolts in neo-colonial territories will also affect those States which have refused to accept the system and therefore neo-colonialist nations have a ready-made weapon with which they can threaten their opponents if they appear successfully to be challenging the system.

These advantages, which seem at first sight so obvious, are, however, on examination, illusory because they fail to take into consideration the facts of the world today.

The introduction of neo-colonialism increases the rivalry between the great powers which was provoked by the old-style colonialism. However little real power the government of a neo-colonialist State may possess, it must have, from the very fact of its nominal independence, a certain area of manoeuvre. It may not be able to exist without a neo-colonialist master but it may still have the ability to change masters.

The ideal neo-colonialist State would be one which was wholly subservient to neo-colonialist interests but the existence of the socialist nations makes it impossible to enforce the full rigour of the neo-colonialist system. The existence of an alternative system is itself a challenge to the neo-colonialist regime. Warnings about 'the dangers of Communist subversion' are likely to be two-edged since they bring to the notice of those living under a neo-colonialist system the possibility of a change of regime. In fact neo-colonialism is the victim of its own contradictions. In order to make it attractive to those upon whom it is practised it must be shown as capable of raising their living standards, but the economic object of neo-colonialism is to keep those standards depressed in the interest of the developed countries. It is only when this contradiction is understood that the failure of innumerable 'aid' programmes, many of them well intentioned, can be explained.

In the first place, the rulers of neo-colonial States derive their authority to govern, not from the will of the people, but from the support which they obtain from their neo-colonialist masters. They have therefore little interest in developing education, strengthening the bargaining power of their workers employed by expatriate firms, or indeed of taking any step which would challenge the colonial pattern of commerce and industry, which it is the object of neo-colonialism to preserve. 'Aid,' therefore, to a neo-colonial State is merely a revolving credit, paid by the neo-colonial master, passing through the neo-colonial State and returning to the neo-colonial master in the form of increased profits.

Secondly, it is in the field of 'aid' that the rivalry of individual developed States first manifests itself. So long as neo-colonialism persists so long will spheres of interest persist, and this makes multilateral aid—which is in fact the only effective form of aid—impossible.

Once multilateral aid begins the neo-colonialist masters are faced by the hostility of the vested interests in their own country. Their manufacturers naturally object to any attempt to raise the price of the raw materials which they obtain from the neo-colonialist territory in question, or to the establishment there of manufacturing industries which might compete directly or indirectly with their own exports to the territory. Even education is suspect as likely to produce a student movement and it is, of course, true that in many less developed countries the students have been in the vanguard of the fight against neo-colonialism.

In the end the situation arises that the only type of aid which the neo-colonialist masters consider as safe is 'military aid.'

Once a neo-colonialist territory is brought to such a state of economic chaos and misery that revolt actually breaks out then, and only then, is there no limit to the generosity of the neo-colonial overlord, provided, of course, that the funds applied are utilised exclusively for military purposes.

Military aid in fact marks the last stage of neo-colonialism and its effect is self-destructive. Sooner or later the weapons supplied pass into the hands of the opponents of the neo-colonialist regime and the war itself increases the social misery which originally provoked it.

11

THE SINGLE MARKET AND EUROPEAN UNITY

Since the fall of Rome in the fifth century of the modern era (or A.D.), Europeans have dreamed of unity. Charlemagne, the Church, Napoleon, and Hitler have all tried—and failed. The latest, and most democratic, attempt is underway by the fifteen European Community (EC) countries. Determined to advance stalled economic integration, they pledged to unite their markets by the end of 1992, creating the world's largest market and trading bloc and taking a major step toward federation—that is, toward political integration. Together with the awareness of North Atlantic Treaty Organization (NATO) members that U.S. and European nuclear arms security interests may not be identical and with the dramatic loosening of the Soviet grip on Eastern Europe, the prospect of a "single market" has revived the old dream of an independent-united Europe.

The chief events in the EC's early evolution are clear: the emergence from the cooperation required by the Marshall Plan; the proposals of French planning commissioner Jean Monnet and French foreign minister Robert Schuman to pool coal and steel resources in Western Europe; the resulting five-nation European Coal and Steel Community; the desire for more economic integration, particularly in view of the British and French failures in Suez in 1956; the 1957 Treaties of Rome establishing both the European Economic Community (EEC), or Common Market, intended to bring an end to customs barriers among its members and a common tariff for the rest of the world, and Euratom, the European Atomic Energy Commission for the peaceful development of atomic energy; French President Charles de Gaulle's 1963 veto of the British application to join (de Gaulle feared Britain's Atlantic ties and Commonwealth commitments and was reluctant to share leadership); the struggles between those who opposed the EEC's becoming a supranational organization, particularly de Gaulle, and integrationists led by Walter Hallstein, who headed the Common Market's executive commission; and the 1966 compromise that reasserted the paramountcy of national sovereignty, with the Council of Foreign Ministers exercising real authority and with each member having veto power. The impetus for a common Europe appeared to have stagnated.

Even so, in 1967 integrationists were able to blend the three European organizations, the Common Market, the Coal and Steel Community, and Euratom into a single European Community, with the right to tax (customs fees) and in some areas have EC law take precedence over national law. Most remaining customs barriers fell in 1968. Membership expanded in 1973 with the admission of Great Britain, Ireland, and Denmark. Closer ties with the Third World were made when a 1975 agreement between the EC and forty-six developing nations allowed the latter to send goods freely to EC markets while members granted greater aid and investment. In 1978 short-term efforts to stabilize currency fluctuations through a European monetary system proved successful, although this fell far short of the common currency sought by integrationists. The direct election of members of the European Parliament was established in 1979. (Previously the Parliament consisted of pro-Europeans sitting in their various national legislatures. But the Parliament, as before, could only discuss the proposals of the EC's executive commission and pass them along to a council of ministers—hence the skepticism regarding integration voiced not only by participants but by social scientists as well.)[1]

In 1981 Greece joined the EC, followed in five years by Spain and Portugal, all three nations having demonstrated their democratic credentials and having allayed fears that these southern European states, because of their lower income, would require subsidies. EC membership now comprised twelve states. By the 1970s it constituted the world's largest trading unit and was a great economic power. A decade later, its total population and gross national product equaled the output of the United States and surpassed that of the Soviet Union and Japan.

Serious problems, however—some new, some recurring—marked the early 1980s. Farming countries such as France continued to benefit from supports, while the British and Germans paid higher food prices as a result. The British insisted that their contribution was disproportionately high, and like de Gaulle twenty years earlier, Margaret Thatcher in 1983–1984 effectively managed to block the EC from functioning until steps were taken to lower agricultural supports. Enthusiasm for the Common Market impetus once again seemed to have evaporated. Member states knew only too well that not all customs barriers were down, that difficulties and delays in border crossings endured, and that rampant regulations in manufacturing showed no signs of easing.

Aware that the EC growth was falling behind that of the United States and Japan and that only the single market originally envisaged provided a solution,

---

[1]Paul Taylor, *The Limits of European Integration* (New York: Columbia University Press, 1983), 299–301.

in 1985 the executive commission under its new pan-European president, the Frenchman Jacques Delors, committed the EC to removing all remaining barriers to the free movement of goods, services, capital, and people among its member states, that is, "to complete the internal market," by December 31, 1992. Three hundred areas were targeted; most important perhaps were the elimination of all border controls, the replacement of unanimity with majority rule (no more veto power) in the Council of Ministers, more power for the European Parliament, the totally free movement of goods and services, and the harmonization of different rules and standards. To take but one dramatic example: an architect qualified to practice in Italy is to be able to practice in any of the other eleven nations.

In 1993 member nations of the EC ratified the Treaty of Maastricht, which endorsed political and monetary (a single currency) union and subsequently transformed the EC into the European Union (EU). In January 1995 Sweden, Finland, and Austria became members of the EU. But in many ways the EU failed to live up to its name. Not all member nations had approved of the Treaty of Maastricht, and many were afraid: traditionalists feared the lessening of national sovereignty; heads of smaller and less efficient firms feared extinction; internationalists feared tariff increases that might produce a "fortress Europe."

Nonetheless, movement toward complete monetary union has gained momentum in recent years. On January 1, 1999, the exchange rates of eleven member countries were put together to create a common European currency, the euro. Though it will not become an open cash currency until 2002, the euro is the unit of exchange for banks and financial institutions. The appearance of the euro showed that member countries were inclined to disregard their monetary policies for the sake of greater European integration. In the wake of the war in Kosovo, leaders within the EU signed a common defense and security agreement. Current president of the European Commission Romano Prodi (appointed in 1999) and other EU leaders have also called for the rapid expansion of the organization from fifteen to thirty members. The four excerpts that follow provide thoughtful analyses of recent developments and future prospects.

Europe's Identity Crisis Revisited

STANLEY HOFFMANN

Stanley Hoffmann is the Douglas Dillon Professor of the Civilization of France and chairs the Center for European Studies at Harvard University. Here he explains the failures of the Maastricht Conference and pays close attention to the structural, economic, and political obstacles to further unity. Why does progress toward building more effective and powerful central institutions remain so "slow and halting"? What are the "deeper" explanations? How, in Hoffmann's view, can greater unity come about?

It is ironic that the crisis of the European Community (EC, now called the European Union [EU]) appears to have begun immediately after the signing of the Maastricht Treaty on European Union, which seemed to promise a major leap forwards. A monetary union, with a single central bank and a single currency, was going, within less than ten years, to crown the enterprise of economic integration begun in 1957 and expanded by the "1992" program of the mid-1980s (the so-called Single Act). The Community's jurisdiction was going to extend to areas beyond the economic realm: social affairs, police matters, immigration—areas close to the core of domestic sovereignty—as well as to diplomacy and defense. A year and a half later, deep pessimism prevails. The French nation endorsed the treaty by the most niggardly of margins. The Danes first said no, and then yes only after having obtained from their partners exceptions that almost amount to exempting Denmark from the Maastricht stipulations. The European Monetary System (EMS) established by a Franco-German initiative

From Stanley Hoffmann, "Europe's Identity Crisis Revisited," reprinted by permission of *Daedalus*, Journal of the American Academy of Arts and Sciences, from "Europe Through a Glass Darkly," Spring 1994, Volume 123, Number 2.

in the late 1970s, and only recently joined by the British, was badly shaken by a colossal crisis in September 1992, which drove the British out, and almost wrecked by a second onslaught in July 1993, which obliged the members to enlarge enormously the margins within which their currencies are allowed to fluctuate. The date of the future monetary union is uncertain, and who will be in it is also in doubt. As for diplomacy and defense, the Community's fiasco in Yugoslavia has been deeply demoralizing. What went wrong?

Two suggested explanations can be rejected outright. The lofty and persistent chorus of European Federalists puts much of the blame on the governments that failed, in Maastricht, to reform the institutions of the Community in a direction that should have been more democratic and more federal. It is true that the treaty, while marginally increasing the powers of the elected European Parliament, consolidated the preeminent position of the Council—composed of governmental representatives—especially because many of the new areas of the EU's jurisdiction shall be dealt with only by unanimity. But the Federalist answer raises a fundamental question. Why have the governments been so timid, why—more than twenty years after the disappearance from the scene of the arch anti-Federalist, General de Gaulle, and three years after the removal from power of that other fierce foe of "supranationality," Margaret Thatcher—does the progress toward more effective and powerful central institutions remain so slow and halting, despite the efforts of a European Court of Justice that has sometimes sounded as if it wanted to imitate the American Supreme Court in the early decades of the United States' existence? The Supreme Court succeeded because it was interpreting a Federal Constitution; the European Court of Justice's attempt to blow Federalist air into the weak lungs of a community based not on a constitution but on a series of treaties could not, by itself, suffice.

The second explanation that does not take us very far is that the current crisis is, as the French would say, *conjoncturelle*. Recession, so goes the argument, is always bad for the Community: remember the years of the oil shocks, during which the governments tried to find national solutions to their countries' problems and "Europessimism" became fashionable. It is true that despite the creation of a single market for goods, capital, services, and (more or less) people, the same causes have tended to produce the same effects. The "convergence criteria" set at Maastricht to prepare for monetary union are promises for the future; until now, state policies have diverged sufficiently to produce a broad spectrum of deficits, inflation rates, and interest rates. It is also true that matters have been made worse at a crucial moment by the unanticipated costs of Germany's unification—the combination of an industrial and ecological disaster whose proportions exceeded all fears, and of imprudent political decisions about the rate of exchange between the Western and Eastern mark and about financing the rehabilitation of the East by loans rather than by taxes. The independent

Bundesbank's decision to combat the inflationary implications of these policies by high interest rates has wreaked havoc on the economies of the countries whose currencies are tied to Germany's, and thus has aggravated the recession. It is also true that the Yugoslav tragedy, which the Community could not prevent or resolve, has proved too complex and too burdensome for the United States and the United Nations as well.

Recessions eventually end. The absorption of Eastern Germany into the new Federal Republic of Germany (FRG) is under way (and the German government has seen the need for greater fiscal rigor) and the ferocity of ethnic conflict in Yugoslavia is not likely to be reproduced elsewhere (foretold disasters in the rest of the Balkans have not occurred—so far—and Serbian bellicosity may well have been dented, if not daunted, by the costs of the wars in Croatia and Bosnia and of international sanctions). There have been other setbacks and crises in the history of the Community, but its march has always resumed; no crisis ever led to an unraveling.

There is some truth in that argument. The Community overcame the paralysis caused by the conflict between de Gaulle and the "Europeans," it came out of the economic troubles of the 1970s and the long battle over Britain's terms of membership, and it may well triumph over the new sources of division and despair. Nobody wants to undo what has been achieved: insofar as it is a construction built on common interests—let us call them peace and prosperity (among the partners)—there are very few voices that express the thought that each member, or even any one of them, would be better off if the edifice collapsed. The EMS did unravel, but if the key members make an effort to coordinate their economic policies and to adopt the same priorities—the fight against unemployment and recession rather than, as in the Bundesbank's case, high interest rates to prevent inflation, and, as in France's case since the mid-1980s, financial rigor and a strong currency—the EMS might be restored and the march toward monetary union might resume.

However, *conjoncturel* factors do not explain everything. The failure to coordinate economic policies predates the recession and explains why a monetary system that tried to preserve narrow margins of fluctuation among currencies, and whose dominant currency was ruled by a *national* central bank intent on following its understanding of a purely national interest, was bound to run into storms once the national situations and policy priorities began to diverge significantly. Even in less troubled times, an attempt by several of the members (such as Italy) to meet the "criteria of convergence" would have imposed enormous strains upon their habits and practices. And while Yugoslavia may well be exceptional, the European performance in the Gulf crisis was not much more edifying. In those two instances, as in the days that followed the loosening of the EMS, the spokesmen for the governments have congratulated themselves on the Community's ability to avoid fatal splits. But if the criterion of success becomes the ability to put in common a good face on retreats and fiascoes, then the European ambition must have fallen rather low.

We must look deeper than the circumstances of the late 1980s and early 1990s, to a number of factors that would hamper the Community's march even if *la conjoncture* improved. They can be divided into two groups: some concern Western Europe's relations with the rest of the world, some concern its internal situation. In both categories, thirty years ago, Western Europe's relation to American society and to America's world role was the heart of the matter. Today, this relation is far less central, although it remains important.

In the first group, we need to distinguish between two kinds of problems: issues of foreign economic and financial policy, a domain which is either predominantly (trade) or largely (money) within the Union's jurisdiction, and issues of diplomacy and security which are still essentially national, despite the halting "European political cooperation" initiated in the 1970s and the promise of Maastricht (but even after the treaty enters into force, unanimity will be the rule here).

The monetary dramas of 1992–1993 have taught two lessons—both of which are damaging to the Union. The first is that as long as there is no single central bank and currency, a large number of private individual and corporate investors (what the French call "speculators" and Americans "the market") will play the game of attacking those currencies they deem overvalued, and they have financial resources far superior to those the national central banks can provide to defend the threatened currencies. These speculative runs point simultaneously to the need for a single currency and to the enormous difficulty of getting one. They undermine the transitory system—the EMS—that is the preliminary and prerequisite to the final monetary union, and they aggravate the distortions among the members' financial situations. The only ways in which the governments can try to thwart the "speculators" are by widening the margins of fluctuations (which defeats the very purpose of the EMS) or by revaluing undervalued currencies and devaluing overvalued ones. But the political costs, and the feared economic ones, of such manipulations deter democratically elected governments. Moreover, when faced with private capital's offensive against public currencies, the elites of the Union's nations have reacted divergently (and predictably) along familiar national lines. In the United Kingdom (as in the United States) currency tends to be seen as a commodity like any other, whose value it is the function of the market to determine: paper barriers are not going to prevail over the wishes of private actors (especially when they seem encouraged by their governments). In Germany, and even more in France, currency is seen as the symbol, instrument, and attribute of the sovereign state, and not as an ordinary good. But until there is a united Europe, Germany's way of protecting that instrument is shaped by the Bundesbank's definition of the German national interest (and therefore it defended the franc but not the pound and the lira in September 1992, and limited its defense of the franc in July 1993), and France's itch to get its partners to agree on sets of regulations and controls that could restrict the operations of outside speculators is not shared by anyone else. Thus, it is not just the *conjoncture* of 1992–1993 that puts the EU at a disadvantage in this realm, by comparison with the United States or Japan. It is its very unfinished nature, its being a halfway house between a group of formally independent states and a genuine union or federation; and the storms to which it is therefore exposed keep it in this unhappy position.

The divergences among the members are just as apparent in trade policy. The difficulties that emerged during GATT's interminable Uruguay Round may have been made more intense, but they have not been created by the recession. What happened is familiar. In the case of agriculture, as in the case of "cultural services" (movies and television programs), the Community had painfully succeeded in putting together policies that reflected, in the former instance, France's attachment to the original Common Agricultural Policy (which had done so much to boost France's export capacity) and, in the latter instance, France's resistance to the "invasion" of American programs. But when the United States began to exert very strong pressure on both fronts, the surface consensus of the EU cracked and divergent combinations of foreign policy traditions and national policy dispositions reasserted themselves: the French being more protectionist, statist, and anti-American; the British being at the completely opposite end; and the Germans riding the middle line, somewhat closer to the British (and to the Americans) while trying not to break up with the French. The split was reflected even in the EU Commission, where French President Jacques Delors and the British commissioner in charge of external trade, Sir Leon Brittan, were not on the same wavelength at all. The French, at the end, skillfully retreated from the brink just enough to get their partners to support most of their demands, but the compromises to which the United States agreed in December 1993 do not resolve the issues once and for all: the showdown was postponed, and surface consensus within the EU was thus restored, for the time being.

❋ ❋ ❋

What this cascade of changes in situations, of forced new calculations, and of difficult and incomplete adjustments explains is the continuing difficulty of the states in the Union to agree on a common diplomacy and security policy. What could not be achieved when they were all together in the "Western" cauldron of the Cold War—because their dispositions toward their own pasts, toward the United States, and toward the Soviet Union diverged—is even harder to accomplish now that the lid is off, and the cauldron abandoned.

The disappointing performance of the Union in the two major post-1989 crises in which it nevertheless tried to speak with one voice—the Gulf war and

Yugoslavia—is the result of both the divisions or divergent calculations mentioned above and of another phenomenon observed by several people, namely the inadequacy of the Union in geopolitical enterprises. The Community, for many of its enthusiasts, including the disciples of Jean Monnet, was going to be an exemplary civilian power, a fine example of supernation building over an economic foundation. As a result, security was left to NATO (i.e., the United States) and diplomacy to the member states. The latter, either because their forces were tied to NATO, or, as in France's case, because their trump card was nuclear deterrence, or because of varieties of pacifism, lost the habit of external military action, except for limited operations to safeguard bits of an empire or a former empire, as in the Falklands, or in Chad. Large-scale military expeditions not caused by a direct threat to physical security have tended to be dismissed as belonging to a distant past.

This explains why, in the Gulf crisis of 1990–1991, the contribution of most of the Community's members was either symbolic or, in Germany's case, reluctant and predominantly financial. The two states that participated far more actively—England and France—saw in the crisis a way of reasserting their rival claims to "global middle power" status and also a wedge for reintroducing themselves into the old diplomatic game of Arab-Israeli negotiations. None of these calculations bore fruit. In the case of Yugoslavia, two facts are most striking: First, the unwillingness of *any* of the Union's members to intervene militarily except as a participant in a peace*keeping* or humanitarian operation—an unwillingness whose first expression had been the early reluctance to take the breakup of Yugoslavia seriously enough. Second, the range of policies was wide. In the beginning, there was a gulf between France and Britain's preference for preserving a Yugoslav state and Germany's push for early recognition of Slovenia and Croatia. Germany dragged its reluctant partners along: they joined Bonn in order to prevent a unilateral German recognition, which occurred anyhow. When Bosnia became the center of the drama there was still an ample gap between Britain's attitude of prudent (some would say disdainful) nonintervention and Germany's awkward combination of anti-Serb feelings and constitutional impotence, with France playing Hamlet in the middle. The Union's own distinctive contribution—Lord Owen—displayed in successive peace plans a bizarre mix of wishful thinking and resignation to the inevitable and a characteristic reluctance to envisage the military means needed to achieve political ends.

What the "external" part of this story shows is simple. With economic integration largely accomplished, two further tasks assumed increasing importance: monetary union, to consolidate the economic enterprise both within Western Europe and in the world, and a common defense and diplomatic policy so that the new economic giant would cease being a geopolitical dwarf. But the outside world's turbulence and the widely different reactions of the key states of the EU have made it impossible to overcome the obstacles. Not the world's turmoil but the same divisions have thwarted a third advance beyond economic integration: the reform of the EU's institutions. But before we examine this failure, we must turn to the internal part of the story.

▧ ▧ ▧

Three new political characteristics interfere with the unification of Europe. The first is, to coin a phrase, the end of ideology. In 1964 communism, Social Democracy, and Christian Democracy were alive, if not well. We all know what has happened to communism, and the Christian Democrats and the Socialists have suffered heavily from the eroding and corrosive effects of power. Economic integration and the attempt to make the EMS function have put serious limits on the leeway of policymakers in the economic and financial arenas. With politics shifting from the enforcement of distinctive programs to the management of constraints, parties that began as programmatic movements lost their programs and their politicians sometimes lost their souls.

The margin of choice among competing partners appears paradoxically narrower than in the United States, whose two parties many Europeans had tended to deride as barely distinguishable. In countries where the state, even when weak, was seen as properly the guide of society, a notion that is far more controversial on this side of the Atlantic, the shift from creative leadership to prudent management was often seen as a fall. The original theory of West European integration had seen the decline of ideology and the prevalence of economic management as a boon for supranational unity: it would be based on a dynamic of interests because interests compromise, ideological passions divide. But managers are not innovators, and if there had not been the ideological drive that animated the Monnet group, or Jacques Delors, little would have been accomplished. Above all, leaders who are primarily managers find it hard to mobilize their publics.

Second, the failure of managerial politics to cope with unemployment and the host of social issues that accompany the recession, or with the relative decline of European industry which aggravates it, and the many scandals that the collusion between the management of state power and the business world has generated have driven many citizens into contempt for politics and politicians (a feature that is most prominent in Italy, but visible also in France, Spain, England, and Germany). It results in political fragmentation, votes for small parties, and above all a great deal of lassitude and skepticism toward the designs of politicians—such as Maastricht. Publics which had often seemed to ask and expect less from politicians than the "revolutions" promised by the latter (remember the French Socialists' slogan of 1981: *changer la vie*) nevertheless expected more and better than what their leaders delivered after they discovered that their promises could not be kept.

Third, new divisions complicate the task of politicians eager to proceed with European unification. In England the gap between the modern industrial and financial sector, boosted by Thatcherism, and the declining parts of the country, the gap between the affluent and the underprivileged, are dangerous for Tories addicted to trickle-down theories and puzzling for Socialists deprived of their old articles of faith. In Germany the many gaps and misunderstandings between the old FRG and the former German Democratic Republic (GDR) will take years to disappear. In Italy we find not only the last supporters of the collapsing old system pitted against a (dis)array of reformers but a division between North and South. Comparable splits exist, of course, in Eastern and Central Europe between those who want their nations to embark on a "normal" course of capitalist free market development with liberal institutions and those who are buffeted by the storms of change, baffled by the new insecurities of employment and social services, and nostalgic about the protection that the state, however authoritarian, had provided for forty years. All these divisions oblige leaders to pay attention to the nation's social fabric first.

▧ ▧ ▧

Thus, the face the Union shows to its members is unfinished. The face it presents to the outside is often unpleasant. Two issues matter here: immigration and the problem of Eastern Europe. Concerning the former there is indeed remarkable European distinctiveness if one compares the Union to the United States, a distinctiveness that is fiercely and systematically buttressed but is anything but admirable. It is as if, having gradually become used to seeing in the citizens of other EU nations persons who, while different from true nationals, are nevertheless not aliens, the inhabitants of each of the EU countries had decided to treat those from outside the magic circle with extra suspicion and severity—a tendency mightily reinforced but not created by the recession. The combination of the Schengen agreements on open borders and new national legislation, especially in Germany and France, is an ugly attempt by each member to push on others the burden of screening asylum seekers and a common policy of the lowest common denominator. Blocking immigration except in the rarest of cases (when asylum cannot be refused under international law), persecuting illegal immigrants with venomous vigor, and, in the French case, making the integration of legal ones more difficult, shows how governments have tried to defuse the arguments and to deflate the growth of xenophobic movements by adopting some of their recommendations and thus by legitimizing their existence—as long, of course, as they do not turn murderous. This is the politics of meanness (it is especially bizarre in Italy, where the Lombard League looks at non-Northern Italians as unworthy foreigners). The opening of borders to foreign goods and services is accompanied by a closing of gates to people.

The prevalence of the politics of fear is evident not only in attitudes toward "invaders" from the poor countries of the Middle East or of North Africa or in fantasies about Islamic or Black hordes besieging a prosperous Europe (which reacts by arguing that the best way to prevent such onslaughts is to help the countries of the Third World keep their peoples at home through a policy of aid to development, an argument that happens to be accompanied by little aid). It is also visible in the timidity with which the Union and most of its members have faced the opportunity provided by the collapse of communism east of the old Iron Curtain. There are, of course, good reasons why Prague, Warsaw, and Budapest could not join the EU at once or quickly. But the Union has behaved as if it was more anxious to protect the fortress of Western Europe from the economic and ethnic turmoil of the East than it was to provide, through close association leading to guaranteed membership if stipulated conditions are met, a safety net for these countries. It is as if the peace and relative prosperity achieved in the West were too precious to be exposed to the turbulence in the East: self-protection is more important than propagation, quarantine than help. The argument that the Union had to choose between "deepening" and "expanding" is specious: so far there has been neither, and a bold expansion might have obliged the members to face sooner the reform of the institutional setup (already too cumbersome for twelve) which Maastricht postponed to 1996, just as the expansions of the 1970s and early 1980s (from the Six to the Twelve) led to the shift to majority vote in the Single Act.

Especially at a time of domestic unhappiness and strife there is no hope for a popular push toward greater unity, for a move from below toward a Union both deeper and wider. As in other historical cases it is from the top that the initiatives will have to come. If there ever should be a European "nation of nations" and a Federal European state above the states that have already lost many of their powers, either through formal transfer to Brussels or through devolutions to "the market" or through simple impotence, it is the elites and the governments that will have to take the decisive steps: exactly what happened in the 1950s and in the mid-1980s. But what is lacking currently is elites and leaders with a daring vision. The convergence of Monnet, Schuman, Adenauer, and de Gasperi was exceptional. What obstructed progress in the 1960s was not the absence of a vision; it was the reluctance of other leaders to accept de Gaulle's vision. A less grandiose but uplifting convergence around the vision of "1992" brought together Delors, Thatcher, Kohl, and Mitterrand.

※ ※ ※

Precisely because of the negative trends and factors on which this essay has dwelled, it would take the convergence of exceptionally bold leaders to transcend the current malaise, timidity, divisions, and retreats. But these same trends and factors make it difficult to see where such leaders would come from and who they would be.

Meanwhile, Western Europe suffers, paradoxically, both from the legacy of the postwar habit of dependence on American leadership in geopolitical affairs and from the decline of an American predominance which had assuredly been a factor of division (between Gaullists and Atlanticists) but also a goad toward a European entity capable of talking back to the United States. And it remains torn by disjunctions it cannot overcome: between politics, which is still national, and economics, national no longer; between economics, which is becoming common, and diplomacy and defense, where the Union still falters; between a settled West and an unsettled East. In 1964 I wondered about Western Europe's spiritual vitality. I still do.

Social Democracy and the Europe of Tomorrow

DONALD SASSOON

Donald Sassoon teaches history at the University of London and writes from a social-democratic standpoint. Does he share Hoffmann's pessimism about the drive for further integration? How does his analysis differ? How does it resemble that of Hoffmann? What problems are created by regional variations and by the possible absorption of Eastern and Central European economies into an expanded EC? Why, in Sassoon's view, is further centralization—that is, a constitution for Europe—the answer?

By the late 1950s all West European socialist and social democratic parties (I shall use the terms interchangeably) had abandoned in practice, and some in theory too, the idea of socialism as an "end-state" or "final goal." What had been short-term aims in the pre-1914 programs of social democracy had now become the only goals: income redistribution, equality and social justice, full employment, the welfare state and the mixed economy. To achieve these objectives it was thought necessary to control the nation-state and its "sovereign" administrative machine. Today this conception is bankrupt; the epoch of construction of social democracy in one country has come to a close. The last attempt in this direction, the French socialist government of 1981–83, provided the resting place for the political ambitions of national social democracy.

Inside the European Community (EC), the irreversibility of interdependence is now widely accepted. Even among nationalists, at least in Europe, economic integration is celebrated because it allows for the viability of new—and sometimes very small—states. On the social democratic left, nonetheless,

Donald Sassoon, "Social Democracy and the Europe of Tomorrow," *Dissent*, Winter, 1994, pp. 94–101.
Copyright © 1994 Dissent Magazine. Reprinted by permission.

although there is plenty of Europeanist rhetoric, there is no European strategy. Instead, we have hybrid "national strategies" that seek to defend national interests within an integrated Europe-wide community. This national obsession is inevitable. Politics is still predominantly *national* politics. Elections are for a *national* parliament. Parties face a *national* electorate. As long as there are no really democratic pan-European institutions, as long as the European Parliament has limited powers, there will not be an institutional framework for the full development of a European strategy.

How should European social democrats think about European integration? First of all, they will have to recognize that national differences and conflicting interests will persist for a long time. To be effective, social democratic strategy must build on traditional social democratic commitments, that is, to welfare reforms and full employment within a regulated market economy under the direction of democratic institutions—whether at the national or European level.

The likely enlargement of the EC to include Sweden, Norway, Austria, and Finland will create the largest and richest market in the world: 360 million consumers in 16 countries.[1] The creation of a single market with a single currency, the establishment of a common commercial law, the elimination of many physical barriers to trade, the erection of common European technical standards, of Community-wide public procurement markets, and the end of transaction costs cannot fail to bring about major economic gains (though these are unlikely to be distributed according to any equitable criteria). But there is a big "if." The process of ratifying the Maastricht Treaty has been far longer and more painful than expected; its outcome is still uncertain. In France, the driving force behind the treaty, only a tiny majority approved it. Two referenda were required to bamboozle the Danish electorate into acquiescence. The Norwegian electorate will prove as recalcitrant as the Danish when they are asked to ratify Norwegian entry. Britain, whose government openly aspires to be Europe's Taiwan, has opted out of the Maastricht's social protocol. And a significant majority of Labour and Conservative supporters in Britain are against further European integration.

What of Eastern Europe?

Outside the prosperous borders of Western Europe, in Eastern and Central Europe, the situation could not be more unstable. Two major scenarios are currently envisaged.

On one hand, the Eastern economics may be turned into free-enterprise areas dominated by a savage and primitive capitalism, characterized by low wages, supervised by more or less stable semi-authoritarian governments—a Slavic

---

[1] As noted in the introductory comments, Sweden, Austria, and Finland joined the union. The Norwegians voted against ratification.

variant of Taiwan and South Korea—with a lower level of productivity and regulation than the newly industrialized Asian countries.

On the other hand, there might be an economic disaster that will bring about severe social tension, massive pressures for emigration, nationalist persecutions, and political and social upheavals as unpredictable as they are dangerous. If the first scenario is unpalatable, the second is intolerable. Some conservatives, however, will find the first quite positive. For them, a period of backwardness seasoned by a local version of Victorian values, a few carrots and plenty of sticks, low wages and hard work: this is the necessary premise, the preparatory Purgatory for a better future. Superior to the communist Hell, this prospect opens the way to the distant but heavenly delights of consumer capitalism.

Social democracy is then faced with a critical dilemma. If the Twelve proceed with the construction of a "social democratic" European space, that is, an integration of their welfare systems "upward" on the basis of environmentally regulated growth, it will be even more difficult than it is now to absorb the Eastern and Central European economies into an expanded EC. Ecologically directed growth, high wage costs, and high taxation in the West would redirect labour-intensive, low-productivity investment toward the East. This would seriously damage any prospect for a return of full employment in Western Europe or the maintenance of existing levels of social protection. It would enable the European right, led by Britain's Conservative government, to destroy the welfare state by deregulating the labor market to conform to the American model. And this, of course, would increase the obstacles to social reform in the United States.

The alternative to a movement of capital from West to East is large-scale labor migration from East to West. But the consequences of this would be untold social problems on both halves of the continent. It would eliminate the possibility of a return to full employment in Western Europe, severely weaken trade unions, contain wages, and narrow dramatically the fiscal reserves available for expanded social programs. Low wages in the East would not provide sufficient demand for a growth of manufacturing in the West. The free-market scenario for the East is a disaster for social democracy on both sides of the former iron curtain. Western socialists, who have had nothing to say to a potential democratic socialist movement in the East, ignore these issues at their peril.

There is no simple way out of the dilemma. The most realistic alternative is to give the electorate in the East a reason to support social democrats or their equivalent in their own countries. At present, East Europeans imagine the West to be a colossal shopping mall, the successful result of free enterprise. The century-long struggle of the European left for political regulation and social reform of the economy is forgotten. This conservative image of capitalism must be challenged: access to the EC and to the possibility of a Western lifestyle should require (since it in fact depends on) not only acceptance of a market and democratic institutions, but also social rights, full employment, non-discrimination, and qualitative growth.

In insisting on this social dimension of European economic integration, the West European left would strengthen emerging social democratic forces in the East, struggling to halt the development of an untrammeled market economy. The precondition for success, of course, is that the social dimension must become the center of the EC's agenda. This is not the case at present. Thus the contest for a social space in the EC, far from being a merely internal matter, is a new form of internationalism. It would offer to Eastern and Central Europe and, indeed, the rest of the world, the model of an advanced society radically different from the neoliberalism peddled by the IMF (International Monetary Fund). It would offer a society in which the values of solidarity prevail over the cacophony of cash registers.

European Monetary Union

To what extent are social democratic principles embedded in the economic and political plans agreed to at Maastricht? Careful textual analysis of the treaties is unlikely to reveal any significant social content. The Economic and Monetary Union (EMU) and the European Political Union (EPU) treaties are in fact asymmetrical. EMU is a carefully constructed document with clear goals and the institutional mechanisms for achieving them—however shaky things may seem after the exchange-rate crisis of the summer of 1993. The EPU is a much more modest document full of good intentions: "harmonious and balanced development of economic activities," non-inflationary growth respecting the environment," "raising standards of living." The more it reaches toward a social democratic agenda the vaguer EPU becomes: the EC will have "a policy in the sphere of the environment," will contribute to the "attainment of a high level of health protection," will contribute to "education and training of high quality," "to the flowering of the cultures of the Member States" and so on. The Social Protocol, binding on all except the British, is not a charter but a framework for action on social security, social protection and some aspects of industrial relations.

EMU offers a sharp contrast to the generalities of EPU. Its "primary objective" is price stability. Its guiding principle is "the open market economy with free competition." Other goals are sound public finances and sustainable balance of payments. It stipulates that the economic policies of member states must be consistent with these guidelines. Their adherence to them will be supervised by a European Central Bank whose independence is established in no uncertain terms: it receives no instructions from the EC's council or the commission or the various national governments. The primary objective of price stability is thus completely removed from everyday political debate, making it impossible to deny that inflation, at a particular moment, is a more serious threat than unemployment. The anti-inflationary guiding principle is thus a constraint on national as well as supranational policies.

One may ponder why inflation is regarded as such an evil when everyone knows how complex it is to identify the winners and the losers. Leaving aside the issue of hyper-inflation, whose disastrous consequences are obvious, it is not clear why a modicum of inflation is regarded as such a threat to economic stability as to warrant the privileged treatment it receives in the EMU treaty. Pensioners and others on fixed incomes could be protected by linking their benefits to the inflation rate. Unstable prices are not necessarily a cause of concern for investors—what worries them are adverse changes in relative prices, and what is adverse for one may be helpful to others.

It is no secret that the pledge on price stability was due more to political and "cultural" than to economic factors. Without it Germany would never have accepted EMU, as the French realized. Should EMU ever come into being, however, a large part of European trade will be "domestic," that is, within the European Community. Would inflation be as bad in such a large market as it may have been in a far more exposed and smaller national economy? Some 59 percent of the trade of member states is with other member states. This proportion of intra-regional trade will certainly grow, making the EC more "introverted" than the United States or Japan. Furthermore the clout of the EC in world trade will be greater than that of any other trading bloc.

▨ ▨ ▨

Unequal Development

Let us imagine that, by 1999, all twelve EC members are part of the single-currency area with, perhaps, the currencies of the other West European states converging into an ERM-type mechanism. Within the EC there are no more national currencies. All transactions are in ECU. Within Europe there will be no further balance-of-payment problems in the same way as Idaho or Alabama or Bavaria or Yorkshire have no balance-of-payment problems. Similarly there will no longer be intra-European "interest rate problems," for the obvious reason that the depositors will be faced with an ECU market competing with the yen and the dollar. Foreign-exchange currency storms, such as that of September 1992, which blew British sterling and the Italian lira off course or that of July 1993, which nearly destroyed the ERM, will be far less likely because speculators will not be able to gang up against individual currencies, which will no longer exist. There will be, at the European level, a different, potentially far more serious, issue: the exacerbation of regional variations. In the absence of any guiding criteria (other than price stability) these differences will become the fundamental issues in the internal politics of the EC. Talk about budgetary

GLOSSARY

European Economic Community, now known as **European Community (EC):** Established by the Treaty of Rome (1957) by France, the Federal Republic of Germany, Italy, Belgium, the Netherlands, and Luxembourg. Great Britain, Denmark and Ireland joined in 1973, Greece in 1981, and Spain and Portugal in 1986.

The Commission of the EC is the EC's executive, the collective name for the seventeen commissioners (two from the larger five countries, one from each of the others). Each commissioner has responsibility for a specific area. Though the commission can initiate policy and has considerable political weight, real power rests with the Council of Ministers. Its current head is [Romano Prodi].

The Council of Ministers is the supreme decision-making body of the community. It is made up of one minister from each country, usually the foreign minister, but it may consist of the agricultural ministers if agriculture is being discussed, or the finance ministers. The council takes the final decision to adopt a proposal. The council is chaired by the minister of the country that holds the presidency. This rotates every six months.

The European Parliament is elected by universal suffrage. It sits in Strasbourg. Each member country sends a number of deputies according to population (Germany has the largest representation, Luxembourg the smallest). Since the European Parliament is devoid of serious power, it is generally accepted to be the most significant instance of the so-called "democratic deficit" of the EC. The EP can make recommendations but the commission is not obliged to accept any. However, the EP can block legislation and the budget. It has also the power—never used so far—to dismiss the commission.

The Maastricht Treaty was finally ratified in 1993. It is made up of two parts: the EMU and the EPU.

and monetary convergence conceals the enormity of the existing differences: in 1991 the unemployment rate was 24 percent in southern Spain but only 2.7 percent in Baden-Wurttemberg. This ten-to-one ratio is about twice the U.S. spread. In other words regional unemployment variations in Europe are 100 percent more severe than in the USA.

What will this European Community look like? As a peculiar multinational state, it will have constituent "sub-states" (for want of a better term), some coterminous with a nation (for example, Denmark, most of France and Italy) and some multinational in themselves (such as Britain and Spain). Some national governments will face considerable differentiations of income and wealth within their borders. In some instances, an entire nation might find the gap between itself and more prosperous lands increasing. In other words the

EMU stands for **Economic and Monetary Union,** which describes a process leading to the establishment of a common European currency in place of the twelve national ones, a common monetary policy, and a single European central bank. This [was] supposed to be in place by 1999. Only countries whose economies converge will be able to join.

EPU stands for **European Political Union,** which is supposed to establish European citizenship, voting rights in local elections for all nationals of member countries, and a common foreign policy. This is the most controversial section of Maastricht and has encountered fierce opposition in Britain and Denmark.

The Social Protocol is attached to the Maastricht Treaty and involves the setting of minimum standards for workers' protection, such as minimum wage and length of the working week. Britain alone has opted out of this.

ECU stands for **European Currency Unit** and is the basic monetary unit used in community transactions. Its value is a weighted average basket of EC currencies on the basis of the relative importance of each national economy (consequently the deutsche mark counts for about half). If economic and monetary union were to become reality, the ECU would be the European currency.

ERM stands for **Exchange Rate Mechanism.** Member states of the ERM keep the value of their currencies within an agreed band in relation to each other. Until July 1993 the permitted divergence was $2\frac{1}{4}$ percent. Following the wave of speculation of September 1992 Britain and Italy left the system while the Spanish peseta and the Portuguese escudo participated in a wider 6 percent band. In July 1993, as the speculators' attack on the French franc intensified, the system was drastically revised, enlarging the permitted band of fluctuation to 15 percent. Some commentators have argued, quite reasonably, that such a wide band negates the whole purpose of an exchange rate system.

unequal growth that has characterized the internal development of most European countries will be reproduced on the European level.

Historically, nations facing these problems have been able to defuse discontent either by repression or by ensuring that the whole population had equal political rights. Democratic institutions forced national politicians to adopt measures aimed at resolving regional problems. These policies required expenditure to modify the disguised terms of trade within the country: tax incentives, direct grants, subsidies, special programs. Equality of social rights meant that the depressed areas had a good chance of obtaining a higher degree of welfare funding than the others. Residents of more prosperous areas sanctioned, grudgingly perhaps, the fiscal implications of this policy, for example, higher taxes. This was sustainable so long as the nation formed some sort of community.

What was a tolerable grumble by taxpayers in the prosperous sixties became a generalized cry of outrage in the seventies and eighties. Even within national communities, solidarity is not a strong currency: many West Germans who welcomed reunification were alarmed to discover that—contrary to what they had been told—patriotism costs money. In Italy the right-wing populists of the Northern League have made inroads into a hitherto moderate electorate unwilling to cough up funds for the apparently never-ending reconstruction of the South.

If this is the situation in a nation-state, is there any reason to think that an effective regional policy could be funded centrally, by a transfer of resources from prosperous European areas to depressed ones? It may be unrealistic to assume that citizens in Stuttgart or Paris will willingly yield "their" money for regional aid to Greece or Yorkshire—after all, they are not so keen for it to be directed to Saxony or Corsica.

There is no easy solution. This much is, however, certain: the neoliberal model of European integration (that is, Margaret Thatcher's)—get rid of constraints, rip the shackles stopping enterprising capitalists from creating wealth, and so on—is a recipe for European disintegration. The alternative is for the left to adopt a clearly federalist approach that accepts the Maastricht rules of convergence in prices, currency, interest rates, and public spending but insists that such constraints on national decision makers are insufficient. Similar constraints, the left must argue, have to be established for regional and social policies. Rules of convergence should not be limited to prices and budgets but should also apply to regional growth, levels of unemployment, social benefits, discrimination legislation, working conditions, and so on.

This strategy has distinct advantages. In the first place it is not new. It is based on widely accepted principles, many already included in the EC treaties, many rooted in the common heritage of social democratic thought but acceptable also to Christian democrats. Social democrats and Christian democrats together constitute a clear majority of the West European electorate. Furthermore, government resistance to these policies in the eighties and nineties has seldom been justified on ideological grounds (Thatcher's Britain was an exception). Usually it was objected that they would make the country in question less competitive or that taxpayers would not stand for them. In an integrated Europe, social convergence and redistribution may be opposed on tax grounds but not for the sake of competitiveness.

The Question of Democracy

Though the present battle cry on both left and right is decentralization, what the EC really needs is further centralization. The present plan charges nonelected institutions—such as the central bank—which are more or less divorced from popular control and uninhibited by elections, with ensuring stable prices, balanced growth, and free competition. Why not the same degree of top-to-bottom commitment to the environment and social rights, to the struggle against unemployment, to equal treatment for women, to help for the handicapped, to safety at work, and so on?

It may be objected that such social integration would leave very little room for party politics. If all governments follow the same guidelines why bother to elect them? This is a serious objection that cannot be dealt with here entirely satisfactorily. It may be sufficient to point out that the construction of any regime entails the establishment of fundamental rules usually embodied in a constitution. Liberal constitutions establish minimum rights that cannot be violated by any government and are therefore removed from normal party competition, but this still leaves room for argument among political parties. The successful introduction of social rights would enhance the democratic process. It guarantees minimum standards that cannot be eliminated by a majority of the electorate and gives the minority (here the underprivileged minority) a stake in the system. Democracy in the full sense (not simply as the will of the majority) is thereby strengthened.

The struggle to entrench social rights will provide a pan-European dimension for the left and thereby set the agenda for left politics in Europe for the foreseeable future. It will not be a utopian fight. It will, actually, renew what used to be called the social democratic consensus, the politics of that golden age in the fifties and sixties when even conservatives favored full employment and did not regard unions as subversive organizations. Of course such consensus politics entails acceptance by all parties—including opponents of socialism—the basic features of a civilized society—yes, a society in which inflation is less than x percent, but also one that eliminates the fear of ill health, poverty and want, the indignities of sexual and racial discrimination, and the dangers of environmental damage.

At issue are political and institutional constraints that cannot be disregarded. These must rest on a consensus so wide that revisions will not be undertaken lightly. I see no substantial difference between this and a written constitution.

A Constitution of Europe is unlikely to come about in a traditional way, that is, through a constituent assembly. It will develop in an ad hoc and largely unplanned manner, for there are no real historical precedents. No successful federal state has ever been peacefully established with such varied national communities, divided by language and tradition. The American example, where a civil war was fought on the issue of centralization, is of little help. In the United States there are no serious language divisions (so far), and state borders do not have the significance they have in Europe. Someone may be proud to come from Iowa, but this is not the equivalent of being Danish or Irish.

European socialists should think of the developing EC in the same way as the constituent assembly for a new state. They should try to inscribe in its articles the central coordinates of their beliefs. They should negotiate, make alliances, try to devise the most effective forms of control and enforcement. They should not boycott it or lag behind. They should not be afraid of being innovative, while realizing that the "document" to be produced must gain wide respect and stand the test of time. They must insist that its guiding principles—on a par with price stabilization—should include full employment, social and environmental constraints, nondiscrimination, and decent welfare policies. The aim is not simply to reproduce across Europe what social democracy attempted on the national level. The criticisms of the old welfare state, from across the political spectrum—its centralized and bureaucratic structure, its paternalism, its frequent indifference to individual needs—have been digested by the more innovative sectors of European socialism. They will now have to invent the basis for the national and local administration of a decentralized welfare system. But such decentralization, to succeed, also needs clear guidelines from the center.

European social democratic strategy cannot be limited to entrenching, in one form or other, its basic principles. The tenet of social convergence, which is closely related to the older democratic commitment to equality, requires the development of transnational democratic institutions, such as the European Parliament, together with transnational political parties and transnational trade unions. The more European integration advances the greater will be the pressures on national parties to defend specifically national interests. This is inevitable: democratic parties respond to their electorates. In circumstances combining unequal development and power shifts to central institutions, clashes between, say, a ruling German Social Democratic party and a ruling Spanish Socialist party are inescapable. Both would be defending national, that is "regional," interests. If they did not do so they would expose themselves to attacks from their national opponents. It seems, therefore, that it would be in the long-term interests of all concerned that significant powers be transferred to the European Parliament, now a weak institution. This would allow regional parties to maintain their own national outlook, to develop national policies, and to lobby the commission and the Council of Ministers as well as the European Parliament in defense of their electorate's interest. Transnational Europarties would have to balance "regional" variations as present-day national parties do. They would be penalized in one region if they disregarded its interests. They would also, inevitably, clash with nationally based parties. In constructing a novel type of federal state, the standard debates between centralists and federalists are to be expected.

There are social democratic pessimists, who under the guise of realism point out that the prospects for a social democratic pan-European strategy are extremely limited. Socialists, they argue, are in bad shape throughout most of Europe: in opposition in Germany, Sweden, Greece, and Britain; cohabiting in France; in minority governments in Belgium, Denmark, and Norway; in total disarray in Italy; and deprived on an overall majority in Spain.

Unfortunately, all this is true. But no one can win battles they don't fight. The current travail of social democracy seems to suggest that a radical overhaul of policies and outlooks might be profitable. Those who believe that a frankly federalist option is too ambitious should bear in mind that every major step toward further European integration has been the consequence of a grand political design. Plans "which will never work" have set the agenda by dangling goals before the old European cart-horse, making it move forward. From Jean Monnet to Jacques Delors, innovative visions have gone hand in hand with hardheaded realism.

This is not a plea for an inward-looking little Europe. The present crisis of European integration, the growing balkanization of Eastern and Central Europe, the horrendous slaughter in the former Yugoslavia point toward a dismal future. Only multinational companies, which have an interest in pitting nation against nation while escaping all forms of national and supranational control, stand to profit. A more integrated Europe, with a revitalized social democratic left, might become a beacon for social advance in the third world. And it might also suggest to Americans, now free from the cold war, new and more promising models of social organization.

The Origins and Evolution of the Single Market in Europe

BILL LUCARELLI

Bill Lucarelli received his Ph.D. in economics from the University of Sydney in 1997 and is a lecturer at the University of Western Sydney in Australia. His research interests include international financial and currency markets, new growth theories, and post-Keynesian economics. The results of his recent research at the Department of Industry in Canberra will appear in his upcoming book *Structural Change and Technological Innovation*. The opening paragraphs, selected from his book *The Origins and Evolution of the Single Market in Europe*, exemplify Lucarelli's idea that the creation of the European Union was a logical response to the economic strains imposed on Europe and the United States in the wake of World War II. He goes on to construct three possible scenarios for the future of the European Union. Which of the three seems the most likely? Why?

Rather than an internal logic of integration, it has been argued that the process of integration has been primarily determined by the configuration of international economic and politico-military relations. Post-war economic reconstruction demanded a supranational response. This overriding necessity was dictated by two fundamental conditions. First, in order to avoid a relapse into the syndrome of economic nationalism and autarchy, the American architects of the European Recovery Programme (ERP) fostered closer inter-State economic co-operation. As a result, the pre-war problems of access to raw materials, investment outlets and markets could be resolved within a supranational framework. At the very core of this problem was the economic reconstruction of the West German economy and the political rehabilitation of the West German State. Franco-German rapprochement was therefore essential.

The second condition in this post-war settlement involved the formation of an anti-Soviet bloc in Western Europe by the Americans in order to deter the perceived threat of Soviet expansionism. Closer European political and military co-operation became a necessary precondition in the formation of the Western alliance after the war. With the onset of Cold War rivalries, the Americans actively supported the anti-Communist forces in the ranks of the Christian Democratic and centrist alliances which emerged as the dominant political power blocs over the next two decades. The Christian Democratic ascendancy in Western Europe provided the political rationale in the birth of the Common Market. This was most evident in the creation of the Common Agricultural Policy (CAP) in which the powerful agricultural lobbies formed a strategic power base for the Christian Democratic parties.

Quite apart from the geo-political imperatives of the Cold War, the American authorities viewed the reconstruction of the European market as an essential means by which to resolve their own impending crisis of overproduction. The European market would provide an outlet for American exports and resolve America's domestic problems of surplus capacity generated during the war. Indeed, the trade imbalance between Europe and the United States only aggravated the dollar shortage in Europe which imposed severe constraints on their ability to launch a programme of economic reconstruction. It was in this context that the Marshall Plan was conceived as a means of resolving the burgeoning U.S. trade surpluses by providing loans and reconstruction aid to European governments so that they could purchase American exports.

Customs union theory had informed the American architects of the recovery programme. It was assumed that a more unified European market would increase the propensity to import American goods while at the same time, improve the economies of scale beyond the limits imposed by the existing national markets within Europe. In other words, American economic planners sought to re-cast European capitalism in their own image through the construction of a "United States of Europe." The "politics of productivity" had governed the American strategy in Europe insofar as the trade imbalance and the dollar shortage were essentially designated as a European problem of production and productivity.

Although the American sponsored recovery programme failed to resolve the trade imbalance and the dollar shortage, the Americans had laid the foundations for a more liberal international economic architecture under the aegis of *Pax Americana*. This new order was enshrined by the institutions of the IMF/World Bank and the GATT Agreements, while the U.S. dollar would perform the international role of reserve currency and a means of payments under the post-war Bretton Woods accords. It was this liberal international environment which ultimately provided the necessary conditions for closer European economic and political integration. American mediation therefore provided the rationalizing dynamic in the process of post-war European integration.

※ ※ ※

Quite contrary to the optimistic projections made by the proponents of Project 1992, this study contends that the liberal and deregulationist logic will merely accentuate regional disparities, erode established social legislation and norms, and severely limit the scope for traditional Keynesian policies of fiscal stabilization and full employment. The restoration of the competitive dynamism of European capitalism through the neo-liberal strategy cannot be taken for granted. The process of negative integration will merely hasten the emergence of centrifugal forces which could threaten further progress toward European union. It is possible to construct three scenarios in the future evolution of the single market.

Scenario One: The Rise of Nationalism and the Disintegration of Supranationalism

In this scenario, the dormant though still powerful currents of nationalism and ethnic rivalries could gain the ascendancy. A relapse into the syndrome of nationalist/imperialist rivalry which had engulfed the continent in the inter-war years is quite possible. This scenario would presuppose an intensification of the current capitalist crisis and the collapse of the prevailing liberal-democratic forms of government. Although the objective conditions and the subjective forces for this kind of scenario appear quite remote, nationalist political tendencies have already emerged in the wake of the collapse of the Soviet bloc. In Germany, neo-fascism has reared its ugly head but is still only confined to the extreme political fringes. In France, the National Front has gained momentum and approached the very threshold of mainstream politics, while in Italy, the Italian Social Movement (MSI) has also acquired considerable political legitimacy.

The deep-seated structural crisis in Europe has resonated in the social and political spheres. With the relative demise of traditional social democratic policies and the ascendancy of the neo-liberal economic paradigm, the post-war consensus based on "social market" policies has been undermined. A single currency and a single market implies the supersession of national forms of State power and the creation of a supranational regime of governance. The neo-liberal strategy of negative integration, however, does not propose to substitute these national forms of capitalist regulation on a supranational level. The political crisis is therefore an expression of the contending national/supranational forms of State power. Although European statehood would not necessarily abolish the existing system of national politics, the remorseless logic of globalization will tend to accentuate these social and regional disparities. Deprived of its traditional armor of sovereignty, nationalism could be re-activated to restore the primacy of the nation-state.

The growing ranks of the unemployed will doubtless provide a fertile breeding ground for the growth of these extremist nationalist forces. Scapegoats can be readily targeted with the presence of foreign workers. With the general shift to the political right, racism has become the dominant ideological expression of this resurgent nationalism. In this sense, the recent Balkan conflict represents the most extreme manifestation of this ethnic/nationalist revival. The triumph of these forces could hasten the Balkanization of Europe. At present, the likelihood of this disturbing scenario appears quite remote. A major economic catastrophe or war could, however, unleash these forces into the maelstrom of history.

Scenario Two: A Confederalist Europe Based on German Hegemony

A more likely scenario which conforms with the argument developed in this study would involve a process of historical continuity with minor variations. The most significant development over the past two decades has been the emergence of German economic dominance. Although the Franco-German axis still constitutes the pivot around which the process of European integration revolves, the German economy occupies the very core of Europe. This is evident not only in the relative size of the German economy but also in the strategic role performed by German capital goods in the dynamics of capital accumulation on a European scale. A central argument of this study has been that the German economy has provided an engine of growth for Europe since the war. The Common Market represented a historical resolution to the issues of markets, investment outlets, and access to raw materials which had been the fundamental causes of inter-state rivalry before the war. In this crucial sense, the making of Europe was the answer to Germany's own making after the war.

German economic dominance is reflected in the politics of monetary union. The German mark has emerged as the nominal exchange rate anchor for the European monetary system while German ideological preferences have prevailed in the creation of a European central bank. Germany is at the very core of Europe surrounded by a concentric circle of peripheral and semi-peripheral countries. In this configuration, the northern industrial regions constitute the centre with the peripheral and semi-peripheral countries in the south and west gravitating around this epicentre. A third concentric circle would constitute the newly emergent capitalist economies of eastern Europe. Given this new enlarged European sphere, the likelihood of European federalism appears difficult to accomplish. A loose confederation is the most likely outcome with Germany acting as the hegemonic centre. A more accurate analogy might be made with the nineteenth century formation of the German Zollverein [customs union] in which Prussia established a base for future expansion. The ultimate question is whether the European Union will become a platform for future German economic expansion.

Scenario Three: European Federalism?

Despite the ideals and aspirations of European federalists, the likelihood of European statehood appears as remote as ever. Indeed, much of the ostensible progress toward European federalism has been imbued with mythology. In the past, European countries have pursued an imperialist policy of territorial acquisition and expansion in order to resolve their domestic problems of markets and access to raw materials. One of the central aims of the post-war political settlement was to reconcile these inter-imperialist rivalries within a pan-European framework. German militarism, in particular, could now be contained and to paraphrase Schuman, "make war not only unthinkable but materially impossible." To this end, supranationalism has succeeded in fostering peace and prosperity within Western Europe. Conceived in the destructive cataclysm engendered by modern war, the federalist cause attracted considerable popular support for a brief period but soon withered away as the nation-state re-asserted its preeminent role in European politics. In contrast to federalist interpretations, this study has generally supported Milward's contention that supranationalism represented a European rescue of the nation-state. The federalist cause might still evoke noble sentiments but has receded in the course of history.

Come Together

Europe's Unexpected New Architecture

ELIZABETH POND

Elizabeth Pond is a well-known journalist and expert on European affairs. She served as foreign correspondent for the *Christian Science Monitor* for twenty years and has written ten books on foreign policy and international affairs, including *The Rebirth of Europe*, which appeared in 1999. Pond is currently stationed in Germany and edits the Berlin-based *Transatlantic Internationale Politik*. In the following selection, Pond considers the strengths and weaknesses of the EU over the past four decades, applauding its performance during the Kosovo crisis and its advancement of a single European currency, the euro. She also paints the growing cooperation between NATO and the EU in a positive light. Given the problematic nature of European unity as discussed in the previous selections, is Pond's optimism warranted?

It must be a new era when the secretary-general of NATO goes out of his way to praise a European Union summit—and when the EU's rhetoric is tougher than NATO's on Russian brutality in Chechnya. Welcome to twenty-first century Europe, in which NATO and the EU routinely meddle in each other's affairs, see themselves more and more as collaborators (and rivals) in joint business, and even fraternize in a manner utterly taboo during the Cold War. It is a Europe in which Lord Robertson, NATO's secretary-general, ostentatiously commended the EU's pledge at its Helsinki summit last December [1999] to

Elizabeth Pond, "Come Together: Europe's Unexpected New Architecture," *Foreign Affairs*, Vol. 79, No. 2., March/April 2000, pp. 8–12. Reprinted by permission of *Foreign Affairs*, March/April 2000. Copyright © 2000 by the Council on Foreign Relations, Inc.

build better European rapid-reaction forces to supplement America's troops in the region and where, for a few days at least, EU leaders talked about imposing sanctions on Russia for its conduct in Chechnya with a severity unmatched by either the United States or NATO.

Increasingly, the chaotic overlapping institutions of post–Cold War Europe are morphing together, led by the premier Western clubs, NATO and EU. Amid the ongoing consolidation, some organizations—for instance, the obsolete Western European Union—are vanishing altogether. Some, like the Council of Europe and the Organization for Security and Cooperation in Europe, are spinning away from the center to focus on heartland Europe's relations with the east Slavs and others who have chosen not to follow the voluntary rules of the European club. And Europe's stronger institutions are finally beginning to define their own niches and refine their mutual interactions.

In short, the continent's long-prophesied post–Cold War "security architecture" is at last appearing—and it is not quite the brick-and-mortar of fixed institutions that analysts envisaged when the Berlin Wall fell a decade ago. It is, rather, a form of what computer aficionados would call systems management— inducing coexisting processes to at best reinforce each other or at least not disable each other.

That the form of twenty-first century European governance is so unexpected should itself have been expected. Heartland Europe is postnational in a way neither America nor Russia nor Japan (nor, for that matter, the Balkans nor the Caucasus) is. Its method of governance is therefore sui generis. Earlier than other, larger countries, the tiny nations of Europe—Germany, the most populous, is physically no larger than Montana—have been forced to realize that they can no longer cope individually with global drug runners, Chernobyl fallout, and instant electronic transfers of billions of dollars. They must band together, and they have by now ascertained that their decades-long cooperation to resist Soviet coercion was no Cold War aberration. However tempted Margaret Thatcher and François Mitterrand were to revert to nineteenth-century balance-of-power games against Germany after the Berlin Wall fell, more sensible habits of cooperation have now become ingrained.

Thus the European Community (EC) promoted reconciliation between the archenemies France and Germany; gradually conferred legitimacy on post-Nazi West Germany; helped France modernize and surpass reunited Germany in per capita output; eased Spain's and Portugal's graduations from autocracy to democracy; turned Ireland into a high-tech center, made it a destination for immigrants for the first time since before the potato famine, and gave it enough self-confidence to facilitate an eventual peace settlement with Northern Ireland; gave Italy an incentive to discipline its finances and qualify for European economic and monetary union; and gave all citizens of its member countries unimagined prosperity and the longest period of peace in Europe's history. Even after the unifying Soviet threat vanished, the EC proved far too valuable to give up. It was retained and even reinforced to create a genuine single market, proclaim the grand goal of a real European Union, open its doors to the new democracies of central Europe, and most astonishingly, meld Europe's many venerable currencies into the freshly minted euro.

Rolling, Rolling, Rolling

All this was achieved by a rolling form of consensus-building, which avoided lowest-common-denominator compromise by repeatedly making the top performances in various fields the "benchmark" standard for all. Essentially, the EU adapted the domestic-consensus political system of Germanic Europe and the Low Countries both to hold disparate nations together and to break out of the EC stasis of the 1970s and early 1980s. In the post–Cold War era, the EU has repeatedly expanded this practice, treating crisis as opportunity, as fluidity, and anxiety about the future in general and German demons in particular as a useful source of energy. The result has been an extraordinary relinquishing of individual sovereignty for the common good in what European governments now perceive not as a surrender but as a positive "pooling" of national sovereignty.

Moreover, this transformation has been helped by developing a culture of peer pressure that defies all conventional institutional or realist analyses. The EU, although already far more than a confederation, will clearly never become a European federation. It has no hierarchy. The European Commission led by Romano Prodi is part manager, part secretariat, part legislature, and part defender of small members' interests against those of the four biggest members. But its staff is tiny (barely matching the number of administrators in Cologne), and it is not an executive. The EU's highest authority remains the European Council, which convenes peripatetic bimonthly summits of semisovereign heads of governments or states who engage in permanent ongoing negotiations.

Nor, after Thatcher banged her handbag on the table in the mid-1980s, will the EU ever have the power of the purse for the mass redistributive transfers that individual European nations make for social welfare and the United States uses for regional assistance programs. The EU budget is limited to no more than 1.27 percent of its members' combined CDP—and half of that is locked into farm-surplus entitlements.

Despite the absence of persuasive carrots or sticks, though, the conclave of equals in the European Council and the councils of foreign, finance, agriculture, and other ministers have mustered the political will to leap forward. Votes are virtually never taken, nor are vetoes exercised (except implicitly, usually by the French or the British). Yet issues are somehow talked to death until the holdouts yield to the informal 80 or 90 percent majority. If anything, this consensus-building process is even more pronounced in the obscure but powerful Committee of Permanent Representatives in Brussels, which solves the vast bulk of intra-European issues at a senior bureaucratic level without recourse to the political echelon. And this custom will probably be blessed formally in this year's Intergovernmental Conference with new rules for "qualified majority voting," which will accelerate EU decision-making.

Until 1999, it looked as if military matters would remain exempt from the EU's spreading supranational approach. To be sure, after some French and Spanish resistance, the EU accepted Germany's priority on trying to replicate western European economic and political successes in central Europe by offering these new democracies EU tutelage and, eventually, membership. This common policy has already had a huge impact on the behavior of the candidates. It may be only soft power, but the lure of possible association with the rich and peaceful EU (and NATO) is highly appealing to nations striving to meet the two club's democratic and market-related preconditions for membership. The chain reaction of Polish-Ukrainian, Ukrainian-Romanian, Romanian-Hungarian, and Bulgarian-Macedonian reconciliation is the best testimony to the positive impact of both the EU and NATO on their eastern neighbors.

Such a coordinated central European policy was already an innovation when the EU set out its road map for admitting new members in 1993. But the EU's grander ambitions about forging a "common foreign and security policy" and a "European security and defence identity" still seemed a pie in the sky. European commonality in the ultimate commitment of blood lagged well behind the pooling of sovereignty in trade, markets, law, and the environment. Clashes between the intervention-prone British and French and the more pacifist Germans and others—as well as the habit of entrusting security decisions to a U.S.-dominated NATO—precluded any meeting of EU minds.

Last year, however, the Kosovo crisis greatly qualified this exception. In only nine months, the EU made a series of firsts. It endorsed a hot war by NATO forces, with the full support of all EU neutrals; came to regard the Balkans not as the barbarian East but as a part of Europe that must be raised to European standards of human rights; was shocked by its own impotence relative to America's electronic-weapons wizardry; held together for 78 days in the face of bitter popular opposition in Greece to the NATO war next door; agreed to fold the Western European Union (WEU) into the EU; appointed the high-profile politician Javier Solana rather than a faceless clerk to be Europe's inaugural "Mr. Foreign Policy" and double-hatted him as interim WEU secretary-general, with the ex officio right to sit in on North Atlantic Council meetings; set the goal of creating up to 60,000 European rapid-reaction troops that could be mobilized within two months for a two-year deployment; held a joint meeting of EU foreign and defense ministers; and put Turkey on the candidate list for future EU membership.

Borderline Schizophrenia

Inevitably, such unwonted European activism in a realm that previously belonged exclusively to NATO has triggered a schizophrenic reaction in the United States and has led to skirmishes with NATO. Washington approves of the European desire to assume more of the common Western military burden but does not want this to prejudice unilateral American action. For their part, the Europeans have differing goals: the French would like to cut the hegemonic "hyperpower" down to size, whereas the British and the Germans want exactly the opposite—relieving the United States of enough of its security burden in Europe to prevent an isolationist Congress from someday yanking U.S. troops home in disgust. But for all their internal differences, the Europeans all insist that contributing more treasure and, potentially, blood to the transatlantic partnership must also mean that Europe gains more say in NATO decisions.

To those fluent in the arts of the Westphalian nation-state and used to America's way of making policy by confrontation rather than consensus, such a European claim seems suspicious. Henry Kissinger, for one, views the development with profound mistrust and asks whether Europe is really turning anti-American and trying to weaken U.S. leadership. The Clinton administration, although more relaxed about a nascent European "defense identity" than its Republican predecessors, praises European efforts in official public statements but then briefs journalists about the risks of Europe's going it alone.

Of course, NATO too has changed in the last ten years. It has shifted not only from large-unit territorial defense to regional crisis management but also from overtly military tasks to more political ones that impinge on EU turf. And for all the new NATO-EU cooperation in the former Yugoslavia, the simultaneous probes by the two organizations for new roles in the present fluid situation sometimes aggravate rather than alleviate transatlantic strains. This is evident in the question of who should handle which future brushfires, American complaints about the EU's slowness to admit new central European members, and the jostling about who sets the agenda in Europe.

Thus such U.S. commentators as former Treasury Secretary Robert Rubin and the editorialists of *The Washington Post*—disregarding poor postcommunist economies' need for complex and time-consuming restructuring to prepare them for EU competition—feel aggrieved at the slowness with which the EU is taking in new members. NATO has moved faster and has had to assume too much of the responsibility for attaching the central Europeans to the West, they argue. The EU is dragging its feet. Meanwhile, they add, NATO has taken the necessary lead in improvising the Partnership for Peace to exert a calming influence and signal the West's interest in security in Ukraine and other states beyond the immediate circle of central European candidates.

But Europeans, many Germans and French retort, are providing the lion's share of assistance and investment for the region. Now that Belgrade has been diverted from old-fashioned Serbian imperialism, the real security threats on the continent today are economic and social rather than military. The normative impact of the EU system is already stabilizing and transforming central Europe. And heartland Europe's more existential stake in what kind of identity its neighbors adopt means that the EU should lead on such issues as using gunboats to enforce an oil embargo against Montenegro's Adriatic port during the war in Kosovo or supplying opposition governments in Yugoslav cities with heating fuel in winter.

To establish a framework for resolving future disputes, the allies have invented some imaginative terminology. Guidelines have been written for "Combined Joint Task Forces"—European-only troops that could mount operations with the help of "separable but not separate" NATO airlift, intelligence, and other assets "when NATO is not engaged." And European rapid-reaction forces are to avoid the "three Ds" of "duplication," transatlantic "decoupling," and "discrimination" against continental countries like Turkey that are members of NATO but not (yet) of the EU.

Such formulas do not guarantee reconciliation of the different movements of Europe's premier institutions, of course. But they do presume a common transatlantic enterprise in which NATO and the EU jointly constitute the indispensable governing apparatus of twenty-first century Europe and in which elite opinion on both sides of the Atlantic is taken into consideration. The natural corollary is that the emerging architecture linking the two institutions can and must be deliberately shaped to maximize that transatlantic interaction and render NATO and the EU not only compatible but synergetic.

12

THE END OF THE COLD WAR AND COLLAPSE OF THE USSR

It is imprudent if not precipitate for studies in history to touch on contemporary developments. The risks incurred in appearing to be left behind by subsequent events are enormous. Yet no European history text that ignores the rapid and exhilarating changes that began in the late summer of 1989 can lay claim to anything resembling completeness. In the wake of Mikhail Gorbachev's twin policies of *glasnost* (opening) and *perestroika* (restructuring), the spectacle of besieged Communist party leaders in Poland, Hungary, Czechoslovakia, East Germany, and Bulgaria granting one desperate concession after another, and then finally stepping aside when emboldened oppositions merely increased their demands, is too astonishing not to be recounted.

Who, earlier in that year, would have predicted the fall of the Berlin Wall, the promise to rebuild multiparty democracy in Czechoslovakia, the amendment of the East German constitution giving up the Communist party's "leading right" to determine policy, the forced resignation and replacement of the discredited Bulgarian Communist chiefs and the equally significant promise of wide-ranging reforms and free elections, or, before the year's end, the flight even of the hard-line Romanian government after its failure to suppress with violence widespread popular protest? By early winter the Polish coalition government, which included the once-repressed trade union "Solidarity," and which was itself formed scarcely three months earlier, was so widely accepted that it ceased to make headlines. These cataclysms all followed Gorbachev's public acknowledgment that the Brezhnev Doctrine (justifying Soviet military intervention in the satellites) was dead and buried and that the Soviet Union would allow each of its Warsaw Pact partners to devise its own *perestroika*, the revolution from above that was being launched within the Soviet Union.

It is clear that events in East-Central Europe were not determined by leaders or committees or summit meetings. As a British columnist (Hugo Young in *The Guardian*) put it, "In Poland, in East Germany, in Czechoslovakia, extraordinary surges of popular feeling, uncontrollable by political leaders or military force, have carried all before them. Decades of oppression and brain-washing turn out not to have extinguished the capacity of these many millions of people to discern not only that communism was a grotesque failure but that they retained the power to overthrow it."

To what extent was the Soviet leader responsible? His promise not to use Soviet troops in support of the satellite regimes was no doubt crucial. Still, Poles and Czechs and East Germans and Romanians showed tenacity, and it was not because of Gorbachev that their democratic instincts survived. Certainly Gorbachev, then a bureaucrat in the Brezhnev government, was not responsible for Solidarity's birth and durability. On the other hand, he perceived the necessity of reforming his own economy and recognized that the greater autonomy of his neighbors need pose no threat to Soviet security—that is, he recognized the direction in which history was taking the Soviet bloc and seemed eager to further that movement.

We may disagree over causes, but we must acknowledge the consequences that have already emerged and will continue to emerge. Most historical periods are transitional, marked by slow incremental change within a seemingly immutable framework of permanence. But every now and then an upheaval takes place that shatters previously held assumptions and opens new perspectives. The year 1989, with the dramatic end of forty-five years of cold war and the chance for a free and whole Europe, brought such an upheaval. For many, it meant the extension of free-market economies; for others, it meant the opportunity to free socialism from its fatal identification with Stalinism (most conspicuously revealed by the Soviet Communist party's decisions to renounce its monopoly on power and to introduce a free market to replace the government-managed, centrally planned economy that failed to produce adequate goods); for most, it meant the extension of democratic forms. Indeed, 1989 may well be remembered, as remarked by Theo Sommer, editor of the West German newsweekly *Die Zeit,* as creating the possibility of putting three things behind us: "the bitter conflict between East and West which began when Stalin rang down the Iron Curtain . . . the horrifying prospect of World War III which has been looming on the horizon for almost two generations now; and, perhaps, even the Great Schism that rent Europe asunder in the Bolshevik Revolution of November 1917. Suddenly, a new order seems to arise out of the familiar array."

"We must now invent another phase in the history of Europe," said François Mitterrand, then president of France. Even so, he, like others, recognized that these changes have given rise to a number of questions, and the responses to them vary. A reunited Germany has become a reality, but its economic dominance worries many in Europe. The future and the credibility of the United Nations, particularly in the wake of the fragmentation of Yugoslavia, also cause concern.

What follows are five assessments of the factors that brought an end to the cold war, particularly the effect of U.S. policy. In insisting that geopolitical as well as ideological motives drove the superpowers, Raymond L. Garthoff denies that the West won through deterrence and credits the new Soviet leadership with greater realism than that shown by its predecessors. Joshua Muravchik, on the other hand, attributes the Western victory to the military buildup initiated and carried out by President Ronald Reagan. Finally, George F. Kennan denies that any country, any party, or any person "won" the cold war and points to the price paid for it by both sides. The final two essays of the chapter, by Michael Mandelbaum and Dominic Lieven, try to explain the USSR's rapid demise, why it was not more readily anticipated by experts, by the "Sovietologists," and whether major reforms ineluctably lead to revolutionary change.

Hard on the heels of—and doubtless related to—the cold war's end came the disintegration of the Soviet Union. For, on December 7 and 8, 1991, during a meeting held at a country estate near the city of Brest and attended by the leaders of the Russian, Ukrainian, and Belorussian (now Belorus) republics, Boris Yeltsin, Leonid Kravachuk, and Stanilav Shushkevich declared that "the Union of Soviet Socialist Republics, as a subject of international law and a geopolitical reality, is ceasing its existence." Their decision came in the aftermath of the ill-fated August coup to overthrow Soviet leader Mikhail Gorbachev, and they invited the other republics in the former Soviet Union to join a Commonwealth of Independent States (CIS).

The unraveling process had gathered momentum when on August 29 the Soviet Congress of Peoples Deputies ratified Yeltsin's decrees denouncing the Communist party as "one of the principal villains" in the attempted coup, suspending its activities and seizing its property. The component republics rejected Gorbachev's plan to salvage the old Soviet Union by allowing self-government for them and demanded complete independence. After the dissolution, Gorbachev resigned to become a private citizen; other states joined the new commonwealth, and the USSR in fact disappeared from the map with Russia taking its permanent seat on the UN Security Council.

However, many great problems remain, ranging from the inflation, crime, and poverty that issued from the abrupt change from a command to a market economy to the disposition of the former Soviet nuclear arsenal and the continued demand for independence by states within the Russian federation. These, however, lie beyond our concern, the downfall of the Soviet empire, a major event in the history of twentieth-century Europe.

Why Did the Cold War End?

RAYMOND L. GARTHOFF

A retired diplomat, Raymond L. Garthoff is a senior fellow at the Brookings Institution and the author of numerous studies on American-Soviet relations. What role did the American containment policy play in bringing the cold war to an end? How does Garthoff view the orthodox-revisionist controversy with regard to its origins and development?

The fundamental underlying cause of the Cold War was the reinforcing belief in both the Soviet Union and the United States that confrontation was unavoidable, imposed by history. Soviet leaders believed that communism would ultimately triumph in the world and that the Soviet Union was the vanguard Socialist/Communist state. They also believed that the Western "imperialist" powers were historically bound to pursue a hostile course against them. For their part, American and other Western leaders assumed that the Soviet Union was determined to enhance its own power and to pursue expansionist policies by all expedient means in order to achieve a Soviet-led Communist world. Each side thought that it was compelled by the very existence of the other side to engage in a zero-sum competition, and each saw the unfolding history of the Cold War as confirming its views.

The prevailing Western view was wrong in attributing a master plan to the Kremlin, in believing that Communist ideology impelled Soviet leaders to advance, in exaggerating Communist abilities to subvert the Free World, and in thinking that Soviet officials viewed military power as an ultimate recourse. But the West was not wrong in believing that Soviet leaders were committed to a historically driven struggle between two worlds until, ultimately, theirs would

Raymond Garthoff, "Why Did the Cold War End?" *Diplomatic History*, Vol. 16, No. 2, pp. 287–293, 1992. Copyright The Society for Historians of American Foreign Relations.

triumph. To be sure, other motivations, interests, and objectives played a part, including national aims, institutional interests, and personal psychological considerations. But these influences tended to enhance the ideological framework rather than weaken it. Moreover, the actions of each side were sufficiently consistent with the ideological expectations of the other side to sustain their respective worldviews for many years.

Within the framework of ideological conflict, the Americans and the Soviets waged the Cold War as a geopolitical struggle, more in terms of traditional balance-of-power politics than in terms of class struggle or global containment/deterrence theory. If ideology was the only thing driving the superpowers in the Cold War, why do we see that conflict as arising from the ashes of World War II rather than as stemming from the October Revolution of 1917? The answer is clear. In 1917 and over the next twenty-five years the Soviet Union was relatively weak and only one of several Great Powers in a multi-polar world. By the end of World War II, on the other hand, Germany and Japan had been crushed, Britain, France, and China were weakened, and the enlarged Soviet Union, even though much weaker than the United States, seemed to pose an unprecedented threat by virtue of its massive armies and their presence deep in Central Europe. Under these circumstances, Joseph Stalin's reassertion in 1946 and 1947 of the division of the world into two contending camps seemed truer and more threatening than ever before.

So the Cold War had both an ideological and a geopolitical dimension. A Manichean Communist worldview spawned a Manichean anti-Communist worldview. Each side imputed unlimited objectives, ultimately world domination, to the other. In addition, each side's operational code looked to the realization of its ambitions (or its historical destiny) over the long term and thus posited an indefinite period of conflict. But even though both sides envisioned a conflict of indefinite duration, and even though policy decisions were pragmatic and based on calculation of risk, cost, and gain, there was always the hazard of a miscalculation that could be especially dangerous, given the historical coincidence of the Cold War and the first half-century of the nuclear age. Nuclear weapons, by threatening the existence of world civilization, added significantly to the tension of the epoch; the stakes were utterly without precedent and beyond full comprehension.

This is not to deny that nuclear weapons also helped to keep the Cold War cold, to prevent a third world war in the twentieth century. Indeed, in the final analysis and notwithstanding their awesome power, nuclear weapons did not cause, prevent, or end the Cold War, which would have been waged even had such weapons never existed. But it is to argue that the arms race and other aspects of the superpower rivalry were driven in part by ideological assumptions. As a result, while the Cold War and the nuclear arms race could be attenuated when opportunities or constraints led both sides to favor a relaxation of tensions, they could not be ended until the ideological underpinnings had also been released. This occurred under Mikhail Gorbachev's leadership, which saw a fundamental reevaluation in Moscow of the processes at work in the real world, a basic reassessment of threats, and finally a deep revision of aims and political objectives.

The West did not, as is widely believed, win the Cold War through geopolitical containment and military deterrence. Nor was the Cold War won by the Reagan military buildup and the Reagan Doctrine, as some have suggested. Instead, "victory" for the West came when a new generation of Soviet leaders realized how badly their system at home and their policies abroad had failed. What containment did was to successfully stalemate Moscow's attempts to advance Soviet hegemony. Over four decades it performed the historic function of holding Soviet power in check until the internal seeds of destruction within the Soviet Union and its empire could mature. At that point, however, it was Gorbachev who brought the Cold War to an end. Despite the important differences among them, all Soviet leaders from Lenin until Gorbachev had shared a belief in an ineluctable conflict between socialism and capitalism. Although Gorbachev remained a Socialist, and in his own terms perhaps even a Marxist-Leninist, he renounced the idea of inevitable world conflict. His avowed acceptance of the interdependence of the world, of the priority of all-human values over class values, and of the indivisibility of common security marked a revolutionary ideological change. That change, which Gorbachev publicly declared as early as 1986 (though insufficiently noted), manifested itself in many ways over the next five years, in deeds as well as in words, including policies reflecting a drastically reduced Soviet perception of the Western threat and actions to reduce the Western perception of the Soviet threat.

In 1986, for example, Gorbachev made clear his readiness to ban all nuclear weapons. In 1987 he signed the INF Treaty, eliminating not only the Soviet and American missiles deployed since the late 1970s but also the whole of the Soviet strategic theater missile forces that had faced Europe and Asia for three decades. What is more, the treaty instituted an intrusive and extensive system of verification. In 1988, Gorbachev proposed conventional arms reductions in Europe under a plan that would abandon the Soviet Union's numerical superiority, and also launched a substantial unilateral force reduction. In 1988 and 1989 he withdrew all Soviet forces from Afghanistan. At about the same time, he encouraged the ouster of the old Communist leadership in Eastern Europe and accepted the transition of the former Soviet-allied states into non-Communist neutral states. By 1990, Gorbachev had signed a CFE Treaty accepting Soviet conventional arms levels in Europe to the Urals that were considerably lower than the levels for NATO. By that time as well he had not only accepted Germany's reunification but also the membership of a unified Germany in NATO. A year later he had jettisoned the Warsaw Pact and the

CMEA economic union and had agreed to verified deep cuts in strategic nuclear forces.

Although Gorbachev may not have expected the complete collapse of communism (and Soviet influence) in Eastern Europe that occurred in 1989 and 1990, he had made clear to the 27th Congress of the Soviet Communist Party as early as February 1986 that a new conception of security had to replace the previous one and that the confrontation of the Cold War had to end. No longer speaking in Leninist terms of contending Socialist and capitalist worlds, Gorbachev spoke instead of one world, an "interdependent and in many ways integral world." He denied that any country could find security in military power, either for defense or deterrence. Security, he said, could only be found through political means, and only on a mutual basis. The goal, he asserted, should be the "creation of a comprehensive system of international security" that embraced economic, ecological, and humanitarian, as well as political and military, elements. Hence, the Soviet decision to give new support to the United Nations, including collective peacekeeping, and to join the world economic system. Hence, the cooperative Soviet efforts to resolve regional conflicts in Central America, southern Africa, the Horn of Africa, Cambodia, Afghanistan, and the Middle East, not to mention the Soviet Union's support for the UN's collective action against Iraq. And hence Moscow's willingness to countenance the dissolution of the Eastern European alliance and Socialist commonwealth, which had been fashioned to meet security requirements and ideological imperatives that had now been abandoned. These moves were all prefigured in the new approach that Gorbachev laid down in early 1986.

In the final analysis, only a Soviet leader could have ended the Cold War, and Gorbachev set out deliberately to do so. Although earlier Soviet leaders had understood the impermissibility of war in the nuclear age, Gorbachev was the first to recognize that reciprocal political accommodation, rather than military power for deterrence or "counterdeterrence," was the defining core of the Soviet Union's relationship with the rest of the world. The conclusions that Gorbachev drew from this recognition, and the subsequent Soviet actions, finally permitted the Iron Curtain to be dismantled and ended the global confrontation of the Cold War.

Gorbachev, to be sure, seriously underestimated the task of changing the Soviet Union, and this led to policy errors that contributed to the failure of his program for the transformation of Soviet society and polity. His vision of a resurrected socialism built on the foundation of successful *perestroika* and *demokratizatsiya* was never a realistic possibility. A revitalized Soviet political union was beyond realization as well. Whether Gorbachev would have modified his goals or changed his means had he foreseen this disjunction is not clear, probably even to him. In the external political arena, however, Gorbachev both understood and successfully charted the course that led to the end of the Cold War, even though in this area, too, he almost certainly exaggerated the capacity for reform on the part of the Communist governments in Eastern Europe.

As the preceding discussion suggests, the Western and above all the American role in ending the Cold War was necessary but not primary. There are a number of reasons for this conclusion, but the basic one is that the American worldview was derivative of the Communist worldview. Containment was hollow without an expansionist power to contain. In this sense, it was the Soviet threat, real or imagined, that generated the American dedication to waging the Cold War, regardless of what revisionist historians have to say. These historians point to Washington's atomic diplomacy and to its various overt and covert political, economic, paramilitary, and military campaigns. Supposedly designed to counter a Soviet threat, they argue, these initiatives actually entailed an expansion of American influence and dominion. The revisionist interpretation errs in attributing initiative and design to American diplomacy, but it is not entirely wrong. American policymakers were guilty of accepting far too much of the Communist worldview in constructing an anti-Communist antipode, and of being too ready to fight fire with fire. Indeed, once the Cold War became the dominant factor in global politics (and above all in American and Soviet perceptions), each side viewed every development around the world in terms of its relationship to that great struggle, and each was inclined to act according to a self-fulfilling prophecy. The Americans, for example, often viewed local and regional conflicts of indigenous origins as Cold War battles. Like the Soviets, they distrusted the neutral and nonaligned nations and were always more comfortable when countries around the world were either their allies or the satellites and surrogates of the other side. Thus, many traditional diplomatic relationships not essentially attendant on the superpower rivalry were swept into the vortex of the Cold War, at least in the eyes of the protagonists and partly by their actions.

It is true, of course, that the Cold War led in some instances to constructive American involvement. The Marshall Plan is a prime example, not to mention American support for some democratic movements, for the Congress for Cultural Freedom, and for the liberal journal *Encounter*. But other overt and covert involvements were more frequently less constructive, and often subversive, of real liberalism and democracy. Apart from the loss of American lives and treasure in such misplaced ventures as the Vietnam War and in the massive overinvestment in weaponry, one of the worst effects of forcing all world developments onto the procrustean bed of the Cold War was the distortion of our own understanding and values. By dividing the globe into a Communist Evil Empire controlled by Moscow and a Free World led by Washington, American policymakers promoted numerous antidemocratic regimes into rewarded members of the Free World so long as they were anti-Communist (or even rhetorically anti-Communist). Washington also used the exigencies of the Cold War to justify assassination plots, to negotiate deals with drug lords and terrorists, and to transform anti-Communist insurgents, however corrupt, into Freedom Fighters. Alliance ties, military basing rights, and support for insurgencies were routinely given priority over such other American objectives as the promotion of nuclear nonproliferation, economic development, human rights, and democracy.

Parallel Soviet sins were at least as great. While Soviet foreign assistance to Socialist and "progressive" countries was sometimes constructive (construction of the Aswan Dam, for example, or economic assistance to India), it was also skewed by both the ideological expectation of moving the world toward communism and by expectations of geopolitical advantage in the Cold War. Often dictatorial regimes, "Marxist" or "Socialist" only according to the cynical claims of their leaders, provided the basis for Soviet support, as with Siad Barre in Somalia, for example, or Mengistu in Ethiopia. In addition, the Soviet Union engaged in many covert political operations and lent support to national liberation movements (some authentic, others less so) that sometimes included elements engaged in terrorism. On both sides, then, ideological beliefs combined with geopolitical considerations to fuel a Cold War struggle that left many victims in its wake.

Although the decisive factor in the end of the Cold War was a change in these beliefs, it is worth repeating that the Soviets could discard a long-encrusted and familiar ideology only because of a powerful transformation in the way Gorbachev perceived reality and because he was ready to adapt domestic and foreign policies to the new perception. Over time the extent of these changes became evident and their validity compelling. I earlier noted some of the cumulative changes in Soviet foreign policy that brought the Cold War to an end. The critical culminating event was the Revolution of '89. The year between the destruction of the Berlin Wall in November 1989 and the European conference in Paris in November 1990 saw the removal of the most important concrete manifestation of the Cold War—the division of Germany and Europe. The division of Europe had symbolized the global battle between the two ideological and geopolitical camps in the years immediately after World War II. When that division came to a conclusion, the consequences for the international balance of power were so substantial that even the most hardened Cold Warriors in the West were forced to acknowledge that the Cold War had ended—even before the collapse of Communist rule in the Soviet Union or of the Soviet Union itself. Moreover, the Revolution of '89 in Eastern Europe was decisive not only in demonstrating that the ideological underpinnings of the Cold War had been removed but also in shifting the actual balance of power. The removal of Soviet military power from Eastern Europe dissolved the threat to Western Europe and also restored a reunified Europe to the center of the world political stage. Russia, and more gradually the United States, even though still closely linked to Europe, will now become less central.

History, including the history of international relations, inexorably moves forward. The Cold War was an important episode, but with roots in earlier history and with ramifications that continue to influence the post-Cold War world. Emerging features of the new world illuminate not only the new agenda of world politics but also the Cold War. We see a return to multi-polarity in a system of great and lesser powers. Related to this development is a shift to wider security concerns and therefore a shift in the elements of world power. Military power is by no means without continuing, and in the most ominous sense, ultimate influence. But military force as a means of registering and influencing power has declined while other factors—above all, economic ones—have become more important. One consequence is an increase in the relative weight of Japan and the European Community (especially with a unified Germany) and a decrease in the relative weight of the United States and the former Soviet Union. There will also be a new pattern of relationships between these countries and the rest of the globe (formerly termed the "Third World," but regarded mainly as an arena for competition between the two worlds led by the superpowers). There are those who see, clearly with some foundation but hopefully in exaggeration, economic and sociopolitical North-South tension replacing the ideological and politico-military East-West confrontation of the Cold War.

Military power will be less salient in world politics, but will remain a factor and on occasion will be used. The Gulf war waged against Iraq in 1991 by a U.S.-led coalition and supported by the Soviet Union was the first significant example. Although probably atypical, that experience did illustrate the enormous change in relations between the former Soviet Union and the West. The possible proliferation of nuclear and other weapons of mass destruction, and the efforts to deal with that danger, will be important elements of the new political agenda—again, in contrast to the nuclear confrontation between East and West during the Cold War.

Above all, there will be a return to the more traditional pattern of shifting blends of cooperation and competition among all nations, including former Cold War allies as well as former adversaries. Countries will pursue their own perceived interests in a more open international context. They will engage not only in new forms of cooperation but also in shifting rivalries and conflicts similar to those that preceded the Cold War. In short, the world will resume a pattern of political relationships free of bipolar superpower and coalition rivalry. We can hope for a new world order, and strive to fashion one. But numerous local and regional conflicts that were largely subsumed into the global confrontation of the Cold War will now assume their own places in the world order—or disorder—and new ones will arise. The most striking new source of potential conflict lies in the former, now-fractured Soviet empire.

U.S.-Russian relations in the new era will remain mixed, although probably with more cooperation and certainly with less competition than U.S.-Soviet relations during the Cold War. There is a distinct possibility that relations, already advancing beyond détente, will move toward an entente, though that outcome would depend on a number of things that cannot yet be confidently predicted. In all, diplomatic history promises to become richer and more varied, though let us hope not *too* exciting.

It is not, however, my present purpose to look into the future, except to sketch how the emerging future differs from the receding Cold War. While attention will naturally and properly be directed forward, it remains useful also to take the opportunity to look to the past. Much has been written about the Cold War and its near half-century of confrontations and crises, and some of it is very good. We know a great deal. But there remains much to learn, both about specific episodes and various dimensions of the epoch and about its underlying causes and effects. With the benefit of new sources, and from a new vantage point, it will now be possible to expand our knowledge of history and understanding of international politics.

How the Cold War Really Ended

JOSHUA MURAVCHIK

❖

Joshua Muravchik is a resident scholar at the American Enterprise Institute and is the author of *Exporting Democracy: Fulfilling America's Destiny*. Here he explicitly repudiates the views
presented by Garthoff in the previous essay.

Up until 1990, the great divide of American politics for at least 25 years, and
perhaps 45, was between hawks and doves. Whatever the relative weight of international or domestic issues in one electoral race or another, the transcendent
issue of the age was the cold war, with its immanent threat of nuclear conflagra-
tion. In the view of the hawks, the Soviet Union was an innately hostile power,
and the keys to peace were strength, toughness, and deterrence. In the view of
the doves, the Soviets were motivated as much by fear as we were, and the key
to peace was mutual reassurance.

The remarkable denouement of the cold war vindicated the hawks. First, the
cold war began to wind down during the administration of Ronald Reagan, the
most hawkish of all U.S. Presidents, and its last remnants were liquidated under
Reagan's heir, George Bush. Second, the hawks' interpretation of Soviet behavior
during the cold war was endorsed by the intellectual and political leaders who
emerged from "under the rubble" of the Soviet Union. Third, as the cold war
wound down, several local conflicts—in Nicaragua, El Salvador, Namibia, and
South Africa—were resolved, thus confounding the doves who had chastised the
hawks for overestimating the cold-war dimensions of these conflicts.

History—which does not consist of controlled experiments—rarely yields so
clear a resolution to an argument. In a better world, many doves would have come
forward, if not in self-criticism, then to acknowledge their error and explore its

Joshua Muravchik, "How the Cold War Really Ended," *Commentary*, November 1994. Reprinted
with permission.

sources. The economist Robert Heilbroner, a sympathizer with socialism, candidly assessed the implications of the Soviet collapse for his discipline, when he wrote in the *New Yorker.* "The contest between capitalism and socialism is over; capitalism has won." But in the field of foreign policy, precious few such voices have been heard.

❊ ❊ ❊

[Far from facing their error, some doves have attempted a] retrospective defense of their position. Now they may have found their champion in Raymond L. Garthoff, a senior fellow at the Brookings Institution and a former diplomat, State Department official, and SALT negotiator. Garthoff is, in other words, an epitome of the liberal foreign-policy establishment, and, accordingly, his newly published tome, The Great Transition: American-Soviet Relations and the End of the Cold War, comes embellished with gushing jacket blurbs from the likes of McGeorge Bundy, Marshall Shulman, and the Washington Post's Don Oberdorfer.

Although Garthoff's purpose is polemical, his method is historical. He depicts the cold-war protagonists as mirror-images of each other: "The fundamental underlying cause of the cold war was the belief in both the Soviet Union and the United States that confrontation was unavoidable, imposed by history." And again: "Each side tended to assume, and see, the worst motivation by the other, to justify its own actions and deny any justification to the other side, and to discount and disbelieve expressions of concern by the other."

In the 1980's, in Garthoff's account, the behavior of the two sides grew less symmetrical. The Soviets sought peace and comity, but the United States under Ronald Reagan sought only confrontation. As Garthoff puts it, while the "pursuit of arms limitations and reductions [was] given highest attention by the Soviet leaders . . . the active pursuit of regional geopolitical competition [was] given priority by the Reagan administration."

But it was not only Reagan's military programs that imperiled the peace, says Garthoff; it was his whole attitude. When Reagan met privately with the Soviet Foreign Minister in 1984, "Gromyko bridled at and rebutted Reagan's simplistic charge that the Soviet Union sought above all to destroy the capitalist system in the United States and the West." Reagan's public pronouncements were even worse, especially when he called the Soviet Union an "evil empire" and the "focus of evil in the modern world." Garthoff chastises the former President for his "unawareness of the diplomatic impact of openly voicing" such sentiments. He also chides Reagan's Vice President, George Bush, for launching in 1983 "a tirade against Soviet hegemony in Eastern Europe."

In general, this book seethes with an obsessive hatred of Ronald Reagan reminiscent of the animus toward Franklin Roosevelt once harbored by diehard Republicans. Garthoff's rage takes in Reagan's closest aides as well: "Some of his team, in particular Defense Secretary Caspar Weinberger, were unhappy even at a limited rapprochement and reduction of tensions" on the basis of "Soviet concessions." He even goes so far as to call Weinberger a liar for declaring that the invasion of Afghanistan demonstrated a "willingness to use military force to invade and coerce other countries." (In general, Garthoff believes, "The prevailing Western view was wrong . . . in believing that Communist ideology impelled Soviet leaders to expand their power.") Given these attitudes, it is no surprise that in every cold-war incident of the 1980's, Garthoff treats the Soviet side more sympathetically. Indeed, in recounting the Reagan administration's charges that the Soviet Union supported terrorism, violated arms-control agreements, or spread disinformation (such as the story that American security agencies had deliberately manufactured the AIDS virus), Garthoff waxes indignant not at the Soviet behavior in question but at the American government for making an issue of it and thereby roiling relations.

Similarly, when the Soviet downing of flight KAL 007 or the nuclear meltdown at Chernobyl resulted in a war of words, Soviet leaders, according to Garthoff, spoke falsely as a result of inadequate information, but American leaders lied maliciously in order to score propaganda points. ("The facts were not considered important; what was important was the opportunity to savage the Soviet leaders.") When the Soviets arrested and framed the American journalist Nicholas Daniloff, their action was an understandable response to the arrest of a Soviet UN employee in New York. (Never mind that the latter was engaged in espionage while Daniloff was not.) When the Soviets shot and killed Major Arthur Nicholson, the U.S. military liaison officer in East Germany, this was a "tragic incident" in which the two sides' claims were equally plausible. (Never mind that if Nicholson was in a restricted area, he could have been arrested rather than shot.) When the Soviets boycotted the 1984 Los Angeles Olympics, it was because they genuinely feared that America would not assure the safety of their athletes. And when the Soviets walked out of the strategic-arms talks, it was because Reagan had turned these into a "charade."

Garthoff's image of a Soviet Union haplessly seeking peace only to be rebuffed again and again by a confrontational American administration reaches back beyond Gorbachev to Brezhnev and the first days of Reagan's presidency. As early as January 1981, the Soviet ambassador to the United States, Anatoly Dobrynin, asked plaintively, "Can't we work out our differences?" When this and similar entreaties fell on deaf ears, Brezhnev was at a loss about how to proceed. Garthoff writes:

> The Soviet leaders had no alternative of "fallback" to their advocacy of détente. They kept hoping that American leaders would eventually recognize that there was no viable alternative to peaceful coexistence and no advantage from confrontation. Hence they continued to wait for signs of a belated recognition of this fact of life by the Reagan administration too.

Brezhnev was succeeded by Andropov, who also wanted peace, but he, too, hit a brick wall. Washington's propagandistic reaction to the tragic downing of KAL 007 proved to be the proverbial straw that impelled a "change from Andropov's own earlier position on giving a little more time for the American administration to come around to a recognition of realities." After Andropov came Chernenko, another seeker of peace. He even, Garthoff tells us, issued "guidance on drafting the [1984 party] program [that] made clear that the prediction of the impending collapse of capitalism and triumph of Communism . . . would be deleted." But again no response from Washington.

How, then, was the cold war brought to an end? Garthoff's answer, of course, is Gorbachev. But Garthoff sees Gorbachev's policy much as Strobe Talbott does—not as a reversal of traditional Soviet policy, but as a distillation of its longstanding essence. In Garthoff's formulation, Gorbachev "recognize[d] that reciprocal political accommodation, rather than military power for deterrence or 'counterdeterrence,' was the defining core of the Soviet Union's relationship with the rest of the world."

When Gorbachev began to act on this realization, however, Reagan presented an obstacle. His hard-line policies, Garthoff insists, "made Soviet movement toward accommodation more difficult rather than more likely. Reagan's line gave ammunition to Soviet hard-liners, not those seeking compromises." Undaunted, "Gorbachev pressed ahead with his unilateral actions and concessionary negotiations not owing to the Reagan hard line and military build-up, but despite it."

Even though Reagan had by now slightly softened his original position, he still gave Gorbachev a hard time:

> He criticized the Soviet Union and called for it to change many practices not only around the world . . . but at home as well. As Gorbachev began to make more and more changes in these practices, . . . Reagan did not reciprocate but asked for more.

As a result,

> Progress in relations came only in areas and to the extent that the Soviet side was prepared to accept U.S. positions. The rapprochement that developed from 1985 through 1988 stemmed from the fact that Gorbachev had been prepared to change Soviet positions and accept American ones.

Lest anyone conclude from this that Reagan policies worked, Garthoff again assures us that the Soviet leaders only made concessions they wanted to make and "did not simply cave in to meet tough American positions."

Now it is certainly true that the Kremlin made the lion's share of concessions. But it is also true that this was the only way the cold war could end—and for a simple reason that doves like Garthoff have spent their careers denying: the cold war was not a two-way street, but rather a function of Soviet policies. America had come out of World War II hoping to maintain its friendly relations with the USSR; but Moscow subjugated Eastern Europe and probed further provoking a defensive response from the United States. Therefore the cold war was always Moscow's to call off. The moment the Kremlin called it off, it was over, except for the technical details which took a couple of years to work out.

✖ ✖ ✖

[Peter] Schweizer complains that "current historiography has given Mikhail Gorbachev the lion's share of the credit for the dawning of the post-cold-war era, . . . giving the vanquished more credit than the victor."[1] But to counterpose Gorbachev to Reagan in this respect is to draw an unnecessary dichotomy. Both men deserve copious credit for the astonishing conclusion to the cold war. It was Gorbachev, and none other, who canceled the cold war. It was Reagan who generated the pressures that led Gorbachev to do it.

Gorbachev did not intend the ultimate effects he caused, especially not the dissolution of the USSR, but he embarked on a path of drastic reform, and like so many other revolutionaries before him, he became radicalized as he went along. Many post-mortems of the Soviet Union have attributed its death to the illness of its economy. Such an analysis is implicit in Schweizer's book, which places economic warfare at the center. But the truth is that even though the Soviet Union could not provide a good life for its subjects, it was far from collapsing economically.

By the time Gorbachev took power, economic growth had slowed to a near halt. But so what? The Soviet military still commanded more destructive power, both nuclear and conventional, than any other on earth. Perhaps the USSR would not have been able to keep up a high-tech arms race with America indefinitely (assuming, implausibly, that America itself would keep up such a race), but for the foreseeable future, its power was secure. Within the Soviet Union, consumers might be unhappy and a few brave dissidents might publish *samizdat*, but the rule of the Communist party faced no challenge whatsoever. Within the party, Gorbachev was firmly in control, even to the point where the party oligarchs, as Charles Fairbanks puts it, drank the Jonestown Kool-Aid he eventually proffered them.

---

[1]In *Victory: The Reagan Administration's Secret Strategy That Hastened the Collapse of the Soviet Union* (New York: Atlantic Monthly Press, 1994).

By all indications, Gorbachev could have ruled unchallenged for the rest of his natural life; he and his cohorts could have continued to enjoy all the luxuries to which the Soviet elite was accustomed, however empty the shops; and they would have presided over a state that, at worst, would have remained one of the world's two superpowers. None of this was in jeopardy when Gorbachev launched the fateful course that brought the whole edifice down.

It is revealing that Gorbachev's main antagonist, Boris Yeltsin himself, takes precisely this view of the matter. In a recent issue of the *New York Review*, David Remnick quotes the following remarkable passage from Yeltsin's first autobiography, *Against the Grain:*

> [Gorbachev] could have gone on just as Brezhnev and Chernenko did before him. I estimate that the country's natural resources and the people's patience would have outlasted his lifetime, long enough for him to have lived the well-fed and happy life of the leader of a totalitarian state. He could have draped himself with orders and medals; the people would have hymned him in verse and song, which is always enjoyable. Yet Gorbachev chose to go another way.

Economic determinism will not suffice to explain this choice. We must endeavor to reconstruct what Gorbachev and his colleagues were thinking.

In spite of the fact that the deteriorating state of the Soviet economy was not a threat to the standard of living or the power of the Soviet oligarchs, it obviously bothered them. Not because their subjects had to stand in interminable queues—these people were not famous for their compassion—but because as ambitious men they did not want to preside over a sinking ship, even one sinking slowly, or one ready for mothballs. They wanted to feel themselves to be captains of a successful venture. (Recall how boastful their public discourse always was.) Hence, by exacerbating their economic predicament—by restricting technology transfers, reducing their hard-currency earnings, and pressuring them in the arms race—Reagan contributed to their malaise.

But he did more than that. If it is true that the economic factor worked not by directly constraining Soviet power but by making the elite feel dissatisfied, these feelings required a context. If the United States had continued, as in the late 70's, to exude pessimism and weakness; if additional countries had continued to fall under Communist rule; if, as the Soviets used to say then, the "correlation of forces" had continued to tilt in their direction, then the slowing of economic growth in the USSR need not have been too discouraging to its rulers.

But Reagan led a revival of American spirit. He restored military strength and diplomatic assertiveness, he spoke eloquently about freedom and democracy, and he challenged Communism rhetorically as no recent President had done, dismissing it as "a sad, bizarre chapter in human history whose last pages are even now being written." This supplied the painful context in which Soviet leaders had to read the bad news about their economy.

This was also the context in which Gorbachev was chosen General Secretary in 1985. The Politburo members surely did not know what he was going to do (or they would not have chosen him), but Gorbachev was the candidate of change, or at least dynamism, while his rivals, Grishin and Romanov, were seen as more conservative.

In struggling, with growing desperation, to get his country moving again, Gorbachev opted for the path of reform, and until he grew too radical, most of his Politburo colleagues apparently concurred. But reform was not the only conceivable approach to surmounting their economic difficulties. An alternative would have been to exploit their military might. They could have sought to appropriate new resources by conquest, either direct or through proxies, in places like the Middle East and South Africa. Or they might have aimed to extort a new inflow of credits, technology, investment, and other benefits from the wealthy countries of Europe, Asia, and the Persian Gulf.

The Soviet economy had long battened on such benefits, won by playing on greed, fear, and illusions. Now that these supplier countries were richer than ever and the Soviet military mightier, perhaps a big increase could have been engineered. Soviet leaders might well have been tempted to try such an approach had the West continued to demonstrate weakness. But Reagan's vigorous defense and foreign policies made this option unattractive.

Reagan's challenge to Soviet political legitimacy may also have affected Gorbachev. It remains unclear why Gorbachev unleashed glasnost as well as perestroika—that is, political reform as well as economic. Several analysts have asserted that economic change required political change but why? After all, things did not work that way in Communist China.

A more compelling explanation is that Gorbachev believed, or came to believe, that the country's economic woes were only a symptom of a larger problem, that Soviet society was somehow off-track. In his 1987 book, *Perestroika*, Gorbachev said that even before coming to power he was convinced that "everything pertaining to the economy, culture, democracy, foreign policy—all spheres—had to be reappraised." And he added: "We know today that we would have been able to avoid many . . . difficulties if the democratic process had developed normally in our country." When he wrote those words Gorbachev still thought of himself as a convinced Leninist. But within a few years, he abolished the Communist party's monopoly of power, thus eradicating Lenin's main legacy.

As Gorbachev evolved, it is hard to imagine that he was not influenced by Reagan's panegyrics on freedom and democracy and attacks on tyranny and totalitarianism (much as Raymond Garthoff was offended by them). We know in fact that Soviet leaders much less supple than Gorbachev were extremely sensitive to ideology pronouncements of American leaders. For example, Brezhnev was so incensed at Jimmy Carter's early gestures regarding human rights in the USSR that Carter soon fell silent on the subject. Reagan was a far more persistent and persuasive advocate, and Gorbachev a far more receptive audience.

No One Won the Cold War

GEORGE F. KENNAN

George F. Kennan, professor emeritus at the Institute for Advanced Studies, was introduced in chapter 3 on the Bolshevik Revolution.

The claim heard in campaign rhetoric that the United States under Republican Party leadership "won the cold war" is intrinsically silly.

The suggestion that any Administration had the power to influence precisely the course of a tremendous domestic political upheaval in another great country on another side of the globe is simply childish. No great country has that sort of influence on the internal developments of any other one.

As early as the late 1940's, some of those living in Russia saw that the regime was becoming dangerously remote from the concerns and hopes of the Russian people. The original ideological and emotional motivation of Russian Communism had worn itself out and become lost in the exertions of the great war. And there was already apparent a growing generational gap in the regime.

These thoughts found a place in my so-called X article in Foreign Affairs in 1947, from which the policy of containment is widely seen to have originated. This perception was even more clearly expressed in a letter from Moscow written in 1952, when I was Ambassador there, to H. Freeman Matthews, a senior State Department official, excerpts from which also have been widely published. There were some of us to whom it was clear, even at that early date, that the regime as we had known it would not last for all time. We could not know when or how it would be changed; we knew only that change was inevitable and impending.

By the time Stalin died, in 1953, even many Communist Party members had come to see his dictatorship as grotesque, dangerous and unnecessary, and there was a general impression that far-reaching changes were in order. Nikita Khrushchev took the leadership in the resulting liberalizing tendencies. He was in his crude way a firm Communist, but he was not wholly unopen to reasonable argument. His personality offered the greatest hope for internal political liberalization and relaxation of international tensions.

The downing of the U-2 spy plane in 1960, more than anything else, put an end to this hope. The episode humiliated Khrushchev and discredited his relatively moderate policies. It forced him to fall back, for the defense of his own political position, on a more strongly belligerent anti-American tone of public utterance.

The U-2 episode was the clearest example of that primacy of military over political policy that soon was to become an outstanding feature of American cold war policy. The extreme militarization of American discussion and policy, as promoted by hard-line circles over the ensuing 25 years, consistently strengthened comparable hard-liners in the Soviet Union.

The more America's political leaders were seen in Moscow as committed to an ultimate military rather than political resolution of Soviet-American tensions, the greater was the tendency in Moscow to tighten the controls by both party and police, and the greater the braking effect on all liberalizing tendencies in the regime. Thus the general effect of cold war extremism was to delay rather than hasten the great change that overtook the Soviet Union at the end of the 1980's.

What did the greatest damage was not our military preparations themselves, some of which (not all) were prudent and justifiable. It was rather the unnecessarily belligerent and threatening tone in which many of them were publicly carried forward. For this, both Democrats and Republicans have a share of the blame.

Nobody—no country, no party, no person—"won" the cold war. It was a long and costly political rivalry, fueled on both sides by unreal and exaggerated estimates of the intentions and strength of the other party. It greatly overstrained the economic resources of both countries, leaving both, by the end of the 1980's, confronted with heavy financial, social and, in the case of the Russians, political problems that neither had anticipated and for which neither was fully prepared.

The fact that in Russia's case these changes were long desired on principle by most of us does not alter the fact that they came—far too precipitately—upon a population little prepared for them, thus creating new problems of the greatest seriousness for Russia, its neighbors and the rest of us, problems to which, as yet, none of us have found effective answers.

All these developments should be seen as part of the price we are paying for the cold war. As in most great international conflicts, it is a price to be paid by both sides. That the conflict should now be formally ended is a fit occasion for satisfaction but also for sober re-examination of the part we took in its origin and long continuation. It is not a fit occasion for pretending that the end of it was a great triumph for anyone, and particularly not one for which any American political party could properly claim principal credit.

Coup de Grace

The End of the Soviet Union

MICHAEL MANDELBAUM

Michael Mandelbaum is the Christian Herter Professor of American Foreign Policy at the Paul H. Nitze School of Advanced International Studies of The Johns Hopkins University and director of the project on East-West relations at the Council on Foreign Relations. Here he argues that political reforms brought about the downfall of the Soviet Union. How did greater democracy help destroy the regime Gorbachev was trying to preserve?

On August 24, 1991, three days after the collapse of an attempted coup by a group of high Soviet officials in Moscow, Marshal Sergei Akhromeyev killed himself in his Kremlin office. Mikhail Gorbachev's special adviser on military affairs left a suicide note: "Everything I have worked for is being destroyed."

Akhromeyev had devoted his life to three institutions: the Soviet army, in whose service he had been wounded at Leningrad in 1941 and through whose ranks he had risen to the position of chief of the General Staff (1984–88); the Communist Party, which he had joined at 20 and on whose Central Committee he had served since 1983; and the Union of Soviet Socialist Republics itself, officially founded a year before his birth in 1923. In the wake of the failed coup all three were disintegrating.

The armed forces were divided and disgraced. Entire units had refused to take part in the coup. A number of the troops sent to besiege the Russian parliament

Michael Mandelbaum, "Coup de Grace: The End of the Soviet Union," *Foreign Affairs,* Vol. 71, No. 1, 1992. Reprinted by permission of *Foreign Affairs,* Vol. 71, No. 1, 1992. Copyright ©1992 by the Council on Foreign Relations, Inc.

building—where a crowd that ultimately numbered 100,000 had gathered to defend the Russian president, Boris Yeltsin, and his government—defected to Yeltsin's side. After the coup had failed Defense Minister Dimitri Yazov and his deputy, Valentin Varennikov, were arrested. Yevgeny I. Shaposhnikov, the newly appointed minister, announced that 80 percent of the army's officers would be replaced because they were politically suspect.

The Communist Party was shattered. As jubilant crowds cheered, statues of communist heroes were pulled down all over Moscow. Gorbachev, shortly after his return from his ordeal in the Crimea, resigned as leader of the party, dissolved the Central Committee, ordered an end to party activity in the military, the security apparatus and the government, and told local party organizations that they would have to fend for themselves.

The union of 15 republics was itself dissolving. In Moscow people began to wave the blue, white and red flag of prerevolutionary Russia. The republics scrambled to declare their independence, the Ukrainian parliament voting for full independence by 321 to 1. For 75 years the vast stretch of Eurasia that was the Soviet Union had been tightly, often brutally controlled from Moscow, which had come to be known as "the center." The president of Armenia, Levon Ter-Petrossian, declared that "the center has committed suicide."

※ ※ ※

On the eve of the coup nine republics were preparing to sign a new union treaty, which would have deprived Moscow of virtually all economic power and left the republics with the right both to challenge any powers the center retained and to secede if they were dissatisfied with the new arrangements. The prospect of this new union treaty probably triggered the coup attempt, for it would have eliminated most of the functions of precisely those organizations that the plotters headed. The coup was a last-ditch attempt to preserve their own power. But that power had already been severely eroded. As the political scientist William Taubman put it at the time: "The coup occurred because of all the changes that have taken place, and it failed because of all the changes that have taken place." The coup-plotters struck to restore the old order; the result of their failure was to put it out of its misery. What began as a coup d'état to preserve it turned out to be the coup de grace for the Soviet Union.

How did all this come about? How did it happen that a mighty imperial state, troubled but stable only a few years before, had come to the brink of collapse in 1991? Who and what were responsible?

The chief architect of the Soviet collapse was Mikhail Gorbachev himself. During the coup, as a prisoner of the junta in his Crimean villa, he was the object of a struggle between the partisans of the old order and the champions of liberal values. But it was Gorbachev who had, in the period between his coming to power in 1985 and the fateful days of August 1991, created the conditions that had touched off this struggle.

The Soviet leader had created them unintentionally. His aim had been to strengthen the political and economic systems that he inherited, to strip away their Stalinist accretions and make the Soviet Union a modern dynamic state. Instead he had fatally weakened it. Intending to reform Soviet communism he had, rather, destroyed it. The three major policies that he had launched to fashion a more efficient and humane form of socialism—glasnost, democratization and perestroika—had in the end subverted, discredited and all but done away with the network of political and economic institutions that his Communist Party had constructed in Russia and surrounding countries since 1917.

The policy of glasnost relaxed bureaucratic controls on information, broadened the parameters of permitted discussion and thereby enabled the people of the Soviet Union to say more, hear more and learn more about their past and present. Gorbachev's purpose had been to enlist the intelligentsia in his campaign to revitalize the country and to generate popular pressure on the party apparatus, which had resisted the changes he was trying to make. He plainly wanted to encourage criticism of his predecessor, Leonid Brezhnev, and to resume the campaign against Stalin that Khrushchev had launched but that Brezhnev had ended.

Glasnost, however, did not stop there. The sainted Lenin, and even Gorbachev himself, came in for critical attention. Gorbachev wanted to foster a reassessment of some selected features of Soviet life. Instead glasnost called all of it into question, including, ultimately, the role of the general secretary of the Communist Party.

More broadly, the people of the Soviet Union were able for the first time to speak the truth about their history and their lives. That meant that they could learn the truth and could acknowledge it to one another. The effect was cathartic, and the catharsis had a profound, indeed a revolutionary, impact on Soviet politics. It began to undo the enduring effects of the terror that the Communist Party had routinely practiced during its first three decades in power. Of the first wave of that terror, imposed not by Stalin in the 1930s but by Lenin during the civil war, the historian Richard Pipes has written:

The Red Terror gave the population to understand that under a regime that felt no hesitation in executing innocents, innocence was no guarantee of survival. The best hope of surviving lay in making oneself as inconspicuous as possible, which meant abandoning any thought of independent public activity, indeed any concern with public affairs, and withdrawing into one's private world. Once society disintegrated into an agglomeration of human atoms, each fearful of being noticed and concerned exclusively with physical survival, then it ceased to matter what society thought, for the government had the entire sphere of public activity to itself.

Glasnost enabled the people of the Soviet Union to lay claim to the public sphere after seven decades of exile from it. Through democratization they had the opportunity, for the first time, to act collectively in that sphere. Gorbachev's purpose in permitting elections, again, was to generate popular support for his program. Democratization was to be a political weapon in his battle against the Communist Party apparatus. That apparatus was deeply entrenched, wholly mistrustful of what he was trying to do and generally adept at frustrating his plans. The experiment in democracy that he launched did not demonstrate, as Gorbachev had hoped, that he enjoyed popular support. Rather it showed that two widely held beliefs about the political inclinations of the people of the Soviet Union were wrong.

Elections discredited the official dictum that the Communist Party had earned public gratitude and support for the "noble, far-sighted" leadership it had provided since 1917. They discredited, as well, the view held by many Western students of the Soviet Union that the party did have a measure of legitimacy in the eyes of the population. Its achievements in defeating fascism between 1941 and 1945 and providing a modestly rising living standard thereafter were thought to have earned it a measure of respect, which was reinforced by the political passivity, the resignation to things as they are, that was presumed to be the dominant Russian approach to public life. The elections of 1989 and 1990 showed the people of the Soviet Union to be neither respectful of nor resigned to communist rule.

Democratization also created the opportunity for the beginnings of an alternative to the communist political elite to emerge. In Russia its main orientation was anticommunism, and Boris Yeltsin became its leading figure. Outside Russia the opportunity for political participation revealed that popular political allegiance was not to socialism, or the Soviet Union, or to Mikhail Gorbachev, but rather to nationalism, which was deeply anti-Soviet in character.

Glasnost and democratization were, for Gorbachev, means to an end. That end was the improvement of Soviet economic performance. Economic reform was the central feature of his program. When he came to power in 1985 the Soviet elite believed that the regime's principal task was to lift the country out of the economic stagnation into which it had lapsed at the end of the Brezhnev era. Without revived economic growth, they feared, the Soviet Union would fall ever further behind the West in economic and perhaps in military terms.

Ultimately it risked being overtaken by China, where Deng Xiaoping's market reforms were producing a surge of growth. Stagnation posed dangers at home as well. Without economic growth the regime would be unable to fulfill its part of the unofficial "social contract," under whose terms the public renounced any say over public affairs in return for a slowly rising standard of living. The revolt of the Polish workers in 1980–81 under the banner of Solidarity served as a cautionary example for the men in the Kremlin.

At first Gorbachev continued the approach that Yuri Andropov had begun in 1982: he tried to impose greater discipline on the work force. The centerpiece of his initial set of economic measures was a highly publicized and intrusive public campaign against the consumption of alcohol. It earned Gorbachev the title of "Mineral Water General Secretary," but did not noticeably reduce Russian drinking. Instead, by forcing people to make their own liquor rather than buying it from the state, the campaign caused shortages of sugar and deprived the government of a large chunk of its income.

This, in turn, contributed to Gorbachev's most enduring and destructive economic legacy: a severe fiscal imbalance. The center's obligations expanded as it poured more and more money into investment and tried to buy public support with generous wage increases. At the same time its income plummeted, as republican governments and enterprises, having gained more power, refused to send revenues to Moscow. In the months before the coup the republics were engaged in what was, in effect, one of the largest tax strikes in history. The fiscal policy of the Brezhnev regime had been relatively strict; Gorbachev's was extremely lax. To cover the widening gap between obligations and income the central government printed rubles at an accelerating pace. By August 1991 the economy was reeling.

In the great historical drama that is the collapse of the Soviet Union Mikhail Gorbachev was neither a villain nor a fool—although in retrospect some of the things he did came to seem foolish. He was not a Western-style democrat, but it is scarcely conceivable that someone committed to Western political principles could have risen to the top of the Communist Party of the Soviet Union. His view of socialism, however muddled and contradictory, was plainly more humane than the reality of the system for which he inherited responsibility. For most of his time in power, moreover, he had to fight against the conservatism of that system, which expressed itself mainly in inertia but occasionally in active opposition to his designs. If he came increasingly to seem a political maneuverer, it was because he had to maneuver—or believed that he had to maneuver—to survive in power and to protect the liberal measures already taken.

Finally, and most important, Mikhail Gorbachev's character, however flawed, was marked by a basic decency missing in every previous leader of the

Soviet Union and indeed in every ruler of imperial Russia before that. He abjured one of the principal methods by which his predecessors had governed. He refused to shoot. He refused—with the exception of several episodes in the Baltics and the Caucasus in which civilians were killed—to countenance the use of violence against the citizens of his country and of eastern Europe, even when what they did dismayed, angered or appalled him. For this alone he deserved the Nobel Peace Prize he received in the fall of 1990 and deserves as well the place of honor he will occupy in the history of the twentieth century.

But after August 21 Gorbachev belonged to history, not to the ongoing political life of what had been the Soviet Union. Although he was rescued from enemies who had only recently been colleagues, the act of rescue swept away the institutional platform on which he had stood. He had made his career as a reformer of communism. In the aftermath of the coup there was nothing left to reform.

Western Scholarship on the Fall of the Soviet Régime

The View from 1993

DOMINIC LIEVEN

Dominic Lieven is a professor of Russian government at the London School of Economics. He has published many books on Russian history and is currently working on a comparison of Russian solutions to the problem of empire in contrast to those adopted by other empires. What does Lieven blame for the failure to predict Soviet events? How useful are his analogies, specifically his comparisons between the Soviet and other empires?

It is the perception of the outside, non-academic, world that Sovietology emerged from the greatest political event of the post-war era, namely the sudden collapse of the USSR, without much credit. Commenting on the profession's failure, on the second anniversary of the August 1991 coup, *The Japan Times* remarked that 'outside a few dissident prophets, mainly in the Soviet Union itself, no expert appears to have grasped the true extent of the system's fragility'.

This is not the place to indulge in a general critique of 'modernization theory', which underlies (Francis) Fukuyama's whole thesis about the Soviet régime's collapse. He is obviously right to argue that the autarchic command economy doomed the USSR to relative economic backwardness and that introducing

Lieven, D. "Western Scholarship on the Fall of the Soviet Régime," *Journal of Contemporary History*, Vol. 29, No. 2. pp. 164–165, 168–173, April 1994. Reprinted by permission from Sage Publications Ltd.

economic freedoms had inevitable social and political consequences. It is also important that the Soviet peoples of the 1980s were better educated and more aware of the outside world than had been the case at Stalin's death. But one should not play down the role of the purely political in one's search for grand sociological explanations for the Soviet régime's collapse. The Soviet peoples were far less terrorized and atomized in Gorbachev's era than in Stalin's. The ruling élite in 1980 was much less ruthless and self-confident, and the régime far less legitimate than in the wake of its defeat of Germany. Nor should one forget the fact that Lenin insisted on authoritarianism both without and within the Party in the early 1920s, precisely because Bolshevik power was too unpopular to survive without it. In 1941 Hitler possessed, and dissipated, many opportunities to exploit widespread potential opposition to Stalin's régime.[1]

Martin Malia and Charles Fairbanks are alike in stressing the central role of ideology in the collapse of the USSR. Malia's thesis is striking in its simplicity. The Soviet Union was an 'ideology in power'. This ideology, promising the end of history, inequality and alienation through the suppression of capitalism, was unrealizable nonsense from the start. The Marxist-Leninist state was therefore bound to collapse in quick order, the only surprise being that it lasted so long. 'If Soviet communism collapsed like a house of cards, it was because it always had been a house of cards.'

Malia is right to stress the essentially ideological nature of the Soviet régime. The USSR shared the same geographical area and therefore some of the same geopolitical interests as the Russian Empire. Stalin deliberately incorporated aspects of 'purified' Russian tradition into his régime, creating something far closer to the Muscovite polity than to the Russia of the nineteenth century. But in its fundamentals the régime was always, and above all, Marxist-Leninist. The Soviet conception of international relations as a zero-sum-game between imperialism and socialism had nothing in common with the Euro-centric and balance-of-power thinking of the statesmen and diplomats of Imperial Russia. The Russian economy in 1900 was much closer to the twentieth-century Japanese economy than to anything that existed in the Soviet Union.

Above all, Marxism-Leninism was a potential world religion, dogmatic and in a sense monotheist like Christianity and Islam, with which it shared a common Judaic ancestry. Such world religions tend to breed splits over dogma, rival interpretations of which are taken up by conflicting political centres within the community of the faithful. The Ottoman Empire's seemingly unstoppable drive to dominate early modern Christian Europe was crucially weakened by the need

---

[1]Fukuyama's, Lieven's, and others' essays appear in the spring 1993 issue of *The National Interest* under the general title, "The Strange Death of Soviet Communism."

to open up a second front against the Shiite heretics in Persia. The Soviet diversion of effort into a second front against China in the 1960s should have come as no surprise.

Ultimately, the survival of the Soviet régime depended on the success of its ideology in weakening religion and combating nationalism as a focus for popular loyalties and a source of values. In this competition, Marxism-Leninism suffered from a number of inherent weaknesses. It lacked religion's transcendental quality or its answers to problems of individual death and morality. Its hold over the emotions proved less strong than that of nationalism, contemporary man's closest answer to the problems of individual isolation, 'transcending oblivion through posterity' and collective identity. Soviet ideology was too rational, down-to-earth and materialist for its own good. Even without Khrushchev's absurd effort to set a date for the arrival of communism, the ideology could be disproved all too easily not merely by scholarship but also by the evidence of the ordinary citizen's eyes. Since the socialist command economy was at the very core of Soviet ideology, the increasingly obvious inability of the USSR to compete with its capitalist rivals severely damaged the régime's legitimacy, not least in the eyes of its more intelligent leaders. This emphasizes the point that the failure of Soviet ideology has to be seen in relative more than in absolute terms. Faced with the onslaught of fascism, the Soviet state proved anything but Malia's 'house of cards'. A siege society and economy was presented with exactly the challenge it was best equipped to meet. In the post-war era, had the much-predicted crisis of capitalism and war between the imperialist states occurred, this would not have made Marxism-Leninism any less inherently ridiculous. But it would have prolonged the life of the Soviet régime.

Charles Fairbanks shares many of Martin Malia's perceptions. He stresses the continuing importance of 'the origins of the Soviet system in a Utopia', agreeing with Malia that the gap between this Utopia and sordid Soviet reality was the key factor in destroying the régime's legitimacy. The core of his essay is, however, the view that the Utopian and revolutionary impulse never died entirely within the Soviet élite and burned strongly within Gorbachev's entourage. To justify this argument he traces the careers of a number of key advisers to Gorbachev back through Andropov's circle to the Zhdanov and Kuusinen factions of the late 1940s and 1950s. He is quite right to stress that much of the political and intellectual leadership of *Perestroyka* had a background in the ideological and security apparatuses, supposedly hardline fastnesses. He traces the origins of these men's views and the way in which they evolved through, to take but one example, exposure to Czech reformist ideas of the later 1960s. The adoption by many of these advisers of essentially Western liberal and non-revolutionary socialist ideas was eased by the fact that 'the "high" tradition of their own régime . . . was highly theoretical and very Westernizing'. Fairbanks tries to illustrate how many of these advisers were linked by birth or marriage to

Old Bolshevik, often intellectual, families. By so doing he seeks to prove that the Bolshevik Utopian and socialist strain was not entirely killed by Stalin but, on the contrary, resurfaced among Khrushchev's 'bright young men' of the 1950s and took its final revenge on Stalinism under *Perestroyka*.

Many of Fairbanks's assertions will require much greater documentation before they are accepted as proven, but his essay is an exceptionally thought-provoking investigation of the most interesting of all the questions linked to *Perestroyka*, namely its intellectual and political origins within the ruling élite. Certainly, Fairbanks's view that Gorbachev and his advisers were hereditary Bolsheviks and, in a sense, true believers may help to explain their naivety in discounting the nationalist threat and imagining that political stability in the Soviet Union could be reconstructed on the basis of democratic socialist principles.

How much should Sovietology be faulted for having underestimated the fragility of the Soviet régime? A number of points should certainly be made in its defence. Though the speed of the collapse was unexpected, many of its ingredients were understood by a large number of scholars. The last major empirically-based study of the nationalities issue to be published in English before *Perestroyka* stressed the sharpening of ethnic conflict, the failure to create a 'Soviet people' and the growing danger of the whole question. Gerhard Simon's book, published in Germany in 1986, made the same points in starker terms. It is also not true either that most non-political scientists (historians for example) foresaw the Soviet collapse or that ideological blinkers were confined to people with left-wing sympathies.

As a historian whose views are not left-wing I am well-placed to make this point. No one had less excuse than myself to underestimate the fragility of the Soviet régime. But when Gorbachev came to power in 1985 I certainly did not expect the demise of Soviet communism within six years. The Soviet Union's international and economic difficulties did not yet seem to me to be sufficiently severe to force the leadership to adopt (and above all sustain) dangerously desta-bilizing reforms. And I had what turned out to be an exaggerated belief in communist leaderships' mastery of the techniques of power and the absolute priority they put on their own self-preservation. As a historian I used a partly historical and comparative approach to understanding Gorbachev-era politics. This approach, though very fruitful, was scarcely infallible. Most great empires, for instance, have been destroyed or fatally crippled by war. Not for nothing did Andrei Amalrik invoke the spectre of war with China in his famous work predicting the Soviet Union's collapse.

In some ways, failure to predict Soviet events was less the fault of Sovietologists than of social science methodology in general. Vladimir Kontorovich comments that 'social sciences are not equipped to deal with individual behavior', but it was precisely individual personality and behaviour, contingency and

accident which contributed hugely to the USSR's collapse. The course and outcome of revolutions is inherently difficult to predict even if one correctly un-
derstands all the ingredients. During an era of revolution, especially in a country
of the USSR's scale and complexity, many new forces erupt on to the political
scene and events move with unprecedented speed and according to erratic patterns. A great deal depends on the precise sequence and timing of these events.
This is the realm of chronology, chaos and contingency—better suited to a historian's retrospective study than to the structural analysis of the social scientist.
Moreover, where the origins of *Perestroyka* were concerned, the Sovietologist
was gravely hampered by the inaccessibility of the Soviet ruling élite and the secrecy with which it shrouded its actions. A country without realistic elections
or opinion polls, with a muzzled press and a government skilled in falsifying
statistics created many difficulties for Western political scientists.

Nevertheless, many problems were very much of the profession's own making. Surveying US doctoral theses written on Soviet domestic politics between
1976 and 1986, Peter Rutland reports that the great majority had entailed no
research in the Soviet Union and many candidates had very limited linguistic
skills. This reflects political science's unwillingness to accept the idea that political systems are rooted in a people's history and culture. Particularly where these
are very different to Anglo-American norms, it is essential to approach them
through a good grasp of language and on-the-spot experience of the society in
question. It is very difficult indeed to understand Russian politics without the
experience of six months of snow on one's boots and of life viewed through a
vodka- and bureaucracy-infected haze. But this, together with listening too
carefully to émigrés' tales, is an anecdotal approach. To maintain his professional status in the eyes of other political scientists, the Sovietologist felt pres-
sured to subscribe to the more 'rigorous' and quantitative methodologies which
alone would enable the discipline to claim academic equality with 'harder' social sciences such as economics. It is impossible to understand any political system through the use of these methodologies alone but in the Soviet context
they were particularly dangerous and difficult to apply. Moreover, even the most
accurate and painstaking analysis of the mechanics of specific areas of Soviet
government did not necessarily lead one to understand the essence of the Soviet
polity. In this sense not only quantification but also social science positivism itself has inherent weaknesses.

Robert Conquest complains that 'the academic mind prefers the comforts
of unifying formulae to the discomforts of reality and of serious thought. The
parochialism of believing that the USSR was not unlike Western politics was sys-
tematized in political science and social science formulae.' On another occasion
he comments that 'the supposed neutrality of an academic is very often, in fact,
no more than the acceptance of the unadmitted prejudice of his time or his
circle'. Conquest's criticisms are harsh but, as applied to Sovietology, not entirely

unfair. The formulae and assumptions brought by Western political scientists to Soviet studies were often parochial. They were rooted not only in Anglo-American history and culture but also in the politics of the very short and perhaps fleeting decades since 1945. Political science can be aggressively contemporary. Most Sovietologists knew very little about pre-revolutionary Russia. For very many, the basic time-frame for understanding contemporary Soviet politics began in 1953. With perspectives as narrow as these, it was inevitable that the existence of a mighty Soviet empire or of bipolarity in world politics should seem as immutable a principle to the Sovietologist as the movement of the earth around the sun is to the astronomer. Soviet politics between 1953 and 1982 was a precariously narrow base on which to perch confident generalizations, let alone predictions. The use of Western political terminology in the Soviet context obscured this. A 'convention' in British politics, for instance, means that no monarch has vetoed an act of parliament since the days of Queen Anne and none is likely to do so in the 1990s. A convention derived from the Soviet politics of 1953–82 is a rather less sure bet. As regards high politics, this period was heavily influenced by the specific circumstances of the Khrushchev and Brezhnev régimes, and indeed by the personalities of the top leaders and their cronies. It is not at all surprising that predictions about the power of the General Secretary derived from these decades should have proved a very inaccurate guide to the possibilities open to Gorbachev when he occupied this position.

In many respects, my own generation, though perhaps more narrowly 'professional' than Leonard Schapiro and Hugh Seton-Watson, were nevertheless inferior to them in wisdom and insight. In part this was simply a matter of experience. Government work during the second world war had taught them down-to-earth lessons about how power is acquired and consolidated, which one does not always absorb from theoretical studies. Having witnessed the dramatic events of the 1930s and 1940s, together with the establishment of the post-war order, they were not inclined to regard the latter as an immutable fact of nature. Hugh Seton-Watson had an immense knowledge, partly hereditary and partly first-hand, of the cultures, histories and life of central and eastern Europe. In addition, neither he nor Schapiro allowed their perspectives to be artificially narrowed by contemporary academic Chinese walls dividing history, politics and international relations, and by false definitions of what are the 'proper' approaches for each discipline. Schapiro and Seton-Watson moved freely across these divisions. They also produced not only detailed work in their own area of speciality but also far more general, indeed in Seton-Watson's case near universal, history.

Sovietology suffered from its lack of knowledge of Russian history. Modern Russian history can to some extent be seen in terms of three great cycles of modernization, each of them initiated from above by the state, and each designed to allow Russia to catch up with its international rivals. The first cycle, lasting from the mid-seventeenth century to 1856, was Russia's attempt to catch up with the great military absolutist monarchies of Europe. Alexander I's defeat of Napoleon reflected Russia's success in this respect, which was then undermined by the impact of the industrial revolution in first western and then central Europe, which changed the balance of power radically to Russia's detriment. Defeat in the Crimean War brought this fact home to Russia's rulers and resulted in their initiation under Alexander II (1855–81) of the second great cycle of modernization. Russia's striving to remain a major power in the industrial era lasted from the 1850s to the 1970s, Stalin's victory over Germany symbolizing success as surely as had Alexander's defeat of France. The conservative and ultimately gerontocratic post-war régimes of Nicholas I and Brezhnev were both rooted in the conviction, bred of victory, that Russia's external prestige and security was safe, and potentially destabilizing radical domestic reform therefore unnecessary. But just as the industrial revolution undermined Russia's international position in the nineteenth century, so the revolution of the microchip and the computer was doing so by the 1970s and 1980s. One layer beneath the gerontocratic top leadership of the late Nicholas and Brezhnev eras, better educated younger officials were more aware of the changing factors of power in the world and chafed at the régime's immobility. Their chance came under Alexander II and Gorbachev, who launched the second and third great 'cycles of modernization' respectively.

The new leaders' reformist régimes aimed to mobilize their country's economic potential. They aimed to liberate economic initiative and energy by dismantling much of serfdom and, in Gorbachev's case, of the command economy. If society was to show initiative and generate wealth, it needed a degree of secure autonomy beyond the reach of arbitrary bureaucratic action. Legality (*zakonnost*) was a watchword of both eras. So too was publicity (*glasnost*). New ideas had to be allowed to circulate. A reformist leader locked in battle with powerful vested interests needed allies who would undermine the intellectual case for conservatism.

Great similarities existed both in the limitations the two leaders tried to put on reform and on the problems it caused them. Neither Alexander nor Gorbachev were democrats: both intended to use public opinion rather than obey it. Basic power was to remain with an authoritarian centralized bureaucracy, without which their own positions, the empire's unity and ordered modernization from above would be undermined. Both régimes were terrified at the prospect of exposing the population to the full force of capitalism. Tsarist legislation, and particularly the commune, drastically constrained its application to the countryside, where the overwhelming majority of the population lived. Gorbachev steered well clear of freeing prices and put high barriers around private property and private enterprise's development. Very soon both leaderships found it much easier to release dissident voices than to silence or satisfy them when they 'went too far'. Given the extent to which some sections of opinion had been radicalized under Nicholas and Brezhnev, it was inevitable that such 'extremists' would emerge and certain that no concession that the régimes could ever realistically be expected to make would satisfy them. Finally, both the Imperial and the Soviet régimes were less legitimate in the empire's non-Russian periphery than in its Russian heartland. Alexander II's policy of liberalization resulted in full-scale revolution in Poland. It was absolutely predictable that Gorbachev's policies would destabilize Eastern Europe and some at least of the non-Russian borderlands. Indeed, knowledge of Alexander II's goals, strategy and dilemmas allowed one to predict very accurately many of the problems Gorbachev was bound to face.

Comparisons between the Russo-Soviet and other empires are also useful. It is true that an empire based on Marxist-Leninist ideology and a centralized command economy is bound to be in some senses *sui generis*. Even without this, a consolidated Eurasian landmass will always differ in key respects from the great European maritime empires that existed between the sixteenth and twentieth centuries. Moreover, there were key differences between the Russian imperial tradition and those even of the continental European empires whose origins, like those of Russia, lay in the late medieval and early modern eras. Unlike the Habsburg empires of Central Europe and mainland Spain, the Muscovite dynasty succeeded in uprooting the institutions and élites of newly absorbed regions, imposing a rigid and arbitrary centralization, unimpeded by any recognition of legality or constitutional restraints, but one which did allow these élites great opportunities in the royal service. The contrast between Novgorod's fate under Muscovy and that of the crowns of Aragon and Hungary is instructive and important. In the eighteenth and nineteenth centuries, it is true, Russia did allow a degree of local autonomy exercised through provincial elected institutions in some of its western borderlands. But these institutions existed at the tsar's pleasure and in time were either greatly weakened (Baltic provinces) or destroyed (Poland).

In forming the Soviet Union, the communists deliberately linked ethnicity and territoriality, giving ethnic minorities states in embryo of their own. The Austrian Social Democrats had bitter experience of the link between ethnicity and territoriality in the crownlands of the Habsburg Empire. For this reason, their Brunn programme of 1899 had advocated the control of all cultural and educational matters by so-called 'National Universities', citizens having the right to register in such 'universities' almost regardless of their place of residence. In many ways this was a modernized version of the so-called millet system, whereby the Ottomans had regulated the affairs of cultural and religious minorities in their empire. The Soviet régime rejected tsarist and Ottoman traditions, as well as Austro-Marxist principles, and instead adopted a seemingly more modern, European and federal approach linked to territoriality. From the perspective of 1992, this looks to have been a serious mistake.

In other respects, too, comparisons with rival empires are of great interest. From the seventeenth century onwards, Russian expansion owed much to the incorporation of Western techniques and technology. As with the maritime empires, in the Russian case too a Christian, European and sedentary society expanded at the expense, very often, of Moslem or animist nomadic ones. The last great example of European expansion in Asia was Khrushchev's Virgin Lands policy of the 1950s, during which the Kazakhs were driven from their ancestral lands and turned into a minority in their own republic.

By encouraging the growth of native intelligentsias the Soviet régime contributed ultimately to its own downfall. In the 1980s, the Russian people, the core of the Union, themselves revolted in part against paying the price of empire. Both phenomena existed to varying degrees in many other great imperial systems too. In addition, the Sovietologist anxious to understand the way in which corruption can rot the moral and administrative fabric of empire, depriving the central authorities of effective control over their regional administrative apparatus, would do well to read Ramsay Macmullen's study of this phenomenon in the Roman Empire. The manner in which the Soviet central élite lost much of its control over local élites and revenues in wide regions of Brezhnevera Central Asia, and then wrecked its legitimacy by attempts to regain control under Gorbachev, also has instructive parallels in the history of the decline and fall of other empires. Soviet demographic patterns, whereby the Russian population grew relative to Asian ones until 1959 and subsequently sharply declined, fit into the broader history of the expansion and contraction of Europe. The rulers of empires, locked in competition with foreign rivals and governing a range of peoples mostly brought under their sceptre by force, must always fear the domino effect of showing weakness, let alone allowing independence to any of their subject populations. In 1849 Lord John Russell commented that:

> the loss of any great portion of our colonies would diminish our importance in the world, and the vultures would soon gather to despoil us of other parts of our Empire, or to offer insults to us which we could not bear.

Still more explicit was the fear expressed by an Austrian foreign minister of Russell's time, that a domino process of dissolution would wreck his 'Empire of nationalities' should independence be granted to any of its peoples. A very similar logic operated in the USSR, as regards both the 'outer' (that is East European) and inner empires. Still more fundamentally, thinking of the Soviet Union as an empire was a useful reminder that huge multi-ethnic states created and sustained by conquest find it exceptionally difficult to hold together as liberalization and democratization gather pace.

Comparative approaches never themselves yield definite answers: their task is to ask questions and open new perspectives. The answers can only come from painstakingly acquired and detailed knowledge of a specific field. In Sovietology's case, however, this detailed knowledge of the inner workings of Soviet high politics was often beyond the reach of Western scholars. Meanwhile, the comparative approaches attempted, mostly linked to concepts derived from contemporary Western politics, often actually reinforced illusions about the stable, modern and basically 'normal' (that is Western) nature of the Soviet polity. Far from encouraging different or thought-provoking new perspectives, they often merely confirmed existing rather conventional, narrow and parochial assumptions.

None of this means that the bulk of pre-1985 Sovietology was without value. On the contrary, it taught us a huge amount about Soviet politics and society. Nevertheless, in the light of post-1985 developments it seems clear that some of the assumptions and judgements of mainstream Sovietology were seriously flawed. In important respects it appears to be 'oddballs' and dissidents from the collective wisdom who had the most valuable insights. In the context of developments within the British social sciences this is an extremely depressing conclusion. Increasingly, what scholarship is considered useful, and which individuals and institutions will conduct it, is going to be determined by quasi-governmental research councils. Those scholars denied their favour will, it seems, be deprived of the time or funds for research. Bureaucracy by definition does not favour 'oddballs'. It is also likely to take a conventional and formal view of what constitute the correct approaches and methodologies for the various branches of social science. Among the scholars whose essays appear in 'The Strange Death of Soviet Communism' are Robert Conquest and Peter Reddaway, distinguished representatives of the older and middle generation of British experts on the USSR. Had Britain's prospective system of research funding already existed in the 1970s and 1980s, it is very hard to imagine either of these scholars enjoying much sympathy from research councils reflecting mainstream opinions in the Sovietological profession.

13

NATIONALISM RESURGENT

The Breakup of Yugoslavia

The end of the cold war and the collapse of communism in the Soviet Union and Eastern Europe brought forth the hope of a new era of peace and prosperity. Yet the end of communism in Yugoslavia unleashed a bitter civil war that threw international leaders into a state of confusion.

The origins of the civil war in former Yugoslavia are complex. They can be traced to creation of the Yugoslav kingdom in 1918, which brought together the regions of Serbia (including the provinces of Kosovo and Vojvodina), Slovenia, Croatia, Bosnia-Herzegovina, Montenegro, and Macedonia under the leadership of a Serbian monarch. Though the peoples of the new Yugoslav kingdom spoke similar languages, they had never enjoyed a common existence and had different cultural traditions. Prior to 1918, only Serbia was an independent kingdom; the others were under the suzerainty of the Ottoman or Austro-Hungarian Empires. The people of Croatia and Slovenia were mostly Roman Catholics. Serbs were Orthodox Christians. Bosnia was almost evenly divided between Muslims, Orthodox Serbs, and Croatian Catholics.

Problems associated with these differences arose in the new Yugoslav state from the very beginning. As early as the 1920s, Croatian leaders complained that the extension of the Serbian constitution to the rest of the country failed to respect the rights of non-Serbs. National unrest forced the king of Serbia to suspend the constitution and convene a dictatorship in 1929.

In 1939, an important compromise between Croats and Serbs was reached. But only two years later, the country was rent asunder by the German invasion of Yugoslavia. Hitler's allies carved out portions of the country for themselves, and a pro-Nazi regime was installed in Serbia. Croat fascists (known as the Ustaše), in cooperation with the Nazi government, founded the Independent State of Croatia (NDH). Civil war erupted when Croat fascists fought Serb royalists. Meanwhile, the communists under Josip Broz Tito fought them both. Tito triumphed over the non-communist forces in 1945 and created a country that emphasized communism over nationalism. During his presidency, nationalist agitators were arrested, regardless of ethnic origin. He endeared himself to his people by casting aside his allegiance to the Soviet Union and fostering trade with the west. Tito's policies bore fruit: Yugoslavia achieved a level of prosperity unknown behind the Iron Curtain. His policy of emphasizing communism over nationalism also appeared to work; in several regions of the country, Serbs, Croats, and Muslims lived side by side in harmony.

But the harmony between the national groups quickly began to unravel after Tito's death in 1980. The post-Tito government was incapable of quelling nationalist agitation, which only gained steam after the collapse of communism in the Soviet Union and Eastern Europe at the end of the decade. Soon communist leaders in the six constituent Yugoslav republics embraced nationalism and began to make a case for nationalist expansion at the expense of the other republics. In 1989 Serb nationalist leaders ended the autonomy of its province of Kosovo, whose population is over ninety percent Albanian Muslim. Fearing that the Serbs, who dominated the Yugoslav national army (JNA), would extend their repression to the other parts of the country, the leaders of the other Yugoslav republics demanded independence. The disintegration of Yugoslavia and the subsequent civil war were the inevitable results.

By 1992, Slovenia, Croatia, and Bosnia had declared independence. The Yugoslav national army fought against all defections. The fighting was the most fierce in Bosnia, where Serbs constituted 40 percent of the population. The Bosnian Serbs favored union with Serbia. Bosnian Muslims favored all-out independence, whereas some Bosnian Croats favored union with newly independent Croatia. The civil war that ensued was horrifically brutal, as radical factions of the Bosnian Serbs, assisted by the Yugoslav national army, used terror to ethnically "cleanse" Bosnia of rival national groups. Bosnian Croats followed similar logic, albeit on a smaller scale. Between 150 and 200 thousand people died in the war. Bosnian Muslims constituted the vast majority of the victims. More than one million people were displaced.

At first, the international community regarded the civil war in former Yugoslavia as an internal matter. But as the scope of the atrocities in Bosnia became known, pressure for intervention increased. The response of the European Union and the United Nations (UN) was muted and weak. Cease-fires in Bosnia were brokered and rapidly broken by the Bosnian Serbs. Areas designated as "safe havens" by the UN were repeatedly attacked, while UN observers watched helplessly. Finally, pressure from the United States and economic sanctions against Serbia bore fruit. Yugoslavia's president, Serbian leader Slobodan

Milošević, withdrew support for the Bosnian Serbs and negotiated a peace agreement with his Croat and Bosnian counterparts. The ensuing Dayton accords of 1995 divided Bosnia into a Serbian republic and a Croat-Muslim federation. The provisions of the agreement were to be enforced by sixty thousand peacekeeping troops, who were to withdraw after one year. Five years after the Dayton accords were concluded, the peacekeeping troops remain. Serb nationalist aspirations were not quelled by the end of the war in Bosnia. In 1999, it became clear that the Serbs were launching another campaign of ethnic cleansing, this time against Albanians of Kosovo. When international pressure to deter the Serbs failed, the North Atlantic Treaty Organization(NATO), with strong backing from the United States, began an extensive bombing campaign against strategic targets in Serbia. In the meantime, about a million Kosovar Albanians fled their homes. After one hundred days of air strikes, the Serbs submitted to peace terms, including the presence of international peacekeepers in Kosovo.

In the final analysis, the combination of force, international pressure, and the presence of peacekeepers have neutralized civil war in former Yugoslavia. However, even despite the presence of peacekeepers, recent years have nonetheless witnessed the outbreak of ethnic violence in Bosnia and Kosovo. And although Servian president Slobodan Milošević was voted out of power in 2000, his successor, Vojislav Kostunica, is regarded as a staunch nationalist who has been very critical of NATO's actions in Yugoslavia.

In the following selections Laura Silber, Allan Little, and Sabrina Petra Ramet discuss the causes for the conflict in greater depth. James J. Sadkovich amplifies the role of the media in making the disintegration of Yugoslavia a subject of international concern.

Yugoslavia

Death of a Nation

LAURA SILBER AND ALLAN LITTLE

Laura Silber and Allan Little, authors of *Yugoslavia: Death of a Nation,* from which this selection is taken, are journalists: the former is the Balkans correspondent for the *Financial Times,* and the latter works for the British Broadcasting Corporation (BBC). Both have been lavished with praise by journalists and historians alike for their coverage of the civil war in the former Yugoslavia. What, in the minds of the authors, are the major causes of the war? How can the ongoing conflict possibly be resolved?

> On that day we'll say to Hell: "Have you had enough?"
> And Hell will answer: "Is there more?"
> *Toga dana mi ćemo reći paklu: "Jesi li se napunio?"*
> *A pakao će odgovoriti: "Ima li još?"*
> Meša Selimović, Derviš i Smrt

Muslim refugees run into the woods, crowd into trucks, some are shot dead while trying to escape a Serb onslaught. Serb refugees form endless convoys of tractors, fleeing a Croatian advance. Blackened skeletons of buildings shape Sarajevo's skyline. Mediators and politicians wring their hands, wondering how to stop the wars in former Yugoslavia, whose waves of wrenching violence have provoked such public outrage.

Excerpts from Laura Silber and Allan Little, *Yugoslavia: Death of a Nation,* pp. 25–26, 30, 388–390. Copyright © 1996 TV Books. Reprinted by permission.

Over the past five years, the images have become familiar. They have faithfully conveyed the anguish of the time.

We wrote this book to shed light on the decisions which led to the horror and destruction. It is an attempt to identify, clinically and dispassionately, the crucial events, the secret meetings, in both the lead-up to war and in its progress once the fighting had started, and to reconstruct those events through the accounts of those people who took part in them—the milestones, if you like, on the road to catastrophe. It does not condemn, or condone, or justify any of the players in the unfolding tragedy. It tries simply to relate what happened, and why, and at whose behest.

The war in Yugoslavia was not the international community's fault. The war was planned and waged by Yugoslavs. It was not historically inevitable. To attribute the calamity that engulfed the peoples of Yugoslavia to unstoppable forces is to avoid addressing oneself to the central dynamic of the war. It is also to let the guilty off the hook. And, it also provides a justification for the failure of the West, for so long, to intervene with sufficient will and vigor to end the war. This book examines why Western governments failed to intervene decisively, and analyzes the means by which they intervened in the end.

. . . Yugoslavia did not die a natural death. Rather, it was deliberately and systematically killed off by men who had nothing to gain and everything to lose from a peaceful transition from state socialism and one-party rule to free-market democracy. We trace the origins of the war to the rise of Serb nationalism among Belgrade intellectuals in the mid-1980s, and the subsequent harnessing of nationalist rhetoric by Slobodan Milošević. [We trace] Milošević's conscious use of nationalism as a vehicle to achieve power and then to strengthen his control first over Serbia and then over Yugoslavia. His original dream was to step into the shoes of Josip Broz Tito as leader of the whole of Yugoslavia. But by 1991, when he found this unattainable, he chose an alternative project, the creation of a new enlarged Serbian state, encompassing as much territory of Yugoslavia as possible. His centralizing, authoritarian leadership and calculated, clever manipulation of the politics of ethnic intolerance provoked the other nations of Yugoslavia, convincing them that it was impossible to stay in the Yugoslav federation and propelling them down the road to independence.

One of [our] central themes . . . is that under Milošević's stewardship, the Serbs were, from the beginning of Yugoslavia's disintegration, the key secessionists. This is not to say that Milošević was uniquely malign or solely guilty. The foot soldiers of Yugoslavia's march to war . . . were drawn from all the nationalities in the country.

This . . . is also a lament for the failed promise of Yugoslavia. As Communism declined in the late 1980s, Yugoslavia was, in many ways, better placed than any other Communist state to make the transition to multi-party democracy, either as a single state, or as a group of successor states. There was a real chance for Yugoslavia to take its place in a new and, at that time, hopeful community of European nations. That this chance was deliberately snuffed out . . . turned out to be Europe's loss and that of all democracies, as well as Yugoslavia's, and a mortal blow to many of the key moral certainties of our age.

Yet in retrospect the appearance of a stable and prosperous Yugoslavia may have been deceptive. Ethnic grievances had been suppressed, not dispelled, by the centralized Communist system. Peaceful change to a liberal political system would have required very careful management, from inside and outside.

It is now clearer than ever that exactly the opposite happened. As the presidents of Yugoslavia's six republics—Bosnia-Herzegovina, Croatia, Macedonia, Montenegro, Serbia, and Slovenia—quarreled in public about the country's future structure in the run-up to war, some of them were cynically plotting the path of disintegration.

※ ※ ※

The fall of Srebrenica and the self-styled Serb state of Krajina in Croatia in the summer of 1995, and the subsequent Serb losses in Bosnia, combined with a massive NATO bombing campaign, heralded a new age in Western engagement. Shuttling among the Balkan capitals, and backward and forward from Washington, Richard Holbrooke, the U.S. envoy, gave the impression that the region was too important, too sensitive to be allowed to fester. In November 1995, the U.S., leading its European allies, compelled the Serbs, Croats and Muslims to sign a treaty to halt Europe's worst conflict since the Second World War. Bill Clinton wanted a foreign policy triumph in the last year of his first term as president; better still a triumph in the very region that repeatedly had confounded all previous attempts at peace-making. But peace became possible only as the result of decisive military victories and the forced exodus of millions of people to areas where their ethnic group predominated.

At the time of writing, the euphoria of the Dayton Agreement had faded. The despatch of 60,000 heavily armed troops met no resistance from any of the three sides. The separation of the warring parties went even more smoothly than envisioned. There remained little sign that the former warring sides were ready to work together. The first test for Bosnia's prospects as a multiethnic state failed when tens of thousands of Serbs abandoned the Sarajevo suburbs before they were handed over to Bosnian government control. The civilian side of the Dayton agreement—the planning of elections and the building of common industries—was the most crucial and yet had the poorest resources. Without full Western backing there was remote hope for rebuilding a climate of trust that would make possible the implementation of Dayton—the right of people to return to their homes.

It remained uncertain whether the parties had truly agreed to a lasting peace or were planning to use the agreement to re-group and re-arm for the next battle.

Washington aimed to cut the Balkan warlords down to size, [but] history suggests that may prove impossible. In the past the region's leaders have proven themselves able to drag more powerful states deeper into conflict than they planned. Yet former Yugoslavia is the clearest illustration to date of a central strategic reality of the post–Cold War world: if the U.S. does not take the lead, then no one does. It was apparent that the only chance for peace is if Washington, with its military and political authority, is prepared to see it through. By spring 1996, Clinton, and his European allies, were still insisting that they would leave within a year, even if that meant leaving behind chaos and carnage. But that would mean the defeat of Western engagement, a price too costly to bear.

※ ※ ※

[By 1995, a] two-week campaign of strategic bombing, together with a joint Bosnian-Croatian offensive, pushed the Serbs back from a third of the territory they had occupied for more than three years.

The war had come full circle. The Serbs, who had launched it with a singleness of purpose that had allowed them to slice through their enemies like a knife through butter, were now divided. They had broken their own pledge that "Only Unity Saves the Serbs." Milošević, who had led them into battle with an apparent clarity of vision that had brought all Serbs together under a single banner, had lost his way. The instigator of Yugoslavia's bloody disintegration, and the guiding hand behind the Yugoslav wars, proved himself no nationalist at all. Milošević, the man once seen as a brilliant tactician, maneuvered himself, and the Serbs, into a corner. For the Serbs, Milošević's rule will be seen as one of the most disastrous periods in their modern history. He had held all the cards in the former Yugoslavia, and one by one, played them and lost. The Serbs, who throughout the wars had been seen as the winners, nearly overnight became the losers. Yet with tight control of the media and the police, Milošević succeeded in channeling public opinion in Serbia. After the fall of Krajina, there was no public outcry; the sense of defeat just set in deeper.

Demonized by the Western press, Milošević was liked by international mediators almost without exception. They found him intelligent and witty—though they frequently failed to appreciate that he would lie to them, play with them like a cat who has caught a mouse. It seemed he met his match in Holbrooke, the first mediator who had an arsenal far bigger than Milošević's, which he had put to use. By the time of the Dayton summit, Milošević already was the most cooperative of the Balkan players. He wanted peace more than his counterparts. In order to secure the lifting of sanctions, he would sell short the very war aims with which he had led his people into battle in the first place. He refused to lift a finger in the defense of the Krajina Serbs, the very people he had claimed to champion. He knew that each day the war continued brought the Serbs closer to total defeat. The fall of Krajina was part of a process that fundamentally altered the balance of power. After four years of indecision and being warned by their allies that military intervention would be disastrous, the U.S. finally demonstrated that a combined use of force and diplomacy could produce a realistic prospect— the first in years—for a peaceful settlement.

As the presidents gathered in Dayton, Ohio, they did so having agreed, for the first time, on a bipartisan division of Bosnia into two distinct entities: one based on the current territory of Republic Srpska, the other on land held by the Muslim-Croat Federation. The land distribution on the ground reflected a territorial share which all parties had, in the past, accepted as reasonable. The U.S. had an unprecedented hold over both sides: over the Serbs, on the one hand, who knew that without a deal now they could face further military defeat and the loss of still more territory; and the Muslim-Croat alliance on the other. Although Zagreb and Sarajevo sensed the war turning in their favor, they also knew that their military prowess depended on the tacit support of the United States.

Further, from successive military victories, there emerged in former Yugoslavia discrete territorial units, on each of which one ethnic group prevailed. The defeat of the Muslim-populated eastern enclaves of Srebrenica and Žepa, and the Croatian victory over the Krajina, though publicly denounced by all sectors of the international community, were privately welcomed by the peace mediators because they offered the prospect of neater maps on which to reach an agreement over territory.

The U.S., like the European Union and the United Nations before it, recognized Milošević as key to finding a solution, and turned a blind eye to his complicity in the crimes that were committed in the prosecution of Serbian war aims. Milošević was rewarded by the lifting of economic sanctions and the gradual return to the international community. But the big winner was Franjo Tudjman's Croatia. His complicity in atrocities committed particularly, but not exclusively, in Bosnia and Herzegovina, has also been conveniently overlooked in the interests of securing peace. Washington brought peace to the Balkans, but there was little talk of honor or justice. It came as a result of treating with the guilty men of Yugoslavia's killing fields. The settlement had the effect of strengthening the hand—in their respective states—of the two men on whose shoulders the lion's share of the responsibility for Yugoslavia's tragedy lies. It was another step towards realizing the vision of Yugoslavia's vision that they first mapped out between themselves at their secret meeting at Karadjordjevo in March 1991: a straight carve up of the spoils between the country's two biggest and most powerful nations.

The losers were Bosnia's Muslims, and those dwindling few Serbs and Croats who have remained loyal citizens of [Alija] Izetbegović's vanishing republic.

They will have as their homeland a landlocked island of territory completely surrounded by both their former enemies. The "Muslim" entity that emerged from the U.S. peace plan is dependent on Tudjman's Croatia,[1] a small and powerless satellite republic, Lebanon to Croatia's Syria. After Dayton, 20,000 U.S. troops were deployed to Bosnia as part of the 60,000-strong NATO-led Implementation Force (IFOR) to make the agreement stick. While its deployment went smoothly, and the rival armies met the Dayton deadlines for withdrawal, the politicians were not ready to comply with the civilian side of the agreement which endorsed the right of return because that would have undermined the very reason why they fought the war. Prospects for peace depended on the survival of the fragile Muslim-Croat Federation. Elections in September [1995] did not change the political landscape. Instead, they were a reflection of the national composition of Bosnia's divided parts; there was scarce sign of the development of a non-ethnic democratic political movement. The initial stages of establishing the joint-governing institutions were a tug-of-war, with international mediators fighting for each inch of ground gained.

What had been achieved so far in Bosnia had nothing to do with a commitment to the peace process, a change of heart among the rival leaders. On the contrary, they each saw their conflicting visions of Bosnia affirmed in the Dayton agreement.

With the fall of Krajina and the weakening of Republika Srpska in Bosnia, the Croats and Muslims came to understand and to apply the great lesson of the Yugoslav wars, a lesson the Serbs demonstrated in the days of their military supremacy: that in the post–Cold War world there is no collective security, no international will to protect the weak against the strong; the lesson that to win freedom and security for one's people requires neither a sound argument nor a good cause but a big army. Victory, in former Yugoslavia, will fall not to the just, but to the strong.

---

[1] Tudjman died on December 11, 1999, at the age of 77.—Eds.

Balkan Babel

SABRINA PETRA RAMET

⊠

Sabrina Petra Ramet is a professor of international studies at the
University of Washington in Seattle. In addition to *Balkan
Babel,* she has written six books dealing with the problems of
nationalism and social conflict in Eastern Europe and Russia.
What are her views on nationalism in general and the causes of
the war in particular? Do her views complement those of Laura
Silber and Allan Little in the previous selection?

Nationalism, . . . in all of its guises, is a false solution which promises much,
but delivers mainly hardship, prejudice, injury, pain, and constant dangers.
Often the product of deliberate stoking by politicians seeking to build a popular power base in support of territorial revisionism or internal repression, "all
nationalism is reactionary in its nature," as Rudolf Rocker has written, "for it
strives to enforce on the separate parts of the great human family a definite
character according to a preconceived idea . . . [and] creates artificial separa-
tions and partitions within that organic unity" which comprises humankind. I
find myself in agreement with Brian Barry that the state community is capable
of generating moral obligations (and concomitant rights), but that "there is
nothing about common nationality *as such* that can make contact with any
morally compelling basis for ascribing special obligations."

. . . [It is] argued that it makes a difference for political practice whether a
given system is legitimate (in the sense in which I have defined the concept of
legitimacy), that nationalism is a form of illegitimate politics from root to

branch, that political dynamics are reflected in, and even adumbrated by, changes in the cultural sphere, and that the religious sphere underpins, and legitimizes actions and decisions taken in the political sphere. The political, cultural, and religious spheres do not exist apart from each other; they are, rather, organic parts of a religio-political-cultural system in which activity in one part has intentions, reflections, and consequences in other parts. Hence, the Serbian Orthodox Church's endorsement of the Serbian military campaign in 1991 heightened the political profile of that Church, deepened and cemented its growing alliance with the Serbian government of Slobodan Milošević, and distorted the Church's gospel itself. Yet so involved did the Serbian Church become in the Serbian nationalist revival and in support for the military campaign that the Vatican, which was overtly sympathetic to Croatian aspirations for independence, sent its Secretary for Foreign Relations, Jean-Louis Toran, to Belgrade on 7 August 1991 to confer with Patriarch Pavle about the crisis.

More broadly, the disintegration of the political fabric in Yugoslavia was presaged by an unremitting fixation, on the part of Serbian writers, with war and war-induced suffering and by a deterioration of interethnic relations in various spheres, including in ecumenical contacts, the media, and even . . . rock music. Later, the rise of nationalist movements in Serbia, Croatia, and Slovenia was reflected in sundry spheres, including in rock music, where the strident tones of Laibach in particular served as a warning, and in the sphere of gender relations, where the new chauvinists expressed disdain for feminists and impatience with demands that women be treated with dignity. More recently, the psychological scarring that the war produced in Serbian society was reflected in the names of some of the newest rock bands. These include bands such as Acroholia, Bloodbath, Bomba za system (A Bomb for the System), Boneblast, Corpus Delicti, Dead Ideas, Ekstremisti, Hands in Ashes, Malfunctions, Mortuary, Napred u Prošlost (Forward into the Past), Pogibja (Catastrophe), Purgatory, and Scaffold. One of Serbia's new breed of "turbo-rock" bands offered this bleak alternative: "We are going to Mars. Life is better there."

Some cultural figures sought to assail the very cultural underpinnings of each other's nations. For example, *Politika* reported claims made by certain Serbian figures at Croats' expense. Milan Paroški, a deputy in the Serbian parliament, told that body that "Croats did not have any literature except for Serbian literature"; and Serbian writer Antonije Isaković declared, "Seeing that they could not constitute a nation on the cakavian and kajkavian dialects [spoken in parts of Croatia], Croats got the idea to take our language [Serbian]." The denigration of the culture of the "enemy" nation even extended to disparagement of specific songs. For example, the Serbian daily *Politika* claimed, in August 1991, that Croats were singing patriotic songs honoring wartime fascist leader Ante Pavelić. The denigration of the other's culture is, thus, one side of the political-cultural coin.

The other side of the coin is that political atavism invariably entails cultural atavism. Hence, just as Croatia restored its medieval coat of arms and its medieval currency, the kuna, there were calls in Serbia for the restoration of the old Serbian coat of arms and anthem. In fact, intercommunal political conflict necessarily has a cultural dimension. And victory or defeat in the political sphere may entail as well corresponding victory or defeat in the cultural and religious spheres.

The Titoists had some sense of this, and this is why they argued back and forth in the 1950s and early 1960s as to whether they should aspire to create a new culture, a Yugoslav culture, which would melt down and assimilate the "partial" cultures of the component peoples of the country, or whether they should rather extend toleration to all component cultures, while promoting a thin overlay of "Yugoslav culture" based ultimately on Partisan mythology from World War II and notions of self-management. In 1964, at its Eighth Party Congress, the LCY [League of Communists of Yugoslavia] opted for the second strategy: toleration while promoting a thin overlay of "Yugoslavism." The internal contradiction here, not noticed at the time, was that in tying this Yugoslavism to the Partisan mythology, this strategy entailed constant reminders of the intercommunal internecine strife of that war. Hence, even while trying to build a concept of "Yugoslavism," Yugoslavia's Communists constantly stirred up reminders of the old fires of intergroup hatred.

Could the alternative approach—energetic homogenization—have produced a happier result? Successful instances of this approach in Europe tend to involve cases where unification and adoption of this policy occurred much earlier (e.g., England, France, Spain). Twentieth-century European attempts to pursue such a policy (the USSR, interwar Czechoslovakia, early postwar Yugoslavia, and Romania in regard to Transylvania) have all run up against serious difficulties.

A 1991 article by Andrei Simić sheds additional light on the dynamics of these processes. Describing the concept of a "moral field" (defined as "an interactional sphere where those engaged typically behave towards each other with reference to ethically perceived imperatives, that is, rules which are accepted as being 'good,' 'God-given,' 'natural,' 'proper,' and so forth"), Simić argues that the membership of a moral field depends on criteria of recruitment which generally are functions of kinship, tribe, or nation. "Within a moral field," Simić points out, "members are expected to act towards each other with reference to a common set of shared ideas by which behavior is structured and evaluated. In contrast, behavior outside the moral field can be said to be *amoral* in that it is primarily idiosyncratic and as such may be purely instrumental or exploitative without being subject to sanctions. Thus, for the individual, those belonging to other moral fields can be said to form part of his or her *amoral* sphere." And hence, actions which might be deemed morally reprehensible when committed against a fellow member of the moral field (such as murder, torture, rape, confiscation or goods) may be seen as morally commendable when committed against persons not included in the group's moral field.

Viewing the issue in this way, it is apparent that the Titoists did not manage to create a common moral field in which all Yugoslavs would be included, much less to inculcate notions of moral universalism. Instead, moral fields remained coincident with ethnic communities, heightening the risks and dangers of political disintegration. Morality, molded and manipulated by politics, culture, and religion alike, ultimately lay at the heart of the breakdown of the Yugoslav system and of Yugoslavia itself and has lain also at the heart of the continuing problems in the Yugoslav successor states.

As long as the politicians and citizens in these states remain "realists," each society content to defend its Nation, the fundamental task will remain unattained. That task, the serious assaying of which will bring in tow the movement toward a positive resolution of a society's social, political, and even economic problems, is no less than the quest for moral excellence. And for this purpose, as Plato urged in The Laws, states should ideally be founded on the following principles:

A. That certain absolute moral standards exist.

B. That such standards can be, however imperfectly, embodied in a code of law.

C. That most of the inhabitants of the [morally refined] state, being innocent of philosophy, must never presume to act on their own initiative in modifying either their moral ideal or the code of laws which expresses it.

The Response of the American Media to Balkan Neo-Nationalisms

JAMES J. SADKOVICH

James J. Sadkovich, associate professor of history at the American University in Bulgaria, has published articles on fascism and the history of the Second World War. The following selection, drawn from a book chapter titled "The Response of the American Media to Balkan Neo-Nationalisms," was published in 1996. It charges the American media with distorting many aspects of the conflict in former Yugoslavia. What conclusions can be drawn about media coverage and its impact on the war?

Although there is no consensus regarding the nature of the American media, they seem to act as a collective gatekeeper and they certainly form part of national and local power structures. Reporters and editors are thus members of elites with vested interests in both the domestic and the international *status quo,* and in matters of foreign policy they are dependent on government officials, and members of universities and think-tanks that have close ties to the government. This puts them in an ambivalent position. As Carl Migdail of *U.S. News & World Report* noted, even though reporters are aware "that government facts are not facts but lies," they still prefer to support their government. Consequently, they reflect the official positions of any given administration and its civilian consultants unless there are strong reasons not to do so. But in the case of the former Yugoslavia no such reasons exist.

☒ ☒ ☒

The media cannot gain perspective nor analyze events, precisely because they cover events on a daily basis. This lack of analytic perspective is especially applicable to television newscasts, which, as an executive of CNN observed, occur in "real time." In other words, everything on the tube is ephemeral and so abstracted from the real world as to form an altogether different reality in the same way that the media form a distinct culture not accessible and often unfathomable to outsiders. Getting one's "side" presented is thus difficult, and sustained analysis is impossible.

Journalists and editors tend to select sources that reinforce their own perceptions; they live for and in the momentary event; they enjoy hobnobbing with and criticizing the powerful; and they focus on personalities and concrete phenomena rather than on ideas and abstract concepts. Consequently, despite disclaimers of objectivity, fairness, and balance, news coverage often reflects corporate concerns, the hidden agenda of government officials, and the unconscious biases of journalists who filter and distort the realities being reported. Put more simply, it is a lot easier for someone like Eagleburger or Kissinger to get on *Nightline* than for most of us to do so.

☒ ☒ ☒

All network nightly news programs covered the crisis in Yugoslavia from 1 through 8 July [1991], when the fighting in Slovenia was both intense and novel, and again on 14 July, when Serbian forces attacked Croatian police stations in the Krajina for the first time. Coverage then became sporadic, and if the networks did not share out the responsibility for mentioning the crisis in Yugoslavia, it seems that the "instinctive" decisions on what is newsworthy are so deeply ingrained that the networks effectively work as a single unit and do not so much cover the news in real time as define what exists in real time on any given day. But if death and destruction, political crises, and human interest stories can catch the medium's attention, they cannot hold it. Episodic and focussed on the novel and the sensational, network coverage has been unable to describe, much less explain and analyze, the political forces that have emerged in the region since the mid-1980s.

☒ ☒ ☒

. . . If the amount of attention that the media has paid to the crisis in the former Yugoslavia has often seemed inadequate, the coverage itself has often seemed to be misinformed and superficial, when not biased and racist. It has tended to focus on the sensational rather than the substantive; it has concentrated on personalities rather than issues; and it has tended to recast what is essentially a Balkan affair in terms of American policy or the role of such international organizations as the EC, the UN, and NATO.

🀰 🀰 🀰

. . . One of the most pervasive misconceptions current in the media is the belief that the ethnic groups of the former Yugoslavia have been at each other's throats for centuries, and that all sides display the same irrational prejudices and harbor the same extreme attitudes. Rather than modern nations, south Slavs are seen as "atavistic tribes" whose psyches thirst for blood, and all sides are depicted as directly or indirectly responsible for the crimes and atrocities that have characterized the crisis ever since the JNA (translates to Yugoslav National Army) attacked Slovenia and the Serbs in Croatia began to seize Croatian towns and villages in the Krajina. Such an approach conforms to the media's idea of being "fair," and Aryeh Neier of the *Nation* is one of the few who have warned that, "Evenhandedness in assessing a conflict in which the overwhelming share of criminal conduct has been committed by one side paints a false picture."

It is thus ironic that after the revelation of Serbian atrocities of Bosnia, the *Nation* ran Alexander Cockburn's disingenuous parallel between current Serbian and earlier Ustaše ethnic cleansing, even though a more apt analogy would have been with the atrocities committed during World War II by Serbian Chetniks, who rationalized their murder of hundreds of thousands of Croats and Muslims as "ethnic cleansing." The *Nation* also provided a platform for Anthony Borden, who diluted the blame for Serbian actions in Bosnia by claiming that Zagreb and Belgrade hoped to create ethnically pure mini-empires, insisting that Croats and Serbs had both resorted to "mass killings and expulsions," asserting that the EC's findings that "Croatia's maltreatment of its Serb minority disqualified it" from being recognized as an independent state, and citing the claim by the Canadian general and UN commander Lewis MacKenzie, that the Bosnians had broken cease-fires and refused to negotiate because they preferred "intervention over negotiation."

Similar efforts to tar all sides with the same genocidal brush and depict all groups as equally aggressive and untrustworthy can be found in the *New York Times*, the *Los Angeles Times*, the *New York Review of Books*, the *Wall Street Journal*, the *New Yorker*, the *National Journal*, the *National Review*, the *New Republic*, *Time*, *Newsweek*, *Foreign Policy*, and *Foreign Affairs*, as well as on the commercial and non-profit networks. For example, in the August 1992 issue of the *New Yorker*, John Newhouse claimed that the cold war had so obscured the past that "all sides were surprised to see the Balkans behaving like the Balkans," and insisted that diplomacy could not "cope with the nationalism, ethnic passions, and capricious behavior" in eastern Europe. He acknowledged that Serbia had been the "aggressor" in June 1991, but then insisted that the Croats "had embarked on a systematic destruction of Serbian villages and enclaves." Although he offered no more than diplomatic gossip as evidence for this, he concluded that, "Both groups had gone back to basics." The only difference between the two sides, apparently was their leadership. Newhouse, who dismissed Izetbegović as ineffectual, reported that "most diplomats who knew them," saw Tudjman and Milošević as "equally odious rogues," but that while the Serb was "clever," the Croat was "stupid" and consequently less dangerous.

※ ※ ※

. . . For a great many journalists and commentators, the situation in the Balkans is simply too emotional, too complex, and too Byzantine for civilized westerners to comprehend. Anthony Borden thus concluded that, "The war in Bosnia is a terrible and murky situation with no easy answers." Contemplating the situation in Croatia in early 1992, Robert Guskind, was "left in shock, asking how something so horrendous could happen in modern Europe and—worse still—why no one has stepped in to definitely stop the fighting." He finally decided that "it is virtually impossible to comprehend the ferocity of what happened here, let alone to fathom the rigid politics, slug-it-out ideologies and centuries-old enmities that encouraged it."

※ ※ ※

. . . The media has repeatedly discussed, and thereby popularized, the argument by policy-makers that they cannot intervene in the former Yugoslavia because doing so would trigger a bloody guerrilla war against the Serbs, who supposedly held massive German and Italian forces at bay for four years during World War II. The image of the Serbs as the only victims of genocide during World War II has also been accepted and popularized by the media.

Alexander Cockburn thus absolved the Serbs of the opprobrium of behaving like Nazis and instead stigmatized the Croats by claiming that "anywhere from 750,000 to 1.2 million" Serbs were "killed in the pogroms organized by the Nazi puppet state of Croatia," even though no more than 850,000 Yugoslavs were killed during the War, and the Serbs, who collaborated with both the Nazis and Fascists, killed hundreds of thousands of Serbs, Croats, and Muslims. Yet Cockburn argued that while the Serbs were "taking a hammering in the press, some but not all of which [was] deserved," the Serbs in Bosnia really felt threatened and "the rhetoric of Western commentators" had gotten "entirely out of hand."

As Serbian forces were overrunning Croatia in late 1991, the *New York Times* reported only the atrocities committed by the Croatian state during

World War II, largely ignored the ethnic cleansing then being carried out by the Serbs in Croatia, and failed to mention either Serbian atrocities in World War II or Serbian collaboration with the Axis. Writing in the *National Journal* a month later, Guskind erroneously claimed that Croatia had "sided with the Nazis, Serbia with the Western Allies," noting that "the gruesome Ustaše World War II record," which included the murder of 500,000 to 750,000 Serbs, Jews, and Gypsies, as well as anti-Serbian and anti-Jewish remarks purportedly made by Tudjman, had lent credibility to Milošević's claim that he was "simply fighting for the unity of Serbia."

This sort of inaccurate and often apologetic history not only rationalized Serbian actions, it implicated Croats and Muslims as equally guilty by blaming one group's past actions for the other's current atrocities. It cannot, therefore, be dismissed, as some in the media have tried to do, as trivial and irrelevant antiquarianism. The net result of imprecise reporting of historical detail has been a generally superficial level of analysis and a tendency to see the victims as carrying the same bad seed as their torturers. Max Primorac was more accurate when he reported that the Serbs were "deliberately terrorizing non-Serbian populations" and waging a "Nazi-like campaign" with "death camps, summary executions, and the creation of millions of refugees."

Yet the media depicted the Serbs as reacting, albeit belatedly, to Croatian atrocities 50 years earlier and as trying to avoid another 500 years of Muslim rule, reporting Serbian claims that they were simply practicing a form of self-defense and self-determination by striking at the Croats and Muslims before they once more became victims of oppression and genocide.

※ ※ ※

. . . It is now over four years since the Serbs initiated the conflict in the former Yugoslavia, and during those years the performance of the journalists and editors of the media has been lackluster, uninformed, and as biased as that of the diplomats and statesmen has been cynical, self-serving, and cowardly. The result has been not only the devastation of Croatia and Bosnia, but the destruction of a people and the evisceration of the spiritual core of the Balkans and the blatant moral failure of the West. As one old Muslim who had lost his sons told David Rieff in late 1992, Bosnia was "a dead country, at least for Muslims." It had become "Serbian," and all that was left for those Muslims who had survived was to try to emigrate to Western Europe or the United States, neither of which was anxious to have them.

José Mendiluce had complained that "we spend our time desperately trying to alert the international community to the depth of the crisis, but whether anyone is paying attention to us—serious attention, anyway—is another question entirely." In fact, as Rieff noted by the fall of 1992 the belief had taken hold that there was really nothing to be done for the Bosnians, just as nothing could have been done for the Beirutis before them; this belief superseded even the horror that so many had felt when the first images of the Serb concentration camps were televised.

Cynicism and "viewer fatigue" had reduced the war to "a long-running *fait-divers*," in which the cosmopolitan Muslim who could not hate was a "hero" and yet "in the context of northern Bosnia during one of the great crimes of twentieth-century Europe, [this] meant that he could only be one thing: a victim." As Peter Jennings said at the end of his special on Bosnia in the spring of 1993, "most of us will go on debating," so rather than abandon the illusory "fairness" that the media had scrupulously observed for two years, he left his viewers with "twelve months of images."

14

UNITY OR FRAGMENTATION?

Europe in the Twenty-First Century

As Europe neared the end of the twentieth century, it was beset by a series of difficult challenges. Though the European Union (EU) made great strides toward economic union, political union still remains elusive. At the same time, the forces of nationalism threaten to destabilize the EU. The disintegration of Yugoslavia presented the EU with a number of formidable challenges ranging from refugee problems to concerns over armed intervention in the conflict. As member countries resist full union and adhere to national allegiances, the question remains as to whether the forces of nationalism and the drive toward a full-fledged European union can be reconciled. The following two selections from Paul M. Kennedy and Francis Fukuyama focus on the problematic nature of European integration and nationalism. Kennedy and Fukuyama have drawn evidence from a variety of fields to paint a picture of the future.

Kennedy's book, *Preparing for the Twenty-First Century,* published in 1993, examines the economic capacities of major regions of the world. It questions the ability of the planet to support a population that might reach 8.5 billion by 2025 and predicts that conflict between the "have" and "have-not" nations is more than likely. Kennedy concludes that a number of factors—including the population explosion, environmental concerns, and the strains of a global economy—will contribute to worldwide instability. Unless nations mobilize their resources to change the planet, the future will be quite bleak.

Kennedy's pessimistic outlook can be contrasted with that of Francis Fukuyama, who attracted worldwide attention with his 1989 article, "The End of History." In this controversial piece, Fukuyama argued that Western liberalism had irrefutably triumphed over all other forms of government. Even Gorbachev's reform proposals were "subversive of some of the most fundamental precepts of both Marxism and Leninism." If implemented, it would be "difficult to know how the Soviet economy would be more socialist than those of other Western countries with large public sectors."[1] Many of Fukuyama's critics argued that his idea of the victory of liberalism was utopian and unfounded. They also decried the notion that the popularity of liberalism constituted the end of politics. As one of them put it, "just because power takes on new forms, it will not cease to exist or cease to define a hierarchy of those who count and those who do not."[2] Responding to his critics, Fukuyama's follow-up book, *The End of History and the Last Man,* revised his conclusions regarding liberal democracy. He argues that liberal democracy has not necessarily triumphed; rather, he considers it *possible* that the greater part of humanity may be led to liberal democracy in the future.

Taking into account the points of view of Kennedy and Fukuyama, what conclusions can be drawn about the future of Europe with respect to the EU and the problem of nationalism? How do these conclusions compare to observations made by scholars in chapter 11 on the European Union and chapter 13 on Yugoslavia?

---

[1] Francis Fukuyama, "The End of History?" *The National Interest. Special Edition* (Summer 1989), p. 9.

[2] Stephen Sestanovich's response to "The End of History?" *The National Interest. Special Edition* (Summer 1989), p. 33.

Preparing for the Twenty-First Century

PAUL M. KENNEDY

Paul M. Kennedy received his doctorate in history from Oxford University in England. After teaching in England for several years, he became the J. Richardson Dilworth Professor of History at Yale University in 1983. A recipient of fellowships from the Alexander Humboldt Foundation and the Royal Historical Society, he has done extensive research on modern strategic and international affairs. Kennedy is the author of eleven books, including the international best-seller *Rise and Fall of the Great Powers*, which was published in 1987. What does Kennedy have to say about Europe's role in world affairs? What is his outlook on European union?

European integrationists often deny that they wish to distance their countries from the rest of the world; but they may have to consider more carefully than hitherto what the various policies for deepening Europe's unity mean *in practice* for others. Much of the world worries that access to markets in the advanced economies will be restricted. There is also considerable mistrust among political and business circles in Japan and (especially) the United States concerning European protectionism. In sum, a broad international feeling exists that the EC, in pursuit of its own destiny, is less interested in boosting global commerce by opening markets and more willing to protect its own farmers and industrial workers, even at the cost of worsening trade relations with the developed world and hurting the prospects of the developing world. This concern may be unjustified, and the forecasts (especially prominent in the American press) that a "trade war" will replace the Cold War could also turn out to be exaggerated. Still, as the rest of the world watches Europe's integration, it clearly is concerned by its meaning for others.

❊ ❊ ❊

It is not simply for economic reasons that great attention ought to be paid to Europe's future. It is engaged in a political experiment of the highest importance concerning how human societies think about themselves and relationships with others. As many experts on world affairs have pointed out, we seem to be witnessing a decline in the traditional loyalties, structures, and associations which have made *nations* the focal point of political and economic identity; instead, there is a growing "relocation of authority" . . . a relocation which concerns both larger (transnational) and smaller (regional, ethnic) units as politicians and peoples strive to discover what size state will work best in our present and future world. This sounds fine in theory, but one wonders what it means in practice. If a civilized and sophisticated people like the Danes vote against further measures of European integration, will there ever come a time when an organization like the EC will appear legitimate in the eyes of its people as national governments were? And how will such an organization relate in a meaningful way to the needs of regional units like Wallonia, Tuscany, the Upper Rhine, and South Wales?[1] Are, in fact, the upward and downward relocations of authority contradictory—or complementary? As we know, the world of the late twentieth century is being moved by two currents. One, driven by technology and communications and trade, tends toward ever greater economic integration. The second is the revived tendency toward ethnic separatism, currently exacerbated by the collapse of a transcendent creed (Communism), the rise of religious fundamentalism, and increasing internal questioning (from Croatia to Somalia) of national borders that were superimposed, often from outside, upon very different ethnic groups; it is also exacerbated at times by economic fears.

In both respects, Europe's role has been critical historically. In the first half of this century, Europe offered dreadful examples of how excessive nationalism, ethnic prejudices, and desire for gain could plunge so-called civilized societies into war. After 1950, however, Europeans have been seeking to learn from past mistakes, creating a structure which would produce economic integration and sink national differences. Considering the fractured relationships elsewhere (East Asia, the Middle East, Central Africa, South Asia), Europe's march towards unity has been remarkable despite its flaws and offers an example to all

---

[1]In 1995, Belgium reorganized its provincial administration along ethnolinguistic lines. In the process, the region of Wallonia was created in the southern half of Beligum. Tuscany is located in west-central Italy, and the Upper Rhine in northwestern Germany. (Eds.)

strife-torn regions. If the leaders of states like Germany and France now wish to be at lasting peace with their neighbors after centuries of conflict and to embed themselves in larger, transnational units, might that not also happen at some time in the future to clusters of countries elsewhere, from South Asia to Latin America? And if it did, would that not be an advance upon today's regional fractures?

Of course, Europe still has a long way to travel and there are innumerable obstacles in the way, not least those thrown up by the new global forces that challenge all societies and—as argued above—pose perhaps special problems for the EC at this stage in its development. Yet it is precisely because of those global forces for change that the integrationists' argument *ought* to prevail over those who merely desire to erect a large trading consortium. In the light of all that is happening in world affairs—the disappearance of the USSR and the possibility of regional conflicts in the successor territories, the rise of East Asian economic power, the emergence of nuclear-armed local Great Powers (India, China), the protracted social and economic difficulties of the United States, the chances of demographically driven struggles, resource wars, and mass migration, the looming population imbalances between North and South, the long-term dangers of environmental damage—Europe surely has no real alternative to *moving forward,* seeking to create an influential and responsible entity capable of meeting these challenges collectively in a way that twelve or twenty separate nation-states simply cannot do. No one will deny that the task is enormous, especially given the tension between "deepening" the Community and "widening" its membership. Yet the profundity of international change, demanding new thinking and new structures, strengthens the position of those who argue that Europe simply cannot stay still.

While the larger logic of historical change favors the integrationists, they in turn need to respond imaginatively to the challenge and opportunity offered. At present, far too much of the rhetoric about Europe's destiny is accompanied by self-serving political maneuvers, bureaucratic infighting, blatant efforts to protect economic inefficiencies, national interests seeking to control and divert pan-European purposes, and protectionist, inward-looking tendencies—all confirming the worst suspicions of the anti-integrationists as well as those of other countries. Furthermore, the typical agenda of EC politics—how to reduce the "butter mountains," for example, or regulate accountancy standards—appears as excessively nitpicking and inward-focused in the light of the enormous demographic and technological forces that are changing the world. Whether any country or group of countries *can* respond effectively to the new transnational developments—some of which may manifest themselves swiftly and unpredictably—is unclear. But if European leaders spend so much time arguing over integration that little or none remains to consider coherent responses to demographic trends, migration, global warming, and the impact of new technologies, then their countries may be completely unprepared to handle the challenges ahead. Even in the early 1990s, it is clear that Europe cannot stand apart from the rest of the world's problems. How much clearer will that be in 2010 or 2030? In sum, the burden is upon European federalists to outline how they can create a thriving unified body which will assume a responsible world role without hiding behind walls, adopting selfish policies, and running against the trends toward globalization; how they can further the EC's internal development at the same time as they seek to cope—and help poorer nations to cope—with global changes. Should it actually manage to reconcile those aims, Europe might find that the next century will be kinder to it than the present century has been. As things now stand, however, resolving such a cluster of major challenges seems unlikely—in which case, both Europe and the rest of the world will suffer the consequences.

The End of History and the Last Man

FRANCIS FUKUYAMA

After Francis Fukuyama received his Ph.D. in political science from Harvard University, he became a member of the political science department of the RAND Corporation. During the 1980s, he also served as a member of the Policy Planning Staff of the U.S. Department of State, where he specialized in Middle Eastern and European political-military affairs. He is currently the Omer and Nancy Hirst Professor of Public Policy at the Institute of Public Policy at George Mason University. His writings focus on democratization and international political economy. Fukuyama is the author of three books, including the worldwide best-seller *The End of History and the Last Man*. In Fukuyama's opinion, is there a solution to the problem of nationalism? Is it tenable? How do Fukuyama's views compare with those of Kennedy expressed in the previous selection?

Those who say that nationalism is too elemental and powerful a force to be vanquished by a combination of liberalism and economic self-interest should consider the fate of organized religion, the vehicle for recognition that immediately preceded nationalism. There was a time when religion played an all-powerful role in European politics, with Protestants and Catholics organizing themselves into political factions and squandering the wealth of Europe in sectarian wars. English liberalism . . . emerged in direct reaction to the religious fanaticism of the English Civil War. Contrary to those who at the time believed that religion was a necessary and permanent feature of the political landscape, *liberalism vanquished religion in Europe.* After a centuries-long confrontation with liberalism, religion was taught to be tolerant. In the sixteenth century, it would have seemed strange to most Europeans not to use political power to enforce belief in their particular sectarian faith. Today, the idea that the practice of religions other than one's own should injure one's own faith seems bizarre, even to the most pious churchman. Religion has thus been relegated to the sphere of private life—exiled, it would seem, more or less permanently from European political life except on certain narrow issues like abortion.

To the extent that nationalism can be de-fanged and modernized like religion, where individual nationalisms accept a separate but equal status with their fellows, the nationalistic basis for imperialism and war will weaken. Many people believe that the current move toward European integration is a momentary aberration brought on by the experience of World War II and the Cold War, but that the overall trend of modern European history is toward nationalism. But it may turn out that the two world wars played a role similar to the wars of religion, affecting the consciousness not just of the generation immediately following but of all subsequent generations.

If nationalism is to fade away as a political force, it must be made tolerant like religion before it. National groups can retain their separate languages and senses of identity, but that identity would be expressed primarily in the realm of culture rather than politics. The French can continue to savor their wines and the Germans their sausages, but this will all be done within the sphere of private life alone. Such an evolution has been taking place in the most advanced liberal democracies of Europe over the past couple of generations. Though the nationalism of contemporary European societies is still quite pronounced, it remains very different in character from the sort that existed in the previous century when the concept of "peoples" and national identities was relatively new. Since Hitler's fall, no Western European nationalism has seen the domination of other nationalities as key to its identity. Just the contrary: the most modern nationalisms have followed Ataturk's path,[1] seeing their mission as the consolidation and purification of national identity within a traditional homeland. Indeed, one might say that all nature nationalisms are going through a process of "Turkification." Such nationalisms do not seem to be capable of creating new empires, they can only break existing empires apart. The most radical nationalists today like Schoenhuber's Republican party in Germany or Le Pen's National Front in France have been preoccupied not with ruling foreigners, but with expelling them and, like the proverbial greedy burgher, enjoying the good things of life alone and unmolested. Most surprising and revealing is the fact that Russian nationalism, usually counted as the most retrograde in Europe, has

---

[1] Kemal Ataturk (1881–1938) was the founder and first president of the Republic of Turkey. He is credited for having modernized the country.—Eds.

been rapidly undergoing the process of Turkification, discarding its former expansionism in favor of a "small Russia" concept. Modern Europe has been moving rapidly to shed sovereignty and to enjoy national identity in the soft glow of private life. Like religion, nationalism is in no danger of disappearing, but like religion, it appears to have lost much of its ability to stimulate Europeans to risk their comfortable lives in great acts of imperialism.

This does not mean, of course, that Europe will be free from nationalist conflicts in the future. This will be particularly true for those newly liberated nationalisms in Easter Europe and the Soviet Union that have lain dormant and unfulfilled under communist rule. Indeed, we can expect a higher degree of nationalist conflict in Europe with the end of the Cold War. Nationalism in these cases is a necessary concomitant to spreading democratization, as national and ethnic groups long denied a voice express themselves in favor of sovereignty and independent existence. The stage was set for civil war in Yugoslavia, for example, by the free elections held in Slovenia, Croatia, and Serbia in 1990, that brought to power pro-independence, non-communist governments in the two former republics. The breakup of long-standing multi-ethnic states promises to be a violent and bloody affair, moreover, given the degree to which national groups are intertwined. In the Soviet Union, for example, some 60 million people (half of whom are Russians) live outside their native republics, while one-eighth of Croatia's population is Serbian. Major population transfers have already started to occur in the USSR and will accelerate as different republics move toward independence. Many of the new nationalisms now emerging, particularly in regions of relatively low levels of socio-economic development, are likely to be quite primitive—that is, intolerant, chauvinistic, and externally aggressive.

Moreover, the older existing nation-states are likely to be attacked from below by the claims of smaller linguistic groups demanding separate recognition. Slovaks now want recognition of an identity separate from Czechs. The peace and prosperity of liberal Canada is not enough for many French Canadians of Quebec, who want in addition preservation of their cultural distinctiveness. The potential for new nation-states, in which Kurds, Estonians, Ossetians, Tibetans, Slovenes, and the like each achieve national identity, is endless.

But these new manifestations of nationalism must be put into proper perspective. First, the most intense ones will occur predominantly in the least modernized parts of Europe, particularly in or near the Balkans and the southern parts of the former Russian Empire. They are likely to flare without affecting the long-term evolution of Europe's older nationalisms in the more tolerant direction suggested above. While the people of the Soviet Transcaucasus have already been guilty of acts of unspeakable brutality, there is little evidence to date that the nationalisms of the northern half of Easter Europe—Czechoslovakia, Hungary, Poland, and the Baltic states—will develop in an aggressive direction incompatible with liberalism. This is not to say that existing states like Czechoslovakia may not fracture, or that Poland and Lithuania will not have border disputes. But this need not lead to the maelstrom of political violence characteristic of other areas, and will be counteracted by pressures for economic integration.

Second, the impact of new nationalist conflicts on the broader peace and security of Europe and the world will be much smaller than it was in 1914, when a Serbian nationalist triggered World War I by assassinating the heir to the Austro-Hungarian throne. While Yugoslavia crumbles and newly liberated Hungarians and Romanians torment each other endlessly over the status of the Hungarian minority in Transylvania, there are no great powers left in Europe that would be interested in exploiting such a conflict for the sake of bettering their strategic position. On the contrary, most advanced European states would seek to avoid entanglement in such controversies like a tar baby, intervening only in the face of egregious violations of human rights or threats to their own nationals. Yugoslavia, on whose territory the Great War began, has fallen into civil war and is disintegrating as a national entity. But the rest of Europe has achieved considerable consensus on an approach to settlement of the problem, and on the need to insulate Yugoslavia from larger questions of European security.

Third, it is important to recognize the transitional nature of the new nationalist struggles now occurring in Eastern Europe and the Soviet Union. They are the birth pangs of a new and generally (though not universally) more democratic order in this region, as former communist empires collapse. There is reason to expect that many of the new nation-states that will emerge from this process will be liberal democracies, and that their nationalisms, exacerbated for now by the independence struggle, will mature and ultimately undergo the same process of "Turkification" as Western Europe.

The principle of legitimacy based on national identity took hold in the Third World in a big way after World War II. It came to the Third World later than it did to Europe, because industrialization and national independence came later as well, but when it arrived it had much the same impact. While relatively few countries in the Third World were formal democracies in the years since 1945, almost all of them abandoned dynastic or religious titles to legitimacy in favor of the principle of national self-determination. The newness of these nationalisms meant that they were much more self-assertive than the older, better established, and more confident ones of Europe. Pan-Arab nationalism, for example, was based on the same longings for national unification as the nationalisms of Italy and Germany in the last century, but was never fulfilled through the creation of a single, politically integrated Arab state.

But the rise of Third World nationalism has constrained international conflict in certain ways as well. Broad acceptance of the principle of national self-determination—not necessarily formal self-determination through free elections, but the right of national groups to live independently in their traditional homeland—had made it very hard for anyone to make military intervention or territorial aggrandizement stick. The power of Third World nationalism has been almost universally triumphant, seemingly regardless of relative levels of technology and development: the French were driven out of Vietnam and Algeria, the United States out of Vietnam, the Soviets out of Afghanistan, the Libyans out of Chad, the Vietnamese out of Cambodia, and so forth. The major changes that have occurred in international borders since 1945 have almost all been cases of countries splitting apart along national lines rather than adding to their territory through imperialism—for example, the breakup of Pakistan and Bangladesh in 1971. Many of the factors that make territorial conquest unprofitable for developed countries—the rapidly escalating costs of war, including the cost of ruling a hostile population, the possibility of internal economic development as a more readily available source of wealth, and so on—have applied to conflicts between Third World countries as well.

Nationalism continues to be more intense in the Third World, Eastern Europe, and the Soviet Union, and will persist there for a longer time than in Europe or America. The vividness of these new nationalisms seems to have persuaded many people in developed liberal democracies that nationalism is the hallmark of our age, without noticing its slow decline at home. It is curious why people believe that a phenomenon of such recent historical provenance as nationalism will henceforth be so permanent a feature of the human social landscape. Economic forces encouraged nationalism by replacing class with national barriers and created centralized, linguistically homogeneous entities in the process. Those same economic forces are now encouraging the breakdown of national barriers through the creation of a single, integrated world market. The fact that the final political neutralization of nationalism may not occur in this generation or the next does not affect the prospect of its ultimately taking place.